New World Dawning:
The Sixties at Regina Campus

New World Dawning:
The Sixties at Regina Campus

by James M. Pitsula

2008

UNIVERSITY OF
REGINA

CANADIAN PLAINS
RESEARCH CENTER

Canadian Plains Research Center
University of Regina
Regina, Saskatchewan S4S 0A2 Canada
Tel: (306) 585-4758   Fax: (306) 585-4699
E-mail: canadian.plains@uregina.ca
http://www.cprc.uregina.ca

Library and Archives Canada Cataloguing in Publication

Pitsula, James M. (James Michael), 1950
        New world dawning : the sixties at Regina Campus / by James M. Pitsula.

(Canadian plains studies, ISSN 0317 6290 ; 56)
Includes bibliographical references and index.
ISBN 978 0 88977 210 6

        1. University of Saskatchewan. Regina Campus History. 2. Nineteen sixties. 3. Social change Saskatchewan Regina History 20th century. I. University of Regina. Canadian Plains Research Center II. Title. III. Series.

LE3.S765R4 2008   378.7124'45   C2008 900492 2

Printed and bound in Canada

Cover design: Brian Danchuk Design, Regina
Cover photo: A love-in at the Saskatchewan Legislative Building, 1967. Photo: Erik Christensen/The Globe and Mail

"Chimes of Freedom" by Bob Dylan copyright © 1964; renewed 1992 Special Rider Music. All rights reserved. International copyright secured. Reprinted by permission.

Canadian Plains Research Center acknowledges the financial support of the Government of Canada through the Book Publishing Industry Development Program (BPIDP) for our publishing activities.

Canadian Plains Research Center acknowledges the support of the Canada Council for the Arts for our publishing program.

For Frances Pitsula

Table of Contents

Preface

I can pinpoint the moment when I decided to write this book. I was sitting in the Hard Rock Café in the Edmonton mall in July 1997, contemplating the video images streaming from the monitors and the music crashing from the speakers. It dawned on me that the sixties, part of my life experience, had become HISTORY, and that it was fitting that I, an academic historian, should write about them. I had many questions. What was the meaning of that turbulent era? What, essentially, was it about? What made it happen, and what was the impact on society? Was the legacy good or bad, positive or negative? I began reading the scholarly literature and started to teach a third-year course at the University of Regina titled "The Sixties in North America."

My students are the children of the baby boomers. They were born in the late 1980s and have no personal memory of any Canadian prime minister before Jean Chrétien. To them, John Diefenbaker and Lester Pearson are distant figures from antiquity. And yet they know quite a lot about the sixties. The music is familiar to them, as are the decade's iconic signposts—the assassination of JFK, Martin Luther King's "I Have a Dream" speech, Woodstock, Trudeaumania, and so on. They are bemused at the self-absorption and self-importance of the baby boomers, but, at the same time, I detect a streak of envy. A student wrote in her essay, "My regret is that my generation will never experience what the sixties generation shared at Woodstock."

One day, I asked the class (about 50 students): "What do you think of Bob Dylan's music?" One-third did not care for it, one-third were indifferent, and one-third really liked it. I asked, "Can you remember the first time you heard it?" A young man with longish hair said: "I was eleven years old. I was sitting on the rug, listening to the record player, when a song caught my attention. I asked my dad what it was. He said it was Bob Dylan singing about Hurricane Carter. I will never forget that moment."

Students are divided about the moral legacy of the sixties. The class on Kerouac is always an interesting litmus test. Some students worship the ground he walked on; they see him as a brave soul, breaking the bonds of convention and searching for ecstatic meaning in life. Others are baffled at his irresponsibility, his refusal to grow up and his lack of consideration for other people, especially women. One day, in a class about the counterculture, I said: "Many of the hippies were trying to find out what it means to be fully human." A student raised his hand and asked: "What does that mean?" … Good question.

This book is for pre-boomers, boomers and post-boomers alike. As you will see, I have a soft spot for the sweetness of the sixties, but I am not uncritical. An important goal is to present the sixties from the point of view of those who made the era what it was. Accordingly, I have tried to interpret the sixties from a scholarly perspective, while also giving space to those who lived it to speak for themselves in the words they used at the time. For this purpose, the *Carillon* is the perfect vehicle. It was one of the best student newspapers in Canada in the sixties, and the royalties from this book are dedicated to the continued pursuit of excellence in student journalism at the University of Regina.

I wish to thank the staffs at the University of Regina Archives and the Saskatchewan Archives Board for facilitating the research; Marilyn Bickford, secretary, Department of History, for technical assistance; Kristine Douaud for proofreading and Patricia Furdek for indexing; and, most of all, Donna Grant, my editor at the Canadian Plains Research Center, for her expertise and enthusiasm in the preparation of this book.

Introduction

"An' we gazed upon the chimes of freedom flashing."

A
s usual when it comes to the sixties, Bob Dylan says it best. In the midst of a thunderstorm he glimpses in flashes of lightning and peals of thunder a clanging church bell. It is tolling, he imagines, "for the rebel," "the searching ones," "the warriors whose strength is not to fight," and "for every hung-up person in the whole wide universe."[1] Although the students at the Regina Campus of the University of Saskatchewan cannot have had the song in mind when they named their newspaper the *Carillon* (the paper predated the song), the title is appropriate. The *Carillon*, like Dylan's "chimes of freedom," tolled the themes of the sixties amidst storms of controversy. This book explores these themes and controversies as they were revealed in the paper and in the lives of Regina Campus students. It is fitting that an era that held such high regard for personal authenticity is here interpreted through documents the students themselves produced—articles, editorials, letters to the editor, columns, cartoons and photos. However, so as not to replicate too faithfully the chaos of the period, the documents are set in a conceptual framework and embedded in an explanatory narrative.

The term "sixties" can be understood in two ways. It can refer narrowly to the decade that began January 1, 1960, and lasted until December 31, 1969, or it can describe more broadly an era of political unrest, social change, and cultural transformation that extended from the mid-1950s to the mid-1970s, the period historian Arthur Marwick calls the "long sixties."[2] In the latter usage, the events define the period, rather than the period defining the events that are taken into consideration. When the sixties are thus understood, it becomes evident that not everything that happened *during* the 1960s is necessarily *of* the sixties. Both Pierre Trudeau and Richard Nixon were elected in 1968, but Trudeau was of the sixties in a way that Nixon was not. Similarly, although both student protests and beauty contests took place during the 1960s, the former were more truly of the sixties than the latter. Gordon Lightfoot is of the sixties, but *Don Messer's Jubilee* is not.

The "sixties" is code for rebellious youth, "sex, drugs, and rock 'n' roll," hippies, flower children, Woodstock, the Vietnam War, civil rights, women's liberation, Bob Dylan, Kent State, "make love not war," the Beatles, and Volkswagen buses decorated with the peace symbol. We do not have another word to comprehend these phenomena in their entirety. US historian Terry Anderson has suggested "the Movement,"[3] but the term is not satisfactory because it implies a unity and singleness of purpose that did not exist. The "sixties," for all its imprecision and ambiguity, is the default word to describe a period of reform and upheaval. Activists, or those we might refer to as "change-agents," have thus been able to commandeer a term that otherwise might have served as a neutral marker for a decade. This is partly because the flow of history has been, to a large extent, on the side of those who promoted change. The Vietnam War is now generally conceded to have been a mistake, the civil rights movement achieved most of its goals, the Quiet Revolution transformed Quebec, the women's movement made major, probably irreversible, gains and the range of socially acceptable lifestyles has greatly expanded.

The "silent majority" of the sixties were so called for good reason. Their story deserves to be told, but that is not the primary purpose of this book, which focuses not on what was old, but rather what was new, in the period from the late 1950s to the early 1970s. The sixties, thus defined, shaped the world we live in today. It is the homeland of today, part of the air we breathe. Whether our society is better off for having experienced the sixties is a matter of opinion. Indeed, the era is a kind of Rorschach test. One sees in it what one is looking for. In the end, how we evaluate the sixties depends on the values we hold. Our conclusions say as much about us as they do about the sixties.

Youth, especially university students, were at the heart of the era. This book puts a spotlight on the University of Saskatchewan, Regina Campus, which became the University of Regina in 1974. At first glance this seems an odd choice. Regina, in the middle of the Canadian prairies, a landlocked city "surrounded by infinite miles of wind-swept nowhere,"[4] seems an unlikely place to find the sixties in full bloom. And yet it was. Regina Campus students embraced the sixties and made it their own, not merely aping what was going on elsewhere, but adapting it to their own lives and circumstances. The Regina sixties was not the North American sixties writ small; it had its own character. This book blends macro- and micro-historical approaches. It is not a detailed local history, but rather the story of how a North American (and to a large extent global) phenomenon expressed itself in a particular setting. It contributes to the literature on the sixties by exploring how the movements and trends of the era were experienced in a specific locale; it adds to our understanding of Western Canada by showing how youth in a prairie city responded to metropolitan cultural influences.

The *Carillon* is the main vehicle of analysis. We see in its pages how issues emerged, generated discussion, caused conflict, evolved and metamorphosed as the years went by. Although the *Carillon* obtained copy from wire services, the focus here is on locally-produced material. The goal is to reproduce the sixties experience of Regina students, to capture how they interpreted the times in which they were living. The *Carillon* enables us to re-enter their world and get a feeling for the emotional penumbra that surrounded events. Scanning the back issues of the paper, one is immediately struck by how much changed from the late 1950s to the early 1970s. In 1961, an article on premarital sex caused a storm of controversy; by 1969, the women's liberation caucus openly and unapologetically distributed birth control pamphlets on campus. First Nations issues were hardly mentioned in the 1950s; in 1965, an entire front page was devoted to racial discrimination. In the early 1960s, the Students' Representative Council (SRC) spent most of its time organizing basketball games and planning sock hops; a few years later, they were marching to the legislature on a regular basis to protest one alleged injustice or another. In 1962, the dean worried about the number of beer bottles that had been scattered outside the gymnasium after a dance; in 1973, faculty and students signed a petition calling for the release of Timothy Leary from jail. Fourteen students staged a protest during the Cuban missile crisis in October 1962; at the close of the decade, 400 protesters marched through the downtown streets chanting "Ho Ho Ho Chi Minh." Something of consequence happened in these years. A line was crossed; a new world was born.

Student newspapers are a rich source of information about the sixties because, unlike general-circulation newspapers, which serve a broad and diverse audience, they cater to the segment of the population that is most in tune with social and cultural change. Moreover, the mainstream media are dependent on advertising, which tilts them to vested interests and the status quo. Student newspapers, on the other hand, are subsidized from student fees and distributed at no direct cost to the reader. Not being subject to the discipline of the market and not having to attend to the bottom line, they have more room for free expression. The underground press of the sixties, while contemptuous of establishment opinion, was circumscribed by its commitment to a particular constituency, either a radical political movement or a subgroup of the counterculture. Underground papers were written "*by* the alienated *for* the alienated."[5] For those in the mainstream, they were chiefly objects of curiosity and derision. Student papers, by contrast, were obliged to maintain contact with the broad mass of students. If editor and staff rode off too far on their own hobbyhorses, the student government, feeling the heat from the student body, reined them in. The student newspaper, therefore, is an excellent source to investigate the sixties. It was neither as blinkered as the underground press nor as middle-of-the-road as the conventional dailies. It was sensitive to change, but not on the fringe.

The student newspaper historically has had a variety of functions. It serves as a bulletin board, listing the time and place of campus activities. It reports university news, including decisions of the governing board and senior administration, student government policies and programs, lectures by visitors to campus, public debates, and other notable events. It usually has an arts section, a sports page, opinion columns, editorials, and letters to the editor. In addition to matters pertaining directly to the university, it covers off-campus news thought to be of interest to students. This is a broad category of subject matter, dependent on the interests of the staff writers at any given time, but it may include civic, provincial, national, and even international affairs. The student press also has a watchdog role. It not only records events, but also offers critical commentary on the actions of university officials and student government representatives. To this end, it digs out information, seeking to expose incompetence and wrongdoing. This may lead to clashes with the university administration, especially when the latter regard the paper as a public relations arm of the university. If members of the general public form a negative impression of the university on the basis of what they read in the student newspaper, senior administrators cannot help but be concerned. If students disport themselves objectionably in print, the reputation of the university suffers.

The sixties was an unsettled time for student newspapers across North America. There were numerous confrontations with university officials, leading to suspension of publication, censorship of articles, confiscation of editions, dismissal of editors, and banning of newspapers from university precincts.[6] These troubles led the University of California to appoint in 1969 a Special Commission on the Campus Press. It recommended that university administrators disabuse themselves of the notion that "student publications constitute a form of official publication for which university administrators bear inherent responsibility." It lauded the free press as "one of the seedbeds of American thought" and a necessary ingredient for "the growth of Western civilization." At the same time, the commission admonished student newspapers to serve their readers in a balanced, fair-minded way, making a clear distinction between news columns and editorial comment and covering both or all sides of controversies. On the vexed question of "obscenity," which was a major source of contention in the sixties, the commission adopted a laissez-faire approach. It said the use of foul language was a minor issue that had been blown out of proportion and recommended that the media pay more attention to major problems confronting society, such as the Vietnam War and racial inequality.[7]

The California study was not the only inquiry into the student press. The American Association of State Colleges and Universities sponsored its own study in 1973. It, too, concluded that the student newspaper had an obligation to mirror the university community and that the opinions expressed on the editorial page should not creep into news reports. In keeping with the great crusading tradition of the free press, the paper should "seek out wrongdoing and duplicity." The study, like the California report, held that the obscenity issue had been overworked. It noted that the language used in college newspapers in the 1960s had made its way into general-circulation magazines and newspapers by the 1970s.[8]

Both studies shed light on the clashes between the *Carillon* and the Regina Campus administration, since the latter at first viewed the former as a student enterprise under the paternalistic supervision of the Board of Governors, not an independent entity controlled by students. The board was keenly aware of the adverse effect the paper could have on public opinion towards the university and, more particularly, on the attitude of the right-of-centre (though nominally Liberal) provincial government led by Ross Thatcher. It was common knowledge that Liberal cabinet ministers did not appreciate the strident and relentless attacks the *Carillon* directed against them. Since the government was the main source of funds for the university, this was no small matter. In addition, the Board of Governors discovered that potential donors to the university threatened to withhold their contributions unless the newspaper was "cleaned up." As in the United States, obscenity was a major concern. The *Carillon* was said to be vulgar and indecent, which was almost worse than its reputation as a "red rag." By the end of the sixties, the struggle was over. The university administration gave up trying to control the paper; freedom of expression prevailed over censorship.

Such struggles occurred all across Canada. At Loyola, Ryerson, University of Montreal, and Simon Fraser, to name a few, universities attempted, invariably without long-term success, to stifle the student press. The Simon Fraser *Peak* went underground for a time, reincarnating itself as the *Free Peak*, while it rode out a faculty-imposed suspension. Left-wing editors at McGill did battle with conservative student councilors and warded off attacks from the engineering society.[9] At Regina Campus, the *Carillon* and student government tended to be of the same political hue, but rifts did appear from time to time between the paper and segments of the student body. Anti-*Carillon* students typically were enrolled in professional colleges, such as the Faculty of Administration and the Faculty of Engineering and, to a lesser extent, the Faculty of Education. These students tended to be more moderate or conservative in their politics than their counterparts in the liberal arts.

The question of how faithfully the *Carillon* reflected the opinions of the broad mass of students during this period is an important one. While it is impossible to know how many students read the paper or agreed with its contents, some indication can be gleaned from letters to the editor and from the opinions expressed at student meetings where the paper was both praised and condemned. It is clear that the students at Regina Campus were not all of one mind. There were radicals, moderates, conservatives, and those who took no interest in what was going on in the political sphere. The *Carillon* in the sixties was always at the centre of controversy. It escaped the worst fate a newspaper can experience—that of being ignored.

News stories reveal that large numbers of students took up sixties causes. Two hundred and fifty students marched to the legislature in March 1964 demanding lower tuition fees and independent university status for Regina Campus. A substantial proportion of students voted in student elections, and large numbers attended annual general meetings. More than 1,600 (out of a total enrolment of about 4,000) showed up in 1969 to discuss the Board of Governors' attempt to shut down the *Carillon*. This suggests a high level of political involvement. Moreover, numbers alone do not measure the impact of a paper. Regardless of how many students read the *Carillon* or agreed with it, the fact remains that it opened up areas of discussion that previously had been closed. It broke the silence on such topics as Aboriginal rights, women's liberation, student power, and nuclear disarmament. The universe of permissible topics expanded. This, in the long run, was the *Carillon's* most important legacy.

This book attempts to dissect the sixties without leaving the corpse bleeding on the table. It strives to conjure the feelings and emotions of the era, as well as the bare facts. The first chapter gives background and an overview. It conceptualizes the sixties as a cluster of complex and multi-faceted phenomena with a distinctive ethos that blended rebellion, idealism, hedonism, self-exploration, political engagement and the search for community. The period was also characterized by an extraordinary sense of generational solidarity, coinciding as it did with the coming of age of the baby boomers. By sheer force of numbers, they wielded great influence in setting the social agenda.

Growing up in the 1950s, middle-class boomers shared common experiences of suburbia, exposure to television, youth-oriented mass advertising, permissive child rearing, progressive education, and the birth of rock and roll. As a result, they developed a strong sense of unity and a belief in their unique historical destiny. Many were alienated from, or dissatisfied with, the conformity, security, domesticity, and materialism of their parents' world. Middle-class boomers, having always known affluence, took it for granted and yearned for something more. Like Benjamin Braddock (Dustin Hoffman) in Mike Nichols' 1967 film *The Graduate*, they felt trapped in a cycle of wealth acquisition and status-seeking that they judged to be phony and shallow. Benjamin is taken aside by his father's businessman friend, who promises to tell him the secret of success. "Plastics," he whispers.

The demographic factor by itself does not explain the sixties. While youth has an inherent tendency to test authority and the size of the baby boomer generation intensified this tendency, there were other variables in play. The changing nature of the economy meant that young people had to stay in university for longer periods of time in order to obtain the credentials required for white-collar jobs. The stage of life between adolescence and the assumption of adult responsibilities (work and family) was therefore prolonged. Being young became a more protracted affair. Further, university students have flexible schedules. They are available for mass meetings and protest marches; indeed, such activities are a welcome relief from the academic grind. And the sixties gave them plenty to protest about. Even without the baby boom, such "trigger events" as the Vietnam War and the civil rights movement would surely have provoked a strong reaction.

The second chapter sketches the local context of Regina Campus, which was in the process of evolving from a junior college into a full-fledged university. Student enrolment jumped from about 300 to over 4,000 in ten short years. A new campus was built on the bald prairie at the edge of the city. Such rapid expansion inevitably brought growing pains, complicated by Regina's relationship with the parent institution, the University of Saskatchewan in Saskatoon. Regina sought to control its destiny and shape its identity by breaking free of the parental bond. Students were very much part of this struggle. They placed themselves at the forefront of the battle for autonomy that suffused the entire period until the University of Regina was established in 1974.

Regina, along with such institutions as Simon Fraser, McGill, University of Toronto, Sir George Williams and Waterloo, drank deeply of the spirit of the sixties. It not only smoked, it inhaled. The radical reputation was acknowledged in a 1964 *Carillon* article, "Are You a Radical?" Student David Adams wrote: "When the Regina campus is mentioned in the presence of one of our big cousins from the Saskatoon campus, the reaction is almost certain to be a scoff accompanied by 'bunch of radicals!' or some such comment." Although the comment was intended as a put-down, Adams refused to take it as such. "Since when," he asked, "has it been shameful for a university student to be a radical?" He argued that the world, more than ever before, was in need of radicals to tackle urgent problems of poverty, over-population, and the threat of nuclear war. Traditional approaches had failed, and it was time to consider new ideas and a fresh vision of the future. Adams concluded: "When we are called a 'bunch of radicals out to save the world,' let's not hang our heads. I see nothing wrong with 'trying to save the world'—a phrase which I take here to mean the avoidance of war and the rearrangement of human affairs in accordance with the ideals of human freedom and reason."[10]

Chapter three is a close examination of the *Carillon*, which won a reputation as one of the best student newspapers of the sixties. John Kelsey, Canadian University Press (CUP) field secretary, so described it in 1968 following
a round of visits to universities in Western Canada. He said that the *Carillon*
was tough and investigative; its approach to issues had "teeth": "[It] doesn't
stop reporting at the campus gates. It has dig-deep features about Regina
city, about jail, about Indians in Saskatchewan, and about provincial law."
Kelsey praised the paper's consistent "editorial attack" and the fact that it
didn't "play stupid games." "All the features and news stories, whether staff-
written or re-printed, are aimed at increasing the awareness of Regina students." He noted the large number of student volunteers who worked on the
paper, a "better criterion of greatness," he said, "than pretty make-up"[11] (the
masthead in March 1968 listed 34 staff members and contributors).[12] Other
newspapers accorded the *Carillon* the sincerest form of flattery—imitation.
The *Globe and Mail* in 1965 picked up on the paper's exposé of discrimination
against Indians, and a story about freedom of the press in March 1969 drew
inquiries from both the *Globe* and the *Toronto Star*. Locally, the Regina *Leader-
Post* relied on the *Carillon* as a source of campus news.[13]

The fourth chapter begins a thematic analysis of the sixties. It recounts
the rise of the student movement, which is portrayed in terms of the transformation of student culture. Traditional extra-curricular student activities
focused on the frosh parade, the crowning of the campus queen, the model
parliament, sports, and dances. Student government was a glorified social
club, and its politics were of the sandbox variety. Students occupied a "pretend" world, a sheltered space, where they prepared for the day when they
would graduate and enter the "real" world. The university functioned in
place of the parent, closely regulating conduct and administering discipline.
Power in the institution was concentrated at the top. Students began in the
early 1960s to expand the role of student government to include such matters as tuition fees, student loans, the quality of teaching and the curriculum.
They adopted a new constitution and established a Students' Union, which
was incorporated under the Societies' Act (later the Non-Profit Corporations'
Act.) The new name implied that students viewed themselves as an organized force in society, analogous to labor unions and farmers' organizations,
with their own interests to defend and rights to protect. They now conceived
of themselves as partners, rather than subordinates, in the university community.

Chapter five studies the liberation movements of the sixties, beginning with the civil rights movement in the United States. Though geographically distant, the movement was emotionally close to many Regina students. They saw direct parallels with the treatment of Aboriginal peoples in Canada. When civil rights activists began lunch counter sit-ins in the southern United States, the *Carillon* reported that Indians were being denied service in Regina restaurants. Students joined the Student Union for Peace Action (SUPA) Neestow Project in Saskatchewan in the summer of 1965, a community development program working on Indian reserves and in Métis settlements. It resembled the Economic Research and Action Project (ERAP), which the Students for a Democratic Society (SDS) sponsored in the ghettoes of major American cities. At the same time, the Quiet Revolution was underway in Quebec. The *Carillon* was sympathetic; for example, it strongly opposed the imposition of the War Measures Act in October 1970. Equally, the paper was at the forefront of women's liberation. The campus climate on this issue changed dramatically in a short time. In 1966, students were still holding annual "slave auctions," which allowed men to purchase female "slaves-for-a-day." Five years later, the women's liberation group disconnected the microphone, pulled down the tables, and permanently ended the event.

Chapter six shifts attention to the peace movement, in particular the campaign against nuclear weapons and the war in Vietnam. A dark, or rather radioactive, cloud hung over the comfortable, complacent 1950s. Families were "nuclear" in more ways than one. Historian Doug Owram pinpoints the symbolic beginning of the sixties in Canada to Christmas Day, 1959, when eight faculty members and students, members of the Combined Universities Campaign for Nuclear Disarmament (CUCND), marched through the empty streets of Ottawa to lay a wreath at the National War Memorial. In Regina three years later, fourteen students braved the jeers of unsympathetic classmates and paraded through downtown Regina to protest the Cuban missile crisis. By 1965, the main focus of the peace movement had turned to Vietnam. It is difficult to overstate the impact of the Vietnam War on the sixties generation. For anti-war activists it was irrefutable proof of the dark evil that lurked at the heart of Western civilization. The *Carillon* brimmed with articles about the war, and in May 1970 twelve students, including the editor of the paper, were charged with participating in a riot at an anti-war protest.

Chapter seven considers the counterculture, which had roots in the Beats of the fifties, a group of poets and writers who rejected 9-to-5 jobs and dissented from mainstream values. The counterculture embraced sexual freedom, expanded consciousness through drugs ("better living through chemistry"), communal living experiments, a desire to "get back to nature," interest in Eastern religions, and alternative styles of speech, dress, and music. As memoirs of the sixties testify, rock music was all-important in creating a feeling of community and shared understanding. It was crucial, writes Nick Bromell, to the "existential and visionary side of the sixties ... an energy that flowed into and powerfully invigorated political ideas and movements."[14] Although few students at Regina Campus could be described as full-time hippies, many participated in the counterculture to one degree or another, and a countercultural sensibility infused aspects of student life. That being said, the dominant mode of protest in Regina was political rather than cultural. This reflected the fact that the campus was located in the capital city of a highly politicized province. Saskatchewan elected the first socialist government in North America in 1944, and elections were always fought with ideological intensity.

Inevitably, the *Carillon* was a bugbear for the establishment. The RCMP kept the campus under close surveillance, and Regina police chief Arthur Cookson declared war on hippies and radicals. More subtly, there was an undermining of dissent through the commercial co-optation of emblems of the counterculture. The *Carillon* published advertisements hyping Contact C capsules "for those 12-hour sit-ins," promoting Rio Algom/Rio Tinto Mining corporation as a "great young rock group," and urging women to "turn on your spring wardrobe." Through such techniques, the counterculture was domesticated and neutralized.

Chapter eight examines the students' critique of mass education and traces the rising tensions at Regina Campus, which reached a crescendo in 1968-69. Around the world, 1968 was a turning point. The assassination of Martin Luther King, Jr., in April touched off riots in over one hundred American cities; the murder of Robert Kennedy in June deepened the mood of anger and despair. At the Democratic party convention in August, police and National Guardsmen clubbed protesters and smashed the cameras of reporters trying to cover the event. Columbia University in New York City descended into chaos that ended only when police forcibly expelled the student occupiers. In France, students and labor unions came close to overthrowing the government, while Soviet tanks were sent into Czechoslovakia to quell the "Prague spring." Although Canada remained relatively peaceful, police had to be called in to restore order at Simon Fraser University, and students at Sir George Williams (now Concordia) went on a rampage, destroying property valued at two million dollars.

Regina Campus, too, experienced heightened conflict in 1968. Students demanded a voice in the selection of the dean of arts and science, turned out en masse at the legislature to confront Prime Minister Pierre Trudeau about the inadequate student loan program, and clashed with the university Board of Governors over control of the *Carillon*. After 1968 the student movement lost momentum. The administration made concessions and gave students the opportunity to participate in university decision-making, including representation on departmental committees, faculty councils, the Board of Governors and the Senate. Although there was another surge of radicalism in the fall of 1972, it became clear that students, while wishing to be treated as partners in the university community, had no appetite for a revolution that would completely overhaul the way the university functioned. That remained the dream of a small minority, who were increasingly marginalized and preoccupied with ideological infighting.

The final chapter assesses the legacy of the sixties. Some see it as a blighted time that eroded the traditional foundations of morality, authority and discipline. They blame the sixties for family breakdown, high crime rates, and a degraded popular culture obsessed with sex and violence. Others celebrate the sixties as the time when oppressed groups—African-Americans, women, Aboriginals, Québécois, students, gays—won their freedom. Espousing a type of sixties triumphalism, they portray the fifties as an era of stifling conformity, thwarted desire and grim repression, a stark contrast to the sixties, which are viewed as liberated, tolerant and creative. A third view maintains that the way we live today represents a compromise between the values of the fifties and ideals of the sixties. In this scenario, the sixties did not overthrow the fifties, but rather melted into them. In certain areas—for example, the role of women in society—we are not likely to return to the fifties. On the other hand, the visionary dreams of the sixties—Che Guevara's "new socialist man" or John Lennon's world without boundaries—have been quietly shelved. The capitalist system today is stronger than ever, notwithstanding the efforts of sixties radicals to undo it. The war in Iraq is a reminder that Vietnam War–style interventions are not a thing of the past.

We live in the world the sixties made. This becomes clear when we read the *Carillon*. The articles published in the 1960s seem up-to-date; they could have been written last week, or maybe a year or two ago. We are treading on familiar ground. When we flip back to the 1950s, the impression is quite different. The students of that decade do not think the way we do. Their view of the world comes across as either charmingly wholesome or annoyingly naïve. They don't seem to understand that nothing is simple and straightforward, and the world doesn't operate according to rules of brush-cut clarity. Not everybody has a happy face and knows exactly what to do. It suddenly hits us. The young people of the sixties are the authors of our present world. So let us give credit where credit is due. Whether we come to praise or bury the sixties, we must acknowledge that the students of that era had minds and were not afraid to use them; they had feelings and were not afraid to express them. They made a difference.

CHAPTER 1

Making Sense of the Sixties

This chapter discusses the what, when, where, and why of the sixties, which is not as straightforward a task as it might appear. Mention of the era brings to mind a stock set of images, events, and ideas: hippies, student protest, the Beatles, and American GIs prowling through the jungle. We have an intuitive sense that these items are somehow related to one another and form parts of a coherent whole. Though separate and distinct, they come together in a single wave of cultural, social, and political change, a movement that jolted the world and shapes our life today. Even so, the several components of the sixties are not always in complete harmony. There is a political side with explicit goals of changing public policy (civil rights, nuclear disarmament, etc.) and a cultural side more focused on values and lifestyle (sexual revolution, drugs, rock music, and so on). The two sides are not mutually exclusive and overlap at many points, but it makes sense to differentiate between them, all the while recognizing that the distinction is somewhat artificial.

As mentioned previously, the "sixties" refers here, not to the period 1960-1969, but rather to a more extended period of political, social, and cultural upheaval. The stirrings of revolt began in the mid-1950s, reached a peak about 1968, and thereafter gradually subsided. The sixties coincided—and this was no accident—with the period when most baby boomers were in their late teens and twenties. It faded out when the leading edge of the cohort reached 30, the magic age when, by their own admission, they could no longer be trusted. By the early 1970s, large numbers of boomers were graduating from university, looking for jobs, starting families and assuming adult roles. The Vietnam War, the most divisive issue of the period, came to a close with the United States withdrawing its military forces in 1973 and surrendering Saigon to the Communists on April 30, 1975. At about the same time, the Organization of Petroleum Exporting Countries (OPEC) dramatically increased the price of oil, triggering runaway inflation and inflicting deep damage to Western economies. The long post-war boom was over. The unemployment rate in Canada climbed from 4.7 per cent in 1969 to 6.3 per cent in 1972;[1] a dollar in 1975 purchased what 72 cents could buy in 1971.[2] Young people could no longer assume that a university degree would lead automatically to a well-paying job. Many of them disengaged from social causes to concentrate on making a living and raising a family.

Even at the height of the sixties, radicals constituted only a small minority. Between 1965 and 1968, only 2 or 3 per cent of US college students described themselves as activists, and only 20 per cent said they had participated in at least one demonstration.[3] However, such statistics can be misleading. As Doug Owram argues in *Born at the Right Time: A History of the Baby-Boom Generation,* the youth of the sixties, despite differences among themselves, shared a highly developed sense of generational solidarity. When push came to shove, they tended to unite against the common enemy. Their hour of destiny—the once-in-a-lifetime opportunity to leave a mark on the world—was the sixties.[4] The times were out of joint, and baby boomers thought that they had been born to set things right. At critical junctures, when it was a choice of "us versus them," the sixties generation formed a solid front against the establishment. At Regina Campus, for example, when the university challenged the right of students to control their own newspaper, the great majority of students rallied in defence of the paper, regardless of whether they agreed with its contents. Good or bad, it was *their* newspaper.

As a political and cultural phenomenon, the sixties transcended national boundaries. Student protests broke out around the world including in Britain, France, Germany, Italy, Japan, and Mexico. However, the epicentre was the United States. It was home to most of the icons of the sixties: Bob Dylan, Haight-Ashbury, Woodstock, Kent State, the Summer of Love, Chicago '68. The Beatles were an exception, but even their music was based on American rock and roll. In addition, the US was the Western country most deeply involved in the Vietnam War. Young Americans faced a wrenching decision: die in the jungle or be a traitor to your country. Canadians were spared this appalling choice. While some volunteered to serve in the American military forces, most watched safely from the sidelines. When Martin Luther King, Jr., was assassinated on April 4, 1968, riots broke out in dozens of American cities. Canadians, meanwhile, basked in the glow of centennial celebrations and Expo 67. The United States plunged into shock and despair in June 1968 when Bobby Kennedy was killed; Canada elected Pierre Elliott Trudeau, our first "star" prime minister. At Kent State in May 1970, the National Guard gunned down four American college students. Nothing like that happened at a Canadian university. Taken as a whole, the sixties in Canada were non-violent, the sole exception being the murder of Quebec deputy premier Pierre Laporte by FLQ terrorists in October 1970.

That being said, Canadians participated intensely, if at second-hand, in the American sixties. Television brought civil rights protests and the Vietnam War into our living rooms. Student power, women's liberation, Aboriginal rights, and the counterculture flourished on both sides of the border. In two respects, Canada was unique. There was no US counterpart to the Quiet Revolution in Quebec, and Americans, by definition, did not share in the 1960s upsurge of Canadian nationalism. Even the "anti-American Americans" who immigrated to Canada to protest against the Vietnam War did not "get it." The perspective from the heart of the empire is always different from that of the colonies. Canadian New Leftists occasionally had to tell their American allies: "We can make our own revolution, thank you."[5]

The Baby Boom

As we have seen, the history of the sixties is intertwined with that of the baby boom generation. The number of births in Canada began to rise in 1941 and continued to increase modestly through the war years. After the war, the number jumped dramatically, peaked around 1959, fell very gradually to 1964, and then dropped off markedly. At war's end, there were just over 300,000 babies born in Canada each year. The figure increased to 372,000 by 1947 and to more than 400,000 in 1952. The total did not fall below 400,000 again until 1966. The birth rate was 22.4 per thousand of population in 1941, 24.3 in 1945, 28.5 in 1947, and stayed above 24 until 1963.[6]

The reasons for the boom in population are many and various. Couples after the war began marrying at a younger age and, consequently, had children sooner. In 1941, the average age of first marriage for women was 25.4 years. In 1961, it was only 22 years.[7] The late 1940s and 1950s were a time when society placed a high value on the comfort and security of family life. The family was perceived as a shelter from the storm, a haven in a heartless world. This was a reaction to the insecurities of the Cold War, as well as compensation for the trials and dislocations of the 1930s depression and the Second World War, when men and women had been denied the opportunity of starting a family. Now, they embraced domesticity.

The economic prosperity of the post-war era was another contributing factor. The feared recession did not materialize, and the economy made a smooth transition from wartime boom to peacetime prosperity. The United States and Canada respectively enjoyed the highest and second-highest standards of living in the world. The unemployment rate in Canada remained well below 4 per cent from 1945 into the late 1950s.[8] Men readily found jobs and earned the money needed to support a family. The structure of the economy was such that high levels of post-secondary education were not required to qualify for well-paying work. Only 6 per cent of Canadians between the ages of 18 and 24 were still in school in 1950. By the mid-1970s, the figure was 20 per cent.[9] Women had entered the paid work force in large numbers during the war to take the place of men serving in the armed forces. After the war, they were encouraged, or even coerced, to return to hearth and home. Neither career nor higher education stood in the way of getting married and having children.

Divorce was practically unheard of. There was a spike in the divorce rate just after the war, as couples exited from hastily considered wartime marriages. The rate tripled from 56.2 divorces per 100,000 married persons in 1941 to 131.9 in 1946. It stood at 88.9 in 1951 and decreased through the rest of the decade.[10] The fifties were the golden age of the nuclear family. Men and women believed in marriage, and, even when the marital relationship was less than ideal, they thought it was important to stay together "for the sake of the children." Besides, a woman who had given up career and independent income for married life faced financial hardship and public opprobrium if she left her husband.

As temptingly plausible as the explanation might be, the end of the baby boom cannot be attributed solely to the availability of the birth control pill, which was authorized for use in Canada in 1961. The pill was certainly a factor in reducing birth rates, but there were other important developments. Because of the changing nature of the job market, both men and women had to stay in school longer, which often meant the postponement of marriage. The participation of women, including married women, in the paid work force rose steadily through the 1950s and 1960s, as new opportunities opened up for women in higher education, the professions, and the public sphere generally. The idealized happy homemaker of the fifties now had more options.

For these reasons, the baby boom tapered off in the early 1960s. The children born in the period from the Second World War to about 1964 constituted a huge demographic bulge that overshadowed the rest of the population. As a result, baby boomers tended to set the agenda. Whatever was of interest to them at any given time moved to the center of general concern—baby food and baby carriages when they were infants; hula hoops and rock and roll when they were teenagers; protests and demonstrations when they were university students; condos and health care as they grow old. Numbers alone do not account for their impact. After all, people are being born all the time. Why do we identify one group as a generation, but not some other group? A generation is a social, as well as a demographic, phenomenon. It is an age group that is shaped by history and in turn makes history.[11] Baby boomers possessed a remarkable cohesiveness and solidarity. They saw themselves as having a unique historical mission that transcended divisions of class, race, gender and region. Their moment in the sun was the sixties.

Growing Up in the 1950s

This generational unity had its origins in the 1950s, when the boomers were still children. Many of them were raised in a permissive environment by parents who heeded the advice of Dr. Benjamin Spock's *The Common Sense Book of Baby and Child Care.* First published in 1945, it sold four million copies in seven years and went through several editions.[12] Of course, people do not always read the books they buy. (I'm glad you're reading this one.) Many copies of Dr. Spock's book sat untouched on coffee tables and bedroom dressers. Nonetheless, his advice encapsulated the expert opinion and conventional wisdom of the day. He articulated in straightforward language what most contemporary child-care professionals were recommending. Parents were advised that children needed encouragement and nurturing more than discipline and punishment. Artificial schedules were said to be undesirable. The markers of child development—toilet training, walking, talking, etc.—must occur on the child's timetable, not the parents'. Children were to be showered with love and affection, their achievements praised and their self-esteem bolstered. The rule "spare the rod, and spoil the child" was turned upside down.[13] Spock was later blamed for the unruliness of the sixties generation, a charge that he said was either unjust or too flattering. Youth were rebellious all over the world, not just in places where his book was read.

Spock's advice in the nursery found an echo in the progressive, "child-centered" classroom. According to American philosopher and psychologist John Dewey, children have a natural desire to learn, a desire that is too often extinguished by authoritarian systems of education. Although Dewey propounded his theories in the early years of the twentieth century, they were not widely embraced until after the Second World War. As with Spock, there was a gap between philosophy and practice. We cannot assume that every classroom in the 1950s was "progressive," but there is no doubt that Dewey's ideas were popular. He believed that the teacher should be a friendly guide, not an authority figure or disciplinarian. The instructor should not drill facts into the child, impose a rigid curriculum, or do all the talking. Topics for study should arise spontaneously from what children are interested in and should be relevant to their experiences outside the schoolroom. Pupils were expected to learn how to work together cooperatively in groups, preferably on some kind of hands-on project, rather than sit in neatly-arranged rows listening to the teacher. The classroom was to be the very model of democracy. Indeed, the whole point of education, according to Dewey, was the training of students for democracy.

This resonated with the wider anxieties of the late forties and the fifties. The West had just emerged from a war against the Nazis, the very antithesis of liberal democracy. The holocaust cast a shadow over the whole period, and people were still trying to come to terms with what had happened. No sooner had the Nazis been defeated than the Cold War broke out. This time the enemy had nuclear weapons and the capacity to blow up the planet. The schools became the first line of defence against communism, the place where future citizens learned to appreciate the benefits of democracy, freedom and equal rights. These lessons were drummed into the heads of baby boomers. It comes as no surprise, therefore, that when the children of Spock and Dewey came of age, they noticed certain inconsistencies in the practice of democracy—for example, the anomaly that many African Americans did not have the right to vote and women were not treated equally with men. The very fact that liberal democracy had been held up as the highest achievement of civilization raised the stakes, laying the basis for the protest movements of the sixties.

Progressive education did have its critics. Hilda Neatby asserted in *So Little for the Mind* (1953) that it amounted to little more than socialization and indoctrination. The true goal of learning, she said, was truth, not attitude formation. Neatby also lamented the decline of academic standards. There was too much emphasis on process over content, on learning how to think rather than mastering a body of knowledge to think about. She pointed out that it was almost impossible to fail anyone (too damaging to self-esteem), and, consequently, schools were turning out graduates who were functionally illiterate. Whatever the merit of Neatby's arguments, they were doomed. The spirit of the age and the views of the education establishment ran against them. As a result, baby boomers encountered John Dewey, not Hilda Neatby, in the classroom.[14]

The children of the fifties were the first generation to grow up with television. Indeed, a baby boomer might be defined as a person who has a childhood memory of television coming into the home. The previous generation first experienced television as adults. The boomers considered it part of the furniture. The first television stations in Canada went on the air in Toronto and Montreal in 1952, and Regina's CKCK TV began broadcasting in the fall of 1954. By 1960, the country had 59 stations reaching 90 per cent of the population.[15] Canadians, except for those who lived near the border and could pick up an American signal, had to choose between the CBC and the privately owned station. Baby boomers grew up watching the same shows, laughing at the same jokes, and idolizing the same heroes. As children, they watched *Friendly Giant, Howdy Doody, Mighty Mouse, Huckleberry Hound, Lassie,* and *The Lone Ranger.* As they grew older, they tuned in to *Father Knows Best, Leave it to Beaver, Gunsmoke, Bonanza, The Ed Sullivan Show* and *Hockey Night in Canada.* Television viewing was a shared experience in a way that today's fragmented, multi-media universe makes impossible.

Boomers, significantly, were exposed to the commercials as well as the programs. It was obvious that this demographic group had enormous market potential. There were so many of them, and parents wanted to spoil them ("I want you to have all the things I didn't have when I was a child"). In addition, the booming economy ensured a high level of disposable income. It was not enough to keep up with the Joneses; you had to keep up with the Joneses' children. The consumer crazes of the fifties—Davy Crockett hats, hula hoops, and Barbie dolls—were all targeted at the baby boomers,[16] who, even as children, flexed their consumer muscles and had a keen sense of their importance in the scheme of things.

Many middle-class boomers grew up in the suburbs with their acres of virtually identical bungalows and split-levels. They typically had a picture window, modern kitchen with electrical appliances, two or three bedrooms, an L-shaped living room/dining room, rumpus room in the basement, back-yard barbecue, front driveway and carport or garage. Because Canada had a severe housing shortage after the Second World War, the government moved quickly to subsidize the construction of single-family dwellings. The Central Mortgage and Housing Corporation, created in 1945, provided mort-gage money at low interest rates. As a result, the number of owner-occupied houses in Canada increased from 57 per cent of all dwellings in 1941 to 65 per cent in 1951 to 66 per cent in 1961, despite the fact that the population of rural Canada, where owner-occupied homes were more common, declined through the period.[17] Between 1945 and 1960, an estimated one million Cana-dians moved to the suburbs.

Baby boomer parents were thrilled to escape crowded downtown apartments and move into homes with a backyard for the children to play in. During the day, when husbands were at work, suburbia was the domain of women and children. It was not always a happy kingdom. Many women felt lonely and trapped by the ceaseless round of childcare and housework. They yearned for contact with the wider world. Betty Friedan, author of *The Feminine Mystique* (1963), called it "the problem with no name." Other wom-en found fulfillment in the suburbs, enjoying married life, taking pride in raising their children, cherishing neighbourhood friends and participating in the community activities of church and school. As historian Veronica Strong-Boag points out, there was no one, single, universal suburban experience.[18] Some people took to it; others did not.

Nevertheless, the suburbs acquired a reputation for bland conformity, mindless banality, and empty consumerism. John Keats's *Crack in the Picture Window* and Sloan Wilson's *The Man in the Grey Flannel Suit* skewered the values it represented. They laid the foundation for the anti-suburbia myth, expressed in Malvina Reynolds' 1961 protest song: "Little boxes on the hill-side, little boxes made of ticky tacky ... and they all look just the same."[19] The suburbs of the fifties acted as a foil to the sixties counterculture. They symbolized materialism, phoniness, and other-directedness—the lifestyle that rebellious youth rejected.

The Teenage Subculture of the 1950s

A dissonant note in the 1950s was the emergence of a distinctive youth subculture. Teenage baby boomers had money to spend, either allowances given to them by their parents or wages earned in part-time jobs, which gave them market clout. Commercial enterprises were more than happy to cater to their needs. In addition, as prolonged schooling became the norm, high school became the institution identified with teenagers and the social space they occupied. Being a teenager was synonymous, increasingly, with going to high school. In 1954, the majority of 14- to 17-year-olds in Canada were in school, and by the early 1960s, the rate was 75 per cent.[20] Teenagers developed their own styles of speech, dress, and modes of interaction. The automobile was an object of fascination, giving rise to the car culture that is nostalgically evoked in George Lucas's film, *American Graffiti*. Souped-up cars, gleaming with chrome, cruise up and down the strip all night (and all movie) long. New magazines catered to the teenage market. Girls pored over *Seventeen*, which began publishing in 1944, eager for information about how to dress, put on makeup, relate to boys—essentially, how to be a teenager.

Nothing was more important to teenagers than rock and roll. Sixties historian Todd Gitlin dwells on its significance:

> The electric subcurrent of the Fifties was above all rock 'n' roll, the live wire that linked bedazzled teenagers around the nation—and quickly around the world—into the common enterprise of being young. Rock was rough, raw, insistent, especially by comparison with the music it replaced; it whooped and groaned, shook, rattled, and rolled. Rock was clamor, the noise of youth submerged by order and affluence, now frantically clawing their way out ... It was an invitation to dance, and at some fantasy level—just as the bluenoses protested—it was an invitation to make love. Even if the lyrics said so subliminally, the beat said it directly: *express* yourself, move around, get going. Rock announced: Being young means being able to feel rock. Whatever it is you're in, kid, you're not in it alone; you and your crowd are where it's at, spirited or truculent or misunderstood, and anyone who doesn't get it is, well, square.[21]

Rock and roll had its origins in the Delta blues, which were adapted by Muddy Waters to a more boisterous, urban sound to create Rhythm and Blues (R & B).[22] It was dance music with a strong beat, basically the blues played faster. At first the main market for R & B records was African American youth—hence the term "black music" or "race music"—but, as the 1950s progressed, the sound attracted white teenagers. According to rock historian David Szatmary, they favoured a more "frenetic, hard-driving version of an already spirited rhythm and blues that became known as rock and roll."[23] Among its progenitors were Little Richard, "a wild-eyed, pompadoured madman who crashed the piano keys and screamed nonsensical lyrics at breakneck speed,"[24] and Chuck Berry, who produced a string of hits including "Maybelline," "Roll Over Beethoven," and "Rock and Roll Music."

As more white teenagers gravitated to rock and roll, disc jockeys gave it airplay. The most ardent promoter was Allan Freed, who hosted a Cleveland radio show, "The Moondog Rock 'n' Roll Party," and sponsored hugely attended rock and roll concerts. He moved to New York in 1954 where he took charge of another highly successful radio program. Freed is credited with popularizing the term "rock 'n' roll," which owes its origins to an African-American euphemism for sexual intercourse. The popularity of the music coincided with the emergence of the civil rights movement, and, in fact, the two developments were related. In nightclubs the common practice was to draw a rope across the middle of the dance floor: "…the blacks on one side, whites on the other, digging how the blacks were dancing and copying them. Then, hell, the rope would come down and they'd all be dancing together."[25] The raucous music triggered a backlash from those who said it appealed to "the base in man" and brought out "animalism and vulgarity." Critics suggested that it was a "plot to mongrelize America."[26] They objected to the music's blatant sexuality, both in the lyrics and the pulsating beat. Parents worried, quite rightly as it turned out, that it would loosen sexual standards. In one volcanic rush, rock and roll channelled youth rebellion, the intermingling of black and white culture, and the sexual revolution.

Sam Phillips, a Memphis record producer, was often heard to say, "If I could find a white man who had the Negro sound and the Negro feel, I could make a million dollars."[27] He found the man he was looking for in Elvis Presley, who recorded "That's All Right Mama," in Phillips's Sun Records studio. When the record aired for the first time on July 7, 1954, the phones at the station rang off the hook. Fans, especially females, reacted hysterically. At a concert at Jacksonville, Florida, in May 1955, they pulled off Elvis's coat and shirt and ripped them to shreds. They chased him backstage, cornered him and forced him to climb on top of a shower stall as they pulled off his shoes and socks. Rescued by security guards, Elvis muttered, "Them little girls are strong."[28] When he appeared on the *Ed Sullivan Show* on September 9, 1956, the cameras showed him from the waist up only so that his swinging hips did not offend anyone. The broadcast attracted 54 million viewers, which represented 83 per cent of the television audience.[29] It was one of the defining moments of rock and roll history. Bono described Elvis Presley as the "big bang." In him African-American culture collided with European white culture to create a new musical universe.[30]

The youth culture of the fifties had a sinister, threatening side embodied in the juvenile delinquent. The film *Blackboard Jungle* (1955), set in a slum high school, featured out-of-control teenagers riding roughshod over their teachers and the school principal. In one scene, a mild, bespectacled teacher tries to ingratiate himself with his students by playing records from his prized jazz collection. The students go on a rampage, smashing his records and leaving him grovelling on the floor trying to find the glasses they have knocked off his head. The soundtrack blares Bill Haley's "Rock Around the Clock," underscoring the point that teenagers do not need adult music—they have their own. The film has a happy ending with the roughnecks being put in their place, but the denouement is less than convincing. The viewer is left with an overwhelming impression of the insolence of youth. The restoration of adult authority seems contrived.[31]

Public anxiety about juvenile delinquency was disproportionate to the actual incidence of juvenile crime. Objectively, it was not a major problem. The number of cases of juvenile delinquency brought before the courts in Canada in the fifties dropped to the lowest point in twenty years, and in the United States the pattern was similar.[32] The panic arose from the emergence of a new youth culture that adults found unsettling. Teenagers created their own world, a world from which parents were excluded. It was natural for them to feel threatened and to give a generous interpretation to the term "juvenile delinquent." A rock and roll band named *Frankie Lymon and the Teenagers* tried to clear up the confusion, recording a song with the lyric: "No, no, no, no, I'm not a juvenile delinquent." Slowly, the panic subsided. A survey that counted the number of articles about juvenile delinquency in

American popular magazines and journals (a rough index of public concern about the problem) showed that the number rose steeply during the Second World War, tailed off after the war, increased sharply in 1953, and then declined in 1957.[33] This suggests that by the late 1950s adults were beginning to come to terms with the existence of a youth culture, which they were able to differentiate from criminal or semi-criminal behaviour. At the same time, it cannot be denied that youth culture had an inherently subversive, oppositional ingredient. The whole point of rock and roll was that your parents did not like it. Parental approval was the kiss of death.

The anti-establishment component of 1950s youth culture remained unfocused and ill defined. *The Wild One*, released in 1953, starred Marlon Brando, who was clad in a black leather jacket, as the leader of a motorcycle gang that terrorizes a small California town. When he is asked what he is rebelling against, he mumbles, "Whadda ya got?" He is against everything in general, but nothing in particular. He has no clue what is wrong with society, much less any idea of how to fix it. Red-leather-jacketed James Dean was another *Rebel Without a Cause* (1955). This classic film of teenage angst, set, not in a working-class slum but rather an affluent, middle-class suburb, portrays unhappy teenagers in a favorable light. The fault lies with their parents who are uncaring, weak, and lacking in self-awareness. James Dean's father (appropriately played by the actor who was the voice of Mr. Magoo) wears a frilly apron and is hen-pecked by his wife; Natalie Wood's father cannot come to terms with his daughter's budding sexuality; and Sal Mineo's parents are just not there at all.[34] The three teenagers improvise their own little substitute family to provide the support and comfort that their parents have failed to give them.

Holden Caulfield, the discontented and profane protagonist of J.D. Salinger's *Catcher in the Rye* (1951), is another emblem of disaffected fifties youth. He sees "phoniness" everywhere, but, as with Brando and Dean, the anguish is more personal than social or political. The youth of the fifties do not organize a movement, write a manifesto, define a mission or forge a purposeful identity. They constitute a subculture, not a counterculture. They are unable to come up with an answer to the question: "What are you rebelling against?" This sets them apart from the youth of the sixties, who were endlessly verbose on the subject.

The Beats

A precursor to the sixties counterculture can be found in the Beats, a literary movement in which Jack Kerouac and Allen Ginsberg figured prominently.[35] Fleeing the boredom and suffocation of middle-class suburbia, the Beats pursued enlightenment and ecstasy in jazz, drugs, sex, travel, and the hip lifestyle. They celebrated "the jagged moment of experience"—not the past or future, but the NOW. For them delayed gratification was a contradiction in terms. Rebelling against jobs and family, they hit the road, seeking joy in the immediacy of pleasure, sensation and motion. Society, they believed, suffered from too much planning and technology, from a rationality that was so all-encompassing that it became crazy. Oddly, this perception was later borne out when US Defence Secretary Robert McNamara's superb technical calculations compounded the catastrophe of the Vietnam War, an outcome that even he came to regret.[36] Norman Mailer in his 1957 essay, "The White Negro: Superficial Reflections on the Hipster," wrote that the hip solution to the problems of life in middle-class America was "to divorce oneself from society, to exist without roots, to set out on that uncharted journey with the rebellious imperatives of the self." The alternative was to be "trapped in the totalitarian tissues of American society, doomed willy-nilly to conform if one is to succeed."[37] This captured the essence of Beat, which led eventually to the sixties counterculture.

The word "beat" was first used in 1888 in a book about the Civil War. It referred to "a lazy man or shirk who would by hook or crook get rid of all the military or fatigue duty that he could."[38] Jack Kerouac updated the term in 1948, when he told an interviewer: "So I guess you might say we're a beat generation."[39] By this he meant a generation that was materially and spiritually beaten down, marginalized, or just scraping by. The word had an affinity with the beatitudes: "Blessed are the meek for they shall inherit the earth … Blessed are the pure in heart for they shall see God." Kerouac said he arrived at this insight while praying before a statue of the Virgin Mary in a church in his hometown of Lowell, Massachusetts. The word also can refer to a musical beat, something that the Beatles picked up on when they changed their name from the Quarrymen. The Beats, however, were pre-rock and roll in musical preference. They favored the bebop jazz of Charlie Parker and Dizzy Gillespie, the sounds and rhythms of which are vividly rendered in Kerouac's pages.

Born in 1922 of French-Canadian stock, Kerouac grew up in a working-class family. His father was a printer; his mother worked in a shoe factory. He won a football scholarship to Columbia University, but soon dropped out, turning instead to a series of menial jobs as mechanic, merchant seaman, and short-order cook. He had a stint in the navy, receiving an honorable discharge after having been diagnosed as a schizoid personality "with angel tendencies."[40] He struck up a friendship with Neal Cassady, a wild character from Denver's skid row, who, by the age of 21, had stolen five hundred cars and spent fifteen months in reform schools. Cassady was, in Kerouac's words, "a wild yea-saying burst of American joy." He was the muse of the Beats, "the straw that stirred the drink."[41]

In April 1951, Kerouac sat down to write *On The Road*, a novel based on cross-country road trips he had made with Cassady. He wrote with feverish

Jack Kerouac (right) and Neal Cassady, the central characters in Kerouac's *On the Road*, the novel that defined the Beat generation. The poster is on the storefront window of City Lights Books, the glass reflecting the streetscape of North Beach, San Francisco, a favorite haunt of the Beats. AUTHOR PHOTO

speed, typing on a 120-foot-long scroll so that he did not have to stop to put pages into the typewriter. In three weeks he produced 186,000 words. When unrolled on the floor, the manuscript looked like an endless road.[42] It was hard for Kerouac to find a publisher. The material was too strange, the style too unorthodox, and the themes too unsettling. Finally, after six years, the book appeared. Gilbert Millstein, who reviewed it in the *New York Times* hailed it as a foundational text: "Just as, more than any other novel of the Twenties, *The Sun Also Rises*, came to be regarded as the testament of the Lost Generation, so it seems certain that *On the Road* will come to be known as that of the Beat Generation."[43]

The novel celebrates the "ragged and ecstatic joy of pure being."[44] Sal Paradise (Kerouac) and Dean Moriarty (Cassady) turn their backs on the stuffy conformity of mowed lawns, Sunday roast beef dinners, and the blue glare of the television set. Their road story is a metaphor for the search for freedom and the meaning of life, or, as Kerouac expresses it, the elusive "IT" that can be fleetingly glimpsed but never fully grasped. The journey into unknown psychological territory foreshadows the yearnings of the sixties. At one point in the story, Sal and Dean hitch a ride with "a tall, thin fag who was on his way home to Kansas and wore dark glasses and drove with extreme care" and a couple of "typical halfway tourists who wanted to stop and sleep everywhere." Dean erupts in an impassioned monologue: "Now you just dig them in front. They have worries, they're counting the miles, they're thinking about where to sleep tonight, how much money for gas, the weather, how they'll get there—and all the time they'll get there anyway, you see." He mimics middle-class thought patterns: "I read recently in *National Petroffious Petroleum News* that this kind of gas has a great deal of O Octane *gook* in it and someone once told me it even had semi-official high frequency *cock* in it, and I don't know, well I just don't feel like it anyway...."[45]

In another passage, Sal yearns to be somebody other than who he is: "At lilac evening I walked with every muscle aching among the lights of 27th and Welton in the Denver colored section, wishing I were a Negro, feeling the best the white world had offered was not enough ecstasy for me, not enough joy, kicks, darkness, music, not enough night ... I wished I were a Denver Mexican, or even a poor overworked Jap, anything but what I was so drearily a 'white man' disillusioned."[46] The novelist is on the outside looking in; he feels like an alien in his own skin. Belonging to the same generation as baby-boomer parents, Kerouac might have been one of them. Instead, he became the anti-parent, the voice of the soul restlessness that many baby boomers felt. They shared his disillusionment and his search; they were, in a phrase that Kerouac invented, "the rucksack generation." *On the Road* is a "hymn to purposelessness, an antidote to what John Fowles once decried as our modern 'addiction to finding a reason, a function, a quantifiable yield' in everything we do."[47]

Kerouac lived with his mother and drank himself to death at the age of 47. Fans still visit his gravesite in Lowell, leaving behind hand-written notes, poems, and half-empty wine bottles.[48] The original typescript of *On the Road* sold at auction in New York in May 2001 for $2.43 million, eclipsing the previous record set by Kafka's *The Trial*.[49] The sales of *On the Road* continue to be strong, averaging 110,000 to 130,000 copies a year.[50] The book still resonates, as in the following prophetic passage: "When daybreak came we were zooming through New Jersey with the great cloud of Metropolitan New York rising before us in the snowy distance. Dean had a sweater wrapped around his ears to keep warm. He said we were a band of Arabs coming in to blow up New York."[51] The book is full of hope and life, and yet profoundly sad. Kerouac's special insight, Allen Ginsberg observed, is that "life is a dream that is already over."[52]

Ginsberg was born in 1926 in Newark, New Jersey, his father a poet of minor reputation and his mother a mental patient. He attended Columbia from which he was expelled for writing obscenities in the dust on his dormitory window. In 1949, at the age of 23, Ginsberg was admitted to the Columbia Presbyterian Psychiatric Institute for eight months of psychotherapy, where his homosexuality was diagnosed as a type of mental illness. The poem *Howl* is dedicated to Carl Solomon, a fellow patient in the hospital. From the opening line—"I saw the best minds of my generation destroyed by madness, starving hysterical naked, dragging themselves through the negro streets at dawn looking for an angry fix, angelheaded hipsters burning for the ancient heavenly connection to the starry dynamo in the machinery of night"—to the impassioned scourging of Moloch—"whose love is endless oil and stone! Moloch whose soul is electricity and banks! Moloch whose poverty is the specter of genius! Moloch whose fate is a cloud of sexless hydrogen! Moloch whose name is Mind!"[53]—the poem raises the flag of revolt. Moloch, an ancient god that demanded the sacrifice of children, was a metaphor for modern America. *Howl* was a declaration of cultural war, a line drawn in the sand.[54]

City Lights Books, San Francisco, publisher in 1956 of Allen Ginsberg's *Howl*, "the poem that changed America." AUTHOR PHOTO

The lane behind City Lights Books, renamed to honor Jack Kerouac. AUTHOR PHOTO

It was read publicly for the first time on October 7, 1955, at the Six Gallery in San Francisco. Kerouac was there, collecting dimes and quarters to buy jugs of cheap wine, which were then passed around to members of the audience. As Ginsberg read, Kerouac interjected shouts of "Go! Yeah!" Published in 1956 by City Lights Books, *Howl* was banned on the charge that the material was obscene and would corrupt America's youth,[55] which only served to increase its notoriety and sales. Norman Mailer said of Ginsberg: "That four-eyed queer was the bravest man in America."[56] He was the living link between the Beats and the hippie counterculture. All through the sixties he showed up at events and rallies, including the Democratic party convention in Chicago in 1968, chanting his poems and lending his support to the youthful rebellion sweeping the nation and much of the world. *Howl*, it has been rightly said, was "the poem that changed America."[57]

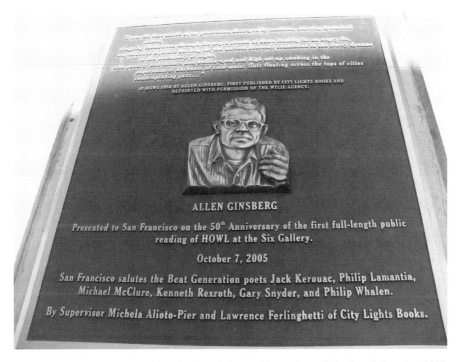

The plaque commemorating Allen Ginsberg's first public reading of *Howl* on 7 October 1955 at the Six Gallery in San Francisco. AUTHOR PHOTO

The Six Gallery, San Francisco, now a furniture store. AUTHOR PHOTO

Setting the Stage for the Sixties

Subversive currents flowed beneath the tranquil surface of the fifties, waiting for the right moment to erupt. The time came when baby boomers in large numbers appeared at the doorstep of universities. In 1956, the Canadian government asked Edward Sheffield to project post-secondary enrolments for the next decade. He predicted an increase from 60,000 to 120,000 by 1965. As it turned out, the numbers were much higher. Undergraduate enrolment in Canada swelled from 96,690 in 1959 to 187,049 in 1965 to 276,297 in 1970.[58] The growth was due partly to the increased numbers of young people and partly to a higher participation rate. Whereas in 1951 only 1 in 20 eighteen-year-olds went to university, by the mid-1960s the ratio was 1 in 10, and by the early 1970s 1 in 6.[59] This was because university graduates were in great demand to fill white-collar jobs in the expanding education, health, financial, and administrative sectors. During the 1960s, graduates with B.A.s had no trouble finding employment; many had offers even before completing their degree.[60]

In addition, the Soviet launch of Sputnik in October 1957, the first man-made satellite to orbit the earth, shocked the West. It was clear that if the USSR had a rocket powerful enough to put a satellite into space, it also had the capability to launch a nuclear missile against North America. Universities were called upon to play a part in the Cold War, especially to secure Western supremacy in science, technology, and weapons research. Money poured into the universities for science and engineering.[61] The humanities and social sciences were secondary beneficiaries, because it was considered important to buttress the cultural heritage of liberal democracy, the "soft" side of the battle against communism. University education was sold, perhaps oversold, as a key to personal success, economic prosperity, and victory in the Cold War. Existing universities were expanded; new institutions sprang up overnight.

The rapid increase in the student population brought problems in its wake. Young people, who had dreamed of a privileged, elite education in the quiet groves of academe, were herded like cattle into vast lecture theatres. The impersonal, bureaucratic nature of the campuses magnified discontent. There is power in numbers, and, in 1966, half the people in Canada were under the age of 21.[62] Students knew they were having a huge impact on the university system, and they were not shy about making their views known. Then, too, the university environment, especially the liberal arts, encourages critical thinking. Debate and disagreement are the lifeblood of a university. It is the ideal setting for radical thought and behavior, and students, who do not have 9-to-5 schedules and skip classes without penalty, can be mobilized for political activity.

The very affluence of the 1960s contributed to youth's discontent. Middle-class baby boomers had always known prosperity. Unlike the previous generation, they had no direct experience of depression or war.[63] Furthermore, boomers had every reason to expect that their standard of living would be as good as or better than that of their parents. Taking all of this for granted, they asked, "Is this all there is?" Such casual anti-materialism baffled and annoyed their parents, who knew the value of a dollar. They had trouble understanding why their spoiled offspring had such low regard for what they had achieved by dint of self-sacrifice and hard work.

While economic and demographic factors provided the structural preconditions for the sixties revolt, they alone do not explain it. Trigger events, such as the civil rights movement, the nuclear arms crisis and the Vietnam

War, activated latent discontent. The denial of equal rights to African Americans exposed a glaring contradiction in the democratic system and a moral failure of the status quo. It ignited righteous indignation and passionate commitment to social reform. Civil rights became a metaphor for the sixties, "We Shall Overcome" the unofficial anthem. Other groups—Québécois, Aboriginals, students and women—saw their own experiences mirrored in that of African Americans. Consequently, the civil rights movement became the model and template for other liberation struggles. In the sixties the marginalized and oppressed stood up and said, "We're not going to take it any more."

The second trigger event was the nuclear arms crisis. Although middle-class baby boomers had been raised in modest comfort, there was a dark side to their white-picket-fence world. This was brought home during the Cuban missile crisis in October 1962, when the world hovered on the brink of destruction. These concerns deepened with the grim spectacle of the Vietnam War. As philosopher George Grant pointed out, other catastrophes of the twentieth century, such as the holocaust and gulag, could be put down to aberrant totalitarian ideologies.[64] The Vietnam War, by contrast, came right out of the heart of liberal democracy. The United States, and Canada, too, through its quiet complicity, were using first-world technology to destroy a third-world peasant society.

The New Left

The New Left emerged as the political arm of sixties radicalism. It took organizational form in the Students for a Democratic Society (SDS) in the United States and the Student Union for Peace Action (SUPA), the Company of Young Canadians (CYC) and the Waffle in Canada. The SDS was by far the largest and most influential of these groups. Founded in 1960, it was a refurbished version of the Student League for Industrial Democracy, a youth club that had been attached to organized labor. The SDS adopted the Port Huron Statement in 1962, marking a philosophical turn from the Old Left to the New Left. The statement began: "We are people of this generation, bred in at least modest comfort, housed now in universities, looking uncomfortably to the world we inherit."[65] It went on to catalogue the sources of malaise, including racial bigotry, the atomic bomb, colonialism, poverty, meaningless work, and dysfunctional politics. Unlike the Old Left, which focused on flaws in the capitalist system, the Port Huron Statement did not name capitalism, as such, as the enemy. Nor did it concentrate, as the Old Left was wont to do, on the needs of the working class. Instead, the New Left moved away from class-based ideology to an analysis based on generational conflict. It saw youth, especially university students, as the "engine force for social reform." The university, fundamentally a middle-class institution, was seen as the bridgehead of social change. Having established a base in the academy, the New Left hoped to find allies in the wider community as part of its plan to renovate society and renew government.

The New Left was not primarily preoccupied with economic issues. The authors of the Port Huron Statement readily acknowledged that they had been "bred in modest comfort," and they did not dispute the material achievements of the American system. Their grievances lay elsewhere. They said the United States had not lived up to the ideals of equality and freedom found in the constitution. Americans were too apathetic. They allowed the elites—political, business, and military—to make the important decisions, they deferred too much to so-called "experts," and they permitted huge bureaucracies, both public and private, to control their lives.[66] Americans had failed in their duties as citizens. They did not care enough about the issues of the day to find out what was going on and try to make a difference in how the society governed itself. According to one Gallup poll, Americans listed "international affairs" a lowly fourteenth on their scale of priorities, yet they also stated that they "expected thermonuclear war in the next few years." The techniques of mass advertising and human relations management (aided by social science research) had been used to immobilize the American people, to substitute a facsimile of democracy for the real thing. The New Left called for the empowerment of the people. In their most famous slogan, they demanded "participatory democracy." This was quite a different focus from that of the Old Left, which had been chiefly interested in the redistribution of wealth and the building of the welfare state.

The Port Huron Statement declared: "We regard men as infinitely precious and possessed of unfulfilled capacities for reason, freedom and love…. Men have unrealized potential for self-cultivation, self-direction, self-understanding and creativity." One had to find "a meaning in life that is personally authentic," not simply conform to "status values." Here the New Left tapped into the concerns of the counterculture, which rejected inherited norms and conventional morality. The idea was not to do what other people thought was right, but rather to look deep down inside oneself to discover what was true and authentic. (The New Left assumed there was a true self to discover. They did not consider the possibility that the self is socially constructed.) To counter the charge that self-absorption leads to "egotistic individualism," the Port Huron Statement made a point of saying, "...the object is not to have one's way so much as it is to have a way that is one's own." Human relationships were deemed an essential part of the good life. Thus, the personal and the political came together. Politics was defined as "the art of collectively creating an acceptable pattern of social relations." It brought people "out of isolation and into community." It was "a necessary, though not sufficient, means of finding meaning in personal life." This highlights the psychological/existential dimension of the New Left.[67] Political involvement was not merely one of the duties of citizenship; it was also a prerequisite of personal fulfillment.

Similarly, a job was not just a job. In the ideal society the New Left envisioned the work one did to make a living not only put bread on the table, but also served a higher purpose. It was "educative, not stultifying; creative, not mechanical; self-directed, not manipulated; encouraging independence, a respect for others, a sense of dignity, and a willingness to accept social responsibility." Workers also had the right to control the workplace and the conditions of work: "The economic experience is so personally decisive that the individual must share in its full determination ... the economy itself is of such social importance that its major resources and means of production should be open to democratic participation and subject to democratic social regulation." Where, one might ask, could one find such a job? ... the university, perhaps?

The Port Huron Statement did not advocate the formation of a political party. Party politics was something the Old Left did. Parties inevitably degenerated into hierarchical bureaucracies controlled by elites, who manipulated people into thinking that their main contribution to democracy was to cast a ballot every four years. This was not participatory democracy, as the New Left understood it. They favoured more direct forms of political action, such as holding demonstrations and boycotts that focused media attention on a particular issue, got people thinking and put pressure on the government. It also encouraged involvement at the community level in co-ops, day care centers, tenants' organizations, lobby groups, student organizations, and other forums where people could have a personal sense of belonging and make meaningful changes. The process was just as important as the end result. The New Left was notorious for its long meetings, where everybody had a chance to say what they had to say until a consensus finally emerged.

The SDS grew steadily, reaching a membership of 100,000 by the late 1960s.[68] In the summer of 1964 volunteers moved into the slums of Chicago, Philadelphia, Newark and other cities to work directly with the poor. They went from door to door, talking with people, becoming familiar with their histories, and learning about their problems. The goal was to work with welfare authorities and other organizations to bring about tangible improvements in the delivery of services. While this work attracted interest, the main growth of SDS did not occur until the escalation of the Vietnam War. An anti-war demonstration in Washington, D.C., April 17, 1965, attracted 15,000 to 30,000 people (depending on the crowd estimate), far more than the organizers had anticipated. SDS president Paul Potter addressed the protesters: "We must name the system. We must name it, describe it, analyze it, and change it. For it is only when the system is changed and brought under control that there can be any hope of stopping the forces that create a war in Vietnam today or murder in the South tomorrow or all the incalculable, innumerable more subtle atrocities that are worked on people all over—all the time."[69] The trouble with the SDS—and this helps account for its ultimate collapse—was that it never did name the system. It did not clarify in specific terms what was wrong with society and how it was to be fixed.

In Canada, the New Left emerged from the cradle of the Combined Universities Campaign for Nuclear Disarmament, a "ban-the-bomb" organization that had been formed to prevent atomic war. The CUCND reinvented itself in December 1964 at a conference held in Regina. The new organization called itself the Student Union for Peace Action. While it continued the anti–nuclear war campaign, it broadened its agenda to include social justice and the empowerment of marginalized groups. Peace, it said, was not possible without justice. SUPA experienced the same difficulties as the SDS. As student leader James Harding put it, SUPA was "an ethical movement in search of an analysis." It needed to "lay out strategies for transforming Canada toward a society where power and wealth are not centralized, but rather remain in direct control of the people."[70] This was a lofty goal that was never achieved. SUPA was still searching for the analysis that Harding had said was necessary when it dissolved in 1967.[71]

The Company of Young Canadians owed its existence to the federal Liberal government led by Prime Minister Lester Pearson. Loosely modeled on the American Peace Corps (except the focus was domestic, not international), it was supposed to be a means for the government to channel the idealism of young people into social action. In practice, it bogged down in mismanagement and chaos. Perhaps it was doomed from the start. How, in all honesty, can a government subsidize a revolution against the establishment of which it is a part? Nonetheless, some useful things were done. CYC workers fanned out across the country to participate in community development projects in city slums and remote rural areas. Although pay was minimal, workers did receive an allowance, which led SUPA activists to jump ship for the CYC, prompting allegations that the government's strategy all along had been to get rid of SUPA. The CYC attracted a certain amount of negative press and attacks in the House of Commons from Members of Parliament, who deplored the hippie lifestyle of CYC personnel. The RCMP described the organization as "a relatively safe haven for subversive, criminal, and otherwise undesirable elements."[72] Plagued by poor leadership, administrative difficulties, and confusion about mandate, the CYC lapsed in 1976. For all the controversy, it helped launch the careers of Lloyd Axworthy, Gilles Duceppe, Georges Erasmus, and Barbara Hall, all of whom signed up with the CYC.[73]

Unlike the CYC and SUPA, the Waffle produced a coherent manifesto. Authored by Mel Watkins, James Laxer, Ed Broadbent and other leftist academics based in Ontario, it laid out a vision "For an Independent Socialist Canada." At one level, the manifesto can be interpreted as a call to the Old Left (in this case the New Democratic Party) to return to its socialist roots. It declared: "Capitalism must be replaced by socialism, by national planning of investment and by the public ownership of the means of production in the interests of the Canadian people as a whole."[74] Specifically, it advocated "nationalization of the commanding heights of the economy, such as the key resource industries, finance and credit, and industries strategic to planning our economy." This echoed the Regina Manifesto of 1933, the founding document of the Cooperative Commonwealth Federation, which evolved into the NDP in 1961. The 1933 statement concluded with the words: "No CCF government will rest content until it has eradicated capitalism and put into operation the full program of socialized planning which will lead to the establishment in Canada of the Cooperative Commonwealth." The Waffle accused the NDP of having strayed too far from its socialist convictions. It needed to return to the purity of anti-capitalist ideology.

However, the Waffle did not merely rehash the Regina Manifesto. It articulated a type of Canadian nationalism that was not present in the earlier document. According to the Waffle Manifesto, "the major threat to Canadian survival today is American control of the Canadian economy." It argued that: "An independence movement based on substituting Canadian capitalists for American capitalists, or on a public policy to make foreign corporations behave as if they were Canadian corporations, cannot be our final objective." For Canada to be independent, it had to be socialist, and for Canada to be socialist it had to be independent. The Waffle also addressed the issue of the separatist movement in Quebec. It said, "...there is no denying the existence of two nations within Canada, each with its own language, culture and aspiration." The only hope for national unity was a common front against American imperialism. Quebec, the Waffle maintained, could be persuaded to stay in Canada under the slogan "two nations, one struggle," which could unite French and English under the common banner of building a socialist alternative to the United States.

The Waffle Manifesto bears traces of the Port Huron Statement. For example, it critiques the welfare state, which is judged to be necessary, but not sufficient: "Much remains to be done: more and better housing, a really progressive tax structure, a guaranteed annual income. But these are no longer enough. A socialist society must be one in which there is democratic control of all institutions which have a major effect on men's lives and where there is equal opportunity for creative non-exploitative self-development. It is now time to go beyond the welfare state." This "going beyond the welfare state" took the Waffle in a New Left direction: "...economic independence without socialism is a sham, and neither are meaningful without true participatory democracy." Workers needed to participate in industrial decision-making and have "effective control in the determination of working conditions and substantial power in determining the nature of the product, prices, and so on." Further, "community democracy is as vital as the struggle for electoral success": "To that end, socialists must strive for democracy at those levels which most directly affect us all—in our neighbourhoods, our schools, our places of work. Tenants' unions, consumers' and producers' cooperatives are examples of areas in which socialists must lead in efforts to involve people directly in their struggle to control their own destinies." The emphasis on process as much as program was very much in keeping with the New Left mindset.

The Waffle Manifesto concluded with a strong endorsement of the NDP as the "core around which should be mobilized the social and political movement necessary for building an independent socialist Canada." This differentiated it from the Port Huron Statement, which, as we have seen, did not support any existing political party or propose the formation of a new one. As a result, the New Left in Canada was less amorphous and more structured than its US counterpart. The Waffle tried to work within or, as some would say, attempted to take over the NDP. The manifesto was debated at the NDP national convention in Winnipeg in October 1969, but the delegates did not approve it. Instead, they voted 499 to 268 in favor of a watered-down statement dubbed the marshmallow manifesto. At the 1971 convention, Waffler James Laxer entered the race to replace Tommy Douglas as national leader. Although he did not win, he made a strong showing, holding on until the fourth and final ballot, won by David Lewis.[75] Significantly, most of the labor unions backed Lewis, marking him as the Old Left candidate. Most of the Waffle supporters were young, many of them university students.[76] Like SUPA and CYC, the Waffle eventually disappeared. The Saskatchewan NDP establishment ignored them in the hope that they would go away, which they obligingly did in 1973.[77] The Ontario NDP took a more heavy-handed approach. Stigmatizing the Waffle as a "party within a party" and "an encumbrance around my neck,"[78] leader Stephen Lewis (son of David Lewis) expelled them from the party in 1972. The Waffle followed a similar trajectory to that of the New Left in the United States. A child of the sixties, it died with the sixties.

The Counterculture

The New Left, as we have noted, conceptualized politics broadly so that it included both fulfillment in human relationships and satisfaction in the workplace. Such a comprehensive understanding of the political provided a bridge to the counterculture, which historian Arthur Marwick defines as "the many and varied activities and values which contrasted with, or were critical of, the conventional values and modes of established society." He adds that "there was no unified, integrated counterculture, totally and consistently in opposition to mainstream culture."[79] This is also the view of Theodore Roszak in *The Making of a Counter Culture: Reflections on the Technocratic Society and Its Youthful Opposition* (1969). Although heavily romanticized, Roszak's analysis provides a good starting point. He describes the counterculture as: "… the embryonic culture base of New Left politics, the effort to discover new types of community, new family patterns, new sexual mores, new kinds of livelihood, new aesthetic forms, new personal identities on the far side of power politics, the bourgeois home and the Protestant work ethic."[80] The counterculture, to him, resembled an updated version of the children's crusades of the Middle Ages. Its adherents comprised a motley band of young people, constantly forming and reforming and never coherently organized, but marching hopefully, if fitfully, to the Promised Land.[81] Their mission was to affirm, in the midst of an overly rational, technocratic society, the transcendent value of the human spirit.

The counterculture involved both alternative lifestyles (dress, music, drugs, sexuality, communes) and oppositional values (spontaneity, self-expression, self-realization, anti-materialism, anti-work ethic).[82] It did not have an organizational structure, a well-defined membership, a clear pro-gram, or a political vehicle. It cannot be called a "movement culture," the term scholars apply to agrarian populist and working class movements that embody coherent, alternative visions to the existing order.[83] The counter-culture was too helter-skelter to qualify for that designation; indeed, it was inherently disorganized and unfocused. This quality comes through in the memoirs of Raymond Mungo, co-founder of the underground press *Libera-tion News Service*:

> It is impossible for me to describe our "ideology" for we simply didn't have one; we never subscribed to a code of conduct or a clearly conceptualized Ideal Society and the people we chose to live with were not gathered together on the basis of any intellectual commitment to socialism, pacifism, anarchism, or the like. They were people who were homeless, could survive on perhaps five dollars a day in spending money, and could tolerate the others in the house. I guess we all agreed on some basic issues—the war is wrong, the draft is an abomination and slavery, abortions are sometimes necessary and should be legal, universities are an impossible bore, LSD is Good and Good For You, etc.,

etc.—and I realized that marijuana that precious weed was our universal common denominator.[84]

There were degrees of involvement in the counterculture—it was not a clear-cut case of being either in or out. A 1967 study estimated that there were 200,000 "full-time hippies" in the United States, 200,000 "part-time summer and weekend hippies," and several hundred thousand others "who use psychedelic drugs, interact, and closely associate with totally dropped-out hippies, yet maintain a 9 to 5 job or student status."[85] Many sixties youth sampled aspects of the counterculture lifestyle or borrowed the trappings, growing their hair long, wearing beads and bandanas, dabbling in Eastern religions, doing drugs, and incorporating hip idiom into their vocabulary.[86] The media projected hippie images to a wide audience, often distorting or trivializing what the counterculture was all about. Advertisements swirled in psychedelic color, the fashion industry embraced bell-bottoms and paisley ties; all manner of products were pitched with promises of "lighting your fire" and "turning you on." After a while, it became difficult to distinguish the authentic from the ersatz.

Politics and culture interacted in diverse and complex ways. Todd Gitlin cites an example of symbiosis, when protesters at a Berkeley rally suddenly and spontaneously switched from singing the labor union stand-by "Solidarity Forever" to the Beatles' "Yellow Submarine," a seemingly innocent children's song about a yellow, lozenge-shaped mind-bending drug.[87] For a moment, hippies and radicals merged into a single community.[88] More often, beliefs and strategies diverged. Hippies generally wanted to opt out of society, in Timothy Leary's phrase, to "turn on, tune in and drop out." The revolution was in your head, not in external social structures or political systems. According to Leary, Ronald Reagan and Fidel Castro were peas in a pod, two ambitious and egotistical politicians lusting for power. The hippies saw in political activists an iteration of their achievement-driven, uptight parents, who turned the counterculture playground into a joyless field of exercise. Those who had a serious political agenda considered the hippie viewpoint naïve and irresponsible. The war in Vietnam was not going to end by itself. Victory for the peace movement required organization and disciplined effort. The hippies, by this reckoning, were inert, self-indulgent and drug-addled.[89]

On the other hand, the counterculture complemented radical politics to the extent that it defied the establishment and undermined traditional hegemonic structures and values.[90] Both the New Left and the counterculture were part of the "Great Refusal." They bound youth together in the common cause of generational revolt. Illegal drugs solidified the "us versus them" mentality, literally turning into outlaws those who were out of step with reigning norms. Music, too, was a binding agent and spiritual force that brought the tribes together.

It is hard to sum up the sixties and to make sense of such a complex, multi-dimensional era. It was the baby boomers' historical moment, the time from the late 1950s to the early 1970s when many of them were of university age. Their demographic dominance, economic security, and existential rebellion against the stale, oppressive fifties combined with trigger issues to de-legitimize the moral authority of the older generation. In the absence of civil rights and the Vietnam War, the youth of the sixties might have found something else to rebel against, but, as it happened, history gave them excellent raw material to fashion a revolt. They were able to cast themselves in the role of liberators, peacemakers and builders of a better world.

Near the beginning of Mike Wadleigh's film of Woodstock, a procession of long-haired, barefoot, weirdly-attired hippies make their way to the concert site. Three nuns dressed in grey habits and wearing old-fashioned glasses suddenly come into view. They look to be in their late twenties or early thirties. As they walk by and peer into the camera, one of them offers the peace sign. She seems to be saying, "I am not one of these hippies, but I have an affinity with them. I understand what they are trying to do." That was how she made sense of the sixties. She felt that there was something happening at that moment in history that connected with her religious beliefs, something that moved her to give a gesture of support. Our own judgment of the sixties depends on who we are and what we believe. It is impossible to be neutral, because the core of the sixties engages our deepest thoughts and feelings about the meaning of life and the kind of society we want to live in. This does not mean that our judgments have to be wholly subjective. We can try to enter imaginatively into the experience of those who lived the sixties, and this is what the next chapters begin to do.

CHAPTER 2

The Setting: Regina Campus in the Sixties

The Regina Campus of the University of Saskatchewan had a reputation for student activism. As alumna Pamela Wallin recalls, it was "a hotbed of radicalism, at least compared with Saskatoon, which we dismissed arrogantly as the traditional, more conservative factory for doctors and lawyers."[1] Part of the explanation for the politically charged atmosphere was Regina's rapid growth from 327 students in 1958 to 4,394 in 1969.[2] It was almost literally an instant campus, taking shape on the bald prairie, without well-established traditions to guide or inhibit development. Faculty and students started with a virtually blank slate. They had to invent an identity and create for themselves a sense of community and purpose. It was soon evident that Regina wanted independence from Saskatoon, a goal that was realized in 1974. There was a strong feeling that the new campus should not be a duplicate of the parent. For many, it became a badge of honor *not* to follow the Saskatoon model. Others felt that it was a mistake to seek novelty for the sake of novelty. They wanted Regina to be a university much like any other university, and, if that meant imitating Saskatoon, so much the better. This difference of opinion set the stage for a vigorous debate about the fundamental aims of higher education.

The Regina Campus Environment

Saskatoon, which began teaching classes in 1909, was home to several professional colleges, such as law, medicine, commerce, education, engineering and agriculture. Regina had professional programs, too, notably education, administration, engineering, and social work, but, compared with the Saskatoon campus, a larger proportion of the student body were enrolled in liberal arts. Humanities and social science students, not having a specific vocational orientation, were more apt to be attracted to open-minded inquiry and challenges to the status quo. Studies of student radicalism in the United States in the sixties reveal that social science majors joined protest movements in greater numbers than those enrolled in professional or vocational studies.[3] The comparison between Regina and Saskatoon seems to bear this out.

Another factor was the hiring of faculty. Out of 369 professors at Regina Campus in 1971, 222 (60 per cent) were Canadian, 73 (20 per cent) were American, 45 (12 per cent) came from English-speaking countries other than the United States, and 29 (8 per cent) originated in non-English-speaking countries.[4] Americans were proportionally over-represented in the Division of Social Sciences, the hotbed of radical activity at Regina Campus, where they made up 34 per cent of the faculty, compared with 20 per cent for the campus as a whole. Some of these expatriates came to Canada to make a political statement or as a gesture of protest against the Vietnam War. Others were simply trying to find a job and advance their academic careers. Later it became fashionable to attribute the discontent at Regina to "Vietnam War draft dodgers," but this explanation lacks credibility. The first major student protest march in Regina took place in March 1964, well before the main influx of American academics and a full year before the escalation of the Vietnam War. When American professors arrived in Regina, they encountered students who already had a high level of political awareness. These students did not have to depend on outsiders for inspiration.[5]

Regina was the capital city of the province that elected the first socialist government in North America in 1944. The Cooperative Commonwealth Federation (CCF), which became the New Democratic Party (NDP) in 1961, enacted legislation that was later imitated throughout the rest of Canada. Shortly after taking power, it established three new departments (social welfare, labor and cooperatives), passed a farm security act, and put in place the most pro-labor trade union legislation on the continent. Saskatchewan was the first province to allow civil servants to form unions, the first to enshrine a bill of rights prohibiting discrimination on the basis of race, color or creed, the first to implement compulsory government automobile insurance, and the first to institute a hospital insurance plan. The CCF also established Crown corporations in key sectors of the economy, such as power, telephones, bus transportation, airline service in the north, fish and fur marketing, forestry products and sodium sulphate mines. In the 1970s, the NDP extended government ownership to potash, oil, and uranium.

Perhaps the most famous initiative was medicare. Premier Tommy Douglas on April 25, 1959, in a speech at Birch Hills, announced his government's intention to create universal, tax-supported, publicly administered medical insurance. After fighting the 1960 provincial election on the issue, winning 38 of 55 seats, the CCF introduced the enabling legislation in November 1961. In one bold stroke, health care was socialized, that is, transferred from the private to the public sector. The doctors, who opposed the plan, went on strike on July 1, 1962, the day medicare was supposed to go into effect. Meanwhile, Douglas had resigned as premier in November 1961 to take over the leadership of the national NDP, leaving his successor Woodrow Lloyd to manage the dispute. Lloyd found the strain almost impossible to bear. "How much punishment can the people take?" he asked; "how much punishment can we justifiably expose them to?"[6] The word "Commie" was spray painted on his house, and health minister Bill Davies resorted to sleeping with a ten-gauge shotgun in the wastebasket next to his bed. Finally, July 23, 1962, a settlement was reached with the doctors, who agreed to practise under the new system. Despite its controversial beginnings, medicare proved popular with the general public. It spread to other provinces, and, in 1968, the federal government agreed to pay a share of the cost. Medicare was on its way to becoming a national institution and part of the Canadian identity.

Saskatchewan in the early 1960s was a lively place on the cutting edge of social change. The economy was strong, the population growing, and the politics intense. The energy and spirit of innovation extended to the world of art. The Regina Five (Art McKay, Ronald Bloore, Ken Lochhead, Ted Godwin, Douglas Morton), a group of young painters from Regina Campus, exhibited their paintings at the National Gallery in Ottawa in November 1961. Reviewers acclaimed it "one of the most significant shows of contemporary Canadian art" and praised the group as "a remarkable phenomenon of the Canadian Prairies."[7] New York art critic Clement Greenberg enthused: "The specialness of art in Regina consists most of all in a state of mind, of awareness, and of ambition on the part of five abstract painters who live there ... I find something wonderful going on in Regina."[8] Ted Godwin, a member of the Regina Five who arrived from Alberta, commented on the atmosphere in the city: "What a place it was ... the Regina of those days. Quite an experience for a Calgary kid to rub elbows at parties with Spanish Civil War veterans, refugees from the McCarthy Communist witch-hunt south of the border, as well as various assorted brilliant committed socialist intellectuals from all over the globe."[9]

History of Regina Campus

This was the environment in which Regina Campus came of age. The school had its origins in 1911 when the Methodist Church established Regina College to offer secondary education to young people in the city and from the surrounding area. High schools at that time were scarce in rural Saskatchewan, and parents welcomed the opportunity to send their children to a church-run residential college, whose stated purpose was to "[train] young people to intellectual mastery and in the principles of Christian citizenship."[10] The college was located on College Avenue to the south of the downtown district and across Wascana Lake from the provincial Legislative Building. Enrolment increased through the 1920s, partly because the college in 1925 entered into an affiliation agreement with the University

Regina College, founded in 1911, which became the Regina Campus of the University of Saskatchewan in 1961. UNIVERSITY OF REGINA ARCHIVES AND SPECIAL COLLECTIONS

of Saskatchewan. This allowed students to take the first year of the three-year Bachelor of Arts course in Regina before proceeding to Saskatoon or some other university to complete their degree. Regina College wanted to extend its offerings to a full degree program, but President Walter Murray of the University of Saskatchewan firmly resisted. He feared that the emergence of a second university in the province would result in less government money for Saskatoon.[11] The Great Depression of the 1930s brought Regina College to its knees. Enrolment slumped calamitously, and the school plunged into debt. Reluctantly, it consented in 1934 to be taken over by the University of Saskatchewan. This meant that Saskatoon was in the driver's seat. Since it now controlled the college, it could block the emergence of a university in Regina, thereby preserving Saskatoon's monopoly over higher education in the province. In the years that followed, the dean and faculty of Regina College repeatedly asked for permission to offer courses beyond the first year, but they were always turned down.

The situation began to change in the 1950s. About 150 Regina citizens gathered at city hall in March 1954 to revive the dream of college expansion. Led by lawyer George H. Barr, they formed the Regina College Citizens' Committee, whose members belonged to a variety of community organizations including the Trades and Labor Council, Chamber of Commerce, Local Council of Women, Public School Board, Home and School Association, Royal Canadian Legion, and Regina City Council. The trade union movement played a prominent role, the Regina Trades and Labor Council being the first organization to contribute money to the Regina College Citizens' Committee. Both the Regina and Moose Jaw Labor Councils persistently lobbied the provincial government on behalf of the college. They drew attention to the fact that in 1954 there were enrolled at the Saskatoon campus 492 students from Saskatoon and 274 from Regina. Regina at the time had a population of 83,000 compared to 61,000 in Saskatoon. It seemed obvious that more young people from Regina would be able to attend university if they had the opportunity to take classes in their hometown.[12]

The province of Saskatchewan had a university participation rate (the percentage of high school graduates who attend university) well below the national average. When the Regina Campus began to offer second-year arts courses in 1961 and the full degree in 1964, the participation rate increased dramatically. While this was part of a national trend based on structural factors, such as the growing need for university credentials for white-collar jobs, it also can be attributed to the increased accessibility of higher education. Regina students from working-class or lower-middle-class families, who previously had not been able to afford to go to university because of the expense of living away from home, now had the chance to pursue their studies beyond Grade 12.

This helps to explain the political atmosphere at Regina Campus. Students who had a labor union background had a different perspective from those whose parents were businessmen or professionals. As we have seen, the unions were among the most stalwart backers of a full degree program in Regina. In addition, Regina was a government town where many people worked for the civil service or Crown corporations. The CCF had been in power since 1944, which meant that the public sector generally had a left-wing cast. Their children were "pink-diaper babies," the Saskatchewan equivalent of "red-diaper babies" in the United States, the term applied to student radicals whose parents had been members of the Communist party in the 1940s and 1950s. Woodrow Lloyd, who was premier from 1961 to 1964 and leader of the opposition from 1964 to 1970, openly admired the sixties counterculture and the New Left.[13] He saw the students of the sixties as harbingers of socialist revival, the best hope to save a world beset by consumerism, racism and militarism.

Bowing to public opinion and the prospect of baby boom enrolments, the University of Saskatchewan Board of Governors and Senate made the decision in 1959 to establish a full degree program at Regina College.[14] The university's forward planning committee reported in June 1959 that the upper limit on enrolment at Saskatoon should be set at "approximately double the present number." Since enrolment in 1958-59 was 4,114, the cap was placed at about 8,000 students. The report went on to say that the limit on enrolment in Saskatoon implied "the development of facilities for university education elsewhere in the Province." In particular, it recommended "that the first step in such a development be the establishment in Regina of a three-year course leading to a Bachelor of Arts degree."[15] Subsequently, in 1966, a Committee on the Organization and Structure of the University produced a report, which was adopted by Senate. It stated that "the Regina campus eventually will approximate the Saskatoon campus in size and activity...."[16] John W.T. Spinks, president of the university (1959-1974), affirmed on several occasions that Regina was to be a well-developed university. In his convocation address in Regina in May 1972, he stated: "Speaking rather more generally about the development of the Regina Campus, it is essential, from the point of view of the impact of a centre of higher education on the surrounding community, that Regina be a real, full-fledged university and not just a large liberal-arts college."[17]

In terms of governance, the initial organizational structure for the two campuses consisted of one board of governors, one senate, and one president, with each campus having its own faculty council reporting to senate. Nomenclature was also revised in accordance with Regina's new status. Regina College on July 1, 1961, became the University of Saskatchewan, Regina Campus. The original plan had been for Saskatoon to rename itself the University of Saskatchewan, Saskatoon Campus, but this was resisted. Saskatoon preferred to be known simply as the University of Saskatchewan, another small sign of the tensions that were developing between the two campuses regarding their status and role.

The university hired a Toronto consulting firm to recommend a site for the expanded Regina Campus. One option was to construct new buildings at the existing location on College Avenue. The other was to acquire land at the south-eastern edge of the city, which was currently in use as a Dominion Agricultural Experimental Station, but owned by the provincial government. The consultants strongly favored the experimental farm site because it was much larger and afforded opportunities for future expansion. The College Avenue property, by contrast, would require the construction of high-rise buildings, forcing students to use elevators to get to classes. Green space would be at a premium, and athletic playing fields reduced to the bare minimum. All in all, the farm site seemed the logical choice. Nonetheless, the Board of Governors rejected the recommendation and asked for a second evaluation of the College Avenue property. The consultants looked at it again, incorporating into their study all the available land in the vicinity, including an island in Wascana Lake. They returned with the same advice they had given the first time, and this time the board accepted it.

As planning proceeded, the scope of the project became more ambitious. The Government of Saskatchewan, the City of Regina, and the University of Saskatchewan formed a partnership to develop the 1,000 acres surrounding Wascana Lake as a "center for government, education, arts, and recreation."[18] The Wascana Centre Authority, as the joint body was called, hired Minoru Yamasaki as master planner of both the park and the new campus. Not yet fifty years old, Yamasaki already had a brilliant reputation. His

Minoru Yamasaki, the American architect who planned the new Regina Campus and designed the first buildings. UNIVERSITY OF REGINA ARCHIVES AND SPECIAL COLLECTIONS

credits included university buildings at Wayne State and Oberlin College, the St. Louis air terminal, and the United States pavilion at the world agricultural fair in New Delhi. Later, he designed the World Trade Center buildings that went down in the 9/11 attacks.[19]

Yamasaki invited Thomas Church, a landscape architect from San Francisco, to work with him on the plans for Wascana Park. Together, they came up with a concept they considered "truly magnificent": "This green centre bounding the shores of Wascana Lake in the Heart of the Capital City of Regina will become a vivid oasis made even more dramatic by the bareness of the Midwestern Canadian prairie; and in this verdant setting will be placed many of the aspirations of the people of Saskatchewan in physical form—The Government Centre symbolic of the Province and the working and living together of its citizens, the University and the aspirations of man for knowledge, and in its parks the reaching of man for beauty."[20] As planner of the Regina Campus, Yamasaki had a blank slate on which to work. There were no roads, buildings, or prominent physical features to interfere with his ideas. His goal, he said, was to design a university that had "great dignity" without being "pompous" and that was "warm and friendly," yet with "the kind of atmosphere which is conducive to study and research."[21]

The forbidding flatness of the site of the future campus in southeast Regina. UNIVERSITY OF REGINA ARCHIVES AND SPECIAL COLLECTIONS

The plan called for the construction of academic buildings on one-storey connecting platforms or podiums, which would elevate the campus above the prairie, forming interior courtyards and sheltering the students as they moved from building to building in winter weather. The main entrance was situated at the northwest corner of the campus, where the road was to pass underneath the podium. On top of it, a 160-foot bell tower was to be constructed, tall enough so that it could be seen from anywhere on the campus and from across the lake.[22] As it turned out, this signature structure was never built. Its sole legacy was that it inspired the students to name their newspaper the *Carillon*.

The Board of Governors approved Yamasaki's plan in January 1962 and awarded him the commission to design the first two buildings, the Classroom and Laboratory buildings.[23] Scheduled for completion in the fall of 1964, they were not ready for occupancy until the summer of 1965 and, even then, students had to pick their way across muddy fields to get to classes since the main road had not been finished. Premier Ross Thatcher, a Liberal who had defeated the CCF in the 1964 election, snipped the ribbon at the official opening ceremony on October 8, 1965. Those in attendance could hear bulldozers rumbling in the background, excavating sites for the Library and

Physical Education Centre.[24] Yamasaki designed the library, which he considered to be the most important building on the campus and the spiritual heart of the university. It was opened in October 1967 by John H. Archer, then archivist and professor of history at Queen's University and later the first president of the University of Regina. He said at the opening ceremony: "Let there be information retrieval … but let there also be value retrieval … Open the doors and let in all mankind who seek answers … Above all, let in youth. Help those to interpret the call of the trumpet notes that sound faint in their ears."[25] The library is now named after him. The Physical Education Centre opened in late 1966, the Education building in the fall of 1969, College West in 1972, and the Administration/Humanities Building in 1973. There were also two federated colleges, Campion College (Catholic), completed in 1968, and Luther College in 1971. In accordance with the federation agreements, the colleges were administratively distinct, but academically integrated with the university.

A shortcoming of campus planning was the lack of space for students. A 1968 study reported: "Conditions of overcrowding on the campus have reached a point at which they should be a cause for grave concern, if not alarm."[26] The space deficiency was estimated at more than 275,000 square

Breaking ground for the new campus in 1963, with Premier Woodrow Lloyd addressing the gathering. UNIVERSITY OF REGINA ARCHIVES AND SPECIAL COLLECTIONS

The Classroom and Laboratory buildings (left) and the Library at the new Regina Campus,
scarcely a tree in sight. PHOTOGRAPHY DEPARTMENT, UNIVERSITY OF REGINA

An aerial view of Regina Campus, 1974. UNIVERSITY OF REGINA ARCHIVES AND SPECIAL COLLECTIONS

feet, but this gross measurement did not take into account the full extent of the problem, since the shortfall was most acute in the area of student services, especially cafeteria, lounge, and student activity space. The cafeteria facilities had been designed to accommodate 1,200 students, not the 3,300 who were enrolled by 1967. Between classes, students sprawled on the floor in the foyer of the library or in front of the elevators. University president John Spinks suggested helpfully: "Had you thought of having a few more settees in the entrance lobby to the Library? This might help to discourage students from lying full length on the carpet."[27] Overcrowding aggravated student discontent. As the previously cited study observed: "... wherever students are located for other than purely academic purposes, they exist on sufferance with respect to some other function of the University. That they are fully aware of this fact does nothing to ease current tensions." The Board of Governors sought a short-term solution in the construction of a temporary student services building.[28] It opened in the fall of 1969 and was intended to last ten years. As it turned out, ten years stretched to thirty. The building was finally torn down in 1997 when the Students' Union and *Carillon* moved into the Riddell Centre.

The Regina Beach Statement

As the planning and construction of new buildings proceeded, the Regina Campus faculty worked on the development of academic policy and programs. A key figure in these discussions was Dallas W. Smythe, chair of the social sciences division. Born in Regina, he studied at the University of California, Berkeley, where in 1937 he obtained a Ph.D. in economics. He worked in Franklin Roosevelt's New Deal administration, serving as chief economist at the Federal Communications Commission from 1943 to 1948. His leftist politics attracted the interest of the FBI, and during the red scare and McCarthy witch hunt of the 1950s, he came to the conclusion that his days as an employee of the US government were numbered. Escaping to academic life, he accepted a position at the Institute of Communications Research at the University of Illinois, Champaign-Urbana. He was interested in the political economy of mass communications, with an emphasis on the role of the media in bolstering capitalism and liberal ideology. His research led to the publication of *Dependency Road: Communications, Capitalism, Consciousness and Canada* in 1981. Both Smythe and his wife were active in the peace movement, and both tended to blame the United States for what they regarded as its overly aggressive posture in the Cold War. For them, the Cuban missile crisis was the last straw. They decided to leave the US and take up residence in Canada.

Smythe took up his duties as chair of the social sciences division in the fall of 1963. The Regina Campus Faculty of Arts and Science was organized on the divisional system, according to which disciplines were grouped in four clusters: social sciences, natural sciences, humanities, and fine arts. This was partly because the departments were still too small to function effectively as independent entities and partly because many (though by no means all) faculty members favored an interdisciplinary approach to liberal arts education. They were of the view that the departmental structure led to the compartmentalization of knowledge and hampered the development of a well-integrated curriculum. Smythe suggested that Dr. Robert Hutchins, former president of the University of Chicago (1929-1951), be invited to address a faculty retreat and assist in formulating the educational philosophy of the new campus. Hutchins was known as an unorthodox critic of mainstream university education. His book, *The Higher Learning in America*, first published in 1936 and reprinted in 1961, argued that the undergraduate curriculum had become fragmented, disordered, and excessively focused on technical training. Students were not given an opportunity to study the classic texts of Western civilization or participate in the "great conversation" about the nature of man and the meaning of life.[29]

After leaving the University of Chicago, Hutchins founded the Center for the Study of Democratic Institutions at Santa Barbara, California, a think-tank where prominent scholars engaged in discussions concerning the issues and problems of democracy. Among the topics dealt with were the role of technology in modern society, the responsibility of the media, civil rights, the women's movement, student unrest, world peace, and economic policy.[30] Although Hutchins was unable to come to Regina for the faculty retreat, he recommended W.H. ("Ping") Ferry, a colleague at the Center, as the keynote speaker. Ferry, like Hutchins, was a severe critic of the status quo in higher education. He believed that universities were failing dismally to deal with the urgent problems facing society. Timid, docile, and conformist, they were, according to Ferry, afraid to offend powerful government and business interests. As a result, they were training students who were able "to make a living, but unable to make a world."[31]

Dallas Smythe could not have agreed more. He grounded his ideas about education in the context of the accelerating, even alarming, pace of global change. The signs were everywhere: uncontrolled development of science and technology, automation of industry, Third World poverty, and, most dangerous of all, the threat of nuclear war. If the planet were to survive, Smythe believed, "mankind will have to change its attitudes and institutions more in the next fifteen years than it did in the last 10,000 years."[32] The university in this context could not be an ivory tower. Its purpose was to extend and transmit knowledge, and the function of knowledge, according to Smythe, was "to provide ways of finding solutions to man's problems." This meant that the curriculum had to be "relevant" (a favorite sixties word) and students had to be encouraged to think critically about the world around them. The university had a crucial role "in forming men's attitudes towards the institutions which provide not only men's consumer goods but his intake of cultural materials of all kinds." The university, in Smythe's opinion, had to be an agent of change.

Allan B. Van Cleave, chair of the natural sciences division, represented the other side of the debate. He maintained that while it was important to build a liberal arts college, the establishment of professional colleges could not long be delayed. "The majority of our students," he pointed out, "attend the university with the view of training themselves for entry into some profession. It is sheer 'ivory towerism' to think that they do not."[33] Van Cleave warned against radical adjustments to the curriculum. Change for the sake of change was not a good thing. "We must be reasonably certain," he cautioned, "that the changes proposed have real merit." Regina Campus would be well advised to concentrate on establishing a reputation for academic excellence and scholarly research. This meant, among other things, the acquisition of "first rate up-to-date scientific equipment … so that a healthy spirit of investigation of the unexplored regions of science may be fostered."

For Smythe and his supporters, the untrammelled development of science and technology was part of the problem, not the solution. They called for a liberal arts approach that subordinated scientific techniques to broader social concerns. It soon became evident that Smythe and Van Cleave had diametrically opposed visions of the future of the Regina Campus. Smythe wanted an innovative liberal arts program that emphasized well-rounded, interdisciplinary education, socially relevant course material, and training for the responsibilities of citizenship. Students were to be prepared not only to make a living, but also, as Ferry had said, "to make a world." Van Cleave wanted a university in the traditional mould. His model was the University of Saskatchewan, where he had been a member of the Department of Chemistry from 1937 to 1962, the year he came to Regina. His colleague in the chemistry department, John Spinks, was appointed president of the university in 1959 and continued in that office until 1974. Smythe suspected that Spinks had sent Van Cleave to Regina to make sure that the new campus did not stray too far from the Saskatoon pattern. Thus, the Smythe/Van Cleave debate about the mission of Regina Campus became entangled in the power struggle between Regina and Saskatoon. Smythe and his supporters came to believe that Regina could not achieve its true destiny until it had secured its independence from the University of Saskatchewan. Van Cleave was branded as "Spinks' man."

These conflicts lay just below the surface at the faculty retreat held December 13-15, 1963, in a freezing hotel at Regina Beach, a small community about thirty miles north of the city. The retreat produced a document titled the "Educational Policy for the Liberal Arts," also referred to as the Regina Beach statement or the Regina Beach manifesto. It opened with a quotation attributed to Socrates—"the unexamined life is not worth living"—and continued in five parts:

I.   The university has traditionally undertaken the role of preserving, transmitting, and increasing the intellectual heritage of man. We reaffirm our acceptance of this task.

II. This affirmation cannot be taken to mean that a university is a mausoleum of possibly interesting but irrelevant and impractical ideas, a repository of the past. No. There must also be an affirmation that the university is an important part of the critical intelligence of society, examining institutions, seeking to penetrate the future, sensitive to change, aware of the past, and of the manifold problems and dangers of the present.

III. Above all, the role of critic, of examiner of institutions and ideas, belongs to the modern university functioning as a community of scholars. Its criticism should be sustained by constant reference to essential human values, which demands a deliberate renewal of the study of the nature of love, of justice, freedom, beauty, science: in fact, all those values which give meaning and substance to life. This implies a de-emphasis of mere topicality in the subject matter of the liberal arts curriculum. Further, this examination requires that all liberal arts students should be involved with a wide range of subject matter, so presented that the student may be able to synthesize his total experience in the liberal arts college. Such a program will frequently call for a kind of intellectual slum-clearance, a breaking up of those conventional myths which are frequently identified with reality. This constant critique must be applied first to the structure and function of the university itself.

IV. The implication for educational philosophy is that, above all, the idea, the general context, the point of view is what should be transmitted to the student. The professor is charged with the responsibility of opening and of sustaining a dialogue with the student: the student must be encouraged to see that his relationship to the educational process, and to the dialogue, is not that of exposure merely, but of involvement. An exceedingly careful choice of basic material has to be made in order to achieve depth of appreciation in a given subject. Material will be continually re-assessed for its relevance and value. The development of critical intelligence in the student calls for considerable attention by the professor to the basic critical assumptions of his discipline. The "mindless counting" approach to knowledge finds scant welcome in the framework; and methodological hobby-horses and peculiarities become secondary.

V. Professors and students must be free to express themselves on all issues, controversial or not, but are responsible to the academic community.

Parts I and V restated traditional goals of the university: the preservation, transmission and expansion of knowledge, and freedom of thought and expression. However, apart from the oblique reference to the "expansion of knowledge," there was no explicit endorsement of scholarly research and publication. Indeed, it may be inferred from the document that the value of such work is doubtful unless it can be related directly to the amelioration of social problems. Nor was there a reiteration of the liberal ideal that truth is worth pursuing for its own sake. As we have seen, Dallas Smythe was influential in shaping the discussions that led to Regina Beach. His fingerprints are all over the document. He characterized research that was driven by the desire to know, and nothing more than the desire to know, as "antiquarianism" or "academic busywork." Significantly, the Regina Beach statement endorsed the principle of free expression for professors and students, but said nothing about free inquiry. This was not just an oversight; it reflected the educational philosophy at the heart of the document. Regina Beach conceptualized the university as an institution that is fully immersed in the world, not an ivory tower standing aloof from society.

This spirit permeated Parts II, III and IV of the Regina Beach statement. Part II declared that a university is not "a mausoleum of possibly interesting but irrelevant and impractical ideas, a repository of the past." It is "an important part of the critical intelligence of society, examining institutions, seeking to penetrate the future, sensitive to change, aware of the past, and of the manifold problems and dangers of the present." Part III elaborated this theme, adding that the university in its capacity as social critic must refer constantly to "essential human values, which demands a deliberate renewal of the study of the nature of love, of justice, freedom, beauty, science." This echoed Robert Hutchins' belief that the modern university had become obsessed with technique and had lost sight of the fundamental questions. Regina Beach reacted against this trend. It affirmed that "essential human values" were worth studying and that they informed the critique of social institutions and practices. The university had to be relevant and practical, but not in a narrowly technical way. Its job was not just to find out how to do things more efficiently but to consider whether they were worth doing in the first place. Such judgments were to be grounded in a sound appreciation of "essential human values."

The remainder of Part III and all of Part IV dealt with curriculum and teaching methods. The student was to encounter "a wide range of subject matter, so presented that [he] may be able to synthesize his total experience in the liberal arts college." Understanding the "general context," "point of view," and "basic critical assumptions" of the various academic disciplines was more important than memorizing quantities of detailed information. The student was to be guided to grasp the "big picture" and to think critically about the course material. For this to happen, professor and student had to engage in a dialogue. Liberal education was not a one-way street: "The student must be encouraged to see that his relationship to the educational process, and to the dialogue, is not that of exposure merely, but of involvement." The student was to be encouraged to think for himself, not merely absorb the ideas of others. This conformed to the liberal ideal of a university as a space sheltered from politics where scholars are free to debate issues in a civil manner. However, if the university is conceived primarily as an agent of social change, the "dialogue" becomes more difficult to sustain. Faculty and students feel pressure to "get with the program." This happened in the sixties at universities where the New Left gained the upper hand. Radicals attacked scholars whose research was deemed irrelevant or inappropriate, even to the point of raiding their offices and destroying their files. This did not happen at Regina Campus; nor was it countenanced in the Regina Beach statement. That being said, the notion of a university as primarily a vehicle for social change has the potential to create an atmosphere not conducive to free scholarly inquiry.

The Regina Beach statement was adopted at a special faculty meeting held February 10-11, 1964. Classes were cancelled for two days so that all faculty members could participate in the discussions. Students' Representative Council (SRC) President Jack Mitchell asked for and was granted permission for student representatives to attend the event. This was quite unusual for early 1964, when students had virtually no role in university councils in Regina or elsewhere. The four students who attended the meetings had full speaking privileges, but were not allowed to vote. The *Carillon* hailed the development as a significant milestone, proclaiming that a breach had been made "in the traditional wall opposed to a student voice in university government."[34] Subsequently, the paper made frequent references to the Regina Beach statement, on more than one occasion reprinting it in full at the beginning of the fall term, as though to remind students of the educational ideals the campus was supposed to uphold. In 1965, it reproduced the document on the front page and pointedly asked: "Is this what you are experiencing in the classroom?"[35] And in 1966 the *Carillon* published an editorial strongly endorsing Regina Beach, thereby making common cause with like-minded faculty.[36]

The latter received a boost from Premier Woodrow Lloyd, who laid the cornerstone for the new campus on September 26, 1963:

We in Saskatchewan have here an opportunity. If our need had just been more classrooms and laboratories this might well have been achieved elsewhere with greater ease and good effect. But something different can be done here—different and worthwhile and needed. So let me express the hope that this will not be just a small-scale model of that which has been done on the Saskatoon Campus.[37]

He went on to say that he disagreed with the "ivory tower" concept of the university. The university had to be "immersed in the lives of those who made it possible," helping people to find answers to pressing social and economic problems. The words were music to the ears of Dallas Smythe.

As the years went by and as the debates about the future of the campus became more intense, the Regina Beach statement acquired symbolic status. It became the receptacle for the hopes and dreams of those who were inspired by a certain vision of the campus. The Regina Beachers found a leader in Dallas Smythe; their opponents rallied around Allan Van Cleave. The two men were surrogates for a wider struggle, the Regina Beach statement serving as the talisman or touchstone differentiating one faction from the other. As physicist Joseph Wolfson, who succeeded Van Cleave as chair of natural sciences in 1969, aptly observed:

No honorable person of good will could possibly find fault with the Policy [Regina Beach statement] … it surely must be realized that it means different things to different people, and it is interpreted by each according to his interests. To some it is a very useful weapon; one simply states that a proposal not to one's liking is in violation of the Policy and forthwith the proposal is defeated. But more than this, the Policy is a magic cloak which provides sure immunity against attack. Like some medieval knight holding out the cross to ward off evil, the wearer presents his own proposals for approval, secure in the knowledge that nobody would be so foolhardy as to attack one manifestly as holy as he. To those skilled in its use the policy is indeed both invincible armament and impenetrable armor.[38]

Academic Program Innovations at Regina Campus

Apart from its symbolic status, the Regina Beach statement had concrete implications. It led in June 1965 to the formal adoption of the division system in the Faculty of Arts and Science. Each division (natural sciences, social sciences, humanities, and fine arts) was mandated to coordinate course offerings in the various subject areas with the aim of offering a well-integrated liberal arts program. The term "department" was deliberately suppressed as a means of deterring faculty members from thinking in departmental terms. Instead, the various disciplines (History, English, Psychology, Anthropology, etc.) were officially referred to as "committees of instruction." (In practice, many people still called them departments.) The overarching goal was to discourage the compartmentalization of knowledge and to promote interdisciplinary approaches to teaching.

Another innovation was the introduction of the semester system in the fall of 1966, a reform that proved more durable than the division system. (The semester system in modified form survives still; the division system has long since disappeared.) At the Saskatoon campus, a full year's work consisted of five classes, each of them meeting for three hours per week over a session that stretched from September to April. Under the new Regina system, students took eight classes per year, four in the fall semester (September to December) and four in the winter semester (January to April). This meant that over three years students in Regina had the opportunity to take twenty-four classes, rather than fifteen, thereby giving them exposure to a broader range of disciplines and subject matter. To ensure breadth of study, arts and science majors were required to take classes in six different disciplines with at least one class in each of the four divisions. Introductory classes were supposed to be designed to delineate "the boundaries of the discipline," cover "the fundamental propositions and statements of the *corpus*," and give an exposition of "the methods of the given discipline."[39] This was in keeping with the Regina Beach statement, which said that "general context" and "the basic critical assumptions of the discipline" were all important, not premature specialization. Even in the second and third years, students had to take a range of courses outside their major in order to achieve a broadly-based interdisciplinary perspective.

Such innovations were by no means unique to Regina. Paul Axelrod (*Scholars and Dollars: Politics, Economics and the Universities of Ontario, 1945-*

1980) notes that "general education" acquired a cachet in the 1960s. First-year students at York University were required to enrol in interdisciplinary courses in the social sciences, humanities, and natural sciences. The University of Western Ontario adopted a new common first-year program that included subjects from "four divisions of Humanities, Social Sciences, Mathematics, Natural Sciences, and Miscellaneous, within certain specified limits." The University of Windsor developed combined programs in sociology and economics, sociology and anthropology, and sociology and political science. The common goal of these initiatives was to design a liberal arts program "which looks first of all to his [the student's] life as a responsible human being and citizen."[40]

Historian Patricia Jasen detects similar motivations in the critique of liberal education offered by student radicals. They decried existing liberal arts programs because, in their opinion, they failed to teach human values. Instead, they trained students for jobs they did not want and inculcated the mindset of passive workers and consumers rather than that of politically active citizens. Radicals demanded that the curriculum be relevant, by which they meant "suitable for a life of effective action." They also denounced overspecialization and the compartmentalization of knowledge in airtight departmental units, a concern, as we have seen, that the Regina Beach statement tried to address. Specialization served the career interests of academics, but was not particularly useful to students who wanted to have a more global perspective on how society functioned, the better to understand how it might be changed or revolutionized. Student radicals also expressed scepticism about the self-proclaimed "value-free" objectivity of the social sciences. They doubted that anyone could be "value-free," and dismissed such claims as a cover to bolster the status quo without overtly appearing to do so.[41] In short, student radicals wanted liberal education to confront the issue of values openly and directly, usually, of course, in conformity with their own wishes and desires.

The critique of liberal education that was abroad in the sixties had a particularly forceful impact on new campuses, such as the one at Regina, which emerged *de novo*, without the entrenched traditions that curtailed experimentation at older universities. In Regina, too, there was a widespread desire to break with the Saskatoon model and strike out on a new path. In other words, it was not just a question of not being bound by tradition, but, rather, actively rejecting it. Only in this way, it was thought, could Regina carve out its own distinctive identity as a university not tied to Saskatoon's apron strings. However, it has to be emphasized that Regina was not of one mind on this subject. Van Cleave and his colleagues in the Division of Natural Sciences found it increasingly difficult to work in the same administrative unit (the Faculty of Arts and Science) with colleagues in the Division of Social Sciences. The natural scientists resented having to obtain approval of course proposals and academic policies from those whose views were so hostile to their own.[42] Accordingly, they attempted in April 1967 to break up the Faculty of Arts and Science and create a separate Faculty of Science, which they alone could control. Dallas Smythe strongly opposed this development, arguing that "scientists should not contract out of the debate on the problems technology creates for human society nor surrender their detachment as scholars to groups who call the tune in technology."[43] Smythe thought that scientists should not be allowed to do whatever they or commercial interests outside the university wanted them to do. He thought that science and technology had become a juggernaut overriding human values and interests, the "Moloch of pure machinery ... whose fate is a cloud of sexless hydrogen" of Allen Ginsberg's imagination. The organizational structure of the Faculty of Arts and Science seems like a small matter in the context of this much larger debate, but Dallas Smythe saw a connection and, for him, it was a battle worth fighting. Van Cleave could not understand what all the fuss was about. Of course, scientific research served the interests of humanity. How could it be a bad thing to have more knowledge? He believed that it was up to politicians, not politically-minded professors, to make ultimate decisions about the uses of technology.

The Task Force on the Future of the Faculty of Arts and Science in April 1968 rejected the proposal for a separate Faculty of Science. To appease the dissenters, changes were made to the division system, the effect of which was to give each division more autonomy. The Division of Natural Sciences now had the authority to "develop its own classes and courses of study, and develop and administer its own budget and recruiting activities" without bringing these matters to faculty council. In addition, departments were officially recognized as the basic units of organization within each division, signalling a weakening of the interdisciplinary approach.[44] Smythe and his supporters had lost a skirmish, and, in the end, they lost the battle, too. By 1974, the natural scientists had their own faculty, separate and distinct from their arts colleagues. The struggle for Regina Beach then moved from the defunct Faculty of Arts and Science to the smaller theatre of the Division of Social Sciences. Even here, in their last redoubt, the Regina Beachers gradually lost influence. As new faculty members were hired, the original cadre was diluted. Many of the newcomers had never heard of the Regina Beach retreat and had no particular commitment to the division system, whose principles they did not understand and whose purposes they could not fathom. For them, it was time for Regina Campus to become a "normal" university.

Demise of the Regina Beach Statement

In September 1970, the Regina Beach statement, the emblem of unorthodoxy, came under direct attack. Frans Rummens of the chemistry department introduced a motion at a meeting of the Faculty of Arts and Science to appoint a committee "for the purpose of assessing the relevance of the so-called Liberal Arts Education Policy as presently worded in the academic calendar ... with a view towards alterations (in clear English!) or removal as dictated by present-day thinking and practices."[45] Rummens argued that the statement slighted the value of the natural sciences by failing to emphasize the importance of "increasing" knowledge through scholarly research, as distinct from merely preserving and transmitting it. He objected to the style of writing, which he characterized as "a quaint hybrid of Jugend-Stil romanticism and hippy-generated jargon of the Sixties." What was meant by "essential human values," he asked, and "why single out human values?" "Is the rest of the Universe not equally important?" Talk of "love, justice, freedom and beauty" he considered little more than "naïve motherhood rhetoric."[46] Physicist Jaroslav Pachner added punctiliously, "It seems to me to be necessary either to define exactly what has to be understood under the nature of love, justice, freedom and beauty (as I see it, there exist only different opinions on those concepts, but no way at all to find out what is their nature) or to omit those unscientific terms...."[47]

Dallas Smythe rallied to the defence of the Regina Beach statement. He summarized its essentials as: the obligation of the arts and science faculty "to the larger community and to its students to be a critic of the status quo"; the duty of the scientist "to be sceptical of received doctrine and 'facts' if he would be more than obedient technologist"; the need for faculty to place emphasis on the "study of values"; and the requirement imposed on students and faculty alike to "synthesize and give meaning to their intellectual activity," constantly critique the "structure and functioning of the University itself," maintain "a sceptical attitude toward conventional myths about the University, about science and about scholarship," and recognize "that education is an active process in which the capacity to evaluate the context and point of view are possibly more important than the capacity to 'absorb' facts."[48] His words were not heeded. The Faculty of Arts and Science in December 1971 approved a new Education Policy statement:

I.   The members of the Faculty of Arts and Science believe in a university whose purpose is the preservation, transmission, interpretation and enhancement of the cultural heritage of man, and the acquisition and expansion of new knowledge and understanding.

II.   They seek to fulfill this purpose by interpreting the past, examining and clarifying contemporary thinking and anticipating the possibilities of the future. Their efforts should be sustained by sensitivity to change, and an enthusiasm for investigation and creativity.

III.   The Faculty derives its strength from a unity of purpose combined with a diversity of outlook which requires it to examine every facet of life and uphold the higher human values implicit in the arts, the humanities and the sciences. The Faculty will serve the needs of society but, in so doing, it will also be society's critic, encouraging independent thinking, free discussion and the pursuit of truth.

IV.   The Faculty is jealous of its freedom, which it will exercise without fear or favor, promoting in its members and students the spirit of courageous inquiry.

V.   The Faculty recognizes that the constitution and function of the university itself should be open to re-examination by the academic community as a whole. The Faculty maintains that to serve society the best the university must be self-determining in academic matters.[49]

A diluted, bleached-out version of the original, the revised statement marked, if not the death, at least the waning of the spirit of Regina Beach.

Its decline was accompanied by the rise of professional colleges. As Van Cleave rightly pointed out, most students come to university to prepare themselves for a career. The ink was hardly dry on the Regina Beach statement when the university Board of Governors in April 1964 approved the

establishment at the Regina Campus of a College (later Faculty) of Education. This was followed a year later by the School of Public and Business Administration, which evolved in 1968 into the Faculty of Administration. Then
came the Faculty of Engineering in December 1965 and the School of Social
Work, which, after a long gestation period, began offering classes in 1973.
As the campus matured, more emphasis was given to research. The School
of Graduate Studies, first created in 1965, became the Faculty of Graduate
Studies in 1968 and the Faculty of Graduate Studies and Research in 1971.
The proliferation of professional programs increased both the number and
range of expertise of faculty members. Regina College in 1959 had a total of
23 full-time instructors, all in arts and science. The complement in 1972-73
stood at 308: 211 in arts and science, 21 in administration, 54 in education,
15 in engineering, and 7 in social work.[50] The Regina Beachers had been mis-
taken to think the future of the campus lay definitively and exclusively in
the liberal arts. On the contrary, Regina rapidly developed as a well-rounded
university.

Creation of the University of Regina

The campus debates of the sixties—general education versus professional
training; interdisciplinary learning versus academic specialization; the ivory
tower versus social relevance; applied knowledge versus pure research;
"human values" versus technology; left versus right—all took place in the
context of the drive to achieve university status independent of Saskatoon. The
inaugural meeting of the Regina Campus Council, April 28, 1964, approved
a motion calling for the establishment of a royal commission on higher
education to determine whether the province should have two universities,
not one. The Saskatoon-dominated Senate objected to the inquiry, and it
did not proceed.[51] Various attempts were made in the years that followed to
devise a workable system of governance for the one-university/two-campus
model, but no solution was found that was satisfactory to either Saskatoon
or Regina.

A joint committee of the Senate, Board of Governors, and the two campus councils in 1966 recommended a reorganization of the administrative
structure. Its report stated:

> The Regina Campus eventually will approximate the Sas-
> katoon campus in size and activity, and the principle of

autonomy of both Councils and campuses has been accepted. Therefore the appropriate organization would appear to
be one that reflects a "University group" and two "campus
groups." The Executive organization of the University group
will be referred to as "The Office of the President," and of
the campus group as "The Office of the Principal."[52]

Accordingly, while the university president and his executive team
coordinated the overall operations of the university, the principal of each
campus enjoyed a substantial degree of administrative autonomy. A General
University Council was created "to ensure the effective coordination of the
academic programs of the two campuses and to make appropriate recommendations thereon to the Senate."[53] It consisted of the president, vice-presidents,
university secretary, principals and vice-principals of the two campuses, the
campus secretaries, and eighteen members elected from each campus council. Although Regina and Saskatoon had equal numbers of elected representatives, the majority of ex-officio members were based in Saskatoon, giving
the latter an overall edge in General University Council decision making.

President Spinks had high hopes for the reorganization, which went
into effect in 1968. He said that "with good will from all concerned, the present structure should prove adequate to meet the varied needs of the Province
for some time to come."[54] The most contentious issues were the distribution
of funds and the rationalization of academic programs between the two campuses. Regina felt that the university administration had a pro-Saskatoon tilt.
Not only was it located in Saskatoon, but also the president and his officers
had built their careers at the Saskatoon campus. Saskatoon was aggrieved
because it believed that President Spinks was bending over backward to appease Regina to the detriment of the older and more established campus.

Tensions increased when enrolment began to fall in the early 1970s. Regina peaked at 4,345 full-time and 299 part-time day students in 1969-70,
for a total of 4,644 (excluding degree, certificate and non-credit classes taken
through the extension program). The student population by 1973 declined
to 4,013.[55] The number of students in Saskatoon reached 10,181 in 1969-70
and fell to 9,714 in 1974.[56] The competition for funds had been intense when
enrolment was rising and government money flowed abundantly. Now, in
a period of contraction, it became positively fierce. Regina Campus principal John Archer asked in January 1971 for clarification about the ceiling

that earlier had been placed on the size of the Saskatoon campus. President Spinks replied: "There is, of course, a firm ceiling on the Saskatoon Campus. When I say 'firm,' naturally I do not mean exactly 10,500, but until the Campus and the Board change their mind, that is where the figure is, and I don't think the present Board would agree to the figure changing very much until Regina has reached something like the same figure."[57] The "ceiling" had risen from 8,000 in 1959 to 10,000 in 1968 to 10,500 in 1971 where it was held firm, at least for the time being.

Regina Campus Council, May 1, 1972, unanimously passed a resolution protesting that the Regina Campus was being "relegated to an inferior status, which is not in keeping with the intention of the Province when the new Campus was inaugurated, nor with the needs of the Province."[58] As the crisis deepened, the provincial NDP government, which had been elected in June 1971 under the leadership of Allan Blakeney, came to the conclusion that the university was unlikely to resolve its internal problems. The government introduced Bill 90 in April 1973. While maintaining the formal unity of the university through an overarching board of regents, the bill gave each campus its own president, board of governors and senate. Regina welcomed the plan, but Saskatoon balked. President Spinks denounced the legislation as "the use of naked and brutal political power … removing any real autonomy from the university."[59]

In the face of this withering criticism, Premier Blakeney retreated. He withdrew the bill and appointed a royal commission chaired by Emmett Hall, former justice of the Supreme Court of Canada, to "report to the government suggested changes in the present university system of government and administration which may be better designed to meet current and future needs."[60] The Hall Commission completed its work in December 1973, reporting that it had found, to paraphrase Lord Durham, "two campus groups warring within the bosom of a single University." Hall's solution was independence for Regina. Spinks remained adamantly opposed. He compared the existing university structure to a "two-division army under one command" and what Hall was proposing to "two separate small armies." He said the aim of the former was "to coordinate and strengthen," of the latter, to "divide and conquer."[61] Blakeney ignored Spinks and followed Hall. The University of Regina came into being as a separate institution on July 1, 1974.

This event brought a symbolic close to the turmoil at Regina Campus. It had been a lively period of rapid expansion. New liberal arts courses were developed, professional schools established, faculty hired, a new campus planned, buildings constructed, and, perhaps most significant of all, the purposes of higher education and the mission of the university seriously debated. The Regina Beach statement had been the focal point. Its supporters held that the university had to serve as a relevant agent of social criticism and positive change; its detractors preferred the university to follow the more conventional path of professional education and scholarly research. The debate helped to make the campus an invigorating, stimulating place. The institutional struggle for self-definition intersected with the turbulence occurring in the wider world: the civil rights movement, the ban-the-bomb campaign, the anti–Vietnam War protests, women's liberation, sexual revolution, the counterculture, and everything else that made the sixties what they were. In the middle of it was the *Carillon*, the voice of the sixties generation at Regina Campus.

"Filthy Rag": The *Carillon* in the Sixties

The *Carillon* in the sixties was synonymous with controversy. Its detractors called it "a dirty, red, communist rag ... [not] fit to line the garbage can"[1]; its admirers considered it to be one of the best student newspapers in the country.[2] It attracted attention, both on and off campus, because it expressed the themes of the sixties, the movements for change that were reshaping society and culture. It caught the spirit of the age, and, in doing so, itself became a battleground. The *Carillon* was not a neutral space where opposing armies fought for supremacy; rather, it was territory held by pro-sixties forces, who were under constant attack from their opponents. It is true that the paper published dissenting views both in articles and letters to the editor—that helped make it lively—but, overwhelmingly, it positioned itself on the side of change, promoting the causes of civil rights, women's liberation, Aboriginal rights, the peace movement, and the counterculture. The struggle over the *Carillon* came to a head in 1968-69, when the university Board of Governors tried to shut it down. When the dust had settled, the paper emerged victorious, having successfully fended off the attempt to censor its contents.

History of Student Newspapers at Regina Campus

Prior to its incarnation as the *Carillon,* the Regina student newspaper had been known as the *Sheet* (1956-62) and before that the *College Record.* In the 1950s, the students at Regina College (predecessor of Regina Campus) had elected the editor of the paper, along with the other members of the Students' Representative Council, namely, the president, vice-president, secretary, treasurer, director of athletics, director of debating, director of music and drama, director of social activities, and editor of the yearbook.[3] Faculty advisors were appointed to guide the various student activities, including

the newspaper. This was in keeping with the *in loco parentis* model of the
day, whereby universities acted in place of the parent in supervising student
life in both its academic and extra-curricular phases. According to the SRC
constitution at Regina College, the student president was "responsible to the
Dean of the College for the conduct of the SRC and of the Students' Assembly
and for the general oversight of all student activities."[4] In addition, the dean
or a member of the faculty had to co-sign cheques for SRC expenditures.[5]

Although students generally accepted these arrangements, they occasionally put up a mild show of resistance. At the beginning of the 1950 fall
term, the faculty advisor to the newspaper invited the editor to a meeting
to talk over plans for the year. The advisor wanted to have the names of the
members of the newspaper staff, the responsibilities they had been assigned,
as well as information about the budget and publication dates. The editor
failed to show up for the meeting, but, in a casual hallway conversation, he
assured the faculty member that everything at the newspaper was proceeding satisfactorily. The advisor in due course read and approved the galley
proofs of the first issue. At the end of November, he inquired of the editor
how the next issue was coming along and was told that it was ready to be
sent to the printers. However, the issue did not appear, and, when the editor
was confronted about this, he had to admit that he was ineligible to continue
as editor because he had failed too many of his mid-term examinations. The
faculty advisor was displeased. He recommended to the dean that in future
the responsibility for starting up the paper in the fall be given to a faculty
member, who would work with the students to ensure that the operation was
established on a solid basis.[6]

The incident reveals much about the way the student newspaper was
perceived in the 1950s. It was considered "a measure of the worth of the
school ... a sort of barometer of the school temperament."[7] An inferior paper
reflected poorly on the college, just as a good publication brought credit to
it. The newspaper was not something that students did on their own and for
which they alone bore responsibility. It represented the college in its entirety—students, faculty and administration combined. Nor was the paper considered a *newspaper* as such. As the faculty advisor in 1951 put it, "The school
paper does not pretend to be a newspaper—it is a record of school events."[8]
Hence the name *College Record.* The boundaries of the newspaper were those
of the college and the activities that took place within its confines.

This had not been the case during and immediately after World War

In the "Joe College" atmosphere that prevailed at Regina College in the 1950s, students did not get involved in politics. Photograph taken September 1958.

SASKATCHEWAN ARCHIVES BOARD R-B8403

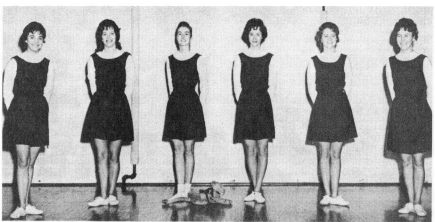

Cheerleaders at Regina Campus in 1962. From left to right, Rose Szala, Maureen Harper, Barb Ingle, Christine Radcliffe, Patty Harding, Delores Fletcher. Regina Campus yearbook, *The Tower,* 1962.

II when large numbers of armed forces veterans had enrolled at
These older and more experienced students had a larger view of   ____,
and they wrote articles that touched on wider interests. In 1948, student G.K.
Piller contributed a piece on the problem of nuclear energy. He observed that
when the atomic bombs had been dropped on Hiroshima and Nagasaki in
1945, there had been a great deal of talk about finding ways to use nuclear
power for peaceful purposes, for example, atomic-powered automobiles and
more efficient ways of cooking food. He wondered what had become of these
projects. It seemed to him that scientists were spending all their time building bombs.[9] Ira Kreel's "A Real Education," also published in 1948, reported
on a series of guest lectures that had been given at the college. They explored
a variety of contemporary issues, including the role of the university in the
modern world, the chances for success of the United Nations, and "the situation in China today." Kreel praised the lectures because they gave students
a better understanding of what was happening in the world. This was better,
he said, than the material found in textbooks, which he considered to be stale
and out of date. He wanted a college education that was connected to the real
world and that would help students come to grips with the problems they
would have to face as citizens when they graduated from school.[10]

When the veterans left the college, the political content of the newspaper largely disappeared with them. The students of the 1950s retreated to a
narrow round of extra-curricular activities: athletics, drama clubs, and dances. Politics was absent from the pages of the *College Record*. There were a few
minor exceptions. The 1958 federal election was hotly debated during study
breaks in the men's residence,[11] and the SRC made an effort to persuade city
council to give students reduced fares on city buses.[12] The request was turned
down in 1955, and again in 1956, and then the matter was dropped.

A brief controversy broke out in December 1955 when the *College Record*
announced: "The articles in this publication were subject to CENSORSHIP!!
Was it good reading?" The faculty advisor gave his reasons:

> You may wonder why a censor stepped in at this point. You
> have freedom of the press, haven't you! You must remem-
> ber, however, that along with the privilege of freedom of the
> press goes the responsibility of printing only the truth (and
> even then a newspaper is subject to libel action). The truth
> of the article is often difficult to establish but the editorial

board is still responsible for it. If an article unjustly damns a person or a situation, a retraction may be printed, but a retraction never completely erases the hard feelings or vicious rumors about the situation. As an advisor I can only advise the editorial board that this be printed in place of the body of the "Sound Off" article. The original article would do no good but only cause hard feelings. Write future articles with these ideas in mind, not with the lurking thought that your paper is subject to censorship (to which it is ordinarily not subject)—Censor[13]

In the sixties, an incident of this type would have caused a major crisis. In 1955, the editor quietly resigned in protest and that was the end of the matter.

The money to pay for the newspaper came from two principal sources: student activity fees and advertising. The total SRC budget in 1950-51 was only $841, of which $156 (18.5 per cent) was allocated to the *College Record*.[14] The paper in 1957-58 (now the *Sheet*) received $500 (22 per cent) from a total SRC budget of $2,261.[15] In 1962-63 (in the *Carillon*'s first year), the amount rose to $2,200 (21 per cent) out of $10,393.[16] By 1970-71, the sum had grown considerably larger, $21,445 (18.8 per cent) out of $114,201.[17] Advertising dollars came from local businesses, such as clothing stores, restaurants, bowling alleys, pool halls, etc., who wanted to tap the student market. Large corporations (Neilson's Chocolate, Coca-Cola, etc.) also placed ads, as did government departments and school boards seeking applicants to fill jobs. In the 1960s and early 1970s, ads from beer companies and cigarette manufacturers were especially prominent, until the *Carillon*, in a spell of puritanism, briefly suspended them. Even the campus administration took out ads to tell students the "real story" about what was happening at the university, an effort to counteract what the administration regarded as the biased reporting of the *Carillon*.

It is difficult to know the exact amount of advertising revenue. Also unknown is the amount of money raised through sales of the paper. Students picked up copies on campus for free (they paid through their student activity fees, but not for individual copies), but the *Carillon* did make an effort to reach the off-campus market. Although there is no indication of how many people bought the paper at the nominal price of 15 cents a copy, the press run in 1973 was 5,000, which was slightly larger than the total student enrolment.[18] Whatever the amount of sales or advertising revenue, it is clear that the paper could not have existed without the student activity fees. The university collected them on behalf of the SRC when students registered at the beginning of the semester, and the SRC paid out a portion of the fees to support the newspaper. The fees were the lifeblood of the *Carillon*. When, in 1969, the university suspended the collection of fees, it threatened the paper's survival.

A New Type of Student Journalism

The year 1961-1962 marked a turning point in the history of the Regina student newspaper. Under the editorship of James Harding, the *Sheet* published a number of controversial articles on topics ranging from sexual morals to nuclear disarmament. Harding said he was not surprised at the strong reaction the articles provoked:

> The *Sheet* editorial policy was based upon a conviction that the world, its societies and respective individuals, must undergo change if humanity is to find new and better ways of living. History has taught us that, through the advocacy of radical ideas, we get change and improved methods of living collectively. The conservative elements of society, who have always failed to "keep up with the times" and adjust to the changing world, are bound to become hostile to such radical ideas since they are a "threat" or "challenge" to their sheltered world. Regina Campus is not different and thus we have observed much hostility toward the *Sheet*. This hostility … is the price people possessing radical ideas must pay.[19]

Harding went on to say that he had faith that "in the long run, men will see the shortcomings of their ways and be prepared to change things without resistance" and that men would "learn to live without war, without hostility, while sharing the products of the world among all humanity." The *Sheet*, he said, "**emphasized world peace and brotherhood over all the other ideas because without these things none of the others are possible** [bold in the original]." Such views did not go uncontested. An anonymous critic wrote:

"Obviously his [Harding's] interpretation of 'Internationalism' is alignment with the 'Internationale.' It seems hardly fitting to credit Mr. Harding and his affiliates with the lofty ideals of unscrupulous Communism. The paper is constantly snowed under with dour 'holier-than-thou' statements of the Ban-the-Bomb movement." Unhappy readers complained that the newspaper was being used to publicize the extreme views of a minority rather than address the concerns of the majority of fee-paying students.[20] This was to become a common refrain of *Carillon* critics.

Don Barker, who succeeded Harding as editor in the fall of 1962, brought a more middle-of-the-road approach to the paper. He said that his intention was to hold up a mirror to the events and personalities on campus, while at the same time giving due attention to "the political and social ideas fostered by the university."[21] Despite the fact that Barker moved in a more conservative direction, he did not return to the old format of merely chronicling social events and athletics. The paper was now committed to publishing articles about off-campus events and engaging the major political issues of the day. It had transformed itself into a paper of the sixties mould. The new name—the *Carillon*—captured the bold, brassy, take-on-all-comers style.[22]

The increasing political content and social awareness of the paper conformed to a nation-wide trend in student journalism. The *Carillon* in December 1963 joined the Canadian University Press (CUP), a national, non-profit organization that allowed editors and writers to exchange information and support one another.[23] Regina Campus student Ken Mitchell attended the national conference in Hamilton in 1965 and was impressed by what he saw: "It is noteworthy that the average college student is becoming less and less interested in panty raids and telephone booth stacking contests, while acquiring more interest in the affairs of the world around him."[24] The student newspaper both responded to and facilitated this transformation. Mitchell came away from the conference thinking that student newspapers across the country were taking their responsibilities seriously.

The relationship between the *Carillon* and the campus administration underwent a change at this time. The old Regina College system, where a faculty advisor was appointed to each student directorate, including the newspaper, was dropped in favor of the creation of three faculty committees (athletics, SRC, and student activities) to oversee student affairs. There was no longer a faculty advisor to the newspaper. Since the paper fell under the jurisdiction of the SRC, it came under the general supervisory umbrella of the faculty SRC committee. The *Carillon* regarded these committees warily, commenting, October 12, 1962: "The faculty emphasizes that these committees are intended to act in an advisory capacity, and not as control bodies.

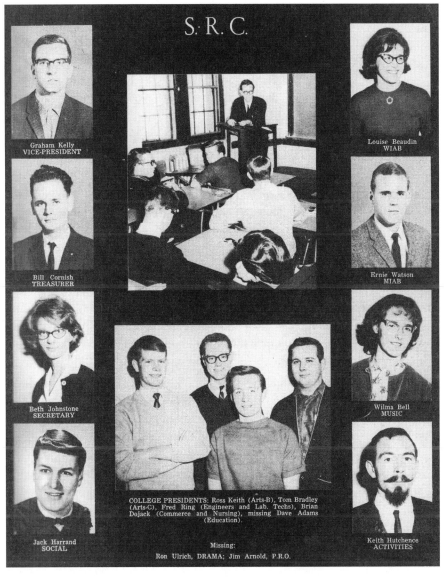

Regina Campus Students' Representative Council, 1964-65, president Simon De Jong (future Member of Parliament for Regina) at the podium. Regina Campus yearbook, *The Tower,* 1965.

If this intention is carried out successfully, then there should be no student objection to the committees. But if these committees unnecessarily intervene in student activities, the students will have every right to object. Let us hope this proves unnecessary."[25]

The SRC constitution was amended in the spring of 1964 to make the editorship of the paper an appointed rather than an elected office.[26] Previously, the editor had been selected by a general vote of the students; now he was appointed by the SRC and served at its pleasure. The pronoun "he" is used deliberately, since all the editors in this period were men: Don Barker (1962-63), Ron Thompson (1963-64), Ken Mitchell (1964-65), John Conway (part of 1965), Don Mitchell (1965-66); Clint Bomphray (1966-67), Don Kossick (1967-68), Norm Bolen (1968-69), Bob Ellis (1969-70), John Gallagher (1970-71), Warren Carragata (1971-72), and Keith Reynolds (1972-73). Women's liberation was already making significant headway at the campus in the late 1960s, but not in the top job at the *Carillon*. It is also worth noting that the editorship was strictly a volunteer position. A student referendum was held in the spring of 1970 on whether to pay salaries to the SRC president and the editor, but the majority voted the proposal down.[27]

In another referendum held in February 1965, students voted 647 to 154 to adopt a new constitution for student government. They created the Students' Union, a significant change in nomenclature because it reflected the growing perception that students constituted a political force within society and that they had interests that they needed to articulate and defend. The sole function of student government in the past had been to organize athletics, social functions and other extra-curricular activities. Now students saw themselves as having a bigger role to play in the education system and in society as a whole. The range of issues that fell within the scope of student government expanded to include all aspects of higher education, including funding, tuition fees, university governance, teaching, curriculum, and program offerings. All of this was encoded in the adoption of the term "Students' Union" to represent students in their collective capacity. The newspaper had a vital function to perform within this reconfigured system of student government. The new constitution spelled out that one of the purposes of the union was to publish a paper, which was "to be an organ of student opinion and information."[28] From the student perspective, the newspaper belonged to them, not to the university. In the 1950s, there had been a different understanding. The student newspaper, complete with faculty advisor, had been seen as a product of the college as a whole. As we shall see, key members of the campus administration still held this view, which meant that there was a divergence of viewpoint between the administration and the students. This led to a crisis out of which a new consensus emerged that affirmed and institutionalized the student point of view.

In the fall of 1965, editor John Conway restated the *Carillon's* editorial policy. He said that the paper would "cover and report on campus events and provide a forum of student debate and dialogue on relevant issues of the times as well as encouraging creativity in the form of short stories, essays, poems, cartoons, etc." In addition, it would "take on a more dynamic role in the shaping of campus events, city events, national and international events." The paper had an agenda. It wanted to go beyond reporting the news to help influence the direction of history. This echoed the CUP charter, which called on student newspapers to act as "agents of social change."[29] Conway continued:

> We do have a stake in the fact that there is an election coming at which we can't vote [1965 federal election], we do have a stake in the fact that there is a war in Vietnam, we do have a stake in the fact that there is a need for a civil rights struggle in North America, we do have a stake in the fact that poverty exists in such a rampant way in Canada, we do have a stake in the fact that our governments have been unable to answer, let alone confront, the major problems and questions of our time. The *Carillon* will speak to these issues throughout the year.[30]

This was the voice of the baby-boom generation coming of age: "The *Carillon* views its role as the forum in which we can begin to articulate our interests and plan strategies in order to use our numbers and our independence from the society to bring about change."[31]

The paper in 1965 refused to accept advertisements that were even "remotely concerned with tobacco or related accessories," even "remotely concerned with beer, wine or liquor," or "concerned with any branch or auxiliary of the military." The latter were banned because "we do not believe that the profession of mass murder should be encouraged on the pages of our newspaper." Not only that, the *Carillon* rejected "any advertisement that it consid-

ered by the editor to be psychologically designed to mislead, misinform or manipulate the reader."[32] Such uncompromising policies stirred controversy. A hand-written poster appeared on a campus bulletin board in October 1965: "STUDENTS ARISE!! Would you accept 'Izvestia' or 'Pravda' as a publication representative of the student body? NO! Then why the *Carillon*?? [33]

The editor was unrepentant. He declared that the paper would not waste ink on "full-page stories describing the exciting dances of the year, or complicated verbal monographs concerning the beauties and delights of

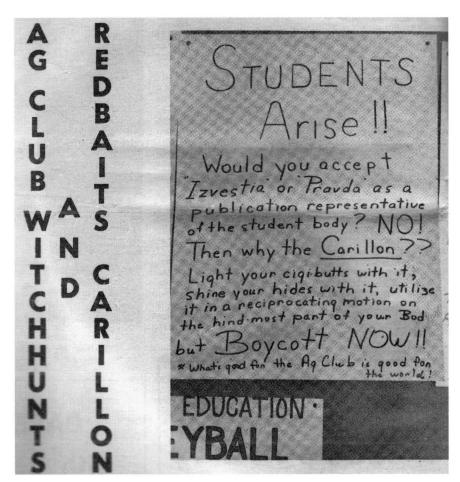

Above: The politicization of the *Carillon* did not please everyone. *Carillon*, 15 October 1965.

Facing page: The *Carillon*, 15 October 1965, changed its focus from student extra-curricular activities to political and social issues.

irresponsibly wasting fee-paying students' fees on ridiculous parades or an alluring character sketch of this year's Frosh Queen."[34] There would be no "column on all the new and glorious cars which are swamping the market" or "several pages of the last six playmates of the year for our unsuccessful Romeos on campus."[35] The SRC president intervened in the dispute, and the editor was removed.[36] The RCMP Security Intelligence Service, which had the campus under surveillance, provided its own account of what happened:

> ... there had been considerable controversy over the editorial policy of the *Carillon* during this term. As a result, [name de-leted] was fired from his position as editor by the Students' Representative Council. [words deleted] it was becoming increasingly apparent to the student body that the student newspaper was controlled by a group of mostly left wing individuals, mostly members of the Student Union for Peace Action, who were using the paper to support their propa-ganda. The particular topic being given constant coverage was the war in Vietnam, which always followed the typi-cal left wing line. Campus activities were not being covered adequately and the newspaper was in financial difficulty. Opposition to the paper was so great that the President of the S.R.C. [words deleted] was under pressure both from the faculty and the student body to do something about the pa-per. [words deleted] was the leader of this group and when he left, a majority of his followers who were on the *Carillon* staff left with him.[37]

It seemed that the SRC and the mass of students were not ready for the editorial policy the *Carillon* had laid down.[38]

After Conway left, the paper toned down a bit, while still pursuing a left-of-center orientation. Clint Bomphray, editor in 1967-68, gave a balanced assessment of where he stood. He said that while concessions had to be made to the "social and athletic froth" on campus, the main thrust was still to bol-ster the "the value of the student as citizen," construct a student community, and expand "the consciousness of the student as to his own worth and value as a person." In his farewell editorial, "Good-bye to All That," Bomphray urged the newspaper to awaken consciousness to what was happening in the world: "It is only in this way, by continually questioning our world, by rejecting the horse-shit we are handed by the 'authorities,' and by discovering our own values and our own meaning, that the *Carillon* will ever find itself becoming a worthwhile contribution to the life of this university. WE ARE ALL ONE!"[39]

The *Carillon's* editorial policy brought it into conflict with the mainstream press. Early in 1968, two *Carillon* staffers reported an encounter with a Regina *Leader-Post* editor: "The gentleman didn't like our paper at all. After describing the *Carillon* as 'c-----,' he turned to a nineteen-year-old female *Carillon* reporter and told her to 'f--k o-f.'"[40] The *Leader-Post* accused the students of allowing personal bias to permeate their entire paper, thereby failing to adhere to the basic journalistic principle that kept news stories separate from editorial opinion. The students replied that the *Leader-Post* did exactly the same thing. The only difference was that the *Carillon* had the honesty to admit it.

The campus newspaper in February 1968 began publishing a feature titled "Follow the *Leader*," which mocked the *Leader-Post* by the simple expedient of quoting its editorials verbatim. A *Leader-Post* article expressed shock and indignation over a CBC television program about bullfighting: "The tormented bull was a pathetic sight. The goring of the blindfolded horse was sickening to see." Why, the *Carillon* inquired, was all this sympathy lavished on the bull and none spared for the napalmed victims of the Vietnam War?[41] The *Leader-Post* said of the Kent State shootings: "… the use of the rifle has one rather serious drawback: if a bullet connects, the target is either wounded or dead." The *Carillon* riposte was: "Jesus, they're all heart. Who else would question the use of rifles on unarmed students as a method of crowd control with such compassion?" The *Leader-Post* went on to say that the most disturbing aspect of the tragedy was that "the guardsmen appear to have used their weapons without having exhausted other possibilities," which provoked the *Carillon* to respond:

> There it is, plain as day. The disturbing thing is not that the students were killed, not that the guardsmen fired on unarmed civilians, but that the guardsmen killed the students before they tried a few other techniques to break up the demonstration. The obvious implication is that if these techniques had been tried and had failed to disperse the

demonstrators then the guardsmen would have been justified in the *Leader's* eyes with killing the students.[42]

What bothered the *Carillon* most was that the *Leader-Post* put the blame on
the students. If the students had not been so unruly, it would not have been
necessary to call in the National Guard and the tragedy could have been
averted. For the *Carillon*, this was all backward: "... if there had been no
unruly disturbances in Vietnam and Cambodia, there would have been no
unruly disturbance at Kent...."[43]

A 1970 *Leader-Post* editorial, "The Wacky Bra-less Battalion," was reprinted in its entirety. It trivialized the women's liberation movement, even
though a federal royal commission had been investigating the issue since
1967 and the topic was hardly new. The editorial stated: "One of the wackiest
aspects of the women's liberation movement is the bra-less battalion. All of
a sudden it has been discovered that the well-known undergarment is nothing more than an instrument of male chauvinism designed to turn women
into sex objects and degrade them as human beings." The *Carillon* added a
postscript to the article: "Honest to God, we haven't changed a word of this.
This is exactly the way the *Leader* wrote it."[44]

The *Carillon* versus the Thatcher Government

The *Carillon's* crusading instincts came to the fore in October 1967 when
Premier Ross Thatcher announced his intention to amend the University Act
in order to assert direct government control over the university budget.[45]
"In essence," the premier said, "the University will be obliged to make
its financial requests to the Legislature in the same manner as any other
spending department. For example, they will have to request so much for
salaries, so much for traveling, so much for new buildings, etc.... from
this time forward, there will be direct financial control."[46] When university
president John Spinks failed to confront the government publicly, preferring
instead to deal with the issue behind closed doors, the *Carillon* went on the
offensive. It filled its pages with articles that strongly condemned Spinks'
soft-pedal approach.[47] A front-page banner in bold letters read: "'Don't Rock
the Boat,'—Spinks; 'Let Thatcher Torpedo It,'—The *Carillon*."[48]

Although the Thatcher government eventually backed down, Spinks
was seriously displeased with how the Regina Campus newspaper had
covered the event. He wrote Principal William Riddell, November 16, 1967:

"This is to let you know in a formal way that I disapprove extremely strongly of the last number of the *Carillon,* dated November 3."[49] The "number" to which Spinks referred dealt almost entirely with the president's handling of the financial autonomy crisis. Riddell replied on November 28, 1967, that the situation had been brought to the attention of the editor of the *Carillon* and the Students' Union president, but the verbal warnings had not produced any result. Riddell believed that "only drastic action [would] be effective." Possible disciplinary actions included withdrawal of permission for the *Carillon* to use the name of the university, refusal to allow *Carillon* staff to use university facilities, and discontinuation of the collection of student fees.[50] The Board of Governors discussed Riddell's recommendation, but decided not to take any action for the time being.[51]

Allan Guy, the minister of public works in the provincial government (and in that capacity responsible for overseeing the construction of new buildings at Regina Campus), told a Liberal party gathering that he had been shocked by what he read in the *Carillon.* He informed Principal Riddell on January 4, 1968: "I, of course, acknowledge their right to write the articles, but I believe I also have the right to criticize their writings should I see fit."[52] On February 1, members of the Board of Governors communicated to Riddell "very grave concern about the *Carillon* and its editorial policy." They "stressed that they [the students] have the right to protest and criticize, but that the vulgarity that permeated the paper was very definitely objectionable both to the University and the public."[53]

Riddell learned in the second week of February 1968 that the *Carillon* was about to publish a story potentially damaging to Allan Guy's reputation. The principal telephoned SRC president Ralph Smith and left a message warning Smith that the article could lead to legal action being taken against the paper. Riddell then got in touch with the printer and delivered the same warning. The printer informed him that the lawyer for the Students' Union had already read the article and given his opinion that it was not libellous.[54] The story duly appeared February 16, 1968. A large photo of Guy dominated the front page with the caption, "The Strange Story of One Student's Loan or How a Guy Gets a Loan." The article charged that, in 1966-67, Guy, then an MLA and not yet appointed to the cabinet, had received a $1,000 federal government student loan, the maximum amount allowable for one year. The student loan program was at that time the subject of vehement controversy. Students claimed that the amount of the loans was insufficient and that they

Official weekly newspaper published by the University of Saskatchewan Students' Union, Regina Campus

Vol. 6   No. 14   Friday, January 26, 1968 — 12 pages

"Academic freedom will be preserved."
—Premier Ross Thatcher, Nov. 8, 1967

"I fully subscribe to the principle long established in this province, that the university is an autonomous and independent institution which must operate free from any government or political interference in its internal management."
—Premier Thatcher, Nov. 22, 1967

"I wish to emphasize that the government will not interfere with the internal operations of the university."
—Premier Thatcher, Oct. 18, 1967

What **Is** Autonomy?

The Premier has assured us that an independent, autonomous university
will be preserved in Saskatchewan. What has he promised to support?

AUTONOMY MEANS:

- The university ESTABLISHES ITS OWN PRIORITIES AND PROGRAMS, under the control of its board of governors—once the elected government has established the total budget.

- The university DETERMINES THE VALUE of its own priorities and programs, by virtue of long experience and democratic tradition.

- The university SELECTS ITS OWN FACULTY AND STAFF, determined by academic standards and a budget set by the board of governors.

- The university IS FREE TO BARGAIN COLLECTIVELY with its own employees.

- The university SETS THE LEVEL OF STUDENT ENROLMENT, according to needs, based on space and funds.

- The university PREVENTS POLITICAL CONTROL OF ACADEMIC PROGRAMS — either indirectly through sub-division of the budget, or by direct political interference.

- The university MUST BE FREE TO PROTECT FREEDOM OF SPEECH. Throughout history, a free university and a free press have always been the first victims of totalitarian governments.

AUTONOMY DOES NOT MEAN FINANCIAL

IRRESPONSIBILITY OR "BLANK CHEQUES"

The budget of the University of Saskatchewan has ALWAYS been examined and approved in detail by the Government of Saskatchewan. The government has ALWAYS determined how much money has been spent each year by the university.

AUTONOMY MEANS THE PRESERVATION OF THE LAWS AND CUSTOMS
WHICH HAVE PROTECTED THE UNIVERSITY'S INDEPENDENCE
SINCE IT WAS FOUNDED IN 1907.

PUBLIC FORUM
THE UNIVERSITY IN THE COMMUNITY
2 P.M. Sunday — Metropolitan Theatre — Admission Free

Facing page: When Premier Ross Thatcher tried to take direct control of the university budget in 1967, the *Carillon* rallied students to defend university autonomy and academic freedom, *Carillon,* 26 January 1968.

Below: The *Carillon* mocked Premier Thatcher's Santa-Claus approach to funding Saskatchewan post-secondary education, *Carillon,* 24 November 1967.

THE CARILLON   Friday, November 24, 1967

You better not shout
You better not cry . . .

were badly administered. Guy had received a loan, when other apparently deserving applicants had been turned down. The insinuation was that his political connections had been helpful in securing the money, though no direct accusation was made to that effect.

Guy had to endure the taunts of Opposition NDP MLAs, who draped the *Carillon* over their desks in the legislature and heckled him about the loan.[55] The controversy also created problems for Principal Riddell, who was in the midst of complicated negotiations with Guy concerning the construction of a new students' residence on campus. The principal was also discredited for having tried to prevent the publication of the exposé. The *Carillon* characterized the intervention as a "flagrant and intolerable violation of editorial freedom."[56] Riddell summoned SRC representatives to a meeting, February 27, 1968, with a committee of the Board of Governors. The SRC was asked to show cause: (1) why the university should continue to collect fees for the Students' Union; (2) why the Students' Union should be allowed to continue using the name of the University of Saskatchewan; and (3) why the university should continue to provide space on campus for the *Carillon*.[57] Riddell said that he knew of instances where individuals had refused to donate money to the university because they had been offended by the contents of the paper. E.C. Leslie, chair of the Board of Governors, described the *Carillon* as an "indecent publication." When asked to identify the articles he considered indecent, he answered, "Read the paper yourself." The board also objected to the paper's "tone of criticism." They said that the Allan Guy story had caused difficulties with the government and that attacks on the university administration had been unwarranted and unfair. Leslie took exception in particular to the *Carillon's* characterization of the Board of Governors as a bunch of "bumbling buffoons." Editor Don Kossick replied that the phrase had to be taken in the context of the article, which had dealt with the university's inept handling of the fiscal autonomy crisis.[58]

President Spinks reiterated at a meeting of the Regina Campus council many of the charges that had been made against the *Carillon*. Some of the faculty members in attendance defended the paper. They said that it was moderate and well behaved in comparison with student newspapers at other universities, and, further, any attempt to impose censorship would backfire and cause more problems than it solved. This statement was greeted with a round of applause, which, as Riddell noted, "appeared to be the result of antagonism to the President." In the course of the meeting, psychology professor Bill Livant distributed mimeographed copies of the letter Riddell had written to the SRC president asking him to show cause why the *Carillon* should not be disciplined. Livant then introduced a motion asking the faculty to uphold the "rights and privileges" of the students. Although the motion was tabled and not voted on, it was a clear sign of the rift that was developing between the Regina faculty and the university administration.[59]

Riddell became increasingly unhappy with the general state of affairs at the campus. He delivered a stern, hectoring speech at the October 1968 meeting of council, which chastised the faculty for not doing more to improve relations with the Regina community. He criticized faculty for not being more generous in their donations to the United Appeal (as the United Way was then called), for not joining service clubs and voluntary agencies, and for "rushing to print on various topics." Students were reprimanded for holding protest marches (though Riddell did admit that some of the protests had been justified), for the "filthy condition" of the cafeteria and library entrance,

And may I go on to say that this ?&($*! rag is beyond a doubt the ?(&$*! crudest ?&($*! vilest ?&($*! . . . . . .   — Sheaf

The *Carillon* made fun of allegations of obscenity leveled against the paper, *Carillon*, 15 March 1968.

and the equally "filthy" articles in the *Carillon*. He said that the irresponsibility of faculty and students had contributed to a "frightening groundswell of reaction against the University" to the point where the government might be tempted to intervene to set things right.[60] This had to be avoided at all costs. The government had already tried to take financial control of the university. It was essential that it not be given an excuse to insert itself into academic decision making, which would do incalculable damage to the institution. It is unclear whether Riddell was merely speculating about possible scenarios or had been given a direct warning from the government. The latter is not at all beyond the realm of possibility.

The *Carillon* responded with an editorial titled "Censor *The Carillon* … Scold the Faculty? … Develop a 'Good Public Image?'…" that attempted to refute Riddell's speech point by point. With respect to the "filthy conditions" of campus buildings, it said that the cafeteria was messy because "it was serving about three times the number it was designed to serve," while the library entrance was littered "mostly with the bodies of students who have nowhere else to go, because facilities are overcrowded and inadequate on this campus, because there is NOT ONE [emphasis in original] student lounge, not to mention residences." The editorial went on to say that faculty members had not contributed to the United Appeal as much as Riddell thought they should because "they consider it little short of criminal that human-welfare programs must depend upon the whimsy of private donations while the military machine is publicly financed."[61] Finally, the paper denied the charge that it was an obscene publication. As a case in point, it cited Jerry Farber's controversial essay "The Student as Nigger." Written by a California English instructor, the essay had been reprinted in student newspapers all across North America. The *Carillon* had published it, too, but only after deleting the more sexually explicit passages. This proved, the editors said, that they were not interested in salacious material. They claimed that the obscenity allegation was a red herring designed to mask the real agenda of the administration, which was to censor the paper because of its criticism of the university and the provincial government. The criticism had been well justified, the paper said, and it made no apologies for it.

Facing page: The *Carillon* hyperbolically compared its plight to that of African-Americans deprived of their freedom. The words "made in Campion" on the padlock related to the fact that, at the time, the university administration had its offices in Campion College, *Carillon*, 29 November 1968.

The students told their side of the story by distributing the *Carillon* on street corners and at various shopping malls in Regina. Liz Sorsdahl, a staffer who spent a Saturday handing out the paper, encountered a range of reactions. Some people looked at her like she was "speaking Swahili and walked right by." Others were hostile, such as the person who said that students drank, smoked and took drugs, and should be expelled from the university. A woman slapped a student's face because he couldn't provide a list of the students who had been refused student loans. The friendliest reaction was at the Northgate Mall in the north end (the working-class/lower-middle-class part of the city) where shoppers willingly accepted the papers and even lined up to obtain a copy.[62]

Riddell made a deliberate effort in November 1968 to bring the *Carillon* to heel. He met with SRC president David Sheard and vice-president Ken Sunquist in an effort to broker a deal. The meetings took place at off-campus locations to keep them secret from the students who did not want to make any concessions to the administration. Sheard and Sunquist agreed that something should be done, but they urged caution. They counselled that overly aggressive action "would cause a major uprising among the students and might probably bring about the formation of a group of the SDS [Students for a Democratic Society]."[63] Riddell came away from the meetings feeling that a settlement was within reach. A *Carillon* reporter told him that the paper planned to change its approach "to make it more objective in reporting news, directing the news to Canadian rather than foreign situations and to limit editorializing to an editorial page." Reassured, Riddell advised the Board of Governors, November 13, 1968, not to take any action.[64]

The Fight for Student Control of the *Carillon*

The situation changed dramatically on December 6, 1968, when the *Carillon* published a controversial image that aroused a storm of protest both within and outside the university. The image, a skillfully executed black-and-white drawing, was a two-page spread in the centre of the newspaper. Largely representational in its various parts, but symbolic in its composition, the drawing juxtaposes stark images of life and death—a womb, a penis, pelvic bones that look like skulls (or vice versa), seeds (or drops of blood?). The appended New Year's greeting—"Happy New Year From The Carillon"— suggests that these images of life and death are expressions of the dying of the old year and the emergence of the new. However, there is undeniably

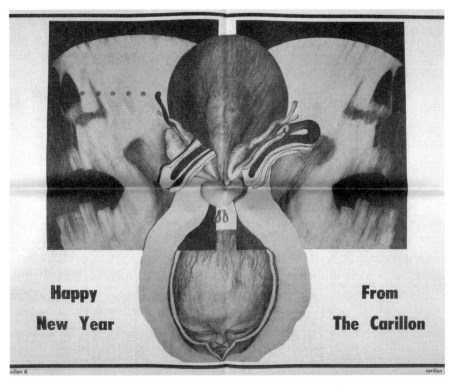

The most controversial image the *Carillon* published. In retaliation, the university Board of Governors tried to shut down the paper, *Carillon*, 6 December 1968.

a further, specifically political, symbolism here, too. While December is normally the time in Western societies for reference to the birth of the Savior, here, instead, the figure both in and emerging from the womb is Ho Chi Minh, leader of the Vietnamese independence movement and president of North Vietnam. When considered in the context of the continuing war in Vietnam and the outspoken opposition to that war found in the pages of the *Carillon* over the years, the skulls and blood are images not only of death but of the violence of war, and the "Happy New Year" greeting itself becomes a greeting dripping with irony.

By today's post–sexual revolution standards, the drawing is hardly shocking. The overall effect is artistic, not pornographic—but that is not the way it was viewed at the time. Attention focused almost exclusively on the sexual content, while all other considerations were swept aside in a deluge of complaint. The possibility of a political allegory was largely ignored. All people could talk about was the affront to community standards of decency and decorum.

Principal Riddell was under intense pressure to "do something." Parents telephoned his office, and he could not walk into a social gathering without receiving a barrage of criticism.[66] Riddell decided that enough was enough. He told President Spinks, December 16, 1968, that the paper had to be disciplined. The *Carillon*, he said, "had continued to attack the University in a most damaging way, it has been extremely biased in its editorial policy and grossly inaccurate in the handling of news. Its general policy appears to be carefully designed to detract from the University, its officials and the Board of Governors and to offend the reader … A rising tide of public resentment directed against the University as well as the *Carillon*, particularly since the last issue for 1968, makes it essential that some action be taken immediately."[67]

The Board of Governors voted by mail ballot to accept Riddell's recommendation and announced on December 31, 1968 (in the middle of the Christmas break when students were not on campus) that it was suspending the collection of student activity fees for the coming semester. Board chair Allan Tubby justified the action on the basis of the need to curb the paper's obscenity. While admitting that the *Carillon's* criticism of the government and the university administration had been matters of major concern, he insisted that the main problem was "the use of offensive and vulgar language."[68] The public had become "enraged," forcing the board to apply a remedy. The *Carillon* shot back: "The charges of obscenity are patently fraudulent and only a cover for the real intentions of those who wish to silence the *Carillon*." The paper alleged it had been harassed since it had taken a strong stand against the university's feeble handling of the autonomy crisis in October 1967. The attacks had multiplied with the publication of the Allan Guy story in February 1968, and they had escalated ever since. The students saw themselves as the target of "an intensive campaign on the part of the provincial government and the university administration to suppress the *Carillon*."[69]

The Regina Campus Students' Union staked out its position in a press release, January 2, 1969: "Can we look to a situation in which only students with 'safe' ideas will be permitted to attend university? Will students a few years from now be expected to demonstrate their political and ideological purity? Will students with 'weirdo' ideas be expelled? Will the Board insist that faculty members teach only 'proper' knowledge and acceptable

Board of Governors news conference, announcing the suppression of the *Carillon*. The body language of board members spoke volumes, *Carillon*, 8 January 1969.

Union Supporters

"The independence of the Students' Union? The Carillon, good or bad? Freedom of Press? Just what are the issues involved in the decision of the Board of Governors not to continue the collection of students fees?

"The Students' Representative Council has taken the position that the main issue at the present time is that of whether there shall continue to be an independent union of students controlling its own destiny. We believe therefore, that the student newspaper, be it obscene or clean, radical or conservative, critical or uncritical, must be CONTROLLED by the STUDENT BODY and by the STUDENT BODY ALONE.

"The administration of the University, by its decision not to collect fees until the Carillon is 'cleaned up,' is stating that it has ultimate control over the Students' Union and its newspaper. This attempt at control must be vigorously opposed.

"To those of you who dislike the Carillon, think of the alternatives. Do you want the student newspaper controlled by your Students' Union or by an organization over which you have no control? Do you want an independent Students' Union that is free to set its own destiny? In short, the issue is ultimately one of control—who shall control the Students' Union—YOU OR THEY?"

—Dave Sheard, president, Students' Union

"The Board's move is somewhat abhorrent . . . . a fiscal sledgehammer being used for censorship.
"The Board is demolishing student activities by choosing not to collect fees."

—Reid Robinson, president, Faculty Association

"Their decision is an infringement on the legal right of the students to organize an independent union under student direction, and free from outside control."

—Students' Representative Council

"We fully support the stand of the SRC and condemn the action taken by the Board of Governors. . . . At no time do we receive financial support from the administration, as other universities do, even though this university has a declared program of intramural and extramural activity."

—Men's and Women's Athletic Boards

"At a time when this university needs the co-operation of students, faculty and administration, I think the administration has let us down."

—Ken Sundquist, vice-president, SRC

"The reform of an organization such as the Students' Union and its publication should come as a result of its own internal examination and not of external influence."

—University of Saskatchewan Employees' Union

"Although we may have internal differences, these are nothing more than family quarrels, and they must be put aside for now so we can act with strength against this threat. If we stand together we have strength and we shall be victorious—we shall be stronger than we were before and all of us will benefit."

—Students' Representative Council

"It looks like the Board of Governors is selling out to some sort of phony public image."

—Eric Olson, president, Saskatoon Campus SRC

"The Board's move opens the door into the internal affairs of the university. If the community should decide it doesn't like the sociology department will the board decide to close that up too?"

—Dr. Alwyn Berland, executive secretary, Canadian Association of University Teachers

"As soon as the governing body (of the university) introduces what is in effect censorship or thought control, the university ceases to be a university as we know it."

—Stan Rands, psychology department

"The Carillon has attempted to provide students with information that is not otherwise available. Obviously the administration of this university is afraid of this information. Their decision is a clearcut attempt to restrict freedom of expression within the university."

—Norm Bolen, editor, The Carillon

"It is the Board of Governors who have chosen a policy of confrontation, not us. . . . Such a serious threat to the right of the students to an independent Students' Union and to a free press are unacceptable and not negotiable."

—Students' Representative Council

"The Canadian Union of Students' National Council, Secretariat and member campuses across Canada, will be watching closely and will be with you in full support as you struggle to resist against this challenge of the right of students to organize. In addition I pledge my personal support and will make available C.U.S. resources to assist your struggle, 'For the union makes us strong.'"

—Peter Warrian, president of C.U.S.

"Above all, the role of critic, of examiner of institutions and ideas, belongs to the modern university functioning as a community of scholars. Its criticism should be sustained by constant reference to essential human values, which demands a DELIBERATE renewal of the study of the nature of love, justice, freedom, beauty, science: in fact, all those values which give meaning and substance to life. This constant critique must be applied first to the structure and function of the university itself."

—Liberal Arts policy as stated in the university calendar

The *Carillon* enjoyed considerable support, both on- and off-campus, *Carillon*, 8 January 1969.

ideas?"[70] With unerring aptness, the students quoted from the Regina Beach statement: "Above all, the role of critic, of examiner of institutions and ideas, belongs to the modern university functioning as a community of scholars … This constant critique must be applied first to the structure and function of the university itself."

Support poured in. Roy Atkinson, president of the Saskatchewan Farmers' Union, expressed "amazement" at the Board's action. W.G. Gilbey, president of the Saskatchewan Federation of Labor, said the decision was reprehensible.[71] Opposition Leader Woodrow Lloyd denounced the attempt to "throttle free speech and freedom of association,"[72] and Reid Robinson, president of the Regina Campus Faculty Association, commented: "The Board's move is somewhat abhorrent … a fiscal sledgehammer being used for censorship." Even the Regina Campus Men's and Women's Athletic Boards, neither of which had leftist leanings, sided with the Students' Union and supported the *Carillon*.[73]

The Board, too, had its backers. When Deputy Premier Davey Steuart was asked whether the *Carillon* needed reforming, he said no; rather, it needed "disinfecting."[74] The president of the Regina Chamber of Commerce praised the clampdown, while twenty-five clergymen signed a petition applauding the board's action.[75] A distraught parent wrote the dean of education complaining that she was ashamed to let her daughter bring the *Carillon* into their home. The parent had seen copies of the *Georgia Straight*, Vancouver's hippie newspaper, and she thought it was positively wholesome in comparison with the Regina Campus paper. The *Leader-Post* declined to support a fellow newspaper caught in a battle for the freedom of the press. It took the position that the principle of journalistic freedom did not apply in this case because the *Carillon* was financed through compulsory student fees, not voluntary purchase. The *Carillon* issued a statement regretting the *Leader-Post's* lack of "any sense of fraternity with another newspaper under attack."[76]

The students held a general meeting on January 8, 1969. It drew 1,600 people, "the largest gathering of students on the Regina Campus for a meeting of its kind in the history of the institution."[77] They voted overwhelmingly to censure the Board of Governors and to hold a referendum on the demand for a contract with the university concerning the collection of activity fees. Despite the outward show of unity, student opinion was mixed. Many made it clear that they did not agree with the paper's editorial policy, but at the same time they objected to the Board of Governors' interference. "The issue," stated Students' Union president David Sheard, "is not the *Carillon*, whether it is good or bad; whether it is obscene, as some have charged, or not obscene, but who has final control of the student newspaper."[78] This apparently was how most students framed the dispute, an interpretation borne out in the report of an RCMP security agent who attended the meeting:

> This vote [to hold a referendum] passed by a large major-
> ity after a number of students chastised the *Carillon* and its
> editor for being a non-representative paper, printing only
> obscenities and a one-sided political view, mainly from the
> left. The mood of the students was generally anti-*Carillon*,
> however, it was obvious that the student body did not want
> to see the Union destroyed because of the *Carillon*. They
> seemed to be determined to save the Union and "get the
> *Carillon*" on their own terms at a later date.[79]

Student Council Sets Terms For Negotiations

Students casting their ballots on Thursday.

An emergency meeting of the Students' Representative Council was held Thursday night to consider the results of the referendum on student fee collection held earlier that day.

The referendum was interpreted by the SRC as a clear mandate from the student body to enter into negotiations with the Board of Governors. SRC councillor Don Mitchell introduced a motion outlining the conditions for negotiation. The motion stated that the SRC is prepared only to negotiate how and when the Board will begin collecting fees. The council is not prepared to discuss the Carillon with the Board of Governors.

The motion also states that, should the Board maintain that it would be impossible for them to collect student fees for this semester at this late date, the Council will expect a grant from the Board to cover the losses.

The contract which is to be negotiated will be drawn up over the weekend for approval by the SRC at a meeting Monday noon. The SRC expects to open negotiations either Monday or Tuesday. The Council has made it explicit that negotiations must be open to all members of the student body.

The deadline for negotiations has been set for Wednesday noon by the Council. Should the Board refuse to comply, another general meeting will be held Thursday to discuss further action.

Council also agreed to release the following press release.

"The SRC regards the refer-

endum results as a clear mandate to take the issue of student fee collection back to the principal with a clear demand for rescinding his unfortunate decision.

"We shall negotiate only the question of how and on what terms the fees are to be collected. We are explicitly instructed to take a position that the union funds are to be controlled by the union. This means the issue of the Carillon cannot and will not be negotiated with the Board. It is an internal matter of the union."

The Saskatoon SRC held an all-day teach-in Friday to which the Regina SRC sent six students as an expression of solidarity. The Council also authorized the publication of two Carillons this week.

Mass meeting censures Board of Governors.

The vast majority of students believed that they, not the university administration, should control the student newspaper, *Carillon*, 13 January 1969.

Cartoon depicting student victory in the 1968-69 battle over the *Carillon*, *Carillon* 13 January 1969.

About 43 per cent of eligible students voted in the referendum: 1,101 in favor of negotiating a contract with the university to force it to hand over student fees to the Students' Union, 539 opposed, and five spoiled ballots.[80]

The negotiations with the Board of Governors proceeded normally until February 3, 1969. On that day, a number of students burst into the room where the talks were taking place and peremptorily demanded that the board representatives present themselves at a teach-in, which was underway in a nearby lecture hall. The board members declined the invitation and attempted to exit the building. However, students linked arms in the hallway, forming a narrow passageway that led directly to the teach-in. The board members succeeded in breaking through the cordon and made their escape. They sped away, pursued all the while by students who held on to the bumpers of their cars and threw snowballs at the departing vehicles.[81] The *Leader-Post* decried this "mob action," calling the student tactics "indefensible" and not to be tolerated by people of the province.[82] Minister of public works Allan Guy hinted gravely that "NDP agitators" and "young Communists" must have been behind the incident,[83] while Premier Thatcher promised that disturbance of the normal functioning of the university would be "met with a firm hand."[84]

Stan Atkinson, a Regina businessman who was a member of the Board of Governors negotiating committee, advised against making any concessions to the students. The general public, he said, was fed up with the *Carillon*. He had overheard at a Christmas party the comment: "Why does the administration permit this filthy rag to carry on?"[85] In his assessment, this was typical of how most people felt. The root of the problem, he thought, was "the attempt by a central organization [the Communist Party?] to use the campus for a base to promote a foreign political ideology through the use of

indoctrinated students and some of the staff who are indoctrinated and that
this purpose to them is of paramount importance above that of education."[86]
The solution was to follow the example of California governor Ronald Reagan, who had put the Berkeley radicals in their place.[87] Atkinson added that
in one respect at least Saskatchewan had an advantage over California. The
cold winters deterred protest marches and outdoor demonstrations.[88]

The students took their case to the public by distributing 100,000 copies of a special issue of the *Carillon* across the province. This was a huge
undertaking, fully twenty times the size of the normal press run.[89] Both the
National Farmers' Union and the Saskatchewan Federation of Labor helped
in the distribution, while students from small towns around Regina took
bundles of newspapers home on the weekend and delivered them door to
door.[90] They felt they were engaged in a momentous struggle and that truth
and justice were on their side. The Board of Governors and the SRC meanwhile continued their negotiations and, finally, on March 11, 1969, came to
an agreement. The students won hands down. The board committed itself
to the resumption of the collection of student activity fees for a period of
one year, the agreement to be renewed annually on August 31, unless either
party gave notice of cancellation prior to the preceding March 1. This meant
that the board could not suddenly and arbitrarily suspend fee collection as it
had done on December 31, 1968. The board had tried during the negotiations
to place the *Carillon* under the supervision of a Publications Board, but the
students vetoed the plan. They did agree to a Board of Governors/Students'
Union Liaison Committee, which was to serve as a forum for discussion between the two bodies. However, this committee was purely consultative and
had no powers of enforcement. Also, the Students' Union promised that the
Carillon would adhere to the Canadian University Press code of ethics, which
the *Carillon* claimed to have been doing all along.[91]

Conservative faculty members criticized the agreement. They thought
the Board of Governors had capitulated meekly to the students. Geography
professor John Chappell fumed: "There was no meaningful penalty levied
for the misconduct of the *Carillon*, and no real guarantee given—except for
the word of the editors, which obviously is not trustworthy—that the same
things will nor recur."[92] Board member Stan Atkinson was equally disappointed. In 1971 he tried to reopen the controversy, requesting that the university lawyer render an opinion as to whether the students were living up
to the agreement. The board quietly let the matter drop, the minutes noting

tersely: "… while a number of members expressed dissatisfaction with the *Carillon*, there was no agreement on appropriate action."[93]

The Waning of the *Carillon*

The students had scored a major victory and firmly established that the newspaper belonged to them and not the Board of Governors or the university as a whole. But the momentum of student power did not carry over into the fall of 1969. When the Students' Union tried to make an issue out of the tuition fee increase (fees were double what they had been in 1963), the effort fell flat. Students ignored the suggestion that they should, as a gesture of protest, withhold the payment of fees. Two "emergency" meetings called by the Students' Union failed to achieve any significant result.[94] A *Carillon* editorial in October 1969 asked plaintively, "Can participatory democracy work without participation?" It bemoaned the fact that "students on this campus really don't want radical social change in this society, a fact that should have been obvious to us."[95]

Seven student journalists left the *Carillon* in the summer of 1969 to work for the *Prairie Fire*, a radical newspaper inspired by the saying of Mao Tse-Tung: "A single spark can start a prairie fire." Funded by a federal government Opportunities for Youth grant, it collapsed in 1971, a victim of money and personnel shortages, poorly defined goals and strategy, and ideological infighting. The dedicated staff worked extremely hard and put in long hours, but to little purpose and with meagre result. As a member of the *Prairie Fire* collective recalled, "We felt as if nobody was reading us anymore; that we could have achieved the same response if we had dumped 500 papers out our office window into the alley below."[96]

The *Carillon*, too, began to lose touch with its readers. In the early 1970s, it grew increasingly shrill and disconnected from the lives and interests of students. It mounted a fierce, unremitting campaign against the Thatcher government, celebrating its defeat at the hands of the NDP in June 1971 with the headline, "Twilight of the Gods: Col. Thatcher's Storm Troops Reduced to Corporal's Guard."[97] The paper also gave enthusiastic support to the labor movement, attacking anti-labor legislation, defending collective bargaining rights, and expressing solidarity with strikers at the Sherwood Co-op and the Parkside Nursing Home.[98] A good deal of space was devoted to agricultural issues, including the National Farmers' Union boycott of Kraft products.[99] Other articles exposed and condemned the practices of Regina's slum landlords.[100] All of these causes may have been worthy enough, but they had little to do with campus life. Earlier editors had always tried to maintain a balance between stories that directly concerned students and those that affected them at one remove. The editors of the early 1970s lost the knack of steering a middle course between the two poles.

Some students became vehement in their opposition to the *Carillon*. A letter to the editor in March 1971 called for a referendum to decide whether the paper should continue to be subsidized by student activity fees. The author of the letter complained that the paper did not reflect his views, and that there was little of interest to read in the "meagre publication." He did not think it was fair that he had to pay $3.00 a year for something that was of no use to him.[101] Another student objected to the publication of a joint *Carillon-Prairie Fire* issue during the 1971 provincial election campaign. He said that he was in favor of upholding the right of free expression, but he did not agree with Students' Union funds being used to campaign against the Liberals, a party he happened to support.[102] Students in the fall of 1971 circulated a petition demanding the impeachment of the editor and, in the space of an hour's canvassing, secured over 250 signatures.[103] A *Carillon* columnist blamed the dissatisfaction on "right-wing freaks from the professional colleges," who were afraid that the radical reputation of the campus would make it difficult for them to get jobs when they graduated. The columnist had no sympathy with such concerns: "We are out to smash capitalism, and we mean business."[104] Students' Union president Larry Schultz admitted that he had heard numerous complaints from students about the paper. He thought the critics had a point: "... there have been many good stories written in the *Carillon* in the past couple of years, and NO one can deny that, and yet at the same time one can say that there is a lot of SHIT written which was completely irrelevant to students and did not relate to them at all."[105]

The editorial policy of the *Carillon*, as stated in October 1973, made no pretence of journalistic objectivity:

> The *Carillon* is a newspaper whose present members share A COMMON interpretation of the weaknesses in their society. We are critical of the all-pervasive influence of the profit motive and its insidious distortion of human values. We believe profit should be outlawed since it promotes disregard for fellow human beings and creates inequalities that cause

unnecessary suffering and hardship given the present tech-
nological achievements of mankind. The values of our society serve to aggravate the material disparities in the society,
and strengthen a mechanism which engineers what are ultimately self-limiting principles ... The paper is not a clique
paper. It does remain open to those of all viewpoints since
the money which supports it comes from student funds.
However, a quorum does dictate the subjects of the stories
which we write since we believe that certain occurrences are
inadequately, or falsely, covered by existing media.[106]

The majority of students at Regina Campus in 1973 did not share the view that
"profit should be outlawed" and that it constituted "an insidious distortion
of human values." The *Carillon's* avowal to the contrary notwithstanding, it
had indeed become a "clique paper."

It is clear in retrospect that the paper's best years were the mid-to-late
1960s when it captured the lively atmosphere of the campus and gave expression to the political, social, and cultural movements of the times. At the
height of its influence, the paper succeeded in both engaging and challenging
its readers. In its declining phase, it assumed a didactic quality, browbeating
students into accepting the "correct" political line, rather than entering into
a dialogue with them. There were still flashes of the old *Carillon*, but, overall, the paper lost its special flavor. Ironically, the year 1968-69 marked both
the paper's greatest triumph in its battle with the Board of Governors and
the beginning of its deterioration as a firebrand journal. The fall from grace
paralleled the trajectory of the sixties as a whole. It, too, began with great
promise and energy, stimulating new ways of thinking about a whole range
of issues both in the university and in society at large, before succumbing, in
its later phases, to ideological rigidity, factionalism, and even violence. We
should not be surprised that the *Carillon*, so richly an embodiment of the sixties, did not escape its fate. But this is to get ahead of ourselves. We need first
to examine the emergence of the student movement in the late 1950s and the
early 1960s, the period when, as the *Carillon* grandly proclaimed, "the giant
awakened."

CHAPTER 4

"The Giant Awakens": The Transformation of Student Culture

S tudents decide to go to university for a variety of reasons, and, once they get there, they occupy themselves in different ways. Helen Horowitz's *Campus Life: Undergraduate Cultures from the End of the Eighteenth Century to the Present* identifies three broad categories of student culture.[1] Although the typology is an oversimplification, it helps us come to grips with the complexities of the topic. The first category is academic student culture, which refers primarily to student involvement in the formal academic program of studies offered at the university. The extra-curricular culture, by contrast, comprises that part of campus life for which no academic credit is given. It includes both formally structured activities (athletics, dances, drama productions, debating clubs, the school newspaper, student government, etc.) and informal, casual pastimes (playing cards, visiting over coffee, partying). The extra-curricular culture is, from the student point of view, more autonomous and self-sufficient than is the academic culture. It is the world students create for themselves beyond the range and direction of adult mentors.

As Horowitz points out, extra-curricular culture, especially the male variant, has traditionally had a hedonistic, unruly side, involving street parades, snake dances, brawls, clashes with the police, and other occasions of misrule. However, these outbreaks of youthful enthusiasm are devoid of political content. It is well understood that the disorder is unfocused and of short duration. Once students have had the chance to "let off steam," they return to normal patterns of behavior. The temporary inversion of authority may even serve to stabilize the power relations within the university because it acts as a safety valve for student unrest. Students are "subject people" in the sense that they have to follow a program of studies and obey rules that are not of their own devising.[2] It is not surprising that from time to time they indulge in disruptive behavior which is excused as youthful exuberance. Such "pranks" and "hijinks" partake more of the spirit of carnival than of rebellion. They do not represent a serious or sustained challenge to the university's hierarchical power structure.

This is what differentiates extra-curricular student life from Horowitz's third category, citizen-student culture. The latter seeks a fundamental change in the role of the student both within and beyond the university. It breaks down what citizen-students perceive as the artificial barrier between the university and the "real world." The campus is seen, not as a sheltered, secluded place where young people are taught to prepare themselves for the duties of citizenship, but rather as an institution fully integrated with the society of which it is a part. From the citizen-student perspective, students are not citizens-in-training, but rather full-fledged members of society and already entitled to the rights and responsibilities of adulthood. This entails both participation in the decision-making processes of the university and involvement in the political affairs of the wider world. Indeed, the university is regarded as the ideal platform from which to launch movements for social change. Youth in such cases often consider themselves uniquely qualified to correct the multifarious errors of their parents' generation.

It must be emphasized that the academic, extra-curricular, and citizen-student cultures are not mutually exclusive. Academic students join protest marches; extra-curricular students have excellent academic records; and citizen-students play on the basketball team. The point of the typology is not to slot students into one category or another, but rather to bring into focus the different ways of experiencing student life. It follows, too, that the balance among student lifestyles can vary over time. Academic studiousness may dominate one period (the Second World War comes to mind), and extra-curricular hedonists another (the Oxford of *Brideshead Revisited*). In the sixties, citizen-students came to the fore. While the other student cultures were not eclipsed, they did recede into the background.

History of Student Activism

Sixties youth did not invent the concept of the citizen-student. Young student revolutionaries in Victor Hugo's *Les Misérables* had "the pure blood of principle flowing through their veins. They stood, without having passed through any intermediary stages, for uncompromising right and absolute duty."[3] Examples may be found closer to home. Historian Sara Burke shows that many students at University of Toronto in the 1880s embraced an altruistic commitment to social reform and to "seek[ing] the highest good" in service to their fellow man. Members of the University College YMCA ventured out to the Newsboys' Home, where they conducted Sunday school classes, told Bible stories, and sang hymns.[4] Female students volunteered to help in the nursery school and playground at Evangelia House, a settlement house that opened in a working-class district of Toronto in 1902.[5] The purpose of the house was to help the poor by living and working among them, thereby sharing their experiences and teaching them a higher standard of life, or, at least, what middle-class students considered a higher standard of life. Arthur H. Burnett, a theology student at Victoria College, helped to organize in 1909 the Students' Christian Social Union, which initiated a series of lectures and a conference on social questions. University of Toronto President Robert Falconer delivered a lecture titled "The University Student and the Social Problem," underscoring the relationship between academic studies and student involvement in social justice action.[6]

Nor were students of this era entirely passive in their relations with university authorities. In 1895, a strike broke out at the University of Toronto. The trouble started when the Political Science club invited agnostic labor leader Alfred Jury and theosophist T. Phillips Thompson to give talks to the students on the subject of labor unions and socialism. The university, disapproving of the men and their ideas, refused permission for the event. The students retaliated by arranging for the lectures to be held at an off-campus location, where over 400 undergraduates packed the hall to hear the speakers.[7] The conflict escalated when the university dismissed Associate Professor William Dale for having publicly criticized the conduct of the university chancellor. The students, led by William Lyon Mackenzie King, future prime minister of Canada, announced a boycott of classes in order to have Dale reinstated. While they did not succeed in this, they were able to convince the Ontario government to establish a Royal Commission to look into the general administration of the university.[8]

The University of Toronto was not the only place where students showed an interest in social issues ranging beyond the academic curriculum. Historian A.B. McKillop finds similar activity at Queen's University and Victoria University, Toronto, in the years before the Great War. Students "complained about 'blind adherence to party' in national politics; believed that socialism, while perhaps 'chimerical,' was 'a very plausible remedy for the ills of humanity'; worried about the jingoistic, expansionist spirit of the United States; decried the existence of industrial combines; and railed that the prohibition question, which had begun as moral improvement, had become 'more and more a football for second-rate politicians, and a subject of mockery by men who have no faith in morals.'"[9] Editorials in student publications debated whether the "modern student" should be actively engaged in solving the issues of the day or defer such involvement until after they had completed their studies. While these students did not engage in demonstrations and protests of the type that became common in the sixties, they at least gave serious thought to the role students might have beyond the narrow confines of the university.

It might be assumed that the 1930s Great Depression acted as a catalyst to student revolt. After all, the economy had collapsed, the capitalist system seemed to have failed, and young people faced bleak job prospects. The time was ripe for social unrest—but not on university campuses. According to Paul Axelrod, at most five per cent of undergraduates in the 1930s joined social reform groups or protest parties, though such participation did increase in the latter half of the decade as the country moved toward war and the possibility of compulsory military service.[10] For the thirties as a whole, however, economic hard times did not produce campus radicalism. Most students came from middle-class backgrounds, and they concentrated on getting a good degree in order to get a good job. The thirties was not a time for collective action to rock the boat; it was a time for individual strategies for survival of the fittest.[11] The sixties, by contrast, drew into the university baby boomers from more diverse class backgrounds than the older elite system had allowed. Further, the buoyant economy allowed students the luxury of shifting attention away from individual career success (which was almost a given) to altruistic social reform movements.

The Second World War ended the depression and restored full employment, but, for other reasons, the climate was not conducive to campus activism. Winning the war took precedence over everything, and dissent from mainstream values was neither welcome nor tolerated. The universities emphasized science and engineering research, much of it under the auspices of the National Research Council, because such work had a direct, practical application to the war effort. There was even an attempt by a group of university officials, including F. Cyril James, principal of McGill University, and

R.C. Wallace, principal of Queen's, to suspend academic programs in such "frill" disciplines as commerce, arts, law, and education. Another group, led by University of Toronto economist and communications theorist Harold Innis, was able to defeat this plan. Nonetheless, the pall of war overshadowed the academy. Universities imposed compulsory military training on male students under the aegis of either the Officer Training Corps or the Training Center Battalion, which required a minimum of six hours per week in military drill and lectures. Male students in arts and science whose grades placed them in the bottom half of the class were eligible for conscription for home defence. Then, in November 1944, 16,000 home defence conscripts were sent overseas. Female students were encouraged to volunteer for the Red Cross or the auxiliary service of the armed forces.[12]

After the war, the Canadian government gave financial benefits to veterans to attend university, and they did so in large numbers. A sudden enrolment bulge placed a heavy strain on post-secondary educational institutions across the country. The veterans, who were older and more worldly-wise than most undergraduates, brought a serious tone to student life. As we have seen, ex-soldiers attending Regina College wrote articles for the student newspaper on topics of a broadly political nature. In "What Price Education?" veteran J.D. Herbert reflected on the irony of the government's offering to pay for a man's university education only on the condition that he had demonstrated a willingness to die for his country. "Isn't it paradoxical," he asked, "that boys should be forced to know the stench of death, the cacophony of the battlefield, cold, strain and exhaustion before they know the good things of life?"[13] Ex–armed forces personnel formed a national organization to lobby the federal government for more generous education benefits.[14] This prefigured some of the 1960s' student campaigns for the reduction or abolition of tuition fees, except that, in the case of the veterans, the agenda was focused on their particular needs, not on those of the student population as a whole.

"Fun and Games" Student Culture

When the veterans graduated, student culture reverted to its more traditional academic and extra-curricular modes and away from the citizen-student pattern.[15] Universities acted "in place of the parent" to regulate closely the lives of students both in and outside the classroom.[16] An unofficial ideology governed extra-curricular activities, which were regarded as both recreational and purposeful because they trained students in the rituals of sociability and taught them how to get along with other people—in short, to have a "good personality." In the words of the dean of Regina College in 1955, extra-curricular activities gave young people the "experience that will assist them in taking a constructive part in the life of their community."[17]

A letter to the editor of the student newspaper in February 1955 said that students were "tomorrow's leaders": "We will be responsible for leading the people in many types of projects and this will require a great deal of talent that can only be learned here and now when we have the opportunity to do so."[18] SRC president Bert Promislow wrote in 1947 that the college experience gave students a chance to learn about democracy through participation in student government, "thereby preparing themselves for their future role as citizens."[19] The key word was "preparing." The students of the 1950s defined themselves as citizens-in-waiting, not citizen-students; extra-curricular activities, for them, were a dress rehearsal for life. They were learning how to get along with other people and how to "fit in." The students of the sixties, by contrast, did not want to fit in; they wanted to shake things up.

One component of extra-curricular student culture had a political aspect. Each year the students elected a mock parliament and pretended to pass laws on matters of national importance. More than 50 per cent of Regina Campus students voted in the mock elections in 1962, casting 167 ballots for the Progressive Conservatives, 162 for the Liberals, and 97 for the NDP. The Conservative platform mingled national issues (nuclear arms for Canada, "reassessment of the government's role with regard to the rights and personal affairs of individual citizens") with local concerns (the establishment of a college of veterinary medicine at the Regina Campus, summer employment of university students). The Liberals promised independence for the Regina Campus from Saskatoon control and offered discounts for students at Regina stores and businesses. The NDP issued its version of the Ten Commandments: "thou shalt reach the age of discretion at 18"; "thou shalt not store, fire, throw or otherwise handle nuclear arms," "thou shalt nationalize thy industry to the best of thy means," and "thou shalt aid thy students."[20] On the surface, the mock parliament seemed to contradict the ethos of extra-curricular culture. The students were talking about the same issues as adult politicians, albeit sometimes in slightly ironic or self-mocking tones. On closer examination, however, we can see that this activity in fact confirmed the essential character of extra-curricular culture. It was, after all,

The annual frosh parade, part of initiation-week celebrations, made its way through the streets of downtown Regina. The "Type B Arts" (social sciences) float featured a giant bee, *Carillon*, 5 November 1963.

a *mock* parliament, not the real thing. Students were pretending to be something that they were not.

Regina Campus in the fall of 1963 celebrated frosh week in the traditional collegiate style. Students entered floats in a parade that progressed through the downtown business section of Regina, the SRC president and female beauty contestants waving to the crowd from open convertibles. Arts "B" (social sciences) won the float contest "with a huge bumblebee surrounded by several drones who were spinning a radar antenna." Immediately following the parade, students headed to the "special SRC drinking section" at the football game between the Saskatchewan Roughriders and the Calgary Stampeders. In the evening there was a dance at the Boat Club: "… with a sloppy roll, our drunken drummer led off the band with such pleasantries as Sharlena, Sugar Shack, and If I Had A Hammer. Within seconds the whole floor was filled with staggering, happy students … Rat fink to the creep who gave Ron Ellingson a knuckle sandwich."[21]

Student Activities Weekend in September 1966 was a melee of shenanigans including a wagon derby, tug-of-war over a mud pit, scavenger hunt, and mud-castle building. The education students won the Volkswagen-stuff-

Above, left: Scavenger-hunt contestants "borrowed" a stuffed hawk from the natural history museum, *Carillon*, 23 September 1966.

Above, right: "Fun and games," frosh week, *Carillon*, 23 September 1966.

Below: Go-cart race, *Carillon*, 30 September 1966

—photo by Woo

Would you believe an accident, on its way to happen?

Left: The police treated college pranks as harmless fun, *Carillon*, 23 September 1966. The real trouble came when students took up political causes and challenged the governance structure of the university.

Below: Engineering students, frosh week parade, 1969, *Carillon*, 3 October 1969.

BRIDGE BUILDERS OF TOMORRROW

ing contest, cramming twenty-one people into a vehicle in fourteen seconds. The Campion College team triumphed in the piano-smashing competition, which involved breaking a piano apart with a sledgehammer and pushing the pieces through a seven-inch hole. Student Ron Thompson pleaded that one of the pianos be saved from destruction and donated to the Orange Benevolent Society, but the idea was unanimously shouted down. There was a tense moment when a police car appeared on the scene: "Any fears of the guilty were quickly dispelled. The officer smiled. He wanted university students to enjoy themselves. All he wanted was the door to the ladies washroom which had disappeared [around the time of the scavenger hunt] ... the policeman drove away with deafening cheers of the crowd in his ears."[22] Students were engaged in destructive, even illegal behaviour, but it had no serious political content. The authorities knew this, and turned a blind eye.

Interest and enthusiasm for frosh week activities waned in later years. The *Carillon* alluded to this development in October 1967 in an article that began: "Another Frosh Week has come and gone and no one even knew about it ... Apparently the students of this campus just are not interested in what's happening or they don't know what is happening as there was a very poor turnout of student spectators [for the parade]." The dance attracted 600 students and featured the crowning of Miss Joan McClinton as Frosh Queen. "All contestants were awarded sterling silver spoons and Miss McClinton was presented with a bouquet of red roses."[23] The frosh parade was still being held in 1969, when engineering students marched down the street carrying a big sign that read, "Engineers Have the Biggest Tools On Campus."[24]

Alcohol figured prominently in extra-curricular student culture, so much so that its consumption was formalized as a competitive sport. The Campus Bacchus Festival in March 1968 highlighted a chug-a-lug contest:

> Friday afternoon hundreds of thirsty inebriates packed the beverage rooms of the Vagabond and the Pig & Whistle for the running of the Administration Society Slop. The contestants formed nine relay teams with the first member of each team guzzling two draught in one beverage room and then running to the other beverage room to drink two more, finally returning to tag his partner who had to follow the same course. Each member of a team had to complete the circuit three times to finish the race. An Arts and Science entry of

Wally C. and Jay A. showed their superiority in the event by tossing back their 24 draught in 18 minutes, 22 seconds to take home the beer steins.[25]

Another version of competitive drinking was the *Carillon* Hotel Inspection Tour (CHIT), inaugurated in 1965 and held every spring. Contestants were required to sprint around a set course through downtown Regina, visiting en route four hotels, at each of which they "inspected" four glasses of beer. The 1967 CHIT attracted 27 entrants, including teams from "Administration, MAB [Men's Athletic Board], Wascana Housing Co-op, Arts C [natural sciences], Hockey Cougars, and Arts and Science." The head judge announced

CHIT ENTRY FORM

NAME:	AGE:	(Can you prove that)
COLLEGE:	YEAR:	
SEX (if any):	WEIGHT (For use in hiring stretcher):	

NAME OF SPONSORING GROUP:

a) Psychiatrist: c) Next-of-kin (Mother if any):

b) Doctor: d) Undertaker:

THIS APPLICATION MUST BE ACCOMPANIED BY PROOF OF AGE

DEADLINE: FRIDAY, MARCH 3

Submit to the CHIT Committee c/o The Carillon

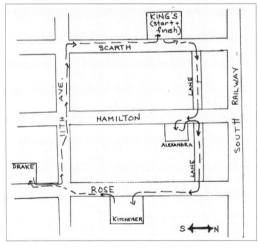

Above: Entry form for the *Carillon* Hotel Inspection Tour (CHIT), a drinking contest-cum-foot race, *Carillon*, 3 March 1972.

Left: The CHIT route in 1972. Contestants quaffed four glasses of beer at each hotel, *Carillon*, 3 March 1972.

Facing page: A CHIT contestant in breach of the "non-regurgitation" rule, *Carillon*, 16 March 1973.

that fifteen judges had been appointed to their positions at the first turn (King's Hotel), second turn (Wascana Hotel), third turn (Queen's Hotel) and home base (Lasalle Hotel).[26] The *Carillon* published the entry form, a course map, and a list of the official rules. Inspectors were immediately disqualified for: "a) failure to drain any glass; b) rupture of the anti-regurgitation clause; c) failure to follow the route; d) exceeding a time of one and one-half hours to complete inspections; and e) breakage of beverage glasses."[27]

Other aspects of student life in the early 1960s may be glimpsed in the

Carillon column "Mitchell and the Mountain," written by Mitchell K. Fantrip, pseudonym for Ken Mitchell, now a well-known author and English professor at the University of Regina. The column took the form of Fantrip's letters back home to his parents on the farm. Fantrip was a Huckleberry Finn–type narrator, naïve and wise at the same time. He described his participation in the Cuban missile crisis protest in October 1962:

> I almost did not get any studying done at all. You remember last week, when Kennedy and the Reds almost blew the world up? They had a big uproar here about that—a bunch of kids decided they were not going to let the Reds blow the world up, and they had a march to stop them. Well, I wouldn't have known anything about the march, except I was walking past and this guy grabbed me by the shoulder. He asked me if I wanted to get blown up, and I said no, not yet until I had my lunch anyway. He said good and stuck this sign in my hand that said "We Want Peace." I could not argue about that—a guy would be crazy not to want peace … so I carried it. At first I thought we were going to march to Cuba or Washington, or even Minot, but all we did was march down to the city hall and back. Some of the kids wanted to throw ink or bricks at city hall, but we did not have enough time because we were on our lunch hour. But I bet we gave them a darned good scare down at city hall.[28]

"Holiday Thoughts," an anonymous December 1963 article, had a more sentimental tone. The writer captured the feelings of students at the end of final exams and just at the start of Christmas holidays:

> Then after your last exam, you take a walk downtown and it's just getting dark, with all the store lights coming on. You meet your girl at Rollie's and have a quiet cup of coffee, then walk on uptown arm in arm with a soft, light snow falling on her brown hair, long and sparkling in the blinking lights and you laugh together at the crazy toys in the windows. Then you walk on home, speaking only now and then, just enjoying the snow and the air and each other. Then there's

that crazy, insane dance at the Hotel, with everyone a little bombed, grinning from ear to ear, people you haven't seen for a year and the boys sneaking down to the Coach Room for a couple, the girls not quite knowing what to do. The guys are all Ivy-sharp and the girls are beautiful but yours is loveliest of all so you don't sneak out but stay and dance with her and no one else ... What do you think of the holiday season? I don't know, but I think that deep inside, everybody has roughly the same idea as mine. But, before I try to justify myself more, I'd best quit. So Merry Christmas, group. We'll see you after the New Year.[29]

Emergence of the "Citizen-Student"

This idyllic scene seems out of character with the sixties, which were more turbulent and unsettled. A sign of the things to come was an editorial in the student newspaper in January 1959. In an English class, the editorial stated, "a certain individual, upon questioning the integrity of Cleopatra, was severely reprimanded, and various not-too-subtle allusions were made as to the licentious nature of his character ... In high school, this would be considered unjust; in a university, it is an outrage." The paper went on to say that such high-handed professorial behaviour and squelching of student opinion was contrary to the basic purpose of university education, which was "to teach reasoning, to gradually unfold the power of the mind, and to point out the road ahead, not to snap rings in noses and drag people down the path the instructor has traveled."[30] A cartoon reinforced the point. It showed a student, his head squeezed in a vice, hands clutching the sides of his desk, while a glowering professor stood over him saying, "Anybody else disagree?"[31]

Anybody else disagree?

A protest against authoritarian teaching methods, *The Sheet*, April 1959.

An editorial in November 1961 developed the concept of the citizen-student. It wasn't enough, the paper said, to vote for the SRC and to participate in college activities. The aim of such involvement was "to provide students with good experience that will be valuable after they graduate … Why wait until we graduate? If each of us doesn't act responsibly now in view of campus, as well as local, national and international problems, we probably won't when we graduate. We won't know how." The paper refused to "stand aloof from the problems which concern us all in this period of turmoil in world affairs. It is the duty of every student to face these problems in the gigantic task which lies ahead."[32]

The first real manifestation of sixties-style student power surfaced in the fall of 1962. The *Carillon* ran a banner headline, October 26, 1962: "WAR IS DECLARED!" The "war" in question was a campaign to obtain preferential student rates on city buses and reduced admission prices at movie theatres. Student president Mike Badham (later a member of Regina City Council) had taken up the demands with Regina mayor Henry Baker, who promised his support. The *Carillon* hinted vaguely that some kind of demonstration was being planned to strengthen the students' bargaining position: "If and when the mobilization occurs, the press and television have tentatively revealed that they will be on hand to cover the situation. Be on hand to put all the legal methods which the B.N.A. [British North America] Act has bestowed upon us to use to get that to which we are entitled."[33]

On October 31, 1962, 250 students "marched on the city of Regina." The demonstration began at the college gymnasium and proceeded north on Scarth Street to the Hotel Saskatchewan where the marchers paraded up and down the halls for fifteen minutes. They advanced to the Capitol movie theatre, chanting, "We want student rates." Next they arrived at National Billiards, where they made off, according to the police report, with seven balls ("black, pink, blue, brown, green, yellow, and white") and three billiard cues—total value, $59.25. Police officers, citing a by-law that required a special permit for demonstrations involving fifty or more persons, ordered the students to disperse, but they refused to comply. Police chief Arthur G. Cookson later complained to Principal William A. Riddell that the students had been disrespectful, rowdy, and ill-mannered, and that they had heaped "abuse, ridicule and insults" on the police.[34] The students in turn accused the constables of unnecessary roughness in their treatment of the protesters.

The marchers regrouped and formed a conga line, which weaved down

11th Avenue to city hall, where they took up the cry, "We want Mayor Baker." He had been victorious in the civic election held that day, and the students took the opportunity to cheer his success because they were grateful for his support for student fares on city buses. The demonstration then broke up: "… tired feet and dimmed spirits prevailed and the protesters quietly returned to the Campus. An invasion of Sammy's P-Za Palace and the 4D [coffee shop] concluded the evening."[35] The police detained four male students, who were later released with no charges being laid.

The *Carillon* headlined its account of the event "THE GIANT AWAK-ENS." It claimed that the march would force the SRC, the faculty, and the citizens of Regina "to reassess their appraisal of our student potential. It ap-pears that students are willing to collectively press for some consideration from the business concerns of this city." This suggests that the SRC had not been involved in planning the march and that the initiative had come from the *Carillon* itself. Student vice-president Harvey Walker later said that the "student council was against it from the outset."[36] In any case, the *Carillon* made the most of the event, emphasizing its importance as a sign of student power.

The *Leader-Post* was not sure what to make of the demonstration. It titled its news report "Snake Dance Leads to Police Warning," but the text of the article placed "snake dance" in quotation marks. Other terms were also used—"march," "parade," "demonstration," "snake dance," "conga line"—none of them, it seemed, quite right. The demonstration blended old and new, combining a prankish element (theft of billiard balls) with political content (chants at city hall). Significantly, the event took place on Hallow-een, a day that had long been associated with revelry, misbehavior, and the temporary inversion of authority. Historian Keith Walden gives an account of Halloween rituals at the University of Toronto in the late 1800s and early 1900s. Every year on October 31, male students marched from the campus to the downtown area where they attended the theatre. They occupied a block of seats in the balcony, and rudely interrupted the performance with shouts, songs, and college yells. Later they paraded through the streets, creating a disturbance and damaging property. This led inevitably to an altercation with the police.[37] The Regina Campus demonstration in 1962 uncannily re-peated this same pattern: march from the campus to the downtown district, attendance at the theatre (in the Regina case a cinema), more marching, riot-ous behavior, and a clash with the police.

There were also local precedents for this kind of behavior. The *Leader* (forerunner of the *Leader-Post*), February 4, 1915, described a hazing ritual: "a tumultuous mob, shrieking and gesticulating wildly, and garbed in the most grotesque of costumes surged through the city streets at a late hour last night, rudely disturbing the peaceful occupations of citizens in their vicinity...."[38] In 1923, Regina College girls "with great green bows added to their hats," marched to the Capitol theatre where they took their places in the front-row seats. When the words "Welcome Freshettes of Regina College" appeared on the screen, the girls stood up and faced the audience while the orchestra played, "Hail, hail the gang's all here."[39]

Halloween at Regina College in the 1950s had been the occasion for raids on the girls' residence:

> Stopping only long enough to barricade the stairs in case of an attack from the rear, they [the male students] raced up to the washroom and smeared sinks, mirrors, doors, and tubs with corn syrup and thick, black molasses. At the sound of the key turning in the latch of one of the rooms, the vigilantes turned as one man and rushed to that room only to realize that they had been duped; they were met by a shower of ink from the transom above the door. No sooner had they recovered from this surprise than they were confronted with an angry Dean of Women who chased them to the staircase where they met—their own barricade.[40]

The girls retaliated the following year with a raid on the men's residence. Dashing from room to room, they tore mattresses from the beds and scattered blankets, sheets, and pillows around the hall. According to the student newspaper, "the raid was a marvelously timed piece of strategy, and we [the girls] were safe behind the locked doors of our own rooms within seconds."[41]

Students in the 1950s also held snake dances in the halls of Regina College as part of frosh week initiation rites. The dance moved out of doors for the first time in 1959, which was the year the decision was taken to expand the junior college to a full degree program. As student Elaine Hamilton explained, "The snake dance is a good idea—should become a tradition at Regina College to make everyone realize that Regina College is a university, not just a glorified high school."[42] Thus, students self-consciously imitated the rituals of older campuses to validate their status as university students. The new ingredient in the 1962 snake dance was politics. The students chanted, "We want student rates" and demonstrated at city hall in support of Mayor Baker. The older style of rowdy behavior—residence raids, snake dances, disruptions in the theatre, clashes with the police, and so on—had a carnival spirit. Such activities did not represent a serious challenge to the established order and lacked political significance. The student protests of the sixties were different. They sought meaningful and permanent changes both in the university and society at large. The Regina Campus snake dance/demonstration of October 31, 1962, borrowed from the past and pointed to the future. It was the symbolic beginning of the sixties at Regina Campus, and the *Carillon* identified it as such.

Doug Owram argues that the baby boomers were a generation with a highly developed sense of collective identity and purpose.[43] This arose in part from sheer numbers. The size of the cohort all but overwhelmed elementary and high schools in the 1950s (portable buildings were often brought into service), and in the 1960s boomers had the same impact on universities. Numbers also translated into commercial power, as young people purchased clothes, records, movie tickets, and automobiles. Appropriately, the first issues Regina Campus students seized on—bus fares and movie prices—related to baby boomer buying power. They seemed to have had an intuitive understanding of where their strength came from and how it could be exercised. All this was latent in the *Carillon's* "THE GIANT AWAKENS."

When the university moved to ban snake dances, the *Carillon* took umbrage. It condemned the action as "gross interference with our right to assemble in protest or to assemble for any reason." This, in the opinion of the students, constituted a breach of the Canadian Bill of Rights, which the Diefenbaker government had recently put in place. Further, the *Carillon* disputed the right of the university to make regulations concerning student actions outside the precincts of the university proper: "Our actions individually or collectively outside the university are our business. They are not subject to University legislation regardless of the circumstances." More broadly, the editorial gave vent to an emerging baby boomer consciousness. It blamed the older generation for "the stinking mess that the world is in today." It suggested that the real motivation for the ban on snake dances was the secret envy of decrepit age for the powers of youth: "… on our first annual snake dance, most Reginans who witnessed our movement wished they had the youth and vitality to take part. These people could see that university students, of necessity, exhibit different ideas and actions that are necessary in producing qualified leaders." Already in 1962 the boomers were making noises about wresting power from their elders and taking charge of society. There is even mention in the editorial of the desirability of revising disciplinary procedures at the university: "There is need for a disciplinary committee COMPOSED OF STUDENTS [emphasis in the original] to enforce discipline on students. If a student acts contrary to rule, let this student be judged by his peers, i.e., other students."[44]

Student Barry Wigmore took the administration and faculty to task for the way they had treated two students who had been candidates in the SRC election. Both were ineligible because their grade-point averages fell below the required minimum. Wigmore did not object to the rule, but rather to the way it had been administered. Neither student had received the courtesy of an official communication prior to the beginning of the election. As a result, they spent time and money on their campaigns, only to be informed by the SRC president that they had been disqualified. "Were they treated with respect?" Wigmore asked; "No—and this is the greatest fault in the whole affair. They were commanded like peasants."[45] The simile seems exaggerated, but it goes to the crux of the matter. Students, increasingly, resented the power relations in the university that placed them in a subordinate position. They felt that they were being treated as though they counted for nothing; they were pushed around and told to do this or that without having any say in the matter. This inferior status was not compatible with the baby boomer sense of entitlement and empowerment.

Discipline became a contentious issue as students registered dissatisfaction with the *in loco parentis* code. Under the existing regime, two faculty "patrons" had to be present at all student dances. The regulations stated:

> Some attempt should be made to see that Patrons are having as enjoyable a time as possible. These functions are more a duty than a pleasure to Patrons, but without Patrons there are no functions ... Patrons must be prevented any annoyance from disorderly students or guests. If a patron leaves a function after reporting to a member of the SRC that he is

withdrawing as Patron, THAT FUNCTION ENDS IMMEDI-
ATELY [emphasis in original].[46]

A Student Activities Committee, composed equally of faculty members and
students, was set up in 1962 to plan the schedule of student social functions.
To the chagrin of the faculty, the students failed to show up for meetings. A
professor observed, "In general there seems to be some feeling among the
SRC that the Faculty aspect of this committee is an encroachment on their
freedom of action in the running of their affairs."[47] The faculty "censure[d]
the S.R.C. very severely for the discourtesy done the members of the Faculty
of the Committee."[48]

In 1965, faculty and students came to an understanding on a new set of
regulations. They decided that the SRC should have responsibility for drawing up a calendar of social events to be held during the school year and for
registering the calendar with the principal by September 15. The SRC was
also entrusted with the task of administering the regulations and supervising
the functions. Even so, two faculty members (the word "patron" had been
dropped) still had to be in attendance at all social events. Student president
Ken Mitchell hailed the breakthrough:

> I received with hearty approval the proposed set of regula-
> tions on student social functions, as suggested by the fac-
> ulty-student committee which met last month. As you, the
> chairman, are well aware, the students' council feels that it
> *has* to assume responsibility for all Regina Campus activities
> if it is going to be in a position to maintain their rights. This
> is what we envisaged in the constitution recently adopted
> by the student union ... I felt that this meeting of faculty
> and students was not only cooperative, but productive. If
> relations between our two respective bodies continue in this
> fashion throughout the year, there is no conceivable limit to
> the amount of concerted action that the two bodies can take.
> All our goals, regardless of their immediate implications,
> can be seen to be the same—improvement of university edu-
> cation—and the atmosphere of the recent meeting can only
> strengthen the progress toward those goals.[49]

The letter spoke not only of student rights, but also of responsibilities. It envisioned an arrangement in which faculty and students worked together as partners towards the common goal of building a better university. This led to a major overhaul of the constitution for student government. The old constitution defined the SRC as the coordinator of student social and athletic activities—planning sock hops, organizing pep rallies, arranging for the publication of the yearbook, and so on. The student council was subordinated to the authority of the dean of the college, who could intervene in its affairs as he saw fit. When four SRC officers—the president, treasurer, vice-president, and social director—resigned in February 1962, Dean Riddell called a general meeting of the students for the purpose of "right[ing] the capsized ship of student government." The newspaper editor tacked a two-page rebuttal to the bulletin board, denouncing Riddell's action as a completely unjustified violation of the independence of the student body. The dean dismissed the protest as "stupid." He insisted that: "The SRC derives its authority from the university's Board of Governors. I'm empowered to step in."[50]

In the fall of 1964, SRC president Simon de Jong (a future NDP Member of Parliament for Regina) outlined a new plan for student government. "We have felt," he said, "that while the SRC has an important duty in coordinating social activities on the campus, we also feel that it must do more than that. It must also act as a union. It must be totally concerned with all student problems and must be willing to act on all such problems affecting students." This included, but was not limited to, "academic programs and how they are offered," "financial difficulties facing students," "conditions students face in their studies," and "the guardianship and expansion of student rights."[51] The new constitution was put to the student body for a vote in February 1965 and passed by a wide margin (voter turnout was about 50 per cent).[52]

A key feature of the new constitution was that it incorporated the Students' Union under the Societies' Act of the Province of Saskatchewan. This gave the union independent legal status as well as the right to own property, borrow money, and enter into contracts. However, this independence was, in a sense, illusory, since the university collected the student activity fees that the Students' Union needed to pay for its operations. Recognizing this, the students inserted into the constitution the clause: "The SRC may contract with the Board of Governors of the University of Saskatchewan for the collection of student fees by the offices of the University."[53] This was the bone of contention of the *Carillon* crisis of 1968-69, a crisis that was resolved, as we have seen, in favor of the students.

Initially, the Board of Governors refused to give its blessing to the legal incorporation of the Students' Union. The *Carillon* was defiant, urging the SRC[54] in March 1965 to proceed with or without the board's consent. The paper said that the "ace in the hole" was the overwhelming mandate the SRC had received from the students in the constitutional referendum: "They [the students] won't allow their hands to be slapped with an admonition of 'Naught, naughty, mustn't touch.'"[55] For two years the SRC tried to negotiate the constitution with the board. The university asked for a legal opinion. Did it have the power to block the incorporation? The answer was no: "… the authority of the Board would only be required in the event that the applicant for incorporation was a trading company or a commercial company and consequently the Students' Union would not require the authority of the Board of Governors."[56] The lawyer added that, after incorporation, the university would not be liable, other than "morally," for agreements entered into by the Students' Union. The latter, as a separate legal entity, was theoretically responsible for its own business affairs. In practice, however, it would be hard for the university to wash its hands of the situation if the Students' Union were to get into financial difficulties. The matter was still unresolved when, in 1967, the students went ahead unilaterally with incorporation.

Student Protests

As we have seen, the first protest demonstration of any size at Regina Campus took place on October 31, 1962, but that had been a hybrid affair blending Halloween hijinks with serious politics. The first unambiguously political demonstration was held March 18, 1964, when 200 students boycotted classes and marched to the legislature to protest a $50 increase in tuition fees and to demand a royal commission to investigate the possibility of a separate university in Regina. Pickets went up around the college buildings at an early hour, and absentee rates in the 8:30 classes ranged from 60 to 90 per cent. At 9:30, speakers gathered at the main doors, the students rubbing their hands and stamping their feet in the chilly weather. Mayor Henry Baker lent his support, as did Professor Charles Lightbody, who traveled from Brandon College especially for the occasion. (Lightbody had taught at Regina Campus the previous year, but resigned in high dudgeon because he believed that Regina deserved independence from Saskatoon.) The speeches over, the students formed a cavalcade and marched three abreast, west on College

Vol. 3   No. 1   U. of S. Regina Campus   Wednesday, September 16, 1964

—Peter Blashill   photo

Why are 250 Regina Campus students marching down Albert Street in the snow? The answer lies below.

The first of many student protest marches to the Legislative Building, 18 March 1964. The photo appeared in the *Carillon*, 16 September 1964.

The protestors demanded a royal commission on post-secondary education to create an independent University of Regina, separate from the Saskatoon campus.

Avenue and then south on Albert Street across the bridge to the legislature. They paraded down the middle of the street, singing, "We Are Marching to Autonomy." At the Legislative Building, a nine-man delegation had an audience with the minister of education, who politely received their brief, but offered only a token response.[57] As one student said, "we were patted on the head like good little boys and told to mind our own business."[58]

As students made the transition from extra-curricular to citizen-student culture, the *Carillon*, on October 15, 1965, published a full page of photographs juxtaposing images of starving Third World children and the "rah, rah, rah" frosh parade[59] (see page 82). The message was clear: university was not for playing games; it was an opportunity for students to confront the grim realities of the world. At about the same time, a dispute broke out over the publication of the student yearbook. The students who identified with the extra-curricular culture valued the yearbook as a souvenir of college days, a record of friendships and fun times. The students who had accepted the citizen-student paradigm considered it a diversion from politics and a waste of money. The *Carillon* editorialized: "We, as students and people, have reached a level of maturity and security that we no longer feel the need to see ourselves reflected in the grey light of poor photos. We don't particularly enjoy thumbing through pages of misrepresentations of what we did at college, designed to call up gobs of nostalgia and the odd tear to shed for the long gone, joyous, misspent days of our varsity youth." The funds dedicated to the yearbook could be better spent on scholarships, to bring in "world famous speakers," or to hire professional psychologists for the counselling service.[60] After prolonged debate, the anti-yearbook faction won out and the tradition was abolished. The outcome was one more sign of the growing ascendancy of the citizen-student over extra-curricular culture.

The battle over the college yearbook symbolized the conflict between traditional extra-curricular student culture and the new student-as-citizen culture emerging in the sixties, *Carillon*, 16 October 1964.

—photo by Wood
Don Kossick chairing the General Meeting last Friday.

Left: The general meeting of the Students' Union in September 1966 attracted more than 600 students. Don Kossick chaired the proceedings, *Carillon*, 30 September 1966.

Below: "Let's for God's sake humanize this place a little bit," declared SRC president Don Mitchell. Note the suit and tie, hardly the attire of a student radical, *Carillon*, 30 September 1966.

"Let's for God's sake humanize this place a little bit." — pres. Mitchell

The two viewpoints jostled uneasily at the annual general meeting of the Students' Union in September 1966. The *Carillon* reported that it was the largest crowd ever to attend such a meeting. Over 600 students participated. Chair Don Kossick opened the assembly by leading each of the colleges in their respective cheers and by warning students of a planned police raid at the float-building sites that evening. Treasurer Jack Harrop gave his report, competing as best he could "with the five Frosh Queen contestants for the attention of the squad of Engineers seated in front of him." Former Students' Union president Simon de Jong gave a speech about the new constitution, which he had introduced in 1965. Students and faculty, he said, "should act together as the guts of the university." He handed the microphone to incumbent president Don Mitchell, who outlined the priorities for his term in office: co-op housing, plans for a Students' Union Building, psychological counseling services, and increased provincial government funding of higher education. He won loudest applause for his criticism of the administration for its "educational mill approach" to running the university. His line, "Let's for God sake humanize this place a little bit," became part of campus lore. After Mitchell's speech came the crowning of the Frosh Queen. Then, with the crowd growing restless as afternoon classes approached, six resolutions were rushed through with little or no debate. These included motions on universal accessibility to higher education and condemnation of the Vietnam War. The latter had to be tabled "as the quorum slowly left the courtyard and Dave Wiffen, singer from the 4th Dimension coffee-house closed the meeting."[61] It was an odd medley of issues. Float building and Frosh-Week Queens competed for attention with tuition fees and the Vietnam War, a snapshot of student culture in the midst of transformation.

Student protest took a new turn December 16, 1966. SRC president Mitchell addressed about 400 students in the Lab building cafeteria on the problems with the semester system, which had been introduced in the fall. Students were under pressure because there was no study period between

Student protest, December 1966. The students wanted more time to study for final examinations, *Carillon*, 20 January 1967.

—G. & W. photo

Part of the crowd sitting in the third floor hallway await the result of a meeting between student leaders and Faculty Council President Dr. A. Berland.

the last day of lectures and the first day of examinations. They also felt
that professors had failed to make appropriate adjustments in the amount
of material they tried to cover in their classes. Some, it seemed, crammed a
full year's work into a half-year class. After Mitchell's speech, the students
marched from the cafeteria to the office of faculty council chair Alwyn Berland. They carried placards reading, "We Like Our Sanity," "A Care for Today is a Cure for Tomorrow," and "Down With the Semester System." The
students refused to budge until Berland agreed to negotiate the operation
of the semester system and allow more time for study before examinations.
The protest had a catalytic effect on the campus. It broke the tension in the
air, and it showed the students that their views counted for something. They
had expressed their grievances, and the university had responded. This set a
precedent for future action.[62]

On another front, Mitchell was less successful. He suggested in September 1966 that the Board of Governors adopt the practice of "open decision
making," that is, holding their meetings in public rather than behind closed
doors. He was allowed to make this proposal in person to the board. In the
course of the meeting, university president John Spinks criticized him for
"ungentlemanly behavior." Mitchell said nothing at the time, but a few days
later wrote Spinks to ask for an explanation:

> It is one thing to direct allegations towards another person
> during the course of a private meeting or conversation at
> which time such remarks can be challenged and refuted, or
> else evidence produced to back them up. It is quite another
> thing I suspect to direct remarks of a personal or deroga-
> tory nature to a participant in a meeting intended for non-
> personal business particularly when those present are not
> familiar with the circumstances or personalities alluded to
> … Without questioning your authority to reprimand me (a
> mere student), I do question the timing of your action and
> the basis for it.[63]

Spinks replied that Mitchell was not a gentleman because he had failed
to discipline the *Carillon* for having published some articles that cast the
university administration in a bad light.[64] Mitchell, of course, did not think it
was his job to censor the student newspaper.

Principal Riddell in 1967 made it clear that he did not like the idea of a student representative on the board of governors. Board discussions, he said, were often confidential, and students could not be relied upon to keep sensitive information private. In addition, he thought that students lacked the experience required "to make a particularly significant contribution" to board discussions, many of which involved complicated financial matters that were difficult for neophytes to understand.[65] The *Carillon* replied with a cartoon that showed a student giant crushing the diminutive Board of Governors under the heel of

By the fall of 1967, students were aware of the power they wielded, *Carillon*, 13 October 1967.

his boot. The student carried a sign that read "Student Power."[66]

By 1967, Regina Campus students were feeling energized and confident. Don Mitchell reflected, in March 1967, on the accomplishments of his term of office. He said that all the issues he had worked on—"housing, student union building planning, activities programming, policy for a more free, more democratic university"—had been directed toward one goal: the building of a spirit of community on the campus. "If we can establish," he wrote, "… an atmosphere in which every individual feels himself a part of the university—an atmosphere which the student can participate in and establish an identity in—an atmosphere in which the learning experience extends beyond the classroom and laboratory—then we have accomplished something important." But what of the future? Mitchell thought the campus faced "a fork in the road." One path led to working with faculty "for more student responsibility in governing bodies … This involves placing a priority in student cooperative enterprise, policy issues for a more democratic university and exercising citizenship responsibilities in the community through the Saskatchewan Students Federation and Canadian Union of Students."

The other road represented "a retreat to a traditional role of students and student government which emphasizes provision of services without policy. Priority in this direction is exclusive to provision of dances, basketball games and yearbook."[67]

It was a choice between the extra-curricular and citizen-student cultures. In one sense, it was a false choice, because the two cultures co-existed all through the sixties and continue to do so today. Along with the core of academic student culture, they make up student life as we know it. At the same time, Mitchell had a valid point. In the sixties the balance shifted decisively from the rampant extra-curricular culture of the fifties to a robust citizen-student culture. Mitchell need not have worried. There would be no retreat.

CHAPTER 5

Building a Just Society: Liberation Movements of the Sixties

reedom, equality, and justice were catchwords of the sixties. It was a
time when excluded and subordinated groups—African Americans,
Aboriginals, Québecois, and women—threw off their inferior status
and asserted their right to equal treatment. The *Carillon* gave full coverage to
these developments, and its editorials displayed a finely tuned awareness of
their significance. But one group stood out because of its special relevance for
Saskatchewan. The *Carillon* surpassed the mainstream media in the attention
it gave to Aboriginal issues. This was the paper's most distinctive commentary on the liberation movements of the sixties.

Civil Rights Movement

The civil rights movement in the United States went to the heart of what
the sixties was all about. The television images were riveting: water hoses,
tear gas, and police dogs turned on peaceful demonstrators; straight-backed
teenagers walking to school under military escort; civil rights activists
clubbed and jailed. It was epic moral drama. The movement taught a
number of lessons: established authority could be in the wrong; the dictates
of personal conscience took precedence over the letter of the law; faith
could move mountains. For those who joined the movement, the experience
had the potential to transform their lives. Many felt ennobled and part of
something much greater than themselves. They were changing the course
of history. Once the moment had passed, veterans of the movement often
transferred their passion to other causes: opposition to the Vietnam War,
women's liberation, environmentalism, anti-poverty work. For such people,
the civil rights movement was the road to Damascus.

It was also a metaphor and template for the sixties. Jerry Farber titled his attack on the education system "The Student as Nigger." Quebec separatist Pierre Vallières wrote that "the liberation struggle launched by the American blacks ... arouses growing interest among the French-Canadian population, for the workers of Quebec are aware of their condition as nigger, exploited men, second-class citizens."[1] Peter Gzowski called his 1963 essay on Aboriginal peoples in Saskatchewan, "This is Our Alabama."[2] The redemptive spirit of the civil rights movement proved an inexhaustible source of analogy and uplift.

The movement grew out of developments in the 1950s, in particular the United States Supreme Court ruling in May 1954 (*Brown v. Board of Education, Topeka, Kansas*) disallowing segregated schools. When Governor Orval Faubus of Arkansas defied the law in the fall of 1957 and tried to prevent African Americans from attending a white high school in Little Rock, President Dwight Eisenhower sent in the 101st Airborne Division to protect the students.[3] A similar scene unfolded at the University of Mississippi in 1962, where 23,000 federal troops were called in to put down riots that broke out in opposition to the admission of black student James Meredith. These incidents made international headlines and focused the attention of the mass media on the desegregation movement.

Students at Regina Campus were aware of the significance of these events. In October 1962, Hans Kieferle wrote in the *Carillon*: "The American Negro's right to equality (a right which no intelligent person will begrudge him) is being violently opposed ... Is it not a fact, that for all practical purposes the Negro in the South still can't vote? Is he not denied admission to numerous educational institutions? And finally is he given the opportunity to mix freely wherever he wants: in public places, theatres, buses, etc...?" Kieferle saw only one solution: "The whites must accept Negroes as ordinary human beings: nothing more, nothing less. Any apologies, especially in the light of recent violence, are simply insufficient. After all, this is the 20th century, the age of emancipation."[4] The *Carillon* Christmas issue in 1964 depicted Santa Claus as a black man, a twist on the stereotype intended to jolt readers' preconceptions about race.[5]

In Montgomery, Alabama, December 1, 1955, Rosa Parks, a 42-year-old seamstress, refused to give up her seat on a bus to a white man. Following her arrest, the black community organized a boycott of the transit system that lasted 381 days. They formed car pools or walked to work. Martin Luther

A black Santa Claus, *Carillon*, 4 December 1964, challenged racial stereotypes.

King, Jr., a twenty-six-year-old Baptist minister, emerged as the leader of the campaign. Despite the fact that his house was bombed, nearly killing his wife and children, he refused to give up. Finally, the courts ruled that the Montgomery buses had to be desegregated. It was an important victory, one that catapulted King into the national spotlight. As head of the Southern Christian Leadership Council, he became the leading spokesman for the strategy of non-violent civil disobedience to win equality for African Americans.[6]

The lunch-counter sit-ins began on February 1, 1960. On that day, four male African-American students from North Carolina Agricultural and Technical College sat down at a lunch counter in a Woolworth's department store in Greensboro and ordered coffee. They were studiously ignored, except for the white customers who shouted insults at them and the black dishwasher, who said they were "ignorant" and "stupid." When they returned to the campus, they were treated like heroes. The college president took their side, defending them against the whites who demanded their expulsion. The next day twenty black students from the college showed up at the Woolworth's counter, and, on the fourth day, the first white student joined them.[7] The movement was unstoppable. It spread through the South, desegregating restaurant after restaurant.

In May 1961, African Americans and whites boarded regular Greyhound buses from Washington, D.C., to New Orleans to force the federal government to enforce the law that required the integration of bus terminal waiting rooms, washrooms and restaurants. The "freedom rides," as the protests were called, continued through the summer. At Anniston, Alabama, a bus was firebombed and the passengers beaten as they fled to safety. When the bus pulled into the terminal at Montgomery, Alabama, a mob attacked with chains and clubs. The police were nowhere to be seen. Jim Zwerg, a white civil rights worker from Wisconsin, seriously injured and lying in a hospital bed, stared into a television camera and said that he was willing to die for the cause. In Mississippi, the freedom riders were jailed, as many as a dozen prisoners crammed into a cell meant for two people. Temperatures soared to over 100 degrees Fahrenheit. But the freedom riders made their point, and "whites only" signs came down across the South.[8]

President Kennedy introduced the Civil Rights bill in June 1963, which outlawed segregation in all public interstate facilities, authorized the attorney general to initiate school desegregation cases and denied funds to federal programs where discrimination was practised. Civil rights workers organized a march on Washington, August 28, 1963, in support of the legislation. The size of the crowd exceeded all expectations. Instead of the hoped-for 100,000 marchers, more than 250,000 turned up, about 60,000 of them white.[9] Standing in front of the Lincoln Memorial, Martin Luther King, Jr., delivered his "I Have a Dream" speech. It was one of the defining moments of the sixties. He called on America to live up to the ideals of its constitution so that "black men as well as white men, would be guaranteed the unalienable rights of life, liberty and the pursuit of happiness." Rejecting the spirit of vengeance, he said: "Let us not seek to satisfy our thirst for freedom by drinking from the cup of bitterness and hatred. We must forever conduct our struggle on the high plane of dignity and discipline. We must not allow our creative protest to degenerate into physical violence. Again and again we must rise to the majestic heights of meeting physical force with soul force." He admitted that this would not be easy: "Some of you have come from areas where your quest for freedom left you battered by the storms of persecution and staggered by the winds of police brutality. You have been the veterans of creative suffering. Continue to work with the faith that unearned suffering is redemptive." The speech was based on two foundational texts, fragments of which King wove into the flow of his oratory: the Declaration of Independence ("we hold these truths to be self-evident, that all men are created equal") and the Bible ("I have a dream that one day every valley shall be exalted, every hill and mountain shall be made low, the rough places shall be made plain, and the crooked places shall be made straight and the glory of the Lord will be revealed and all flesh shall see it together.") This gave the speech extraordinary resonance and power, as in the peroration: "And when we allow freedom to ring, when we let it ring from every village and hamlet, from every state and city, we will be able to speed up that day when all of God's children—black men and white men, Jews and Gentiles, Catholics and Protestants—will be able to join hands and to sing in the words of the old Negro spiritual, "Free at last, free at last; thank God Almighty, we are free at last."[10]

Civil rights workers, many of them members of the Student Non-Violent Coordinating Committee (SNCC), went to Mississippi in the summer of 1964. African Americans made up 64 per cent of the voting-age population of the state, but were only 9 per cent of registered voters. About 800 white college students, many of them from major universities such as Yale, Berkeley, Michigan, Princeton, Harvard, Wisconsin and Stanford, volunteered to assist in registration drives. Once in Mississippi, they were warned not to drive at night or to travel alone. Three of them (two whites and one black) were murdered on June 20, 1964. Walter Cronkite, CBS news anchor, said the eyes of the world were on the American South.[11] (In Saskatchewan, CCF members of the legislature took up a collection for the widow of a Unitarian minister from Boston who was bludgeoned to death in Selma, Alabama.[12]) The 1964 Freedom Summer succeeded in registering only 1,600 African American voters.[13] Blacks feared for their jobs and even their lives. Unlike the college students who could go back to school at the end of the summer, they had to stay in Mississippi and live with the consequences of their actions.

While King's non-violent strategy achieved tangible gains, such as the Civil Rights Act (1964) and the Voting Rights Act (1965),[14] many African Americans thought that progress was too slow. Attention shifted from the South to the ghettoes of northern cities, where blacks were equal with whites before the law, but a type of *de facto* segregation was practised. They lived in the poorest districts with the worst schools and the least opportunities. The Black Power movement preached nationalism, rather than integration; militant action rather than acceptance of suffering through civil disobedience. It was the opposite of what Martin Luther King stood for. Malcolm X (formerly Malcolm Little) declared: "Our enemy is the white man!" "Black people," he said, "are fed up with the dillydallying, pussyfooting, compromising approach that we've been using toward getting our freedom. We want freedom now, but we're not going to get it saying 'We Shall Overcome.' We've got to fight until we overcome."[15] He mocked King, who had been given the Nobel Peace Prize in 1964: "If I'm following a general, and he's leading me into battle, and the enemy tends to give him rewards, or awards, I get suspicious of him. Especially if he gets a peace prize before the war is over."[16]

Whites were expelled from SNCC in 1966, a worrisome development for white middle-class liberals. H. "Rap" Brown raised the spectre of widespread violence: "If America don't come around we're going to burn it down."[17] In August 1965, a six-day riot in Watts, Los Angeles, resulted in 34 deaths (32 of them black), 900 injuries, and 4,000 arrests.[18] Disturbances in Detroit in 1967 left 43 dead,[19] and the dismal pattern repeated itself in other American cities. The *Carillon* kept track of the developments, publishing an article written by two Regina students who visited Detroit in the wake of the riot. They reported that it was "essentially a civil war fought on the basis of the have-nots against the haves" and predicted "rebellion on a broader scale," if things did not change.[20]

In October 1966, Huey Newton and Bobby Seale, two young blacks from Oakland, California, founded the Black Panther party. They issued a ten-point platform demanding jobs, housing, education, justice, and peace for African Americans.[21] More controversially, the Panthers alleged that the police were guilty of using excessive force against poor blacks, and they asserted the right to take up arms in self-defence. They referred to the police as an "occupying power." The Panthers also called for "an end to the robbery by the CAPITALIST [emphasis in the original] of our Black Community." Drawing eclectically from Mao Tse Tung, Frantz Fanon, and Che Guevara, Black Panther ideologues asserted a socialist solidarity with oppressed peoples around the world, whom they considered victims, like the blacks of America, of US imperialism. Clad in black leather, mysterious behind dark glasses, armed to the teeth, the Panthers projected a macho, menacing image quite unlike that of Martin Luther King and the Southern Christian Leadership Council. By the end of 1968, they had chapters in over twenty cities and a membership of about 2,000.[22]

The Regina student council voted funds to invite Black Panther leaders to speak on campus, and November 18, 1969, Fred Hampton, chair of the Illinois chapter, addressed about 600 students in the Education auditorium. "The only difference between Canada and Chicago," he said, "is that you're a further north part of Babylon." He talked about the social welfare side of the Panther agenda, for example, the free breakfast programs and health clinics, and emphasized the severity of party discipline. Members "could be expelled for the use of narcotics, not including marijuana, for pointing a weapon at someone or using it unnecessarily, for not defending himself if attacked, or

Black Panther Fred Hampton at Regina Campus, *Carillon*, 21 November 1969.

for crimes against the people ... Each panther below a certain level in the party is required to read for three hours a day." With respect to the use of force, Hampton said the policy was based on self-defence: "If people break down our doors, we'll blow their brains out." "However," he continued, "the only people who need worry about getting their brains blown out are the ones who are going to kick down our doors."[23]

Two weeks later, on December 4, 1969, Fred Hampton was killed. Illinois state police shot him and fellow Panther Mark Clark in an early morning raid on their Chicago apartment. As soon as the *Carillon* staff heard the news, they published a special bulletin.[24] The violence that was occurring in the United States had been brought closer to home. The police had fired more than eighty shots through the door into Hampton's apartment; only one shot was fired from the inside. Despite the physical evidence, the Panthers were charged with attempted murder, and the police claimed they had acted in self-defence. The charges were so ludicrous that they had to be dropped. The Hampton and Clark families sued the State of Illinois and the police, settling out of court for $1.85 million.[25] The building where Hampton died was later razed as part of an urban development project, and his son, Fred Hampton, Jr., tried to get the street named after him. He described his father as "a hero who boldly demanded rights for black people, pressed for meals for black schoolchildren and died at the hands of the police."[26] But the wounds of the sixties are slow to heal, and the proposal was rejected.

Aboriginal Rights

The *Carillon* was quick to make the connection between the civil rights movement in the United States and Aboriginal rights in Canada. The latter issue, while intensifying in the sixties, had been building for some time. After World War II, Indian and Métis veterans came home to reserves and communities where they faced poverty, discrimination, and paternalistic government control. There was a wide gap between the ideals they had been fighting for—liberty, equality, and democracy—and the reality of their daily lives. The war had been fought against racism; yet, here in Canada, another form of racism was practised, and nothing was done about it. All over the world in the post-war years, colonial empires were being dismantled. Britain gave up India in 1947; France was pushed out of Vietnam in 1954. The days of global white supremacy were over. Likewise, within Canada, Aboriginals initiated a process of decolonization and asserted their right to self-determination.

The Government of Canada in 1946 appointed a joint committee of the House of Commons and Senate to consider revisions to the Indian Act. After a series of hearings and discussions, Parliament passed a number of amendments in 1951. Some of the more oppressive measures in the Indian Act, such as the ban on traditional religious ceremonies like the Potlatch and Sun Dance, were deleted. The Department of Indian Affairs could no longer prevent an Indian organization from raising money or hiring a lawyer, and the practice of compulsory enfranchisement, whereby individuals could be forced to give up their Indian status, was also brought to an end. Band councils were allowed a modest increase in decision-making power in the administration of reserves. Nonetheless, despite improvements, the basic purpose of the Indian Act remained the same. Indians were still expected to assimilate into the mainstream of Canadian society.

The federal government in 1960 extended the federal franchise to Indians without requiring them to give up Indian status or treaty rights. At about the same time, the provinces granted the provincial vote on the same terms.[27] The Indian Affairs department in 1963 appointed a team of social scientists led by Harry Hawthorn, a sociologist at the University of British Columbia, to conduct a national survey of living conditions on reserves. The results were appalling. Thirteen per cent of Indian homes had running water, compared with a national average of 92 per cent. Forty-four per cent had electricity, as against 99 per cent nation-wide. The average life expectancy for Indian males was 33.3 years, for all Canadian men, 60.5 years. For women, life expectancies were 34.7 and 64.1 years respectively.[28] It was obvious that a new approach to Indian policy was needed.

The Hawthorn report recommended a policy framework based on the concept of "citizens plus." It urged the federal government to abandon its longstanding policy of assimilation in favour of extending the full rights of Canadian citizenship to Indians, while simultaneously recognizing special privileges arising from Aboriginal and treaty status. The Trudeau government rejected the advice and, in 1969, released the "Statement of the Government of Canada on Indian Policy," better known as the White Paper. Based on the premise that Indians had no claim to special legal status, the document recommended repeal of the Indian Act, the dismantling of the Department of Indian Affairs, delivery of government services to Indians through the same channels as to all other Canadians, conversion of reserves from crown land to Indian ownership in fee simple, and the "equitable" termination of treaty rights. It amounted to a crash course in assimilation.

The Alberta Indian Association countered with the "Red Paper," which was subsequently endorsed by the National Indian Brotherhood. It asked that the existing legal status of registered Indians be respected and treaties honored. It reminded the federal government that it had a constitutional duty to protect Indians and Indian lands, a responsibility that it could not hand over to the provinces. Reserve land was held in trust by the Crown and could not be transferred to fee simple status and sold. As a result of the outcry against the White Paper, Indian Affairs minister Jean Chrétien promised in 1971 that the government was not going to implement it.[29]

The controversy revealed the extent to which Aboriginal peoples had developed political organizations to work effectively on their behalf. The National Indian Council was formed in 1961 to represent Indians, Métis and non-status Indians. It split into two parts in 1968, the Métis and non-status Indians regrouping as the Native Council of Canada and the Indians as the National Indian Brotherhood. Progress was also made at the provincial level. The Federation of Saskatchewan Indians (later the Federation of Saskatchewan Indian Nations) evolved from an advisory body to a program-delivery organization. Its annual budget grew from $70,000 in 1969 to more than $1.5 million in 1972, when it employed 119 people to run its programs.[30] Under the leadership of Walter Deiter and David Ahenakew, the

FSI began to restructure the relationship between Indians and non-Indians, replacing paternalism and subjugation with Indian cultural affirmation and self-determination. The touchstone was treaty rights, which were invoked at every opportunity, especially when the federal government threatened to remove them, either directly, as in the White Paper, or indirectly through devolution of federal Indian programs to the provincial government. The FSI committed itself to negotiation and the non-violent approach. As Chief Walter Deiter said in 1968, "I don't go along with the idea of Black Power or Red Power ... [Indians] don't have any of these ideas of revolution or wanting to control the whole world."[31]

Métis and non-status Indians in Saskatchewan in the sixties adopted a more radical tone and style. The Saskatchewan Native Action Committee (SNAC), founded in April 1968, distributed a leaflet, "Up the Revolution," proclaiming, "Integration is not the solution, especially not forced integration. We oppose Whitey's attempts to assimilate our people, our culture, traditions, and philosophies into his supreme society." The leader of SNAC was Howard Adams, who grew up in St. Louis, a Métis community south of Prince Albert. Adams studied at Berkeley, graduating with a doctorate in 1966. He analyzed the colonization of Aboriginal peoples in his book, *Prison of Grass* (1975), which laid out a program for national liberation, linking the Aboriginal movement with Black Power ideology:

> The more I became involved, the clearer colonialism became. I was very moved when I heard Malcolm X speak to the students [at Berkeley] about black nationalism. Afterwards I wanted time to think of the beautiful things he had said. The ideas he expressed about black nationalism were so important that I could not put them out of my mind. I kept trying to fit them into the Indian/Métis situation at home. Nationalism seemed to be a spirit that motivated black people to a new sense of pride and confidence. Like the black people, I began to reject my feeling of inferiority and shame, and to become proud of my Indian heritage and native nation.[32]

Although Adams did not think that violence was the preferred method to achieve Aboriginal liberation, he did not rule it out altogether. He argued that a call to arms under existing conditions would be suicidal, but "there may come a time when guerrilla violence will be necessary and appropriate, and we must not hesitate to use it."[33] Possibly because of his willingness to contemplate the use of force, Adams became an object of fascination for the media, which referred to him as a "militant" and "red power advocate." *Leader-Post* reporter Eric Malling interviewed him at his suburban bungalow in Saskatoon. A portrait of Louis Riel hung on the wall, and, in the course of the conversation, Adams pulled down from a bookshelf the diary of Che Guevara and Frantz Fanon's *The Wretched of the Earth*.[34] All this fed the "red power" image.

The Toronto *Globe and Mail* in July 1967 published excerpts from a draft report titled "Indians and the Law," which had been prepared by the Canadian Corrections Association for the Department of Indian Affairs and Northern Development. According to the *Globe*, the report warned that "in many communities in the West, with substantial numbers of Indian people living on the fringes of cities and towns, relationships between the Indian and non-Indian residents are severely strained, and a precarious and explosive situation exists."[35] The Regina *Leader-Post* ran the front-page headline, "Indian-White Racial Hostilities Said Near Explosion Point in West." It was placed next to an article titled "Death Toll in Detroit Riots Climbs to 33," leaving the impression that Canada could soon have its own version of the events roiling American cities.[36]

The leadership of the Métis Society[37] in 1969 passed from Howard Adams to Jim Sinclair, a "tough fighter" who had picked himself up from skid row and completed a high school education. He read Eldridge Cleaver and met with the three Black Panthers who visited Regina Campus in late 1969.[38] The *Prairie Fire,* a radical newspaper put out by ex-*Carillon* staffers, saw possibilities in the encounter: "What the Indians and Métis hopefully learned from the Panthers is that it is possible to control one's destiny, and if white racist capitalists stand in the way and use terror, then it is only natural to defend oneself—by whatever means necessary."[39] While eschewing violence, the Métis Society asserted their demands forcefully: "We, the Métis people demand recognition as a People. Through legislation and rejection by our two parent cultures, we are now a whole new nation of people. Vive le Métis."[40] A new paradigm of Aboriginal rights and affirmation replaced the old paradigm of colonization and assimilation.

The *Carillon* was in the forefront of reporting on these issues. "Racial Prejudice and the Regina Indian," published March 15, 1963, drew a parallel with the civil rights movement: "During the Mississippi incident emotional condemnations of our neighbors reached an all-time high and U of A [University of Alberta] went so far as to offer the persecuted Negro an escape. However, before we assume the responsibility of judging someone else's backyard we should proceed to clean out our own." The article recounted an incident that had occurred in a Regina coffee shop: "Only a few weeks ago while enjoying coffee in a downtown restaurant I observed two Indians enter the establishment. Except for skin color, their racial origin (using the popular term) was unobservable. That this had some bearing on the case appears certain, as after a 15-minute interlude they left without being waited on. Somehow that coffee didn't taste like Nabob coffee should!"[41]

The entire front page of the September 29, 1967, *Carillon* was devoted to a story about racial discrimination at a hotel beverage room in Montmartre, a small town an hour's drive southeast of Regina. The beverage room was divided into two sections, one for men and the other for "ladies and their escorts." The men's side was "plain, uncarpeted and not decoratively lit," the women's side, slightly more pleasing in appearance. Indians were not permitted to sit on the ladies' side. If they did so, they were either ignored or told to move to the other side. On the other hand, white men, even those without a female escort, could drink on the ladies' side. As a result of the students' investigations, the manager of the hotel was convicted on seven counts of discrimination under the Fair Accommodations Act and fined a minimum of $25 on each count.[42]

Carillon reporter Barbara Cameron wrote a piece about Sandy Bay, an isolated community in northern Saskatchewan with a population of about 600 Indians and Métis and a few whites, including the priest, the nurse, two local storekeepers and a small number of teachers. Most of the houses were unpainted, ramshackle cabins, topped with huge TV aerials. Cameron visited a house that had two rooms: "There was a huge TV-stereo against one wall, a wood stove, and a partitioned bedroom. It was in above-average condition. Most of the houses consist of only one room. One family has five children and only one cup in the house." Although there was no liquor store, wine and hard liquor were shipped in. The locals also made a beverage called "molly," which was a kind of malt beer. Cameron attended an Alcoholics Anonymous banquet and dance held in one of the school buildings. After a huge meal, the priest proposed a toast to the school principal and his wife, who were about to leave the community, and to two long-time members of the A.A. group, who had successfully stayed away from "molly" for over a year. Cameron observed the scene with a keen eye: "All through the meal children were clamoring outside the windows of the school to get a look inside. The native women who had organized the party had seated most of the natives at one table and the white people at the other table, which struck me as ironical." She said the school was a "beautifully designed and modern structure, equipped with everything new in the way of school furniture, including indoor-outdoor carpet on all the floors and on the front steps." Once again, the irony was inescapable: "When I think of the children coming here from filthy shacks to a beautifully modern carpeted school, I wonder how the white population here can justify it."[43]

Regina Campus student Zenon Topuschak headed an Indian and Métis tutoring program, which aimed to assist high school students with their studies. Staffed by volunteers, it received funding from the Department of Indian Affairs. There were about 12 to 15 tutors, each of whom met once or twice a week with a group of 5 or 6 students.[44] An even more ambitious undertaking was the Student Neestow Partnership Project, which defined itself as "a two-way learning process where the students learn the problems of Saskatchewan people of Indian ancestry by living in the communities and sharing the problems, and hopefully, with the students and community people working together, seek to find solutions for these problems."[45] In the summer of 1965, nine students lived in seven different locations in the province, in each case at the invitation of local Indian and Métis leaders. Richard Thompson and Pat Uhl lived in Green Lake, a town of 1,100 Métis and 100 whites, where they worked on a plan to help farmers obtain land from the provincial government and became active in the Métis Association of Saskatchewan. In October 1965, Robertson Wood, who had finished his work with the Student Non-Violent Coordinating Committee (SNCC) in Mississippi, joined them at Green Lake. Linda Seese, another SNCC worker, was also part of the team. They brought the experience they had gained working on behalf of blacks in the southern United States to the situation they found in Saskatchewan.[46]

The Company of Young Canadians (CYC) undertook similar projects in Saskatchewan, much to the consternation of politicians who regarded the whole enterprise as a boondoggle. Premier Ernest Manning of Alberta was concerned about "the CYC's incredible waste of money and about agitators and radicals among the volunteers." Conservative M.P. James Ormiston from Melville, Saskatchewan, said he had been swamped by requests that "something be done to get these people out of here." The *Carillon* pointed out that the volunteers received only $35 a month plus living expenses, and it defended John Ferguson, the CYC coordinator at Fort Qu'Appelle, who had been accused of stirring up trouble among the Indian and Métis population. Ferguson denied that CYC workers were agitators: "If a man who has been getting less than the minimum wage all of a sudden learns to read and write and realizes that he is getting gypped or cheated and he makes a complaint about this I don't see that this is inciting to riot ... For a person to ask for their rights in our society should not be construed as riotous. I think we should be happy that people are aware of what their rights are."[47]

Aboriginal rights brought the sixties to Regina Campus students in a direct and personal away. Unlike the civil rights movement in the United States and the Quiet Revolution in Quebec, which were experienced mainly second-hand, this issue was right on their doorstep. The fact that they took it up shows they had internalized the spirit of the sixties. They did not just read about civil rights and watch the reports on television. They applied the lessons concretely to their own city and province. Louis Riel was just as much a hero to them as Huey Newton or Che Guevara. The front page of the *Carillon*, November 15, 1968, consisted of a large photo of Riel's grave with the caption "On the 83rd Anniversary of the Murder of Louis Riel by the Canadian government—Has anything changed?"[48]

Quebec's Quiet Revolution

The Quiet Revolution in Quebec, while of interest to the *Carillon*, did not have the same salience. Nonetheless, the paper was fully aware of the importance of what was happening, not only for Quebec but also for the rest of Canada. The Quiet Revolution challenged the power of the Anglo-Canadian and Anglo-American business elite that had dominated the province since the Conquest. The people of Quebec wanted to be "maîtres chez nous" ("masters in our own house"). The pace of change accelerated when the Liberals led by Jean Lesage took office in the 1960 provincial election. On election night, Lesage began his victory speech with the word "désormais" ("from now on"). It was as though a current of electricity had passed through the room. Everybody realized that nothing in Quebec would ever be the same again.[49] The new government kept up a frantic pace of reform: expanding and secularizing the education system, putting in place new social welfare programs, and nationalizing the hydroelectric industry.[50] Quebec singers,

Commemoration of the execution of Louis Riel, *Carillon*, 15 November 1968.

writers, and other artists ushered in a cultural renaissance, while a new class of Francophone business entrepreneurs vied with Anglophones for control of the commanding heights of the economy. General James Wolfe had taken the heights in 1759; now the French were retaking it.

The revival and renewal of Quebec nationalism led to a movement for separation from Canada and the formation of an independent state. René Lévesque, who had been a cabinet minister in Jean Lesage's government, broke with the Liberal Party in 1968 to found the separatist Parti Québécois. An extremist group, the Front de Libération du Québec (FLQ), launched a terror campaign, committing 232 acts of violence, including 163 bombs (47 of which did not go off or were defused) between 1963 and 1970.[51] The targets were mostly federal government buildings, mailboxes, and other symbols of Anglo-Canadian domination, such as the Montreal Stock Exchange.

On October 5, 1970, the FLQ kidnapped James Cross, the British Trade Commissioner in Montreal. The terrorists laid down a number of conditions for his release, including the broadcast of the FLQ manifesto, a large ransom, and the freeing of FLQ members serving jail sentences (so-called "political prisoners"). The federal government rejected all the demands, except for the release of the manifesto, which was broadcast on radio and television on October 8. It summoned the workers of Quebec to rise up and take back "your factories, your machines, your hotels, your universities, your unions," and ended with the fervent declamation:

> We are the workers of Quebec and we will continue to the bitter end. We want to replace the slave society with a free society, functioning by itself and for itself; a society open to the world. Our struggle can only lead to victory. You cannot hold an awakening people in misery and contempt indefinitely. Long live Free Quebec! Long live our imprisoned political comrades. Long live the Quebec revolution! Long live the Front de Libération du Québec. [52]

The FLQ on October 10 carried out a second kidnapping. This time the victim was Pierre Laporte, Quebec's minister of labor and immigration and the deputy premier. As the crisis deepened, labor leader Michel Chartrand stated that his union executive gave "unequivocal support" to the FLQ manifesto. Students at the University of Quebec at Montreal and other schools threatened to go on strike to secure the freedom of the "political prisoners," whose release the kidnappers demanded. A crowd of several thousand people gathered on the evening of October 15 to hear pro-FLQ speeches, capped with Chartrand's rallying cry, "The FLQ is each one of you." He urged the people of Quebec "to organize the fight for liberation in each district, in each plant, in each office, everywhere."[53] Despite the fiery rhetoric, the crowd dispersed quietly and went home, rather than taking to the streets.[54]

Prime Minister Trudeau, October 14, 1970, gave members of his cabinet a stern warning: "The population was already being excited by people like Chartrand and Lemieux [lawyer for the FLQ], and there would be a real danger of the movement gaining many converts, resulting in the creation of a popular movement. In order to prevent this from happening, it would be necessary for the government to act before it lost the power to act."[55] Trudeau invoked the War Measures Act in the early morning hours of October 16, 1970, justifying the measure as a response to "apprehended insurrection." This gave the police extraordinary powers to enter buildings without a search warrant and to detain persons without laying a charge. Of the 436 persons taken into custody, only 62 were ever brought to trial and a mere 20 convicted.[56] The War Measures Act stabilized the situation through the application of massive federal force. Those who had expressed sympathy for the FLQ were silenced. The terrorists holding Laporte killed him on October 17, leaving his body in the trunk of a car for the police to find. James Cross was released unharmed on December 3, 1970, and his captors were given safe passage to Cuba. Later, they returned to Canada to face trial. The men who killed Laporte were also convicted and spent time in jail.[57]

The *Carillon* covered these events extensively, devoting entire issues to the story. Generally, it supported the FLQ's aims and ideology, if not their methods. Trudeau had been viewed with deep suspicion since 1968, when the paper debunked the Trudeaumania sweeping the nation. An article "Trudeau's Our P.E.T." was laced with sarcasm: "Everywhere he goes girls mob him, hoping for a kiss (or at least a handshake). And we know it's mainly because it's the 'in' thing to do. As long as we know that's all it is, it can't do any harm. Can it?" The paper mocked Trudeau's hip image: "He spent some time in Morocco, and everyone knows that anybody who goes to Morocco is a head: how much more 'in' can you get? So he's just bound to liberalize the drug laws. Again it's sort of irrelevant that he won't say a word about that sort of thing. We know he's just hiding his real feelings until all the 'straights' elect him. Isn't he?" The bottom line for the *Carillon* was that the people who bankrolled the Liberal party called the tune. Tongue in cheek, it commented: "We all know that he's just using the Liberal party to get in and then he's his own man again. We just love the way he's sucked in all those stupid reactionary big money corporations; like General Motors, Westinghouse, the American Potash Company of Canada, Molsons."[58]

The *Carillon* thoroughly disapproved of Trudeau's handling of the FLQ crisis in October 1970. An editorial expressed sympathy for what the FLQ was trying to accomplish. It denied that the kidnappings were the acts merely of "a few desperadoes on the margins of society"; rather, the kidnappers shared "the same frustrations, the same understandings with the average Quebecer, but perhaps feel more anger and are willing to go much further in order to do something about it." An editorial published before the imposition of the War Measures Act urged the federal government to "negotiate the release of the two hostages, even if this means meeting all the demands of the FLQ." Trudeau had stated that he could not negotiate because to do so would only encourage the terrorists to carry out more acts of violence. The *Carillon* reversed the logic, arguing that since terrorism and unrest in Quebec were going to continue anyway, it was folly to refuse to negotiate, thereby sacrificing the lives of the two men who had been kidnapped.[59]

Under the War Measures Act, the Canadian government had the power to limit freedom of speech and censor newspapers. Defying the government, the *Carillon* went ahead and published the FLQ manifesto. It also drew heavily on the Canadian University Press for articles written from a non-government point of view. Its self-assigned mission was to bring readers "a part of the story you will not find in the bourgeois media."[60] About 1,000 students gathered in the courtyard in front of the Classroom building to discuss the imposition of the War Measures Act. Opinions divided sharply, and the debate took on an ideological flavor, with strong epithets exchanged on both sides. About 200 students marched downtown to the post office, which was chosen as the protest site because it was federal government property.[61]

The *Carillon* summed up the situation in an editorial titled "The Story is Wearing Thin." It claimed that Trudeau's justification for invoking the War Measures Act had no basis in fact: "What is becoming clear is that there never was an insurrection—real or imaginary. Trudeau is using the lynch-mob mentality created by the killing of Pierre Laporte to try to destroy the separatist movement." The editorial predicted that the tactics would backfire:

—Photo by Zenon

Part of the crowd at the emergency meeting last Friday. About 1,000 students showed up in the classroom building courtyard to hear discussion on events in Quebec and the invocation of the War Measures Act. There was agreement by the majority in opposition to the act, but bitter division over attitudes toward the FLQ. About 200 participated in a later demonstration downtown. About 800 participated in a similar meeting Monday.

Protest against the War Measures Act, *Carillon*, 23 October 1970.

"Trudeau should have known better. He has unwittingly all but guaranteed the eventual separation of Quebec by his actions, disgraced himself politically, and guaranteed himself a role as a villain in Canadian history."[62]

Women's Liberation

Of all the liberation movements of the sixties—the Quiet Revolution, Aboriginal rights, civil rights—women's liberation was the last to make an appearance in the *Carillon*. The roots of the movement go back to the so-called "first wave" of feminism in Canada, the period from the late nineteenth century to the First World War, when women obtained the vote. The second wave began in the sixties and, arguably, continues to this day. This is not to say that women from the 1920s to the 1950s were inactive in pursuing feminist goals, merely that their activities were largely conducted at the local level or in the non-government sector and, as such, did not receive much attention in the national media.

As was the case with other liberation movements, the fifties was a seed-bed of women's emancipation. On the surface, everything seemed settled and calm. Men were expected to be the breadwinners, women the keepers of the hearth. Only 5 per cent of women and 4 per cent of men in a 1960 Gallup Poll thought it was appropriate for young mothers to enter the paid labor force.[63] However, beneath these entrenched gender roles there existed a contradiction, scarcely noticed at the time, but full of implications for the future. All through the 1950s and 1960s, increased numbers of women entered the paid workforce. Women constituted 22 per cent of waged and salaried workers in 1951, 27.3 per cent in 1961, and 34.4 per cent in 1971.[64] Equally significant, the proportion of married women in the labor force grew from 30 per cent in 1951, to 49.8 per cent in 1961, to 56.9 per cent in 1971.[65] The problem was that, although women were gaining a foothold in the workforce, it was at the bottom rung. They faced systemic discrimination and limited opportunities for advancement. To make matters worse, they had to work a "double day," combining full-time employment outside the home with the main burden of housework and childcare.

Shifts in the gender composition of the workforce coincided with changing trends in education. Female undergraduate enrolment in Canadian universities rose steadily from 13,866 in 1950 to 26,629 in 1960, 101,351 in 1970 and 155,554 in 1980. Male enrolment increased, too, but at a slower pace, so that the ratio of male to female undergraduates decreased from 3.6:1 in 1950 to 1.2:1 in 1980.[66] As more women earned degrees, they were increasingly conscious of the fact that their talents and skills were under-utilized in a world that thought of them, first and foremost, as wives and mothers. Higher education acted as an incentive to challenge gendered job ghettoes.

Regina Campus women in the early 1960s still belonged to the pre-liberation era. "Amid tears and cheers, seventeen-year-old, green-eyed Nora Best was crowned Campus Queen at the Christmas Prom" in December 1963. "'I can't believe it,' she exclaimed, clutching her 23 victory roses." Best was described as "an active co-ed, a cheerleader and member of the Cougettes basketball team." Also, as the *Carillon* hastened to add, she "had a mind of her own." "I believe in college education for women and in a greater role for women in modern society," she affirmed, after she had, as the *Carillon* reported, "regained her composure."[67] The campus candidate for the Miss Saskatchewan Roughrider contest in 1964 was Miss Pam Gawley, "a 5' 1", 106 lb. package, topped with blonde hair and sky blue eyes."[68]

Above, left: Nora Best, Campus Queen, *Carillon*, 17 January 1964.

Above, right: Pam Gawley, Regina Campus candidate for Miss Saskatchewan Roughrider, *Carillon*, 2 October 1964.

Right: Female student "slave auction," *Carillon*, 10 November 1964.

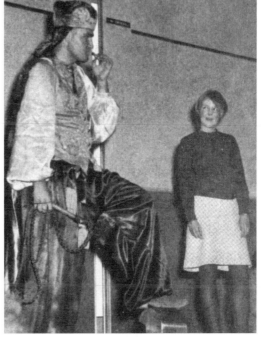

The Campus girls' club, Tap-Way (derived from a Cree word for "true")[69] sponsored an annual female slave auction. In 1965, male students were invited to place bids on "twenty of the most tempting, tantalizing and fun-loving coeds on campus." The rules were simple: "The slave will be yours to do with as you please according to the code of slave ethics from 8:30 a.m. until 12 o'clock midnight Friday, November 5th."[70] The auction was repeated in 1966, with the auctioneer costumed as "heartless Pasha Abdul" and carrying a whip. On Slave Day "the girls were forced to dance in the cafeteria, give rubdowns, and sell kisses (who but mercenary engineers would submit females to such heartless cruelty)."[71] The day culminated with a Slave Dance, also known as "Bondage A-Go-Go."

The slave auction caricatured the gender inequality that second-wave feminists were beginning to analyze in such books as Simone de Beauvoir's *The Second Sex*, published in French in 1949 and translated into English in 1953, and Betty Friedan's *The Feminine Mystique* (1963). *Chatelaine* magazine, under the editorship of Doris Anderson, published articles that critiqued the prevailing norms. For example, Christina McCall wrote a series of articles in 1961 and 1962 ("Working Wives are Here to Stay," "All Canadians are Equal—except Women," and "Why Can't We Treat Married Women Like People") which encouraged women to consider wider horizons beyond the domestic sphere.[72] Anderson's 1969 editorial, "Women: a Chance for Change" quoted American psychologist Dr. Richard E. Farson, who predicted: "I think we will see within the next two years a massive rebellion of women that is at least comparable in magnitude to the black revolution or student protest."[73]

The feminist movement in Canada gained momentum with the formation of the Voice of Women (VOW), an organization that sprang up shortly after the failure of the 1960 Paris summit peace talks between the United States and the Soviet Union. The two superpowers resumed nuclear tests in the atmosphere, heightening Cold War tensions and polluting the environment. *Toronto Star* reporter Lotta Dempsey wrote a column asking, "What can women do?" The article touched a nerve and galvanized women into holding a meeting at Massey Hall in Toronto, which led to the founding of the Voice of Women on July 28, 1960. By the fall of 1961, membership had increased to 5,000.[74]

Historian Elaine Tyler May posits a link between Cold War foreign policy and the prevailing gender and family ideology of the 1950s. The stable family of breadwinning husband and full-time wife and mother was deemed a necessary building block for a strong, healthy society capable of withstanding the threat of Communism. As the family went, so went the nation.[75] It is fitting, therefore, that the first women's liberation group of the sixties called into question the reigning ideology of the Cold War. Women voiced opposition to both nuclear arms and the nuclear family, as it was then constructed. The Voice of Women urged Prime Minister Diefenbaker not to support President Kennedy's hard-line stance against the Soviet Union during the Cuban missile crisis, and they lobbied against the installation of nuclear missiles on Canadian soil. Maryon Pearson, the wife of Leader of the Opposition

Lester Pearson, joined the VOW, justifying her stand with the statement that, whereas "men get casual and used to talking about piles of bombs here and piles of bombs there," women "produce life and want to see their children live."[76] The organization gradually broadened its agenda to include a range of other issues: bilingualism, environmentalism, anti–Vietnam War activism, birth control, and improvement of the status of women. What began as a peace group, evolved into a multi-faceted feminist organization. In this respect, it paralleled the student peace movement, which also had roots in ban-the-bomb agitation and then took on a more wide-ranging and ambitious New Left agenda.

In 1966, Laura Sabia, president of the Canadian Federation of University Women, brought together representatives from about thirty national women's organizations, including the YWCA, IODE, Canadian Federation of Business and Professional Women's Clubs, and the National Council of Women, to form the Committee on Equality for Women. Jointly with the Quebec Federation of Women, they asked Prime Minister Pearson to appoint a Royal Commission on the Status of Women.[77] At first, he did not see the need for the inquiry, but thanks to the prodding of Laura Sabia, who threatened to have a million women protesting on Parliament Hill, and Judy Lamarsh, the only woman in the cabinet, he changed his mind. The commission, appointed in February 1967, took on the character of a national consciousness-raising event. It received 469 briefs and 1,000 letters and held dozens of hearings in downtown hotels, church basements, community halls, and shopping malls all across the country. Everywhere the stories were the same. Women discovered that their issues were not merely personal and individual; they had a social dimension that needed to be dealt with in public policy.

When the commission released its final report in 1970, Anthony Westell of the *Toronto Star* said it was "packed with more explosive potential than any device manufactured by terrorists. As a call to revolution, hopefully a quiet one, it is more persuasive than any FLQ manifesto. And as a political blockbuster, it is more powerful than the famous report of the controversial commission on bilingualism and biculturalism."[78] The report contained 167 recommendations organized around four principles: women should be free to choose whether or not to take employment outside the home; the care of children was a responsibility shared by mother, father, and society at large; women needed special consideration in the workplace so they would not be penalized on account of pregnancy and childbirth; and affirmative action was justified in certain areas to compensate for historical discrimination against women. In summary, the royal commission gave second-wave feminism its agenda.[79] It was a shock to the status quo. The National Action Committee on the Status of Women was formed to make sure the report did not sit on the shelf and gather dust. It settled on three priorities: the expansion of daycare facilities, legal reforms to prohibit discrimination on the basis of sex, and the decriminalization of abortion.

The third item was especially controversial. Prior to 1969, abortion was a criminal act punishable by lifetime imprisonment. Under the revisions to the criminal code in that year, a woman could obtain an abortion if a hospital-appointed therapeutic abortion committee, consisting of at least three doctors, ruled that continuation of the pregnancy threatened her life or health.[80] Feminists organized the Abortion Caravan in April 1970 to lobby the government to remove these restrictions. They traveled from Vancouver to Ottawa, stopping en route in Kamloops, Edmonton, Regina, Winnipeg, Toronto, and other cities. The protesters carried a coffin filled with petitions, symbolic of the women who had died from botched illegal abortions.[81] The caravan culminated in a disruption of the proceedings of the House of Commons, with demonstrators chained to seats in the visitors' gallery chanting, "Free Abortion on Demand" and "Every Child a Wanted Child."[82] Eighteen years later, January 28, 1988, the Supreme Court of Canada invoked the Charter of Rights to strike down the abortion law, effectively removing all legal restraints on abortion.[83]

Although the caravan did not bear immediate results, it served the purpose of raising consciousness and stimulating the formation of women's groups at the community level, including at university campuses.[84] Women came together in small, informal groups to talk about their experiences and share ideas. As a result, women's centres sprang up to provide services that were otherwise not available: birth control information, abortion referral, feminist literature, and a safe place to talk.[85] As awareness of the problem of violence against women increased, communities established rape crisis centres and shelters for victims of domestic abuse.[86] In this way, the feminist movement took hold at the grassroots level and offered immediate, practical help for women whose problems had previously been ignored or glossed over.

The feminist movement at Regina Campus followed the broad outline of what was happening at the national level. In March 1963, a campus club

called "Fraternitas" held a discussion on the role of women in Canadian society. The panelists were Dr. Cecil French, professor of sociology; Rev. Owen
Still, a clergyman who later served as campus chaplain; and Louise Million
and Margaret Winters, two students in second year arts and science. Dr.
French stated that the role of women in the home and in business sometimes came into conflict, and that men were generally averse to taking orders
from women. It was, therefore, "hard for women to fill any high positions
in society except in careers such as nursing, which often require especially
women." The two students were of the opinion that "on the whole, women
do not wish to compete with men to be like men, but they merely wish to
gain higher positions when they are capable of doing so. There should be
more understanding between the two sexes."[87]

The discussion of women's issues had evolved considerably by 1965,
when student May Archer wrote the *Carillon:*

> I am married; I have two children; I am a part-time student.
> Both children were born in the midst of my studies. Conse-
> quently, I have had to think about what womanhood meant
> to me very carefully. I like being a woman. But from time to
> time, I have bitterly resented members of both sexes for what
> I considered attitudes crippling to human growth, both male
> and female … It takes great courage to grow but I am hope-
> ful that now, when so much of the straitjacketed thinking of
> the past is fading, that more and more women will achieve
> what they conceive to be a balanced life, with both emotion-
> al and intellectual relationships enriching each other.[88]

In a second letter titled "Mothers Arise!" Archer advocated the setting
up of a child daycare centre on campus. She said the facility was necessary for
three reasons: "there are a number of women attending university here who
have families, who are obtaining elsewhere at considerable cost, and often
inconvenience, part-time care which they feel is suitable for their children's
needs"; "there are numerous other women who would continue their educa-
tions, if they were certain of good care for their children"; and "psychology
majors and education students need to get a good look at the raw material of
personality under normal conditions."[89] A daycare centre was established in
1969, though it operated in the early years on a tenuous financial basis.[90]

The *Carillon* in 1968 took a leaf from the Royal Commission on the Status of Women to launch a column titled, appropriately, "Status of Women." The first article set the tone: "If a woman ceases to develop her human potential because she is afraid that it will hurt her in the marriage sweepstakes, because she has accepted society's presently unworthy goals for herself rather than her own, rising out of her own abilities, then she is guilty of bad faith … In black parlance she is a 'handkerchief head.'"[91] Subsequent columns dealt with topics ranging from women's role in the economy and the image of women's bodies presented in the mass media to the issues surrounding birth control and abortion.[92]

By the fall of 1969, Regina Campus had an organized women's liberation caucus. One of the founders explained how the group had been formed:

> Initially, we came together as a group of women who felt limited by the roles we were expected to play and those we expected of ourselves. We had no clear understanding of these very real feelings. Gradually, on talking to one another, we began to realize that these were not personal difficulties or deficiencies but instead problems with a common root, social problems. We realized that the abnormality was not within ourselves but within the society and that our difficulties and frustrations had broad implications for men as well. We came to the conclusion that equality with men should not be our goal. Men, in this society, suffer the same frustrations but manifest them in different ways. Despite appearances, women's problems are not caused by men and therefore we ought to work together to change the society which forces us all to assume basically anti-human roles.[93]

The women's liberation caucus handed out birth control pamphlets on campus in the third week of September 1969. Reactions varied. Some of the men "felt it necessary to seem either amused or super-cool and casual about it. Others picked it up surreptitiously looking the other way." At first, very few female students showed any interest, but gradually, as the week went by, they became more receptive. According to a women's liberation caucus member, "In this society honest sexuality has 'dirty' connotations. Boys have to regard sex as a joke and girls fear that any display of interest will label them as 'an easy lay.' This is only another manifestation of this society's and our own attitude toward women. We are seen as either 'mothers' (pure and sweet) or whores. There is no in between."[94]

The rising tide of campus feminism was evident in a *Carillon* editorial, October 10, 1969, that called for the abolition of the Frosh Queen contest. Women, the editorial said, "were tired of being treated as objects, as walking vaginas ... paraded around like cattle to be ogled at by flesh connoisseurs." Such contests reinforced the idea that women were second-class citizens: "As long as women are judged by the standards set up by Max Factor or Revlon, they will not relate to one another or to men as human beings but as objects of competition and attraction respectively."[95] The women's liberation group took matters into their own hands in November 1971, disrupting the "Beaver Auction" sponsored by engineering students. The women stood on top of the table used as the auction block, seized the microphone and drowned out the proceedings. They then disconnected the microphone and collapsed the table, bringing the auction to a halt.[96]

Students established a women's centre in September 1970 under the auspices of the Students' Union. It was partly an outcome of the Abortion Caravan to Ottawa that had taken place earlier that year. Following that demonstration, women made a decision to carry on the struggle in their home communities, and this included action at the Regina Campus. The women's centre had two main purposes: "to disseminate birth control information and make referrals to competent doctors" and "to provide literature, both as a means of information and as a means of discussion on the fundamental questions which affect women's lives."[97] Funded by the Students' Union, it was given space in the Student Services building. The demand for its services was described as "overwhelming."[98]

There was also a backlash to campus feminism. Colleen Slater, in "Women's Liberation: Hog Wash and Lye Soap," mocked the women's liberation group:

> The initiation rites demand dedication to the cause: one must abandon her cosmetic bags, cast off her padded undergarments, and denounce any previous appearances in morality plays; then one must don the checkered cloth [the red-and-black checkered lumberjack shirt that some campus feminists wore] and devote all energy to parading about the

halls spouting the changing role of women in society. Need-
less to say, this is an exacting task, and not for the faint of
heart.[99]

Slater's main point was that women had long since secured the legal right
to enter any profession they might aspire to. All they had to do was work to
achieve their goals: "Whether a liberated woman decides to run for Prime
Minister or to remain at home and raise a family is a matter of personal
decision, however, women must liberate their minds before they can attack
and remove the remaining barriers to their acceptance in society."[100]

The women's liberation group countered that Slater's individualistic
perspective blinded her to the structural conditions that governed gender relations. The problems facing women, they said, were not "primarily personal
problems, but social problems." They could not be

solved by individual women acting on their own, but require organized social action ... The oppression of women
runs deep in the seams of this society. Women's demand for
responsibility for themselves cannot be met in this society
for the motivating force in this society is profit and to make
profit one group of people must exploit and consume other
groups—the exploited are becoming aware of their condition and will create solutions which negate exploitation altogether.[101]

This analysis blamed the oppression of women on the capitalist system,
placing feminism squarely within a Marxist framework.

Opposition to women's liberation surfaced at a meeting of the student
council in September 1972, when an attempt was made to abolish the abortion loan service. The women's centre gave money to women seeking a legal
abortion, the loan to be paid back when the woman was able to do so. Debate
focused on the questions of whether the unborn fetus was a human being
and whether the mother alone had the right to terminate her pregnancy. Jim
Gallagher, arguing against abortion, said: "You'll have to show me that there
is a greater right than the right to life." Fred Storey responded: "We pompous
men sit around making regulations governing women's lives." Gallagher answered that while he could not be aware fully of what women went through

in these circumstances, he "could make a moral judgment regarding the destruction of life." At the end of the debate, the council voted 8 to 2 to maintain the abortion loan fund.[102]

It is difficult to know how deeply feminism penetrated Regina Campus student life in the late 1960s and early 1970s. In 1969, the Aquarius club, which had 150 female members, promoted two raffles. The prize for the

Aquarius . . . Club With a Future

From Greek history comes this explanation of Aquarius — "the butler of goodness, gods and youth." With a little luck and a lot of enthusiasm from the members, (not to mention support from Administration, Engineering, McFetridge, etc.) approximately 150 girls on Regina Campus will be able to call themselves Aquarians in the true sense of the word. It's the objective of the club to give the members an opportunity to meet new people, take part in University events and introduce a few new ideas to the Campus in general.

We feel that the club has already begun to fill these three important requisites. What better start for a new club with a whole new membership, the majority of them being Frosh, than to have a prize winning float in the Frosh parade. The girls worked very hard all through the week and certainly deserved the honor. The float was beautiful and we were all very proud of it.

We are sure that the students are aware of the two raffles that Aquarius is promoting. One is a chance for the buyer to win their choice of a $5.00 gift certificate from a beauty salon of their choice or a 26 of their favorite beverage. Tickets are 25 cents. The second is a combination: If a girl wins, the prize is a fully expense paid evening with one of the Saskatchewan Roughriders; two boys win an evening with seven — count 'em — seven Aquarians of their choice, also fully expense paid. Tickets go for 35 cents each or two for 50 cents. We hope you all will support these raffles.

Plans have been settled for the Sadie Hawkins dance for the 69-70 school term. Because of problems with possible road conditions and heating we aren't able to hold the event in a barn outside of Regina as we had hoped. As a result, it will take place in Campion's cafeteria. There will be a free hayride going to sections of the surrounding countryside, free food provided and music by the Transmigrated Soul. Tickets, girls, go for $3.00 a couple. Anyone wishing to attend stag, may buy tickets at $1.50. There will be advance sales as well as available at the door. Grubby attire is encouraged so here is a dance that is going to be a lot of fun. So girls, get up your courage and ask for a date! Sadie Hawkins is November 8th!

The present executive: Dawn Lockhart, Georgia McVeigh, Liz Rsit, Linda Durham, Sharon Wheale and Louise Gerein wish to thank all members for their hand work and devotion to the club. We hope it continues with strong bonds between the members themselves and Aquarius in relation to the campus.

The Aquarius Club, backlash against the women's liberation movement, *Carillon*, 24 October 1969.

first was a "choice of a $5.00 gift certificate from a beauty salon" or "a 26 of their favourite beverage." The prize in the second raffle, if a girl won, was "a fully expense paid evening with one of the Saskatchewan Roughriders." If two boys won, they were awarded "an evening with seven—count 'em—seven Aquarians, also fully expense paid." The club also had plans for a Sadie Hawkins dance (women invite men) including "a free hayride going to sections of the surrounding countryside, free food provided and music by the Transmigrated Soul."[103] The cultural and countercultural confusions abound.

The *Carillon* in October 1970 conducted a snap poll, interviewing six students who were asked to respond to the question: "What do you think of the Women's Liberation Movement?" Two responses were negative (Joan Miller: "Women's Liberation is trying to get superiority for women, not equality with men ... Men should be on top and in control as they are naturally suited to having the final authority" and Carol Turner: "I suppose that it is important to all women, but somehow I just don't feel that it concerns me personally"). Two answered equivocally (Carol Harbottle: "I have changed my mind about it so many times that I am afraid to give any answer. Right now I think that they are completely right about the need for equality with men" and from a person who chose to remain anonymous: "I agree with what they are doing, but not how they do it"). The final two gave strong endorsements (Brian Page: "They are justified in the position they take on issues like the rights of women to equal opportunity in jobs, business, and so on, and should be supported" and Eleuthan Noel: "It is a worthwhile movement and has many good points to recommend it. For example, women should be able to get equal pay and equal opportunity in jobs. They should have full rights of their own in everything, and should not always have to have a man behind them").[104] The sample, while unscientific, suggests uncertainty and fluidity of opinion in a time of social transition.

Ironically, one of the bastions of male chauvinism was the New Left itself. In the early phases of the radical movement, men assumed leadership roles in the SDS and SUPA, relegating women to menial tasks, such as making coffee or stuffing envelopes. The situation began to change when women at national SUPA headquarters in 1967 produced a manifesto, which said in

Facing page: Student views on women's liberation, *Carillon*, 16 October 1970 (more on page 166).

What's That You Said?

—PHOTOS AND INTERVIEWS BY ZENON AND ENA

QUESTION: What do you think of the Women's Liberation Movement?

Carol Turner
2nd Year Education

I suppose that it is important to all women, but somehow I just don't feel that it concerns me personally. I guess I have too many things to do already to get involved, and besides I feel satisfied with my own life now.

The Birth Control Center on campus is a good thing if it does what the posters says it does: refer girls to doctors who are willing to prescribe birth control pills, and gives information on the how and where of legal abortions.

Brian Page
2nd Year Education

They are justified in the position they take on issues like the rights of women to equal opportunity in jobs, business, and so on, and should be supported.

Women's Lib, like every movement, has its extremists who get carried away, often because it is the "in" thing to do. They trip out on trivia, like agitating against the wearing of bras, something that should be just a matter of personal choice.

Carol Harbottle
3rd Year Education

I have changed my mind about it so many times that I am afraid to give any answer. Right now I think that they are completely right about the need for equality with men. Certainly women are not inferior to men intellectually or otherwise, and they must cease being a subjugated lower class.

About abortion I am not sure. While I can agree that abortion could be a good thing if the child won't be properly taken care of, everything in my upbringing and in my personal feelings makes me doubt that I could make such a decision for myself.

I can't afford to give my name

I agree with **what** they are doing, but not with **how** they do it. The main problem for women is that their lives are restricted to the home, and they should be freed of this. For example, the best argument in favor of abortion is that otherwise women are tied to the home by children, whether they want to be or not.

The problem with Women's Lib is that it is made up almost exclusively of younger women. Older women, who have been through the problems, don't speak. Maybe they don't come forward, but I think that those who might wouldn't be listened to by the young women.

Eleuthan Noel
2nd Year Arts and Science

It is a worthwhile movement and has many good points to recommend it. For example, women should be able to get equal pay and equal opportunity in jobs. They should have full rights of their own in everything, and should not always have to have a man behind them.

They were wrong, however, to make an issue about bras. Bras serve a functional purpose—for women who are plump they are a necessity, for others they are not. Women should wear them or not, as their personal need or wish decides; they should not make of it a cause.

Joan Millar
1st Year Arts and Science

Women's Liberation is trying to get superiority for women, not equality with men. They are trying to turn things around from the way they are now.

Men should be on top and in control as they are now because they are naturally suited to having the final authority. Can you see what would happen if women took over leadership? They would just mess up everything, including themselves.

Friday, October 16, 1970

Above: More student views on women's liberation, *Carillon*, 16 October 1970.

Facing page: None of the candidates for student office at Regina Campus in 1971 were women, *Carillon*, 11 February 1971.

Candidates For President

LARRY SCHULZ

—Fourth year administration student majoring in economics. To be objective I will implement monthly expenditure publications of the Students' Union funds in the Carillon. I feel it will be my responsibility as president to make students aware of how their funds are spent. Our summer employment program must be revamped, as in the past it has suffered from inefficiency and personal bias. I do not associate myself with any political organization: my duty will be to portray student views on specific issues rather than handle issues with preconceived political attitudes. As president, it is my duty to ensure that the S.R.C. will not be subservient to the Administration. Total communications; total involvement; make the Union work for YOU! VOTE.

BRUCE SHEPPARD

It is evident that there will be two broad areas of concern for next year's student council. The first of these is the obvious need for action on the immediate problems of: (i) phoney rent schemes hitting first-year students; (ii) high student unemployment in the summer and after graduation; (iii) hints of a faculty cut; (iv) continuing traffic and parking problems around the university. However, there seems to have been a tendency on the part of past councils to relegate long-range considerations to collecting dust on backroom shelves. Strengthening faculty level has been raised before and the need for this type of program is obvious.

FRED STOREY

I am running on a slate because I feel that with the extensive program which we are planning it would be pompous to pretend that any individual could carry it out alone. I know Rick and Dale are the best people to aid me in implementing our program. Aside from our extensive program of services and academic activities I feel that student employment and financial assistance are of utmost importance and rise above the needs of petty politicking. I will be speaking extensively on these problems at the election speeches today. Please attend.

Candidates For 1st Vice-president

KEN BADLEY

The S.R.C. should represent a cross-section of the student body. The moderates lack of representation is a result of their not voting. Representation is not an impossibility. I am prepared to represent what I feel is a majority in this university, in the coming year.

DALE BUTLER

Aside from these more political services we recognize the need for tangible services to reduce costs to the student for necessities or recreational activities. In this respect Rick has successfully served as S.R.C. film director bringing first-class films on campus at a low cost. This philosophy has been extended to the Thursday social evenings in the service centre and to the student-operated bus service which Fred organized last summer. We plan to extend these services to include such things as a secretarial pool which will provide employment for students as well as low cost typing on campus for students.

BRYAN FOLEY

1. Housing—Student participation in managing of residences control living costs, residents establishing their own rules of conduct. 2. Loans—At present our student loan is $600 (tuition $230, leaving $370 per semester which is of a four-month duration. $17 per week is not enough to feed, house and clothe a person. Think: Can we not better this desperate situation by virtue of planning a credit system to be managed and run by the student body with help from the federal government. A student credit system will enable us to operate a business which will give students a better living standard.

ROD McDONALD

I strongly disagree with the statements about students being an "apathetic" group who are at university to get a degree to raise their standard of living. I believe that given the facts many students have and will continue to take part in various struggles on the campus and off. I feel that the Students' Union cannot be a sectarian group and engage in nothing but reformist politics. I feel that the number one struggle in Canada and therefore in the university is the anti-imperialist struggle. To be an anti-imperialist student is to also stand up against arbitrary rules and regulations. I support all students in this struggle.

Candidates For 2nd Vice-president

DON ANDERSON

Bacchus is here and all students are taking part! Or are they? Do first and second year students really realize what Bacchus is and are they really encouraged to participate? In my opinion they aren't and is one this is typical of most activities at Regina Campus. The S.R.C. does not communicate with the students, especially the first and second year students.

What we really need is an S.R.C. that can inform and encourage all students to take part in university life. The first and second year students make up a large portion of the student body yet the third and fourth year students benefit most from student activities. Let's inform all students as to what is happening and encourage them all to participate.

RICK AUGUST

We have decided to run as a slate for the executive of the Students' Union as we see no reason why this coming year cannot be a year of greater activities by the students on behalf of the students. Last year we were successful in originating an academics committee which would serve to assist students. Under this committee we established a forum through which student grievances were given a fair hearing and in most cases a successful outcome. Where this failed we established a legal-aid fund so that the student could take further recourse. In light of the problems of education, interns and the recent changes in regulations regarding "incompletes" these activities are even more important.

DON CARNIE

I am an anthropology major in second year and believe I can be a contribution to the Students' Union because there are obvious improvements to be made by "fresh" personnel. I am conservative in philosophy with a little room for new projects. I believe that financial matters in the union should be examined and publicized and justified.

Candidates For Senate

CAMPBELL BOWER

Always question certain operation of university government relations with the university such as: (1) operation of the bookstore, how much profit and why? (2) the different marking systems in the two campuses class credit honors and better co-ordination between the campus in all regards. (3) Try to influence some members of Senate to remove education tax from educational books sold at book store. (4) Priorities for employment to the unemployed Canadian prof.

CHRIS CHEESMAN

If elected Senator I intend to propose to the Senate, when in turn must get an answer from the Board of Governors, that a system of financial restitution be made to interning Education students. In regards to the handling of incompletes the Senate must be made aware of the problems for the individual student created by the adoption by the Dean of the Faculty of Arts and Science of the present policy. The Senate and Board of Governors must clarify the question of faculty cuts in the very near future.

BOB ELLIS

Responsible to student body. Make it more representative of Saskatchewan people. Take part in any meaningful committees, example — student financing committee work in conjunction with S.R.C. and Sask. Assoc. of Students. Work to remove Senate from the absolute power of President Spinks.

CHARLES INGRAM

Why am I running for the Senate? I have two main reasons: (1) I am disturbed by the unfair treatment given students at Regina Campus. Students transferring to Saskatoon can have their class G.P.A. reduced by as much as a full grade. (2) I am opposed to the practice of profs marking on the curve. The fallacy that some students should fail, and only a limited number can excel, is simply that, a fallacy. If elected I will press for the eradication of both of these practices immediately.

KEN NICHOLS

Responsible to student body. Make it more representative of Saskatchewan people. Take part in any meaningful committees, example — student financing committee work in conjunction with S.R.C. and Sask. Assoc. of Students. Work to remove Senate from the absolute power of President Spinks.

part: "... until the male chauvinists of the movement understand the concept of liberation in relation to women, the most exploited members of any society, they will be voicing political lies."[105] Regina Campus student Barry Lipton broached the issue in March 1974 in an article critical of "Macho Marx" politics. He accused male radicals of using the jargon of women's liberation to oppress women—"to get them into bed or get them to do the shit work of our great projects." There were two choices: "We can ignore the blatant contradictions in our practice and say they will go away after the revolution; or we can start accepting women and men as people."[106]

In a short time, a long distance had been traveled. A wide gulf separated the Frosh Queen contests of 1963 from the women's centre in 1970. The same was true of the other liberation movements of the sixties. The Quiet Revolution transformed Quebec and forced national unity to the top of the agenda. Aboriginal issues moved out of the shadows and into the spotlight. And behind all three was the civil rights movement—Rosa Parks refusing to give up her seat on the bus, the lunch-counter sit-ins, the freedom rides, the oratory of Martin Luther King, Jr.—which set the backdrop and provided inspiration for the other crusades. In each case, the *Carillon* fed the fire. All the liberation movements of the sixties captured the interest of Regina Campus students, but if there was one that had a special local resonance, it was Aboriginal rights. Here, the *Carillon*, through investigative journalism and support of hands-on projects, made a distinctive contribution.

CHAPTER 6

"A Mad Frenzy in the World":
The Peace Movement

T he ban-the-bomb movement, like civil rights, was one of the main-springs of the sixties. It emerged in the context of the Cold War that erupted after the Second World War and continued until the collapse of the Soviet Union in 1989. The 1950s conflict between democracy and communism was portrayed in stark black-and-white terms. In the United States, Senator Joe McCarthy led a witch hunt, searching out communists, real or imagined, and having them fired from their government or private sector jobs. In Canada, the war against subversives was carried out more subtly. Individuals were either refused employment or dismissed from their positions, without ever being told why they were under suspicion or given an opportunity to defend themselves.[1]

The Cold War and Threat of Nuclear Holocaust

In the early 1960s, the Cold War entered a new and more dangerous phase. When the USSR shot down an American U-2 spy plane flying over Soviet territory, President Eisenhower lied about it. This caused embarrassment for the United States when the Russians produced both the plane wreckage and the pilot, who had survived the crash and now confessed to what he had done. Partly for this reason, Soviet leader Nikita Khrushchev stormed out of the Paris summit conference in 1960, escalating the tensions between the two superpowers. In April 1961, newly elected President John F. Kennedy suffered the humiliation of a failed invasion of Cuba, which the CIA had organized in an attempt to overthrow Fidel Castro. The Bay of Pigs fiasco cast the United States in a bad light and allowed the Communists to score a propaganda victory.

The rise of nationalist independence movements in the Third World in the post–Second World War period also had a major bearing on the geopolitical situation. The United States had the disadvantage of being allied with Britain and France, whose crumbling colonial empires were now largely in disrepute, at least among non-Europeans. Moreover, the US often found itself in the invidious position of supporting reactionary, repressive regimes for the sole reason that they were not Communist. The Soviet Union and, after 1949, China presented themselves as brothers-in-arms of the world-wide proletariat seeking to overthrow their colonial rulers. From the communist perspective, capitalism and imperialism were two sides of the same coin.

The nuclear arms race continued at a feverish pace, casting a pall over the 1950s suburban dream of domestic security and an ever-rising standard of living. US defence policy was based on the concept of "Mutually Assured Destruction" (MAD for short). Since the United States did not have the technology required to intercept and destroy intercontinental ballistic missiles (even now missile defence is not a sure thing), American security depended on the delivery of a retaliatory strike against the USSR that would be so devastating that the Soviets would not dare to launch an attack in the first place. The Russians, of course, made the same calculation, with the result that there was an escalating arms race. Even if MAD worked in principle, there was always the possibility of a ghastly mistake that would accidentally trigger a nuclear war, a scenario satirized in Stanley Kubrick's 1964 film *Dr. Strangelove, Or How I Learned to Stop Worrying and Love the Bomb.*

The Campaign for Nuclear Disarmament originated in Britain under the leadership of Bertrand Russell. Members of the group marched in 1958 from London to the Aldermaston nuclear weapons plant. Russell invited artist Gerald Holtom to design a logo for the movement. He came up with the idea of incorporating the semaphore code letters "N" and "D," which stood for nuclear disarmament. A flag straight up and one straight down represented "D," while two diagonal flags pointed downward formed "N." He then drew a circle around it, giving Nuclear Disarmament its symbol, and, as it proved, an icon for the sixties.[2]

In Canada, the Combined Universities Committee for Nuclear Disarmament (CUCND) came together in 1959. Members of the Regina branch of the CUCND made a point of attending Remembrance Day ceremonies, November 11, 1961. Their purpose was to persuade others that the best way to "remember the death and destruction of the two Great Wars is to prevent it from happening again." The campus newspaper also published stories describing what would happen if a 20-megaton atomic bomb were dropped on Regina. At ground zero there would be a 200-foot crater, and the blast would destroy everything within a 400-square-mile radius. In addition, over one thousand square miles would be covered with radioactive fallout.[3] The Regina CUCND circulated a petition in 1961 protesting against the resumption of Soviet nuclear testing. Eighty per cent of the students who were approached signed it. The activists "hoped that more students now will accept some responsibility for averting war and securing world peace; for if the younger generation doesn't, who will?"[4]

An inkling of new thinking about the Cold War can be detected in Peter McCallum's essay "Canada—A Theoretical State," which appeared in the Regina Campus student newspaper in April 1961. McCallum argued that Canada worshipped a false god called "Standard of Living," the Western equivalent of the communist hammer and sickle:

> We claim that our society is based upon "Christian" principles, when our economic system is one based upon the arch-vice of greed and our leading citizens are mere gluttons whose avarice we laud and whose greed we worship. Our civilization is based on the principle of waste while that of the Russians and Chinese is based on economy. Our rivers run filth, our air is clogged with industrial byproducts, our food is coated and saturated with poison, all in the holy name of "Profits."[5]

The only solution was "to establish a planned economy upon the gradual dissolution of our present system." Otherwise, Canada's epitaph would be: "Here lived a decent, godless people, their only monument the asphalt road and a thousand lost golf balls." The essay won second prize in the "Golden Jubilee Essay Contest" (the 50th anniversary of the founding of Regina College), the first prize going to a piece titled "Trinidad Carnival."[6]

In October 1962, President Kennedy demanded that the Soviet Union withdraw the nuclear missiles it had secretly planted in Cuba. For thirteen stressful days, the world awaited Khrushchev's response. Regina Campus students held a protest march. As arts and science student Hans Kieferle explained, the demonstration was directed against both the Russian shipment of nuclear arms and the American naval blockade of Cuba: "We are not taking sides but are protesting against everything." The students, he said, felt there was a "mad frenzy" in the world, and they were trying to do something about it. The city police told them that a parade of more than fifty people required a permit, but, as it turned out, only fourteen students showed up. They marched north from the campus on Scarth Street, east on Twelfth Avenue, and north on Rose Street to the city hall (the old city hall, which has since been torn down). The signs they carried read: "An Atomic War Will Destroy You Too"; "No More Military Bases"; "We Protest Against All Military Action;" and "Stop Military Action, Talk It Over At The U.N." At city hall, they paraded up and down the street for a while and then returned to the college. Most of the people on the sidewalks ignored them, except for a few who shouted out, "Better red than dead" and "Where's your red flag?" There was also jeering from fellow students, who rode in cars beside them and hurled insults.[7]

Student Sylvia Meier defended the protest. To the critic who had said, "everyone who marched should be tried for treason," she replied, "Is this

The first peace march at Regina Campus, October 1962; photo published in *Carillon*, 29 March 1963.

not a denial of the very freedom which this 'conservative' group professes to defend, even to the point of nuclear war?"[8] A few weeks later, the Regina Campus Young Progressive Conservatives, dressed up as followers of Fidel Castro, staged a mock invasion of the college cafeteria and abducted at "gunpoint" one of the leaders of the student model parliament. They said they wanted to dramatize the fact that democracy did not exist in Cuba.[9] Student Garth Hibbert wrote an article refuting the notion of nuclear disarmament and supporting Canada's acquisition of nuclear warheads. Communism, in his opinion, was inherently expansionist and aggressive, and "Canada without nuclear weapons is like a fortress without walls."[10]

A tempest blew up in the fall of 1964 when Kenneth More, the Progressive Conservative Member of Parliament for Regina, charged in the House of Commons that a Russian professor was indoctrinating Regina Campus students with Communist ideas. A.B. Nicolaev, professor of economics at Moscow State University, was spending a year at the campus as part of a cultural exchange program between Canada and the USSR. More said he had received complaints from several parents who were perplexed to learn that a Communist was teaching their children.[11] The student council accused the Conservative MP of trying to interfere with the academic freedom of the university, and Principal Riddell said that to deny Nicolaev the right to teach would be an action characteristic of totalitarian societies: "… the purpose of education is to develop critical and analytical intelligence and it's automatic that a university must be a place where students may gain the capacity to criticize and analyze all points of view."[12] The storm blew over, and Nicolaev was allowed to stay.

The Vietnam War and the Peace Movement

In early 1965, attention turned to the Vietnam War. The roots of the conflict went back to the end of the Second World War, when the Japanese were driven out of Southeast Asia. France tried to retain its former colony of Indochina (Vietnam, Laos, and Cambodia), but met stiff resistance from a nationalist, revolutionary movement led by Ho Chi Minh. United States policy was to support the French, whom they considered an important ally, because the US wanted to contain the spread of Communism. By 1953, the Americans were footing the bill for eighty per cent of French military expenditures in Vietnam, which added up to over $1 billion per year.[13] France suffered a catastrophic defeat at Dien Bhien Phu, May 2, 1954, forcing them to pull out of the war.

With Ho Chi Minh's forces poised to achieve total victory, the international community intervened to impose a settlement. Delegates from the Soviet Union, United States, Great Britain, France, Communist North Vietnam and non-Communist South Vietnam gathered in Geneva to negotiate a cease-fire agreement. They drew the boundary between North and South Vietnam at the 17th parallel and promised that there would be an election in two years' time to choose a government for a reunified Vietnam.[14] It is important to note that neither the United States nor South Vietnam signed the final Geneva Accord.

An International Commission for Supervision and Control (usually referred to as the International Control Commission or ICC) was set up to supervise the agreement and monitor its implementation. It had three members: India, Poland, and Canada, with India serving as chair. Poland was a satellite of the Soviet Union, Canada aligned with the United States, and India was considered to be neutral. The commission had no powers of enforcement. All it could do was carry out investigations and file reports on how well or poorly the parties were adhering to the terms of the agreement.

President Ngo Dinh Diem took power in South Vietnam and forced the French to leave. With the assistance of his brother, chief of police Ngo Dinh Nhu, he ruthlessly suppressed all opposition to his government. In 1956, he refused to agree to the all-Vietnam election that had been promised in the Geneva Accord because he thought the Communists would win. The United States supported this decision, thereby deepening their involvement in Vietnamese affairs. The Communist opposition within South Vietnam to the Diem regime coalesced as the National Liberation Front (NLF), which the Americans and their South Vietnamese allies referred to as the Viet Cong. In 1959, North Vietnam resumed armed conflict against the South, sending men and equipment to help the NLF via a network of roads known as the Ho Chi Minh Trail. As the struggle intensified, the United States increased its flow of aid to Diem. It had sent, by 1963, 13,000 military "advisors" to assist the South Vietnamese army.[15]

The United States became increasingly disillusioned with Diem because of his crude and impolitic repression of Buddhist dissidents. Government forces opened fire on a Buddhist assembly in Hue, May 8, 1963, killing one woman and eight children.[16] Resistance spread throughout the countryside and met with brutal reprisals. On June 11, 1963, an elderly Buddhist monk was soaked with gasoline and set on fire. The photo (news services had been given advance warning) appeared on the front pages of newspapers around the world. The United States government decided that Diem had to go and gave the green light for a military coup to overthrow him on November 1, 1963. Diem and his brother fled to a Roman Catholic Church in Cholon, the Chinese suburb of Saigon. After attending Mass, they agreed to be picked up in an armed personnel carrier. They thought they were being given safe passage out of the country, but this was not the case. After boarding the vehicle, they were shot and stabbed so many times that the floor of the vehicle was awash with blood. President Kennedy was dismayed.[17] He himself died of an assassin's bullet three weeks later. It is doubtful that the United States gained much advantage from Diem's removal. The military juntas that followed in quick succession failed to bring political stability to Vietnam, much less defeat the National Liberation Front.

In June 1964 the United States asked Blair Seaborn, the Canadian representative on the ICC, to deliver a secret message to Hanoi. The message warned North Vietnam that if it did not withdraw from the South, it would face massive American bombing. If, on the other hand, North Vietnam made peace, it could count on abundant American economic development aid. Hanoi rejected the carrot-and-stick approach. It would accept nothing less than a unified Vietnam under Communist rule. In addition to acting as a go-between, Seaborn passed along information to the Americans based on what he had seen in North Vietnam.[18] This was not in keeping with the neutrality expected of an ICC member. In any case, the Seaborn mission failed. President Lyndon Johnson launched his bombing campaign dubbed "Operation Rolling Thunder" in March 1965.

Students at Regina Campus followed these developments closely. The SRC in February 1965 debated a motion condemning American aggression in Vietnam and calling for the withdrawal of American troops. Jim Arnold, who moved the resolution, started the debate by saying: "It is the duty of students to take a stand on the great moral issues of our times. Greater tension is developing in Vietnam, and there is a growing trend of American involvement in this area, which could involve Canada. We could see the beginnings of a nuclear war developing here." One of the students asked whether it was proper for the university to get involved in political questions. Discussion revolved around this point. Treasurer Bill Cornish argued that the SRC "was not elected by the students to express opinions on public issues." Dave Adams, college of education student president, disagreed. He said that "students should take a stand on important world issues. Passing resolutions on questions such as this is a good way to get them thinking about critical questions; then the students will elect those who represent their opinions on these issues." Cornish countered that the SRC did not have enough information to form a judgment: "We don't know the situation in Vietnam and we won't find out from our press. I would rather see research done and a program to influence public opinion started."[19] In the end, council voted 4 to 2 against the resolution. The exchange revealed much about the student mindset in early 1965. Students were still unsure whether it was appropriate for the SRC to take a stand on public issues. Very soon, this would not be a matter for debate.

The anti-war movement on campus received a boost when the CUCND transformed itself into the Student Union for Peace Action (SUPA) at a conference held in Regina, December 28, 1964 to January 1, 1965. The conference, which was attended by 150 delegates from universities across Canada, elected James Harding of Regina Campus as the chair of the national council. SUPA regarded itself as a "social action group with interests in all aspects of society, but maintaining the peace issue as its focal point."[20] It organized a march to the Legislative Building in February 1965 to ask the provincial government to pass a resolution "denouncing the American policies of expanding the war in South Vietnam."[21] About fifty people joined the march. The police were on-site to provide security, but there were no untoward incidents, except for a few eggs thrown at the protesters as they crossed the Albert Street bridge.[22]

The US, by 1968, had dropped more bombs on North and South Vietnam than had fallen on Germany and Japan combined during the Second World War, an average 800 tons per day for three and a half years.[23] Nonetheless, North Vietnamese morale remained high, and supplies continued to move down the Ho Chi Minh trail. By contrast, the morale of the American troops steadily deteriorated. It was difficult for them to distinguish friend from foe; the enemy lurked everywhere. Gains were hard to measure, and the same territory was won and lost several times over. North Vietnam launched the Tet offensive in January 1968, simultaneously attacking most of the major cities in the South. Even the American embassy in Saigon came under fire. Although the Communists were not able to hold on to their gains, they scored a brilliant propaganda coup. Contrary to what the American public had been told by their military leaders, the war was far from being won. President

Richard Nixon, who took office in January 1969, implemented a policy of "Vietnamization," that is, the phased withdrawal of American troops and their replacement by South Vietnamese forces. The American army in Vietnam, which peaked at 550,000, now began to shrink. Concurrently, the United States opened peace talks in Paris with the Hanoi government.

The war slowly wound down. Nixon struggled to achieve "peace with honor" against an enemy that was intent on total victory. The anti-war movement in the United States, a loose coalition of "church people, organized women, traditional peace workers, intellectuals, students, and assorted leftists,"[24] kept up the pressure. Membership in anti-war organizations in the early 1970s swelled to between 300,000 and 400,000. The number who participated in demonstrations of various kinds could be counted in the millions.[25] Nixon faced enemies on two fronts: the war in Vietnam and the war at home.

At Regina Campus in 1968, the student council endorsed the International Day of Protest to be held October 26. The *Carillon* lectured: "We are as guilty as the Nazis if we sit back and do nothing. We are hypocrites if we demonstrate for ourselves and not for the Vietnamese, who suffer far more."[26] The day of the protest was cold and windy, and only about twenty people showed up. They handed out pamphlets to shoppers, or at least tried to hand them out:

> People would just walk by or would say things like "not to-day thank you." Well some of their excuses sounded pretty silly to me so I started thinking up dramatic lines like "kids are still dying in Vietnam." But then they'd say "not my kids." And if I said "Jesus Mr. does it matter whose kids they are?" they'd shove their faces close to mine and scream "commie!" And I wouldn't know quite how to feel about that; whether to get mad or hate or feel bad or what; and so I'd just go on kind of mechanically handing out pamphlets while I tried to decide how to feel. After quite a while though, I realized that I felt tired, so I crammed the rest of the pamphlets into my pocket and went home.[27]

The demonstration held on the International Day of Protest in November 1969 was more successful. Over 400 people marched through the streets

---

INTERNATIONAL DAYS OF PROTEST

AGAINST THE WAR IN VIETNAM

SATURDAY, OCTOBER 26, 1:00 P.M.

The S.R.C. of Regina Campus has endorsed the International Days of Protest against the American war of aggression in Vietnam and Canadian complicity in that war.

In conjunction with similar rallies on other North American campuses, the S.R.C. has called for students and the public to rally on Saturday afternoon at the bandstand in Wascana Park.

OPPOSE THE WAR IN VIETNAM

---

of downtown Regina, chanting "Ho Ho Ho Chi Minh," "Big business gets rich, GI's die," and other slogans. The marchers included students, members of the Regina Committee of American Deserters and a number of trade unionists. There was not too much interaction between the protesters and the people watching, although one bystander was heard to say: "Let's hear it for the Americans; they're fighting for your freedom, too."[28] Dr. Benjamin Spock, the renowned childcare expert and anti-war activist, spoke in Regina in October 1970. He described the Vietnam War as "the dirtiest war possible" and urged protesters not to be "intimidated by the law." As for the violence that sometimes occurred in connection with demonstrations, he said it was "miniscule when compared to the violence that occurs through established channels, such as the war in Southeast Asia."[29]

The most unruly anti-war protest in Regina occurred on May 14, 1970, at a US Army Band concert held at Sheldon-Williams Collegiate under the auspices of the Kinsmen Club. Scuffling broke out when the protesters tried to force their way into the hall. Some of them shouted slogans, one of the girls yelling, "You're damn right we're going to stop this concert." Members of the audience shouted: "Go back to your red campus," "Get these bastards away," "Go back to Russia you bums," and "Send them to Mao." The Kinsmen became especially enraged when a few of the demonstrators began to

Facing page: The Students' Union took a firm stand against the Vietnam War, *Carillon*, 25 October 1968.

Below: The *Carillon*, 13 November 1969, encouraged students to protest the war.

chant "Up against the wall mother f-----s." A girl removed her shirt and paraded topless before the startled concertgoers. The police, who by this time
had arrived on the scene, chased her out of the hall. Another female pro-
tester had her hair pulled and face scratched by an angry fifty-year-old who
screamed repeatedly, "Kill her, kill her." One of the American bandsmen took
a calmer view. "This happens everywhere we go," he said, adding, "When I
heard I could avoid going to Vietnam by joining this band I sure learned to
play this horn in a hurry."[30]

The incident, which the police referred to as a "riot," led to charges
being laid against twelve students, including the editor of the *Carillon*. This
made national news and prompted a telegram of support for the "Regina

Left: Anti-
Vietnam War
demonstration
in Regina, 14
May 1970, at
which twelve
protesters
were arrested,
Carillon, 21 May
1970.

Facing page: The
"Regina Twelve"
included the
Carillon editor,
Carillon, 18 June
1970.

Carillon Editor One Of Twelve Charged With Rioting

The editor of the Carillon, a senior Prairie Fire staffer, the head of the Regina Committee to Aid American Exiles and the head of the Regina Internationalists were among 12 people indicted for "rioting" as a result of the Sheldon-Williams demonstration May 14.

The summons were issued almost a month after the protest took place, on June 8.

John Gallagher, Carillon editor, and Barry Lipton, Prairie Fire staffer and SRC representative, were both charged with participating in a riot.

Lipton was also charged with disturbing the peace by shouting.

The charge of participating in a riot is an indictable offence and carries a maximum penalty of two years imprisonment.

Among those summonsed were four women who were also charged with shouting obscenities.

All twelve are scheduled to appear, as we go to press, Tuesday, June 16.

(See pictures pages 1 and 3)

Twelve" from several prominent Torontonians including Pierre Berton, Dalton Camp, Robert Fulford (editor of *Saturday Night*), Rev. A.C. Forrest (editor of the *United Church Observer*), Melville Watkins (professor of economics, University of Toronto), Tim Reid, M.P., Stephen Lewis, M.P.P., William Kilbourn and John Sewell (aldermen, City of Toronto).[31] The evidence did seem flimsy. For example, one of the persons charged was not even in Regina at the time of the riot.[32] Magistrate H.J. Boyce noted "several ghastly lapses by crown witnesses,"[33] and, in the end, nobody was convicted. Two weeks after the trial, the FLQ crisis broke out and the War Measures Act imposed. The "Regina Twelve" were fortunate that their cases had already been dealt with.

The anti-war activists felt strongly that Canada's "quiet complicity" in the Vietnam War had been swept under the carpet. Canada was selling large quantities of war material to the United States: nickel, iron ore, lead, zinc, copper and oil, as well as grenades, personnel armor, navigational systems, bazooka barrels, gun sights, rocket warheads, ammunition, radio sets, napalm, and even green berets.[34] Under the terms of the Canada-US Defence Production Sharing Agreement, Canadian industry furnished some $2.47

billion worth of military equipment to the US between 1965 and 1973. At least 37 per cent of these supplies went to the Southeast Asia theatre.[35] American bomber pilots trained in Canada and practised carpet-bombing runs over Suffield, Alberta, and North Battleford, Saskatchewan. Agent Orange was tested at the Canadian Forces base in Gagetown, New Brunswick, and manufactured at a Uniroyal plant in Elmira, Ontario. The United States dumped over eleven million gallons of the defoliant on Vietnam. It was later learned that the chemical causes genetic defects, cancer, and numerous other health problems. The United States government compensated American personnel who came in contact with the chemical, but not the Vietnamese victims.[36]

When the Canadian Defence Research Board interviewed job applicants at Regina Campus in November 1969, protesters disrupted the proceedings. They shouted slogans and pounded on the doors and walls of offices where the interviews were being held. One of the students being interviewed protested that his rights had been infringed: "These people [the anti-war demonstrators] do not believe that a person has a right to a private interview. This they demonstrated by listening at the door between their childish outbursts, and loudly reporting overheard pieces of conversation to their fellows. In this they exhibited a level of ignorance that I did not expect to find at this university."[37]

Prime Minister Lester Pearson, for the most part, kept quiet about the war. The exception was a speech he gave accepting the World Peace Award at Temple University in Philadelphia on April 2, 1965. While he did not condemn directly American involvement in Vietnam, he suggested that a bombing pause might be useful to get North Vietnam to come to the negotiating table. The next day President Lyndon Johnson administered a stiff dressing down. He told Pearson he had no business coming to the United States and "piss[ing] on [his] rug."[38] Pearson thereafter kept his own counsel and even sternly rebuked cabinet minister Walter Gordon when he ventured a few words of criticism of the war.[39] Prime Minister Pierre Trudeau, who took over from Pearson in 1968, was as reticent as his predecessor had been. In terms of *realpolitik*, Canada had nothing to gain from speaking out and much to lose. The United States would do what it wanted anyway, and Canada depended too much on American goodwill to damage recklessly the bilateral relationship. In January 1973, late in the war, the House of Commons passed a resolution with all-party support condemning the US bombing of Hanoi and Haiphong. President Richard Nixon put Canada on his "shit list," and

Canadian diplomats were given the cold shoulder in Washington.[40]

Many Canadians sympathized with the American predicament in Vietnam. The Canadian Institute of Public Opinion reported in May 1966 that 35 per cent approved of President Johnson's handling of the war, and 34 per cent disapproved. In February 1968, 35 per cent expressed gratitude for US efforts, while 37 per cent wanted Canada to dissociate itself from the American position. Not until February 1972 did 51 per cent hold the opinion that the United States had made a mistake sending troops to Vietnam (a different thing from saying they were morally wrong to do so), with 27 per cent disagreeing.[41]

Canadians were also divided on the question of admitting anti-war Americans into the country. An estimated 50,000 (including wives and girlfriends) sought refuge from US draft and military laws, the largest political exodus from the United States to Canada since the American Revolution. Whether evading the draft or deserting from the armed forces, they found a haven north of the border. Male students in American universities lived under a Damocles sword. As soon as they graduated, they lost their deferment and were subject to the draft. The brightest students were often the ones most skeptical about the war. Robert McNamara, secretary of defence in both the Kennedy and Johnson administrations, recalled that when he received an honorary degree from Amherst College in June 1966, many of the graduates wore anti-war arm bands: "I counted the number and calculated the percentage of protesters in each of four groups: graduates, cum laude graduates, magna cum laude graduates, and summa cum laude graduates. To my consternation, the percentages rose with the level of academic distinction."[42]

For such students, appeals to patriotic duty fell flat. John Hagan, author of *Northern Passage: American War Resisters in Canada*, recounts a speech given by General Louis Hershey, head of the Selective Service System, at Dartmouth College. Hershey borrowed a sports metaphor: "The United States is a football team, we have elected its captain, he calls the plays, the rest of us might not agree with them, but the team can't win the game unless it listens to the quarterback." At the end of the speech, a student at the back spoke up: "I just wanted to congratulate General Hershey—Generals Goebbels, Goering, Hesse, and Hitler—for over eight million touchdowns in winning their football game."[43]

Canadian immigration policy initially imposed barriers against the admission of war resisters. Immigration Department Operational Memorandum (OM) number 117, January 14, 1966, permitted the entry of draft evaders, but not deserters.[44] The anomaly in the ruling lay in the fact that nothing in the Immigration Act excluded either draft *or* military resisters, and in the past Canada had accepted military deserters from such countries as Hungary and Czechoslovakia. The immigration department in October 1967 adopted a point system, according to which applicants were evaluated on nine criteria on a 100-point scale. The factors taken into consideration included age, education, employment, occupation, knowledge of French or English, financial resources, and relatives in Canada. Although nothing specific was mentioned about military resisters, immigration officers had the authority to turn down applicants who earned more than 50 points "if in his opinion there are good reasons why these norms do not reflect the particular applicant's chances of establishing himself in Canada and those reasons have been submitted in writing."[45] Many border officers used this clause to deny entry to both draft and military resisters. The fact that 234 of 353 immigration officers in 1969 were veterans of the armed forces helps account for their attitude.[46]

Toronto columnist Ron Haggart wrote a series of articles exposing the contradiction between the law, which did not ban draft and military resisters, and departmental procedures, which effectively did. Five York University undergraduates working for the student newspaper posed as American deserters at five border crossing points. Four were turned back, and the fifth was asked to fill out an application form.[47] The United Church of Canada and the NDP lobbied on behalf of the resisters and publicized the fact that Canada was not following its own laws. Immigration minister Allan MacEachen finally announced on May 22, 1969, that American draft and military resisters would be admitted to Canada without regard to their military status.[48] This was later followed by a special amnesty for those who had entered the country illegally during the time when the rules had been stricter. From August 15 to October 15, 1973, war resisters living underground were allowed to come forward and have their status legitimized.[49]

Sympathizers in Canada assisted the newcomers, lobbying government on their behalf, loaning money, helping them to get jobs, and finding them places to live. The Regina Committee to Aid Deserters was one such group. It criticized the Canadian government policy that immigration minister Allan MacEachen put forward in May 1969 on the grounds that it made it more difficult for unskilled, uneducated Americans to come to Canada. These were the very people who were over-represented in the lower ranks of the American military. They were not able to earn enough points on the 100-point scale to qualify for entry.[50] The Regina committee operated a hostel for war resisters until November 1971. When the hostel closed, the committee found accommodation for draft resisters in private homes or arranged transportation to a larger city. Those who offered assistance did not necessarily share the political beliefs of the people they were trying to help. One draft dodger turned in amazement to a Regina aid worker and said, "Why, you're a goddamn Commie!" The worker replied, "Who else do you think would help you?"[51]

The long war finally drew to a close. On January 23, 1973, after five years of negotiations, the United States signed a peace agreement with North Vietnam. It provided for the withdrawal of all US troops from Vietnam, a cease-fire along existing battle lines, and the return of American prisoners of war. South Vietnam's President Nguyen Van Thieu strongly opposed the agreement and at first refused to sign it. The "cease-fire along existing battle lines" meant that North Vietnamese troops were allowed to stay in the South where they were well positioned to resume the battle. Under heavy pressure from the Americans and much against his better judgment, Thieu gave his consent. It was a death sentence for South Vietnam. The US pulled out all of its troops and in August 1973 withdrew air support. South Vietnam's pleas for American military assistance went unheeded, the Communists pushed southward, and on April 30, 1975, Saigon fell.[52] Nearly 60,000 Americans and an estimated 3 million Vietnamese had died, roughly 20 per cent of the population.[53] The economic cost approximated $200 billion; Vietnam and its people had been devastated.[54]

The reasons for the tragedy are much debated. The United States government maintained that it was fighting to defend South Vietnam from Communist takeover. It believed, in accordance with the domino theory, that Vietnam was the key to Southeast Asia. If Vietnam succumbed to the Communists, other countries were sure to follow—Burma, Thailand, Malaysia, India, Indonesia, and so on. Vice-President Nixon had warned in December 1953, "If Indochina falls, Thailand is put in an almost impossible position. The same is true of Malaysia with its rubber and tin. The same is true of Indonesia. If this whole part of Southeast Asia goes under Communist domination or Communist influence, Japan, who trades and must trade with this area in order to exist, must inevitably be oriented towards the Communist regime."[55]

Those who defend the American record in Vietnam War draw an analogy with the Munich Pact that led to the destruction of Czechoslovakia in 1938. They argue that if the Western democracies had stood up to Hitler, rather than trying to appease him, the Second World War might have been averted. According to this logic, the United States had to resist Communist takeover in Vietnam in order to send a strong signal to the USSR and China that aggression would not be tolerated. When the issue is viewed from this perspective, the Americans did not "lose" the war; rather, they exacted a terrible price for relatively modest Communist territorial gains in Vietnam and, by doing so, kept most of Southeast Asia out of the Communist orbit. Apologists for the war maintain that the United States fought for a noble cause—to make the world safe for democracy. The justice of the cause was confirmed, they say, by the misery visited upon the people of Vietnam when the Communists took complete control. Although there was no bloodbath, the new regime sent teachers, civil servants, and middle-class professionals to political "re-education" camps, while thousands of "boat people" risked death on the high seas to escape Communist rule.[56] After the war ended, Hanoi sent captured American military equipment to countries where Communist insurgencies were underway, including El Salvador in 1980. The Vietnamese Communists, by this reckoning, were not naïve nationalists fighting only for the unification of their country. On the contrary, they shared a deep commitment to messianic Marxist-Leninist ideology.[57]

Opponents see the war in an entirely different light. For them it was a "metaphor for horror"[58] on a mass scale. If they drew an historical analogy, it was with the Nazi holocaust, not the Munich policy of appeasement. The spectacle of the richest and most powerful nation on earth bombing a third-world peasant society into oblivion transformed the war into "a self-evident symbol of evil."[59] Leftists believed that US intervention in Vietnam could not be put down to accident, blunder or misstep; it was the logical outcome of American capitalism and imperialism. Historian Gabriel Kolko, for example, interpreted the war as part of the "intense commitment" of the United States "to create an integrated, essentially capitalist framework out of the chaos of World War Two."[60] The US fought in Vietnam to make the world safe for capitalism and to build a global order according to American specifications.

By this interpretation, the United States was and is an inherently imperialist power, and the Vietnam War was not an aberration. It was symptomatic of America's plan for the world.

Prime Minister Pearson, as we have seen, said almost nothing in public about the war. Privately, he thought that while the Americans had honorable motives for fighting, it was the wrong war at the wrong place at the wrong time. [61] Pearson did not consider the South Vietnamese government to be a strong or dependable ally, and he questioned the validity of the domino theory. The defeat of South Vietnam would not, in his opinion, lead inexorably to the collapse of all the pro-West regimes in the region. He was also appalled at the destruction visited upon Vietnam in the David-and-Goliath struggle. At the same time, he was cognizant of Canada's economic and military dependence on the United States. There was no getting around the fact that we were partners with the US in NATO and NORAD and that American trade and investment sustained our high standard of living.

Canada and the "American Empire"

The *Carillon* gravitated to the view that the Vietnam War was an outcome of American imperialism, and that the Canadian government's complicity in the war could be explained by Canada's status as a willing satellite of that empire. A mock job advertisement in January 1970 featured a photo of Prime Minister Pierre Trudeau with the caption, "Graduating from University this Spring? Looking for a good job? Try American Empire. Like this young man."[62] Another "ad" depicted Saskatchewan Premier Allan Blakeney, who defeated Ross Thatcher in the 1971 provincial election, under the headline "American Empire: The Company with the Human Faces." The accompanying text read:

> American Empire has been in business a long time. Long enough to read the pulse of the people, long enough to know that we must give the people what they want. That's part of the reason why we have been so successful. So when the people of our Saskatchewan branch started to show displeasure with our branch manager, Col. Thatcher, we reproached him immediately. Our new man in Regina, Allan Blakeney, we feel, will promote the interests of American Empire as well as Mr. Thatcher, but he will do it in a nice way.[63]

The *Carillon* depicted Prime Minister Pierre Trudeau as chore-boy for the "American Empire," *Carillon*, 23 January 1970.

American Empire
The Company With The Human Faces

American Empire has been in business a long time. Long enough to read the pulse of the people, long enough to know that we must give the people what they want. That's part of the reason why we have been so successful.

So when the people of our Saskatchewan branch started to show displeasure with our branch manager, Col. Thatcher, we reproached him immediately. Our new man in Regina, Allan Blakeney, we feel, will promote the interests of American Empire as well as Mr. Thatcher, but he will do it in a nice way.

That's what American Empire is all about. Doing things in a nice way.

Allan Blakeney has been working his way up the ranks of our company for many years.

Last year he was responsible for soundly defeating an attempt by Godles radicals to take over one of our Sask. subsidiaries. He has shown that when dealing with those who seek to impose their will on the majority and institute Communism and other varieties of Hitlerism, he can be firm.

Our Saskatchewan customers have shown that they were concerned with our previous policies of economic development. They didn't understand that by taking a lot of money out of a subsidiary and sending it to head office, that the capital would be spent developing technology so that we could help you even more.

But at American Empire, the customer is always right. So we changed our economic policy. Mr. Blakeney has pledged that he will attempt to formulate a policy that will satisfy both the customer, and its servant, the empire.

Of course, Mr. Blakeney has not been given a Carte Blanche. If he doesn't produce, or if he falls under the influence of the Communist Waffle we will replace him as quickly as we replaced his predecessor.

THE
American Empire©
CANADA LTD.

Washington. Ottawa. London. Lisbon. Madrid. Rome. Bonn. Bern. The Hague. Copenhagen. Brussels. Vienna. Oslo. Dublin. Canberra. Saigon. Manila. Bangkok. Seoul. Rangoon. Kuala Lumpur. Taipei. New Delhi. Tel Aviv. Karachi. Johannesburg. Lagos. Salisbury. Brazilia. Buenos Aires. Quito. Panama City. Lima. Bogota. Santiago. Mexico City. Tegucigalpa. San Juan. Guantanamo. Paris. Vientiane. Caracas. and many, many more to serve ya'you.

The *Carillon* made sport of the watered-down socialism of the Saskatchewan New Democratic Party, *Carillon*, 8 September 1971.

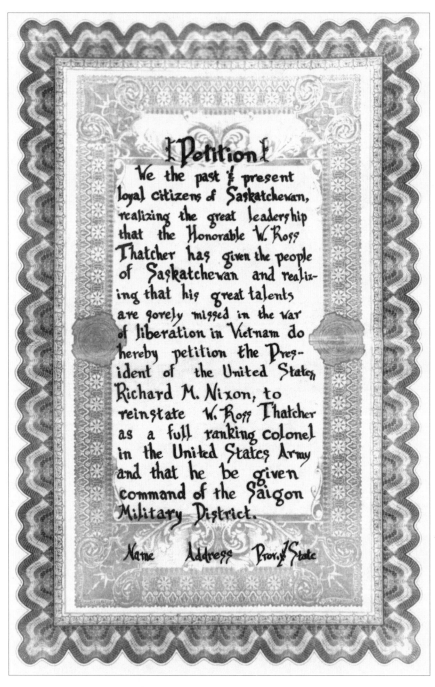

Facetious *Carillon* petition, 22 January 1971.

"Colonel" Thatcher received satirical treatment in a bogus petition that requested his appointment "as a full ranking colonel in the United States Army and that he be given command of the Saigon Military District."[64] The *Carillon* also printed a large poster and inserted it into the July 9, 1971 issue of the paper. It showed a large map of North America entirely covered in the stars and stripes with the slogan "CONTINENTALISM IS TREASON!" written in large block letters.[65]

Large poster insert, *Carillon*, 9 July 1971.

Nuclear Testing and Environmentalism

Even as the Vietnam War continued, the US resumed its nuclear tests. A major detonation was scheduled to take place in the Aleutian Islands in Alaska in October 1969. Protesters mobilized, including two busloads of Regina Campus students who journeyed to the US border crossing at North Portal to hold a demonstration. The Students' Union second vice-president Rob Milen said the reason for the protest was "concern over dangers of seismic disasters, possible disruption of the ecological balance and possible environmental poisoning." The students gathered along the highway to slow down cars and talk to the people crossing the border into Canada. Their signs read: "Remember 1812," "We Love Your People But Your Overkill Slays Us," "The Illegal Eagle Strikes Again," and "Use Texas." Most motorists proved quite sympathetic to the cause and listened patiently to the students. Indeed, two Canadian families were so supportive that they stopped their cars on the American side, blocking the border crossing for over half an hour. However, one truck heading for Alaska bulldozed its way through the barricade. The protest lasted for about an hour and then broke up.[66]

The students staged the "Vietnam-Amchitka Day of Protest" on November 3, 1971. It combined a rally against the war with a protest against the

Shown here is a small sample of the approximately 100 students who blocked the North Portal border crossing.

Regina Campus students at the American border, protesting nuclear test explosions, *Carillon*, 3 October 1969.

Vietnam - Amchitka Day of Protest

Program

The Students' Union has declared today "A day of Protest Against the War in Vietnam and Against Amchitka.

The agenda for today's activities is:

10:30 - 12:00 — FILMS ON THE WAR IN VIETNAM AND ATOMIC TESTING
        —"DAY OF THE LOCUST"
        —"WHAT DO WE DO NOW"

12:30 - 2:00 — SPEAKERS ON VIETNAM AND AMCHITKA
        —David Lord, Minnesota co-ordinator Vietnam Vets Against the War
        —John Richards, NDP-MLA from Saskatoon
        —Mary-Jo Kinzel, Regina Pollution Probe

2:30   — DEMONSTRATION AND RALLY
        Meet at the College Building (Old Campus), march to Legislative Building, down College Avenue to Albert Street. Rally at Legislative Building, to be addressed by a Cabinet Minister in the Provincial Government.

Stop The Nuclear Madness

Double-barreled protest (the Vietnam War and nuclear testing), *Carillon*, 3 November 1971.

American plan to explode a five-megaton nuclear bomb at Amchitka Island. The students asked Regina Campus principal John Archer to cancel classes for the day, but he denied their request. However, he did have some sympathy for what they were trying to do. After they left his office, he wrote: "It was really a very good discussion and I must say that I have a certain admiration and respect for these young people who find time and energy to be concerned over the future of their world."[67] The *Carillon* published an account of the day of protest titled "The American Empire Will Eat You Up." The speakers were David Lord, Minneapolis-St. Paul coordinator of the Vietnam Veterans Against the War; John Richards, a Saskatchewan NDP MLA; and Mary Joe Kinzel, president of Pollution Probe. Kinzel focused on the possible environmental damage caused by the Amchitka blast, including higher levels of radiation that had been linked to genetic damage and leukemia.[68]

Her speech was typical of a growing tendency to link imperialistic corporate capitalism with the deterioration of the environment. In October 1970, Regina Campus held a three-day "Environmental Teach-in," which examined a range of topics from "pesticides and soil pollution" and "the rise and fall of the Great Lakes" to "the problems of human population growth."[69] In keeping with this trend, the biology department revised its curriculum to include courses dealing with ecological issues.[70] The campus group Ecology Probe, founded in January 1970, distributed information about pollution, encouraged environment-friendly consumerism, and studied the long-range effects of the use of insecticides and other toxic chemicals.[71] The *Carillon* embraced these

ANOTHER VIEW: THE AMCHITKA BLAST

Cartoonist's view of the Amchitka nuclear blast, *Carillon*, 5 November 1971.

ENVIRONMENTAL TEACH-IN

PROGRAM SUPPLEMENT FOR THURSDAY, OCTOBER 22, 1970
ROOM ONE CLASSROOM BUILDING

2:30 p.m. Pesticides and Soil Pollution

A brief review of what is known and what isn't know about the long term effects of pesticides on soil fertility . . . by Dr. Roy Cullimore, Dept. of Biology, Regina Campus.

3:00 p.m. Film: The Erie Report

A comprehensive look at the pollution of Lake Erie.

3:45 p.m. The Prince Albert Pulp Mill: The effect of deforestation on the ecology of Northern Saskatchewan.

Ecologists are concerned about the long-term effects of clear-cutting timber over large areas of the north. Dr. Maureen Rever of the Biology Dept., Saskatoon Campus, will explain why.

4:15 p.m. The Prince Albert Pulp Mill: Pollution of the North Saskatchewan River.

Patricia Tones, a graduate student at the Dept. of Biology, Saskatoon Campus, has recently completed a thesis on water pollution caused by the Prince Albert Pulp Mill. She will present her assessment of the seriousness of this pollution problem.

4:45 p.m. Film: The Rise and Fall of the Great Lakes.

A humorous look at the geological and recent history of the Great Lakes, including pollution.

5:00 p.m. Mercury Pollution of Saskatchewan Waters.

Dr. Gary Wobeser of the Dept. of Veterinary Pathology, Saskatoon Campus, conducted the first studies of mercury in fish from the Saskatchewan River System. These studies led to the closure of sport fishing and the confiscation of commercial fish. Dr. Wobeser will explain why mercury is dangerous and will discuss some of his recent work.

7:30 p.m. Panel Discussion on the Pollution of the Qu'Appelle Lakes.

The discussion will be introduced with a talk by Dr. Andrew Hamilton of the Fisheries Research Institute in Winnipeg on "Phosphates and Water Pollution." The panel will then discuss the specific problem of the pollution of the Qu'Appelle Lakes. Panelists will be: Dr. Roy Cullimore, Biology Dept., Regina Campus. Dr. Cullimore is conducting surveys of weed and algal growth and coliform bacteria for the Qu'Appelle Basin Study Board; Mr. Peter Dubois, representative of the Federation of Saskatchewan Indians; Dr. Ted Hammer, Biology Dept., Saskatoon Campus. Dr. Hammer has conducted long-term studies on the growth of algae in the Qu'Appelle Lakes; Dr. Keith Johnson, Dept. of Chemistry, Regina Campus. Dr. Johnson is conducting water quality studies for the Qu'Appelle Basin Board Study; Mr. Peter McCart, Biology Dept., Regina Campus. Mr. McCart became interested in the pollution of the Qu'Appelle Lakes last summer when he observed heavy growths of blue-green algae and dead fish washing up on the beaches of Echo Provincial Park. He has been critical of the Qu'Appelle Basin Study; Mr. S. P. Regan, president of the Qu'Appelle Valley Development Association; Rev. John Sloan, staff associate of the Prairie Christian Training Centre (P.C.T.C.).

PROGRAM SUPPLEMENT FOR FRIDAY, OCTOBER 23, 1970

1:30 p.m. The Problem of Human Population Growth.

Dr. Russ Zacharuk of the Biology Dept., Regina Campus, will outline the problem and suggest possible solutions. Dr. Zacharuk has been concerned with the overpopulation of our planet for a long time and has spoken at numerous public gatherings.

2:00 p.m. Film: Boomsville.

A satirical look at the belief that growth is invariably and completely good.

2:15 p.m. The Problem of Economic Growth.

Our present economic system relies on growth in population and in resource exploitation to sustain employment, wages, and profits. Is this the only system possible in a democracy? Dr. Alex Kelly of the Economics Dept., Regina Campus will consider the question.

3:00 p.m. Coffee.

3:15 p.m. Film: Before the Mountain Was Moved.

The film examines some of the sociological results of strip-mining in West Virginia.

4:00 p.m. Resource exploitation and conservation of the environment.

Mr. John Livingston, featured speaker for the teach-in, will consider the conflict between our increasing resource requirements and the destruction of natural environments. Can we prevent resource exploitation in our provincial and national parks? Should we allow private enterprise to extract profits from our public parks?

4:45 p.m. To be announced.

SATURDAY, OCTOBER 24, 1970

8:00 p.m. A panel of politicians will discuss the political reality of recommendations resulting from the teach-in.

Politicians that will attend are: Mr. John Burton (NDP), MP for Regina East; Mr. Walter Smishek (NDP), MLA for Regina Northeast. Others to be announced.

Environmentalism, a popular cause by 1970, *Carillon*, 16 October 1970.

issues, publishing "Corporate Obscenity—The Rape of the Environment,"[72] an exposé of wasteful timber-cutting practices in north-eastern Saskatchewan, as well as numerous articles dealing with the ban on Styrofoam cups, the inadequate sewage treatment facilities in Moose Jaw, DDT poisoning of wildlife, and the activities of Greenpeace, the peace group synonymous with the birth of the environmental movement.[73]

Che Guevara as Sixties Icon

Leftists tended to blame war, nuclear arms, and the destruction of the planet on the capitalist system, especially the United States, its imperial centre. Their answer was "revolution," a word that gestured in the direction of an ill-defined utopia. These vague yearnings converged in the person of Che Guevara, the man who became hero, martyr and revolutionary icon. Born in Rosario, Argentina, in 1928, Ernesto ("Che" is a nickname derived from his Argentine habit of using "Che" to mean "Hey you")[74] Guevara trained as a doctor, but abandoned the practice of medicine to pursue the life of a guerrilla fighter. He joined Fidel Castro in the overthrow of the Batista regime in Cuba in January 1959. An ardent Marxist-Leninist, he grew disillusioned with what he considered to be the Soviet Union's betrayal of the pure principles of Communism. He was furious with Khrushchev for capitulating to President Kennedy during the Cuban missile crisis, going so far as to tell a reporter that the missiles should have been fired on the United States rather than dismantled.[75] Guevara decided to leave his job as economic planner for Cuba (a project that was not going very well in any case) to lead a guerrilla insurgency in Bolivia. There, at age 39, he met his death at the hands of the Bolivian military and the CIA. In his knapsack was found a verse from the Spanish poet Leon Felipe: "Christ: I love you, not because you came down from a star, but because you showed me the light. You taught me man is God, a poor God in sin like You, and he on Your left on the Golgotha, the evil thief, is God too."[76]

The manner of his death, together with his lifetime commitment to the poor and oppressed, transformed him into a secular saint. After falling into relative obscurity in the 1970s and 1980s, he made a comeback in the 1990s as "an enduring symbol of passionate defiance to an entrenched status quo."[77] In Latin America today, only images of the Virgin Mary are more ubiquitous. His picture is on T-shirts everywhere, for reasons that are not completely clear, even to those wearing them. When he died on October 9, 1967, his persona already had a grip on the popular imagination. The *Carillon*, November 3, 1967, published a eulogy:

> Che Guevara was a prototype of a new form of man, which has begun to make an appearance on the horizons of history. The beginnings of a change in human nature emerging from changes in the historical and social conditions of men. It is only within the context of revolutionary change that Guevara the man becomes understandable. Che was a revolutionary, in that he was involved in the process of revolution. And it was in that process that he was formed … The man Che Guevara was an alternative, a prototype—a socialist man.[78]

It is hard to imagine an article of this kind in the Regina Campus newspaper ten, even five, years earlier. Students in the fifties had not concerned themselves with the problems of the world. Their interests lay elsewhere. They were busy with academic studies and harmless, self-improving extracurricular activities. Marching in the streets was unheard of, unless it involved a Halloween prank or a high-spirited conga line. With the arrival of the sixties, the student mindset and behavior began to change. The Vietnam War marked a turning point. In February 1965, just before the start of the major bombing escalation, the student council debated a resolution condemning the United States. The motion was defeated mainly because some students were still unsure whether the council should be taking a stand on political matters outside the narrow range of student affairs. The SRC was accustomed to planning dances, not making statements about foreign policy. Very quickly, the atmosphere changed. Led by the Regina branch of the Student Union for Peace Action, protests against the war multiplied. The *Carillon* took up the cause, condemning the war on humanitarian grounds and linking it to American imperialism and capitalism. The terrain of debate had shifted. What formerly had remained unsaid now moved into mainstream discourse. It was now taken for granted that students could have opinions about the Vietnam War, nuclear disarmament, the power of multinational corporations, environmental pollution, and Third World revolution. The meaning of "normal" had changed.

CHAPTER 7

"What It Is Ain't Exactly Clear": The Counterculture and Its Critics

T he movements of the sixties were not just about politics; they were also concerned with values and lifestyles. The sexual revolution, drugs, music, and the counterculture formed the context in which the anti-war and liberation struggles were carried on. Critics of the sixties often failed to make a distinction between politics and culture; they conflated zonked-out hippies and Marxist revolutionaries. This was an oversimplification. It is possible to separate the strands of the sixties, while acknowledging how tightly they were interwoven. The *Carillon* both explored and endorsed the counterculture. That being said, the general tenor of the paper was more political than cultural. This reflected the personal interests of the staff, but it may also have had something to do with the political culture of Saskatchewan, with its legacy of socialism and intense ideological rivalry. Perhaps the writers of the *Carillon* were too much the sons and daughters of their parents not to place politics front and centre.

Defining the Counterculture

It is not easy to define "culture," since it encompasses almost everything we think, say, do, or invest with meaning. Arthur Marwick defines it as "the network or totality of attitudes, values and practices of a particular group of human beings."[1] John Tomlinson prefers: "the order of life in which human beings construct meanings through practices of symbolic representation."[2] Culture surrounds us; we are immersed in it. It is what people draw on, consciously and unconsciously, to make sense of the meaning of their lives, not only the books they read and the movies they watch, but also "the trip around the local supermarket aisles, or to the restaurant, the sports hall, the dance club or the garden centre, the conversation in the bar or on the street corner … [all the] mundane practices that directly contribute to people's ongoing 'life-narratives.'"[3] The counterculture runs against the core tendencies of the mainstream culture, or, as Arthur Marwick says, it comprises the values and activities that contrast with or are critical of the values and activities of established society.[4] The key point is that the counterculture is oppositional. This differentiates it from a subculture, which is more a variation on the status quo than an alternative to it.

The clash between culture and counterculture can be glimpsed in an exchange of letters in the *Leader-Post* in 1968. A businessman complained about hippies lounging in downtown Victoria Park:

> I have been in Regina for more than 50 years and for 35 years I used to have my business on 12th Avenue across from Victoria Park. The beautiful park seems to be the center where the young and dirty generation known as "hippies" stay day and night, sleeping on the grass or on the benches, using profane language or using improper gesticulations to others walking through. When they are leaving, they leave behind them a lot of rubbish. Is it good in a public place like this, where our kiddies are playing in the playground and where some of our retired businessmen try to pass a few hours? I am wondering why no one is taking responsibility to stop this activity by hippies. There is no reason for spending so many thousands of tax dollars each year to keep up the parks, if they are to be taken over by this group and I think it would be better to turn them over into parking lots or other enterprises.[5]

A few days later, a "hippie" responded:

> This is a reply to the gentleman who wrote the other day complaining about "hippies" in Victoria Park. We seem to be called "hippies" just because we sit around the park. Is there something so awful about just sitting around there and having fun? We seem to be known as the dirty generation. Well, that just takes the cake; everyone I know there is

neatly dressed and clean. There always has to be some people who do not like the younger generation. This gentleman
says that he would like to see us moved out of there. If we
leave, where are we going to go? Maybe he wants us to hang
around street corners and get charged with loitering. If we
have to leave, the other people who go there should leave
as well. What are parks for if not to sit around and pass the
time in? Can someone answer that question for me? We do
not cause trouble around there so why should we leave?[6]

The letters set up a series of polar opposites: age versus youth; work
versus play; taxpayer versus freeloader; clean versus dirty; messy versus
neat; profane versus polite; doing versus being; parking versus parking
lot (reminiscent of the Joni Mitchell song). To this we could add numerous
other oppositional terms: short hair versus long hair; tie versus beads; shoe
leather versus bare feet; alcohol and cigarettes versus marijuana and LSD;
easy listening/jazz/classical versus rock; procreational versus recreational
sex; processed versus organic foods; mainstream Christian denominations
versus Buddhism and other Eastern religions; nuclear family versus communes; delayed versus immediate gratification; planning versus spontane-
ity; "follow the rules" versus "do your own thing"; realism versus romanticism; technology versus nature; good manners versus "sincerity"; respect for
authority versus rebellion; ambition versus "live for today." More could be
included in the list, but the point is made. The counterculture was complex
and multi-faceted, not uniform or monolithic, but while it pulled in several
directions at once, it had an overall anti-bourgeois tendency. It opposed traditional middle-class values and lifestyles. In short, the dominant culture stood
for "materialism, order, regularity, custom, rational thinking, self-discipline,
and productivity"; the counterculture valued "creativity, rebellion, novelty,
self-expression, anti-materialism, and vivid experience."[7] Significantly, the
counterculture as an anti-bourgeois phenomenon was largely a product of
the bourgeoisie, or the children of the bourgeoisie. It was a case, as Allan
Bloom has observed, of "the bourgeois need to feel that he is not bourgeois,
to have dangerous experiments with the unlimited."[8]

The counterculture was not something completely new. It had familial
ties, as we have seen, with the Beats of the 1950s. More distantly, connections
may be drawn with the Romantic movement of the late eighteenth and early

nineteenth centuries, in particular the Romantic cult of feeling and spontane-ity and nature worship.[9] Jean-Jacques Rousseau declared that men are "born free" but "everywhere in chains." He believed that civilization, with its rules and customs, has a corrupting influence; the authentic self is the self in the state of nature—pure, unspoiled, and inherently good. Self-assertion against artificial social constraints and legal obligations is, therefore, more than jus-tified. Such ideals have inspired Bohemian subcultures, from New York's Greenwich Village to the Left Bank in Paris. The heroine in Puccini's 1896 opera *La Bohème* leads a life that is poor in material possessions but rich in feeling. She takes pleasure in simple things like the single flower that bright-ens her attic garret and the first warming rays of the April sun. Her lover and their artist friends live outside the world of work and family. They make fun of the uptight, hypocritical bourgeoisie, and they have no qualms about tak-ing advantage of them to pay for meals and rent. Mimi is a flower child; she and her friends are proto-hippies. They are on the fringe of society, an aberra-tion from the prevailing norm, exotic and excluded. In the sixties, the fringe moved into the mainstream, setting the tone for middle-class youth culture.

The Sexual Revolution

A key component of the counterculture was the sexual revolution, defined by Marwick as a permissiveness that entailed "striking changes in public and private morals and … a new frankness, openness and indeed honesty in personal relations and modes of expression."[10] It encompassed premarital and extramarital sex, common law relationships, the birth control pill, legalized abortion, and the wide diffusion of X-rated material. British poet Philip Larkin was not far wrong in suggesting that sexual intercourse was invented in 1963.[11] The basic rule in the 1950s was that sex was for married couples, a tacit exception being made for activities that stopped short of intercourse, such as necking (kissing and caressing above the neck) and petting (below the neck). The important thing was to not "go all the way."[12] Men were cast as sexual aggressors, while women were assigned the role of "limit setter." Hers was the final "yes" or "no." It followed that if things went too far, it was her fault. She lost her "reputation" and was branded as "fast," "loose," "cheap"—"damaged goods on the marriage market." If pregnant, she had three options: hasty marriage, concealment or removal to another town until the baby was born and given up for adoption, or an illegal abortion. It was frowned on for an unmarried mother to raise a child born out of wedlock.

The 1950s was the era of "going steady," the apogee of a dating culture in which gender roles were clearly defined. Boys asked girls to go out on dates; girls waited by the phone. Boys opened the car door and picked up the tab. A 1955 Philip Morris ad made fun of the inadequate male who went "dutch": "Today Finster goes everywhere and shares expenses fifty-fifty with Mary Alice Hematoma, a lovely three-legged girl with side burns."[13] Going steady was rehearsal for marriage. Men were the breadwinners and women the dependent homemakers, roles that were scripted in the popular television sitcoms of the day. Canadians looked to the British royal family for a model of domestic normalcy: "The Duke and Duchess of Edinburgh are young, modern parents who, like many other young people, in an anxious and insecure world, find their deepest happiness and satisfaction in the warm circle of family life."[14]

Parents and school authorities enforced the norm of no-sex-before-marriage. The doors of the Regina Campus women's residence were locked each night at 11:00 p.m. The girls could apply to the warden for late leaves until 12:30 a.m. on Wednesday, Thursday, and Friday, and until 2 a.m. on Saturday. The warden could also authorize overnight and weekend leaves, provided the student's parent or guardian signed a form indicating where the girl was allowed to stay. The girls had to sign a register each time they left the residence and again when they returned. Unauthorized visitors were strictly forbidden. The college considered the breach of this rule to be a serious matter that had to be referred to the faculty committee on discipline.[15] In one case in February 1953, four boys entered the girls' residence reception room at about 10:30 in the evening. They were rowdy and sang "boisterous songs to such an extent that two of the residence girls and their escorts left the room to visit elsewhere." At 11:20 p.m., after the residence lock-up, the warden found two male students on one of the floors of the girls' residence. One claimed to have gone up to borrow a book, while the other explained that he had followed to look for his friend. According to the disciplinary report, it had been obvious that "some of the group at least had been drinking." The guilty parties were placed on probation; a second offence would result in expulsion.[16]

With the arrival of the sixties, the dating culture became obsolete. Couples abandoned the rituals and protocols of the formal date and began to think in terms of "relationships." The line between going out and having sex was blurred. The dating ritual had required a huge investment in time and energy in settling the sex question. Now it was less of an issue. Historian

Beth Bailey suggests that this allowed young people to have more authentic relationships with deeper levels of companionship and mutual understanding.[17] But she admits that the dating ritual did have romantic appeal: the waiting and the telephone calls, nervous boys clutching corsages, the thrilling moments of risky privacy, the rush to sign in on time. All this was lost when sex became more matter-of-fact.[18]

In the spring of 1968, Linda LeClair, an unmarried student at Barnard College in New York, was expelled when it was discovered that she was sharing an off-campus apartment with her boyfriend. The media fastened on the story because it seemed to epitomize the decadence of the young generation. Leclair was denounced as a "whore," and it was suggested that the school be renamed "Barnyard" College. The young woman explained in an interview that sex was just one aspect of the relationship she had with her partner. He was her friend, companion, and roommate as well as her lover. Nor was she concerned that her reputation had been tarnished or that now she would be unable to find a suitable husband.[19] The scandal and her response to it signalled a shift in sexual mores; the rule of chastity before marriage was being openly and unapologetically defied.

The dawn of the sexual revolution at Regina Campus can be dated with some precision. On December 1, 1961, the student newspaper devoted its entire front page to the topic. An editorial stated: "In our society codes which prohibit the free discussion of sex have led to several unfortunate consequences. Most of us suffer from the most pervasive of all anxieties—that which comes from sex guilt ... Cruelest of all, our way of life condemns premarital pregnancy to such a degree that many lives are wasted because of self and societal shame, and yet on the other hand, facts are not made available to stop the birth of undesired children."[20] The paper said that its aim was neither "to justify premarital intercourse" nor to defend "present mores." It wanted merely to start a discussion and throw light on a subject that too long had been hushed up and hidden away in darkened corners. This was somewhat disingenuous, since the paper, while claiming to be open to all points of view, in fact advocated a liberalized approach to sexual attitudes and conduct. It advised readers to be "as accepting, non-critical, and democratic about the sex behavior of others as you can possibly be ... Work, in whatever way you can, for rules and laws which seek only to discourage sex acts whereby one individual needlessly, gratuitously, and distinctly harms another human being, rather than statutes and mores which are based on superstition, igno-

The *Sheet* (predecessor of the *Carillon*), 1 December 1961, lifted the lid on the discussion of taboo sexual topics.

rance, and sadistic 'sex morality.'"[21] The articles communicated several messages: "reputable doctors and scientists" could find little that was harmful in masturbation; homosexuality was "neither harmful or undesirable, only unaccepted as our society norm"; prostitution had been outlawed on moral grounds, overriding "evidence and scientific and social considerations"; and abortions were dangerous "only because they are illegal."[22] In sum, science and reason demanded a reassessment of the traditional code of sexual morality.

The articles aroused a storm of controversy.[23] Ron Chapdelaine, president of the Newman Club (a Roman Catholic student association), said they were "an insult to Christians" and an attack on marriage. The detailed discussion of methods of contraception constituted "an encouragement to the unmarried to commit premarital intercourse, alias fornication." "The good of society," he continued, "depends intimately on the sanctity of marriage. Newman Club hates to see the ideal of married love confused with a counterfeit love which denies the altruism of the marriage act by rejecting ahead of time all limit to sex-gratification." Chapdelaine argued that the student newspaper had set up a false dichotomy—puritanical prudishness versus enlightened liberation. It had tried to discredit anybody who took a different view by labeling them "bigots, ignoramuses, etc." The Newman Club, he said, "has no desire to return to an era of furtive secrecy on sex, but neither does it wish to see a sense of reverence for it forgotten."[24] The secretary of the campus Student Christian Movement supported the stand that Chapdelaine had taken. Sex had been "given to man for enjoyment, but only within the bonds of marriage. It is only in marriage that the responsibilities involved in the sex act can be dealt with as they ought."[25]

The sharp exchange was typical of the times. The Regina Public Library in 1961 banned Henry Miller's *Tropic of Cancer* because the chair of the library board had read it and found it disgusting. The *Leader-Post* contacted Regina Campus librarian Betty Henderson to see whether the university had a copy of the book. She said the book had not been ordered, but this had been merely an oversight: "I am putting in an order for it immediately." She was then asked whether the book would be placed on the open shelves. She hedged. It would be kept on the restricted shelf, but not because of its salacious content. All rare books—and *Tropic of Cancer* was considered a rare book—were held in the restricted area.[26]

By 1963, the atmosphere had changed. The "*Carillon* Counsellor" offered satirical advice "about those intimate problems that befall all varsity students:"[27]

> Dear C.C.: My mother told me to be careful around boys because no matter what they said, there were only after ONE THING. But my mother would never tell me what this ONE THING was. She would pat my head and smile and say I would understand some day. My girl friend is going steady with this real nice guy, only sometimes the other girls sneer at her behind her back and say it's because she gives him WHAT HE WANTS. Well, I don't care any more. I've missed the last two formals and I'm sick of going to the 4-D with the girls to stare at those chicken-hearted boys staring at us chicken-hearted girls. I will give a nice boy THE ONE THING THAT HE WANTS. Only what is it?—Willing.

> Dear Willing: Boys simply want companionship, someone they are proud to be seen with, someone who can share their defeats and triumphs, someone whom they can place on a pedestal and respect. That's all, Yup.[28]

An article in late 1963 took the view that sex was morally correct as long as "both parties love each other."[29] Whether or not they were married was a secondary consideration. An editorial "Think for Yourself" advised "the college girl" to have sex if that's what she thought was the right thing. The decision was strictly a matter of individual conscience; there were no hard-and-fast rules to follow.[30]

The birth control pill, which was approved for sale in Canada in 1961, made it easier to prevent unwanted pregnancy. The pill was 99 per cent effective, and, unlike condoms, its use was not dependent on the cooperation of the woman's partner. However, the Criminal Code still made it illegal to advertise, sell or make available "any means of preventing contraception." Though rarely enforced, the law stayed on the books until 1969. A doctor's prescription was required to obtain the pill, and, initially, most doctors were reluctant to prescribe it for unmarried women. Women resorted to subterfuges such as wearing a fake wedding ring when they visited the doctor's office, and feminists campaigned for unfettered access to birth control. Many university health clinics gave out prescriptions to female students, and, by the early 1970s, adult women in Canada, whether married or not, had little difficulty obtaining the pill.[31]

The *Carillon* in March 1967 conducted an informal sex survey of campus students. Ten girls said they had had premarital sexual relations, and 44 said they had not. This compared to 16 boys who said yes, and 8 who said no. In answer to the question, "if the circumstances were 'right' would you engage in premarital sex?" 28 girls replied yes, and 25, no. For boys, it was 23 and 3 respectively. A few of the girls admitted they were on the pill, which they said they had obtained from "friendly" doctors, "especially European doctors," or from "the girl next door" or "a married friend."[32] The Saskatchewan Department of Health was so concerned about the spread of sexually transmitted diseases that it ran ads in the *Carillon* warning that VD rates in the province among 15 to 19-year-olds had risen 26 per cent from 1972 to 1973. It urged at-risk individuals to get in touch with the VD Information Centre.[33]

The sexual experimentation of the counterculture, in its more extreme manifestations, went well beyond the transgressions of premarital sex. John Sinclair of the White Panther Party in the United States boldly declared: "Our position is that all people must be free to fuck freely, whenever and wherever they want to, or not to fuck if they don't wanna—in bed, on the floor, on the streets, in the parks and fields, 'back seat boogie for the high school kids' sing the Fugs who brought it all out in the open on stage and on records, fuck whoever wants to fuck you and everybody else do the same."[34] The Weather Underground, a violent splinter group of the Students for a Democratic Society, instructed its members to have sex with as many partners as possible, as part of their indoctrination in shedding bourgeois hang-ups and building loyalty to the movement.[35] Radicals used sex as a weapon because they knew it had shock value. John Thompson, a student at Berkeley, was arrested for standing on a street corner holding a sign inscribed with a "one-word poem"—"Fuck." Upon his release, he amended the poem to "Fuck!" and went back out onto the street. Using the four-letter expletive was the verbal equivalent of throwing a bomb. Sexual revolution and anti-war protest came together in the slogan "Make Love, Not War." The Vietnam War, the protesters said, was obscene; sex was not. By this strategy, those who broke the sexual code regained the higher moral ground. Sex was a battleground between the old and the young, the establishment and the rebels.

In society at large during the 1960s, censorship eased and standards of propriety were relaxed. The risqué off-Broadway show, *Oh! Calcutta!* (the title derived from the French phrase "Oh! Quel cul tu as!" or "Oh, what a nice ass you have"), opened in June 1969. The first act of the 1967 musical *Hair* ended with the entire cast naked in front of the audience. *Georgy Girl*, a 1966 British film, presented actors in the nude, and *Ulysses* (1967), based on the James Joyce novel, gave the word "fuck" its cinematic debut.[36] The Canadian Supreme Court ruled in 1962 that D.H. Lawrence's novel *Lady Chatterly's Lover* was not obscene. Judge Judson wrote in his decision: "That the work under attack is a serious work of fiction is to me beyond question. It has none of the characteristics that are often described in judgments dealing with obscenity—dirt for dirt's sake, the leer of the sensualist, depravity in the mind of the author with an obsession for dirt...."[37] Judge Taschereau submitted a minority opinion. He thought that over three-quarters of the book dealt with "filthy, obscene descriptions" unrelated to the alleged literary purpose of the book. The citizens of Fort William and Port Arthur sided with Judge Taschereau and ceremoniously tossed the offending book into a bonfire.[38]

The Supreme Court in 1963 adopted "contemporary community standards" as their criteria for determining whether or not a work of art was obscene. According to the ruling, the standards were not to be set by either "those of lowest taste or interest" or those of "rigid, austere, conservative, or puritan taste and habit of mind." A middle way had to be found, one that was adjusted to the "general average of community thinking and feeling."[39] As a result, a more liberal public pushed the judiciary in a more lenient direction, and vice versa. Standards were eroded, and the range of what was

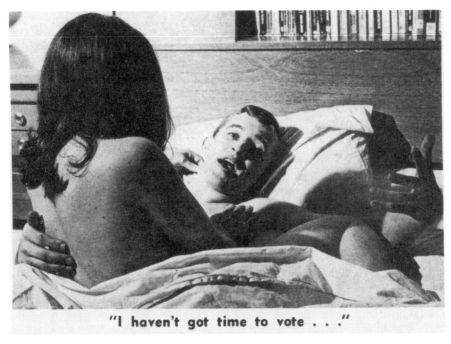

"I haven't got time to vote . . ."

The *Carillon*, 22 February 1967, used sexual innuendo to promote voter participation in student elections.

considered unwholesome for decent society grew ever narrower.[40]

The *Carillon's* treatment of sexual material was conservative compared to other publications in the sixties. A photo in the February 22, 1967, *Carillon* showed a man and woman under the sheets in bed. The man looks into the camera and says, "I haven't got time to vote,"[41] a coy reference to the student elections. An article promoting the World University Service "SHARE" campaign to raise funds for needy students and professors in the Third World featured an image of an almost naked female model, partially censored, with the caption "SHARE..." written underneath.[42] The cover of the March 22, 1968, issue presented, for no apparent reason, a backside view of a naked woman posing in front of a high-wheeled bicycle.[43] But the coup de grace, the image that led the Board of Governors to try to shut down the *Carillon*, was a drawing published in the December 6, 1968, issue (already discussed at some length in chapter 3). The administration seemingly failed to look past the drawing's depiction of human reproductive organs and insisted that

Provocative *Carillon* front page, 22 March 1968.

the bounds of good taste definitely had been breached. They took a strong stand—from which they were forced to beat a hasty retreat.[44]

Gay rights did not emerge as an issue until the late 1960s. The Supreme Court of Canada in 1967 ruled 3 to 2 to uphold the conviction of Everett George Klippert, who confessed to having had sex with men. The acts were consensual and had not been performed in a public place. Nevertheless, Klippert was sentenced to a three-year jail term. Even more serious, he was classified as a dangerous sexual offender, which meant that he could face indefinite imprisonment.[45] In December 1967, minister of justice Pierre Trudeau introduced an omnibus bill to amend the criminal code, which included a section legalizing homosexual acts in private between consenting adults aged twenty-one or older. The bill passed May 14, 1969 by a vote of 149 to 55 and took effect in August of that year.[46]

The Carillon first mentioned gay rights in October 1971. Interested persons were invited to a discussion group to talk about "the psychological, sociological, and legal hassles concerning the gay way of life." The notice of meeting assured potential participants that "there is no thought involved in any way of conversion, but rather a sincere desire to discuss the problems associated with accepting and understanding the gay person."[47] A February 1973 article had a less defensive tone. It announced that "an organization has been formed to affirm the dignity of gay people and to publicly uphold their right to full equality with heterosexuals." The association promoted the belief that "homosexuality is an integral part of human sexuality" and sought "to eliminate anti-homosexual content in courses and textbooks which perpetrate false and negative conceptions of homosexuality," as well as promote "consciousness raising and solidarity among gay people."[48]

When the Regina student newspaper first opened up the discussion of sexual mores and behavior in December 1961, there had been an outcry, especially from the religious groups on campus. By the end of the sixties, the tables had turned. Momentum shifted in favor of a more liberal code. Birth control was no longer much of an issue, and premarital sex was being normalized. Censorship standards were watered down, both at the campus level and in society at large. Gay rights were being talked about. The Carillon had been in the middle of the sexual revolution, often provocatively so, but it had not indulged in flagrant, sixties-style "fucking-in-the streets" rhetoric. By the measure of the more radical fringes of the counterculture, it was relatively tame—though people in Regina did not always think so.

Marijuana and LSD

"Sex, drugs, and rock 'n' roll" immediately come to mind whenever we think of the sixties counterculture. Drugs, the second part of the triad, were justified as the royal highway to an altered consciousness and enhanced perception. They were part of the project to turn away from the middle-class view of the world to something that was supposed to be much better and more meaningful. As historian David Farber rightly says: "… those academicians who have written about the 1960s, without any attempt to seriously or analytically relate drug consciousness to the events of the 1960s have done so at the cost of warping and misconstruing much of what went on."[49] Drugs facilitated the spiritual quest and the search for community inherent in the counterculture.

Prior to the sixties, illegal drug use (not including alcohol) had been a fairly minor problem in Canada. There were only 516 charges laid under the Narcotics Act in 1960, compared to 8,596 in 1970.[50] It was estimated in the latter year that 30 to 50 per cent of university students had used drugs (meaning LSD or marijuana), and as many as 25 per cent of Grade Twelve students.[51] This contrasted with 1955 when a House of Commons committee reported that marijuana was a negligible factor that constituted no threat to Canadian society. Drugs became a marker for the sixties, an indicator of whose side you were on. The penalties were harsh—as much as six months in jail for possession of marijuana. This meant that the stakes were high, much more serious than wearing your hair long or playing music that other people didn't like.

The counterculture invested LSD (lysergic acid diethylamide) with mystical properties; the establishment media said it damaged chromosomes and drove people to suicide. Dr. Albert Hofmann first synthesized the drug in 1938 in the laboratories of Sandoz Pharmaceuticals, Basel, Switzerland. After accidentally swallowing 250 micrograms (a millionth of an ounce), he experienced a strange sensation: "My field of vision swayed before me, and objects appeared distorted like images in curved mirrors … I thought I had died. My 'ego' was suspended somewhere in space and I saw my body laying dead on the sofa."[52] Sandoz made the drug available to medical researchers and psychiatrists around the world, including Dr. Humphry Osmond, clinical director at the mental hospital in Weyburn, Saskatchewan. Osmond theorized that LSD was a "psychomimetic" drug, that is, it simulated in normal people "some of the unbelievably unpleasant and sometimes quite terrifying mental agonies of the schizophrenic patient."[53] He ingested LSD as a means of "getting into the skin" of the mentally ill and understanding how they "perceive the world—its dimensions of time, space, and color." LSD also had potential for the treatment of alcoholism. One Weyburn study reported a recovery rate of 50 per cent among alcoholics who were given the drug.[54]

LSD was not exactly a hallucinogen. It did not produce visions of things that did not exist; rather, it enabled the user to see the world in a different way. As Osmond observed of his own LSD experiences: "A sense of special significance began to invest everything; everything was brilliantly sharp and significant ... A plain wooden chair was invested with a 'chairiness' no chair had ever had for me before."[55] British novelist Aldous Huxley, who was then living in California and writing scripts for Hollywood movies, learned of Osmond's work and invited him for a visit. Under Osmond's supervision, Huxley took mescaline in May 1953, which inspired him to write *The Doors of Perception*. After trying LSD for the first time in 1955, Huxley became a convert. He said the drug had taught him that love was the centre of all being and the secret of the cosmos.[56] He thought the world would be a better place if intellectuals, political leaders and other influential people took the drug and shared the insights he had experienced. Like Osmond, Huxley believed the word "hallucinogen" did not do justice to the wonders of LSD and proposed instead "phanerothyme." He composed a little poem: "To make this trivial world sublime, Take half a Gramme of phanerothyme." Osmond replied with a poem of his own: "To fathom hell or soar angelic, Just take a pinch of psychedelic."[57] Psychedelic means "mind-manifesting," that is, bringing to the surface what the mind already knows, but lies hidden in the depths of the unconscious. The psychedelic experience varied from person to person. It depended very much on the individual taking the drug and the circumstances in which it was taken. This was what LSD researchers referred to as the "set" and the "setting."[58]

Osmond joined forces with Dr. Abram Hoffer, a biochemist and psychiatrist at the University of Saskatchewan hospital in Saskatoon, and Dr. Duncan Blewett, professor of psychology at Regina Campus, to make the province of Saskatchewan a leader in LSD research.[59] Regina Campus student Dianne Leibel took the drug under Dr. Hoffer's supervision, January 29, 1963, and wrote up the experience for the *Carillon*:

> I could float about my hospital room at will. I still kept my
> eye out for my comfort, because I always took my bed on

these excursions. The bedspread, which was the usual hospital variety, seemed to be very heavy, to be bound with silk,
and to reach from ceiling to the floor … I have mentioned
that I didn't care about eating, but I did have a piece of toast.
I have never enjoyed chewing anything so much in my life,
and the honey smelled deliciously out of this world … For a
time I was much more conscious of light [the author of this
account was blind], and my sense of touch for a few days
was improved to the extent that I could trace lines of print
in ordinary books.[50]

By January 1964, Dr. Hoffer was sounding the alarm about students
taking hallucinogenic drugs, such as the cactus plant peyote, under unsupervised conditions. When not used properly and under the guidance of "properly trained and competent physicians," the compounds could aggravate
latent psychosis and trigger serious depression. "Even more dangerous,"
Hoffer warned, "is the use of certain morning glory seeds. They contain substantial quantities of ergot and consumption of these could lead to serious
poisoning.…"[61]

The *Carillon* in 1966 deplored the lurid stories and sensationalism surrounding the media discussion of psychedelic drugs. "It is time," the paper
editorialized, "to approach LSD as a scientific phenomenon, time to determine the extent of the minimal hazards of psychedelics and to explore in a
responsible, formal, investigative manner the proven potential of LSD." To
that end, it proposed the formation at the Regina Campus of an Institute of
Psychedelic Research. Drawing upon the expertise of scholars from a variety
of disciplines, "such an institute could prove to be a huge academic boon to
this university, providing it with a flame of rationality to hold against the
dark, fear-filled cavern of ignorance surrounding us."[62]

As it turned out, LSD moved out of the research laboratory and into
the street. Timothy Leary, a psychology professor who was fired from his job
at Harvard, advised everybody to "turn on, tune in, and drop out." Allen
Ginsberg, the living link with the Beats, took psilocybin (a synthesized com-
pound similar to magic mushrooms), stripped off his clothes and proclaimed,
"We're going to teach people to stop hating … start a peace and love movement."[63] The psychedelic lifestyle bloomed in the Haight-Ashbury district of
San Francisco, where the first human "be-in" took place on January 14, 1967,

Letter of Do-o-o-o-m . . . .

The Editor:

I wonder if you would mind alerting the student body to certain dangerous habits presently being carried out by some students.

It has been brought to my attention over the past year that some students are playing around with the hallucinogenic cactus plant Peyote. This plant contains mescaline as well as twelve other alkaloids. Mescaline and LSD are used in psychiatry and in psychiatric research for investigating aspects of behaviour, and as a treatment for certain mental diseases, especially alcoholism.

When used by properly trained and competent physicians these compounds are safe and effective. But students who take Peyote on their own, or who are given it by pseudo scientific students are running grave risks of doing harm to themselves. The dangers are that when not properly supervised they may suffer aggravation of a latent psychosis leading to serious depression. There is on record now a suicide in California as a result of the self use of these compounds.

Mescaline is a prescription drug and listed under Part I of the Schedule F of the Food and Drug Act. According to the act "These drugs must be sold only on prescription. Violations of these regulations will result in court action". Since mescaline is an ingredient of Peyote, it too must be considered a prescription drug.

Even more dangerous is the use of certain morning glory seeds. They contain substantial quatities of ergot and consumption of these could lead to serious poisoning or ergotism.

Students using these compounds should be aware (1) the use of Peyote under Canadian law is illegal and (2) there are grave risks to health.

A. Hoffer, Ph.D., M.D.
Director, Psychiatric Research

Early warning of the dangers of drug use, *Carillon*, 17 January 1964.

at Golden Gate Park. Over 25,000 men, women and children celebrated with music, poetry, sunshine, bells, incense, feathers, flags, and marijuana. Acid flowed "like lemonade."[64] In June, the tribes gathered at the 1967 Summer of Love Monterey Pop Festival where Janis Joplin, Jimi Hendrix, the Who, and the Grateful Dead performed before an audience of nearly 50,000.[65]

"Be-ins" and "love-ins" spread across North America. At Regina Campus the 1967 fall semester began with a love-in in the courtyard of the Classroom building. Four hundred students, many in bare feet, grooved to *Sgt Pepper's Lonely Hearts Club Band.* "Girls stood in long velvet dresses alongside a rectangular pool and gazed for endless minutes at its concrete bottom or played with rocks." Other students were "deeply engrossed with [the] stones of a sidewalk." They said they were "writing rock poems." David Fairley, an instructor in the English department who had helped organize the event, described it as "an outside in for those who are inside out."[66]

The psychedelic culture fascinated the mainstream media and the purveyors of popular culture. Gray Line Bus Company gave organized tours of "psychedelphia" (Haight-Ashbury), which it advertised as "the only foreign tour within the continental limits of the United States."[67] As the buses rolled by, hippies held up mirrors to the faces of the gawking tourists. Hordes of runaway teenagers and sensation-seekers flooded into the area, as did criminals who had nothing to do with the counterculture, but saw an opportunity for profits in the drug trade. Violent crime increased, and malnutrition, hepatitis and VD took their toll. As Martin Lee and Bruce Shlain, authors of *Acid*

The Haight-Ashbury district of San Francisco, the heart of the counterculture in 1967, now a commercialized tourist-trap. AUTHOR PHOTO

Dreams: The Complete Social History of LSD: The CIA, the Sixties, and Beyond, relate, "the acid ghetto was trampled to death during the Summer of Love, leaving a social sewer in its place."[68]

Reports began to appear in the mass media linking bad "trips" to mental illness and suicide. Although the dangers were real enough, some of the articles took on a hysterical tone. LSD was said to cause leukemia, chromosome damage, narcotics addiction, blindness, birth defects, and brain damage, not to mention rape, murder, and suicide.[69] Research studies had established that taking LSD in unsupervised settings sometimes had seriously negative consequences, including psychotic breakdowns.[70] The popular press took this scientific evidence and pushed it to the limit, churning out sensational stories that found a ready audience among middle-class parents, who were trying to figure out what had gone so badly wrong with their children. Drugs were an easy answer, an all-purpose scapegoat.[71] Just as Timothy Leary and other LSD advocates hyped the so-called benefits of the drug, the anti-LSD establishment sensationalized the dangers. LSD was not just a chemical substance; it was a symbol in the culture wars.

Duncan Blewett admitted that there was a downside to using the drug, especially if the conditions were not right: "When young people started using it, they'd go to a party or something and get stoned out of their gourd. There was no support system if they freaked out. They'd end up in a mental ward somewhere and get a shot of niacin or something to put them down. That wasn't a very effective way of getting them to consider what they were learning."[72] However, at a symposium on drugs held at Regina Campus in November 1969, he was upbeat, saying that: "… the whole trend of social evolution has been along a dimension of being. People are slowly becoming able to be themselves. Psychedelic drugs open up areas of your head, providing a link between the conscious and unconscious mind. Any method of extending your being can never be repressed or 'legislated out of existence.'"[73] Others on the panel were less sanguine. Gary Fields spoke of his own drug experiences. He said he had "started using acid quite often and enjoyed where he was at, however, it was still not enough. He had been through the revolutionary thing and couldn't find peace, or joy; drugs also couldn't help him—then he found Christ!"[74] In the early 1960s, government authorities in both Canada and the United States began to tighten restrictions on the use of LSD in scientific research.[75] This effectively shut down the Saskatchewan experiments that had been conducted by Osmond, Hoffer and Blewett. From there it was but a short step to banning the drug altogether.

In February 1973, fifty students and faculty at Regina Campus signed a petition calling for the release of Timothy Leary from jail. Leary, they said, "had found his people locked in the psychic prison of cynical, competitive materialism, riven with hatred, greed, despair and fear. He tried to give each of them the key to freedom, self-knowledge and self-actualization ... He has helped millions to find new love, life, beauty, joy and discernment. We owe him!"[76] Closer to home, John Gallagher wrote an editorial in the *Carillon* making the case for the legalization of marijuana. He observed that, by "some curious process of mental gymnastics," alcohol was legal, but pot was not. Indeed, society did not even recognize alcohol as a drug. Drugs were "something that dope-fiends take, while normal people enjoy a 'sociable drink' or 20 or 30 of them."[77] It was unjust to send people to jail for smoking pot, "a drug that is relatively harmless while in watering holes all over the city others escape their problems by drinking another drug that is physically harmful." Alcohol and pot, Gallagher argued, were both a means of social control. They kept people from "fac[ing] up to reality and attempting to change it." For this reason, he predicted that eventually pot would be legalized: "Industry will come to see it as an even more effective social control than alcohol. It interferes much less with the work-process than does alcohol, and it is probably a more complete form of escape." The major stumbling block was the beer and liquor industry, who "[stood] to lose substantial sums of money if society changes its consumption habits to another drug." In the end, Gallagher predicted, the "barons of booze" would be overruled. "One small segment of capital cannot long prevent the majority of capital from manifesting their will."

Gallagher's piece was typical of *Carillon* articles in that it located the counterculture in the framework of politics and economics. More specifically, Gallagher applied a Marxist analysis. Rather than talking about marijuana as a lifestyle or values issue, he discussed its role in the capitalist system. He argued that recreational drugs—whether alcohol or marijuana, it didn't matter—functioned (almost literally) as the opiate of the masses. Equally, Gallagher did not think the debate over legalization hinged on culture. He did not expect the hippies to win over the establishment with their arguments or vice versa. In his view, the economic power of the beer and liquor industry was the key factor. As long as it maintained its dominant position, pot would be illegal.

Notwithstanding the impression left by Gallagher's editorial or the petition supporting Timothy Leary, Regina Campus students were divided on the question of drugs. The Students' Union held a referendum, November 27, 1969, asking: "Are you in favor of the Students' Union presenting a brief for the legalization of marijuana to the Commission on Non-Medical use of Drugs?" Thirty-eight percent of eligible voters turned out, and, of these, 794 said yes and 635 no, hardly a ringing endorsement of the pro-drug position. The size of the negative vote is significant, especially given the fact that the referendum was held only a few months after Woodstock, the rock concert that is taken to represent the apex of the counterculture.[78] If the question had been asked about LSD, rather than marijuana, the negative vote would have been even higher.

Rock Music: The Sixties Soundtrack

As much as sex and drugs, if not more so, rock music put its stamp on the counterculture. The sixties had a soundtrack. James Miller, in *Flowers in the Dustbin: The Rise of Rock and Roll, 1947–1977*, remembers the impact the music had on him when he was growing up: "Still, if I'm honest, the most thrilling moments all came early, in the Fifties and Sixties, when the music was a primary focus of my energy, shaping my desires, coloring my memory, and producing the wild fantasy, widely shared, that my generation was, in some inchoate way, through the simple pleasure we all took in rock and roll, part of a new world dawning."[79] Myrna Kostash recalls the first time she heard Bob Dylan's "Desolation Row":

> It was late afternoon, I was drying dishes, and from the radio came a song, a song by Bob Dylan, and I stood transfixed, hand with plate poised mid-air, as the light went out of the room and, yes, I said, the war, the naked, the dead and the dying, the lies and the treachery and the filth heaping up in the streets around my room, yes, we are targets of the riot squad and ambulances of Desolation Row, we are the rearranged faces and assumed names of Desolation Row. Yes, we accept this grotesque and suffering self these songs make us an offering of. And all the rest of my life I will know this hour.[80]

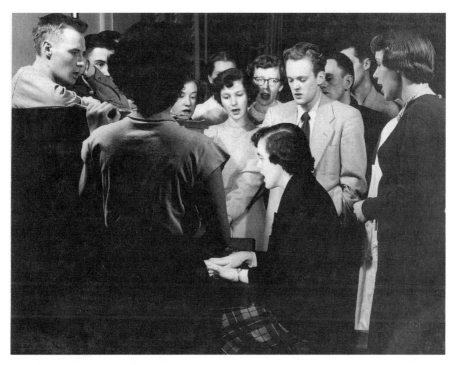

Students singing together at Regina College in the 1950s. SASKATCHEWAN ARCHIVES BOARD R-B6489

Such experiences were not uncommon. Music gave young people in the sixties an almost mystical sense of communion, an "affiliation with something larger and more powerful than themselves."[81]

The late 1950s and early 1960s witnessed a revival of folk music that was the immediate precursor of the golden age of rock. Groups such as Pete Seeger and the Weavers, the Kingston Trio, the Limeliters and New Christy Minstrels were popular. The Travellers had a hit with "This Land is Your Land," a Canadian version of the Woody Guthrie classic ("From Bonavista to Vancouver Island, from the Arctic Circle to the Great Lake waters, this land was made for you and me").[82] In Regina, the student newspaper pinpointed the arrival of the folk music craze on campus: "Folk-singing has finally hit Regina Campus. It came thundering in on Monday, November 7, 1961 … The songs we sing are expressive of our culture and our heritage. These folk songs will endure, even after we finish singing. So if you want to join us in re-

UNIVERSITY OF SASKATCHEWAN REGINA CAMPUS
STUDENTS' REPRESENTATIVE COUNCIL

presents

The Travellers
CANADIAN FOLK SINGERS
EXHIBITION AUDITORIUM

Saturday, Sept. 28, 1963
9:00 p.m.

$1.50 per person   —   University   — $1.50 per person

Above: Ticket for The Travellers' concert, *Carillon*, 25 September 1963

Right: Gordon Lightfoot, popular with Regina Campus students, *Carillon*, 3 March 1967.

Gordon Lightfoot

MARCH 9

Boyle Memorial
Gymnasium

There are
some tickets left
$2.50 - $2.00

viving old favorites, sea shanties, and good ol' drinking songs, then come out to folk-singing."[83] The SRC sponsored well-attended concerts by the Travellers in 1963[84] and Gordon Lightfoot in 1967.[85]

More than any other artist, Bob Dylan took the folk tradition and adapted it to the sixties vernacular. Born in 1941 in Minnesota, Dylan traveled to New York in January 1961. He wanted to visit his folk music hero, Woody Guthrie, described by music critic Greil Marcus as "troubadour of the dispossessed, poet of the Great Depression, ghost of the American highway, a man blown by the wind and made out of dust."[86] Guthrie, who suffered from Huntington's Chorea, a degenerative neurological disorder, was living in a New Jersey state hospital. Dylan was able to see him, and they struck up a friendship. He wrote "Song to Woody" for him and recorded it on his first album. For Dylan, folk music was the key to understanding America and the world. As he said: "Folk songs played in my head, they always did. Folk songs were the underground story ... It was what the country was talking about. Everything was simple—seemed to make some kind of splendid, formulaic sense."[87]

Dylan went one step further. He began to use the folk idiom to talk about things that were happening around him and in society at large. He tried out this material at Greenwich Village clubs, alternating his songs, delivered in talking-blues style, with funny, ironical patter. Eight months after arriving in New York, he had a contract with Columbia Records. His first album, released in March 1962, had only two of his own songs and did not make much of an impact. The second album, *The Freewheelin' Bob Dylan* (May 1963) broke new ground. The Beatles, just on the brink of Beatlemania, were touring in France when it came out. They played it non-stop for three weeks in their Paris hotel.[88] The tracks included "Oxford Town" (about racial segregation at the University of Mississippi), "Masters of War" (an indictment of the arms trade), "A Hard Rain's A-Gonna Fall (inspired by the Cuban missile crisis), "Talkin' World War Three Blues" (the world after the bomb goes off), and "Blowin' in the Wind," which became an instant sixties anthem.[89] Dylan's songs did not preach, but rather made the listener think about issues in a new way. The answer was "blowin' in the wind." Did that mean it was obvious, borne on the winds of change, or did it mean that the answer was elusive, as difficult to grasp as a will-o'-the-wisp?

Dylan became the golden boy of folk, the poster boy of the Left. He traveled to the South and performed at civil rights demonstrations. He sang in front of the Lincoln Memorial in Washington, D.C., in August 1963 when Martin Luther King, Jr., gave the "I Have A Dream" speech. But, at the height of his folk music fame, Dylan turned away from what he called "finger-pointing songs." The decisive break occurred July 25, 1965, at the Newport Folk Festival. He scandalized the audience by going electric, abandoning folk music for rock and roll.[90] His fans booed him, not just at Newport, but also through the months of concert touring that followed, both in the United States and Britain. The betrayal operated at more than one level. Folk music was perceived as pure, non-commercial, traditional, idealistic, and leftist; rock, by contrast, was considered to be corrupt, selfish, mass market, vulgar, and not political. At Newport, Dylan made a political, as well as a musical, statement.[91] The crowd reacted as they did partly because the music was loud and they couldn't make out the words. More importantly, they sensed that Dylan was turning his back on the sixties they wanted to believe in, that is, the sixties where people joined hands and sang "We Shall Overcome," their hearts burning with the certain knowledge that they knew how to make a better world. They reacted angrily to Dylan's Newport statement because they knew deep down that he was right: things weren't so simple.

Dylan released "Like a Rolling Stone" in July 1965. Greil Marcus claims that the song "melted the mask of what was beginning to be called youth culture; and even more completely the mask of modern culture as such."[92] Superficially, it is about a high-class woman who has fallen on hard times ("Once upon a time you dressed so fine … Now you don't seem so proud about haven' to be scrounging your next meal"). The narrator sneers at the woman, insistently asking, "How does it feel?" Metaphorically, the song addresses the sixties generation, who also have been riding high. They had come from comfortable, middle-class homes ("bred in at least modest comfort" the Port Huron statement said), had attended the best schools, and felt that they had everything under control. They freed themselves from old ways of thinking and from traditional morals, philosophy and religion. What had been the result? Dylan doesn't say. He just asks, "How does it feel? To be on your own, With no direction home, A complete unknown, Like a rolling stone."[93]

The song is a critique of the sixties from the heart of the sixties; it is an anti-*Howl* or, perhaps, *Howl* updated. Dylan does not advocate turning back the clock or pretending the sixties never happened. His point is that freedom is problematic. It's exhilarating not to be tied down or homebound, to explore ideas and do what whatever you want to do. But there is a price, a spiritual impoverishment that parallels the physical destitution of the fallen woman on the streets, who asks, "Do you want to make a deal?" When Dylan wrote "Like a Rolling Stone," the worst of the sixties had not yet happened: the riots, the Weather Underground's "days of rage," the assassinations and bombings. That came later. But already in 1965, he sensed where the sixties were heading. After his motorcycle accident in 1966, he retreated to family life and seclusion. "I don't know what everybody else was fantasizing about but what I was fantasizing about was a nine-to-five existence, a house on a tree-lined block with a white picket fence, pink roses in the backyard. That would have been nice. That was my deepest dream."[94] "Whatever the counterculture was," he added, "I'd seen enough of it."[95]

"Like a Rolling Stone" changed the direction of popular music. It gave rock and roll permission to deal with serious subject matter, not just "She Loves You, Yeah, Yeah, Yeah." Paul Simon acknowledged Dylan's contribution, saying, "He made us feel at a certain time that it was good to be smart, to be observant, that it was good to have a social conscience."[96] The impact on the Beatles was noticeable, as their music became more introspective and thoughtful, beginning with *Rubber Soul* in the fall of 1965. The barriers dividing musical genres broke down, and a new world of artistic possibilities opened up. The political content and social awareness of folk merged with the mass appeal of rock and roll. These developments transformed rock and roll into rock, marking it as the distinctive cultural idiom of the sixties.

The *Carillon* had a regular music column titled "Records" written by

John Blewett. He commented on the changes that had occurred in popular music: "Eight years ago hit parades were about little boys and girls who tried to get something going at the high school prom or in daddy's Ford ... This kind of crap persisted in an unadulterated stream from our radios for half the decade ... In 1965 a new theme was added to pop music's repertoire. It happened when Bob Dylan, Barry McGuire, P.F. Sloane and the Rolling Stones demonstrated that songs with polysyllabic lyrics were still commercial."[97] In true *Carillon* style, Blewett took direct aim at the business side of the rock music industry:

> Rock and roll was, is, and probably ever shall be a commercial enterprise. The recording companies that merchandise the music are ultimately profit-oriented. If it can be said that the recording industry is among the best industries in North America in terms of racial integration, then the rationale is financial expediency rather than good Karma. If the recording companies produce music that motivates people to examine, challenge and restructure their environment, this can only be attributed to blind fate. Organizations like Columbia, RCA Victor, and Capitol are steeped in the materialistic technocracy that permeates this continent. To attribute any motive other than greed to the executive moguls at RCA is to be naïve.[98]

In like manner, the *Carillon* portrayed Woodstock as primarily a money-making enterprise. This went against the grain of most interpretations of the event its organizers advertised as "The Woodstock Music and Art Fair: An Aquarian Exposition," held August 15-17, 1969, at Max Yasgur's farm in upstate New York. Fans were invited to spend $18 for a ticket to hear Jimi Hendrix, Janis Joplin, Joan Baez, Arlo Guthrie, The Grateful Dead, Jefferson Airplane, Creedence Clearwater Revival, Country Joe and the Fish, and Crosby, Stills, Nash and Young, among others. The expected crowd of 100,000 swelled to 400,000, making it impossible to collect the admission fee and forcing the organizers to throw the gates open to all comers. Despite horrendous logistical problems, including shortages of food, water, toilets, and medical supplies, a mood of peace, harmony, and cooperation prevailed.[99] "Woodstock is the great example of how it is going to be in the future," exulted Timothy

Karl Marx as rock star, *Carillon*, 11 September 1970, symbol of the complicated relationship between radical politics and the counterculture.

Leary. "We have the numbers. The loving and peaceful are the majority. The violent and authoritarian are the minority. We are winning. And soon."[100]

The *Carillon* did not quite see it that way. It noted that it cost $2.25 to see the movie about the "free" festival: "Woodstock—the whole thing—the festival, the records, the movie, and myriad other promotional gimmicks—amounts to the biggest, grossest heist pulled in public for some time." According to the *Carillon*, it was a classic instance of turning culture into a commodity:

> Woodstock functions by mystifying the youth culture and then selling the product back to North American youth. Because they are essentially buying themselves in a processed and packaged form, the customers must be manipulated by the promoters into identifying with the product. Woodstock, therefore, must become something that all young people are proud of, a monumental accomplishment of the generation. Since part of the product is the anti-profit-making ethic, this necessarily involves a little sleight of hand. The customers just can't figure out that a profit is being made off of them. So far "the most aware generation ever" appears to be too dumb to notice what's happening to them.[101]

Not all of the *Carillon's* coverage of the music scene was as stringently political as the Woodstock commentary. When Pink Floyd came to town in October 1970, student journalists took delight in a lengthy interview with Dave Gilmour, Roger Waters, Rick Wright and Nick Mason.[102] Larry Day wrote a laudatory review of a Joni Mitchell concert in Saskatoon, though half of it dealt with the trials of driving from Regina to Saskatoon in the middle of a prairie blizzard. "To hear that fluty, hauntingly pastoral voice of hers echoing through a totally silent full house," he said, "is enough to make anyone temporarily forget about blizzards, or accommodations or academic pressures."[103] The *Carillon* also reviewed the big albums of the sixties, such as the Rolling Stones' *Let it Bleed*, which it described as "music that will send shivers up the spine and scare you a little":

> 'You Can't Always Get What You Want' is the last cut and the album's crowning achievement. They use horns, three female vocalists, plus the London Bach Choir … Play it often and remember, as the dust jacket says, 'This Record Should Be Played Loud.'[104]

When Jimi Hendrix and Janis Joplin died, both at a young age, the *Carillon* published eulogies. It said of Hendrix:

> Who really gives a damn if Hendrix found relief in the drug scene? Who actually needs to be told over and over again that that habit snuffed out his life after only 27 years? The importance of drugs to Hendrix has absolutely nothing to do with the impression he made on the minds of acid rock lovers throughout the world. Why can't the fast buck press people put the emphasis where it belongs … on his musical contribution to the younger generation … Somewhere out there a "purple haze" surrounds the soul of Jimi Hendrix. A purple haze that encases a challenging and changing light that left mortal man with one of the finest gifts ever. The gift is a simple one. The expression of one's innermost feelings through music that meets the needs and challenges of today's generation. Jimi Hendrix was a big, big man.[105]

The tribute to Joplin was equally heartfelt: "When she sang, she didn't sing from thoughts but from pure raw feeling. Her voice could be a high feline scream or a rasping growl. But it was a voice of a person driven by pure emotion … We loved her—God knows."[106]

The Spiritual Heart of the Counterculture

While sex, drugs and rock and roll were important elements of the counterculture, there was much more to it than that. As historian James Farrell remarks, the counterculture challenged society's dominant myths— "the work ethic, utilitarian individualism, repressive sexuality, Cartesian rationality, technocratic scientism, denominational religion, industrial capitalism, lifestyle suburbanism, and compulsive consumerism."[107] The word "hippie" derives from "hip," which, in turn, is rooted in the Wolof (an African language spoken by slaves who came to America from Senegal and coastal Gambia) "hepi" ("to see") or "hipi" ("to open one's eyes").[108] It was used on this continent as early as the 1700s. The slaves also brought "dega," a Wolof verb for "understand," which entered English as "dig." They had to talk in a coded language of in-group communication because it was too dangerous for them to speak openly and directly in words that their masters could understand. Consequently, "hip" connoted enlightenment, that is, knowledge that was hidden from others.

By 1860, there were almost 4 million slaves in the United States, out of a total population of 31 million. But, unlike the huge sugar plantations of Brazil and the Caribbean, where slaves lived in a separate world apart from their white owners, farms were relatively small and required few slaves. This meant that the races lived together, "unequally but intimately."[109] Many whites did not own slaves and worked alongside them in the fields as indentured laborers or low-class wage earners. There were many opportunities for the races to mingle with one another, each culture influencing the other. This interpenetration accounts for much of the dynamism and creativity of American culture, for example, in the development of jazz and rock and roll. Just as the Beats were drawn to African-American lifestyles, so, too, the counterculture bears the imprint of its influence. As Norman Mailer noted, the hipster was a white negro.[110]

The notion of hip seeped into Regina Campus in the early 1960s. A party in the college residence in November 1960 had a beatnik theme:

> Bill Taylor set the theme with the rhythmic beat of his bongos. Miriam Promislow recited poetry to the accompaniment of wailing jazz. Traditional Beatnik candles in wine bottles

added to the effect by their mysterious flickering light. One courageous soul came costumed as a conformist, but the Beatnik crowd soon turned him into a cool cat with disheveled hair and a black shoe polish beard.[111]

A jazz concert at the campus in 1961 advertised "The Street Swingers," who were described as "a septet of local college hippies."[112] (It is interesting that the word "hippie" was being used in the Regina Campus newspaper in 1961, well before 1965, the year most secondary sources say it was coined by Herb Caen of the *San Francisco Chronicle* in reference to the cultural rebels of Haight-Ashbury.[113]) "Cool jazz and poetry readings" were also on offer at the Village Coffee House, which opened its doors in 1965.[114]

The campus newspaper in 1961 published "On Chianti," a critique of mainstream culture's obsession with "Detroit's last bloated offerings, pastel toilet paper, and togetherness and television programs that always end happily, and never offend minority groups, but which always manage to offend everybody else with their commercials."[115] A set of cartoons in November 1969 also developed a countercultural theme. The last frame taught the lesson: "The way for us all is within ourselves. To find it one must take one cosmic step in the mind. One must stop running. Only then do we see."[116] Student Howard Halpern went so far as to suggest that weather reporters stop giving specific numbers for temperatures in their broadcasts:

> Our differences must be emphasized, no matter how small or meaningless. Similarities (for example, the fact that we're all cold) are overlooked. Scores are kept. Highs and lows are always given, as though Saskatoon with a temperature of 40 below was "beating out" Regina, which has only 13 ... A report on the condition of the environment, potentially one of the most unifying forces in society, turns out to be something that categorizes, delimits, and divides. What is even more typical, and of greater concern, is the way people are quantified, measured, "broken down," and precisified [*sic*] to the point where they, and we, become meaningless. Quantification in such cases, is at best an intellectual exercise; at worst, self-mockery.[117]

The importance of "being," as opposed to "doing," *Carillon*, 7 November 1969.

Jesus Christ, represented as hero of the counterculture, *Carillon*, 2 December 1966.

Thomas J. Burns assailed the tyranny of the automobile: "Not only does the air of our fair 'Queen City of the Plains' reek with its fumes, our junkyards and dumps bulge with its remains, a large bulk of our real estate caters to its whims, the streets run red with blood and a mixture of glass and tin, but now pedestrians are legally required to stay in a place of safety, i.e. indoors."[118]

Enemies of the Counterculture

The counterculture had its critics, and at times the battle was fierce. The conflict was dramatized in the 1969 movie *Easy Rider,* in which Peter Fonda and Dennis Hopper played hippies riding their motorcycles from California to New Orleans on a symbolic journey down freedom road. They are arrested in a redneck town, where they meet up with Jack Nicholson, a small-town lawyer and former football hero turned disillusioned drunk. The journey ends tragically. Nicholson is beaten to death, and Hopper and Fonda are shot down and killed from their bikes. The *Carillon* published two reviews. James Henshaw described the film as a "brutal indictment of the American way of life," but added: "… to say that *Easy Rider* is talking about America alone is very untrue. Many of the sequences could easily have been filmed in rural Saskatchewan and Regina. Don't kid yourself, man. I've lived many of the film's scenes personally and so have most of this town's long hairs, rock bands and freaks."[119] Peter Larson, the other reviewer, agreed: "If you're a head or a radical or an Indian, or a Black, you'll recognize Saskatchewan writ large. The valleys are more spectacular, the heads are hipper, the flower people have real flowers, the rich are richer, the poor are poorer, the pigs are even more piggier, the whores have more paint on their faces, the New Orleans Mardi Gras is the Regina Chamber of Commerce's ideal conception of Buffalo Days, and at least the bigots are honest. But the stakes are the same."[120]

The conflict between mainstream culture and counterculture created tensions between town and gown. The Regina Chamber of Commerce prepared a brief, "The Role of the University in the Community," which condemned university professors who used "legitimate dissent as a cover to promote riots" and "orgies of destruction." According to the brief, "students [were] entering society without the ability to make seasoned judgments in respect to social and political factors because of biases emanating from contemporary teachers who, themselves have been given incorrect informa-

Easy Rider advertisement in the *Carillon*, 24 October 1969. The paper saw close parallels between the movie and the attitudes towards the counterculture in Saskatchewan.

tion."[121] Regina Campus principal John Archer defended the students in a speech to the Kiwanis Club, praising them as "a fine generation—the brightest, best prepared, most sensitive generation ever to go to university." Justice R.L. Brownridge stood up and disagreed with Archer. The judge "estimated that about five per cent of the young were at war with society and yet they expect the older generation to applaud their efforts ... Let's not be the first generation to run up the white flag. Let's not defend the indefensible." He did not want to see "every hoodlum who parades under a university banner defended by university professors." Archer held his ground. He said that he thought that students should sit on university committees and boards, and that "universities will probably be much better for it."[122] The *Carillon* thanked the principal for his support.[123]

Relations between police and students constituted another arena of conflict. The RCMP had Regina Campus under surveillance, along with other universities in Canada.[124] Even minor events, such as the showing of a documentary film, "The Guerrilla Struggle in Venezuela," September 30, 1966, were targets of police investigation.[125] The RCMP followed anti-war activities with interest, one officer reporting, "The subtle workings of the left-wing element continued and an indication of their success was seen during May 1967 when 47 out of 210 faculty members of the University signed a petition urging Canada to support UN proposals in Vietnam and the prohibition of arms shipments to the US."[126] The *Carillon* reported in December 1963 that the RCMP had attempted to recruit a student to spy on his fellow students. The paper condemned this activity as a breach of academic freedom:

> A university must remain an institution where scholars can congregate in an atmosphere conducive to thought, discussion and learning. Such an atmosphere is destroyed completely with the thought that one of your classmates might be a police agent making up a dossier on the basis of your comments in discussions—a dossier that could affect your future livelihood. Even the most completely devoted academics are liable someday to have a wife and children to support and will have to consider all his remarks in the light of such ...What student is going to profess—because he believes in it, or simply for the sake of argument—a belief that Marxian Communism is the answer to the world's problems

when an RCMP agent is noting beside his name the tag, "Communist"?[127]

Radicals referred to police as "pigs," and the *Carillon* published a picture of a pig in RCMP uniform mounted on a horse.[128]

The hostility to city police was just as intense. The *Carillon* collected quotes, which it attributed to police chief Arthur G. Cookson. He was alleged to have said:

> These people [radicals] are trying to change everything. They're trying to push out on the boundaries of knowledge. We've got Maoists, Marxists, Cheists, Freudists, any kind of ist ... how many concessions are you going to grant these dissidents? Are they going to be satisfied when you do grant them? ... It's got to be tied to an international organization. Anything I've heard here—revolution is the only answer—the people will rule—these are stock slogans. I'm satisfied it's an international organization. They're left of the left, Maoists quarrelling with Leninists and Marxists, I think it's a matter to be concerned with. They're undermining our youth, clouding their brains with drugs.[129]

On Victoria Day, 1971, a crowd gathered around the band shell in Wascana Park for a concert. Someone went to the microphone and said he had acid for sale. Nobody paid much attention to him or tried to make a purchase. Three police officers approached the seller and carried out a body search. He was clean, but when the police tried to search another man sitting close by, he made a run for it, the police in hot pursuit. One of the officers made a flying tackle and brought the man down. The police started to drag him out of the park. Several hundred people gathered around and began to chant, "Let him go, let him go." The officers started "beating upon the prisoner's head like a bongo drum." A man in a suit stood up and said, "The cops have no right to harass us!" The crowd roared its approval. The police arrested him, too. The spectators kicked in the headlights of the police cruiser and grabbed the aerial of the car. Twenty more city police officers arrived on the scene, along with four RCMP. Isolated battles broke out as the police arrested or attacked other men and women. Ultimately, eleven people were charged. The *Carillon* put the blame squarely on the police: "Trouble could have been avoided if the cops didn't beat people. It was interesting to note that the crowd was made up of old and young, short haired and long haired, straights and freaks, all of them wanting to fight the cops."[130]

The *Carillon* questioned why the Moose Jaw police needed to be equipped with mace. The US surgeon-general had warned that the gas could cause "death from respiratory arrest or peripheral vascular collapse." The real purpose of the chemical, the *Carillon* charged, was not riot control, "but rather in immobilizing an individual prisoner when he talks back or doesn't 'cooperate.'"[131] In another incident, a Regina student hitchhiked a ride with "a lad from Philadelphia who had, among other things, long hair." The car was pulled over near Brandon and the vehicle searched. The police officer found a quantity of "cannabis sativa, better known as grass." The two men were taken to the station for questioning. "Take off your clothes, son," the officer instructed. The student complied: "So there I stand, in all my glory … in my shorts … I mean … well you know what I mean. Then he says, take off your shorts. MY SHORTS … Keerist, where in hell does he think I'm hiding it?"[132]

While confrontations with the police could be frightening and dangerous, they were at least open and direct. Other attacks on the counterculture were more subtle. Co-optation was the process by which the "emblems of dissent were quickly translated into harmless commodities, emptied of their content and sold to their very originators as substitutes for the real things."[133] Through commercialization, the idealistic essence of the counterculture was neutralized. Pepsi launched its youth-oriented "Pepsi Generation" advertising campaign in 1963, Dodge "Challenger" ads in 1969 pitted a hip nonconformist against an obnoxious policeman, Buick promised that its 1970 models would "light your fire," and Clairol in 1967 introduced "psychedelicious beiges" for lipstick and nail polish.[134] People were encouraged to rebel through consumption. A letter to the *Carillon* described this phenomenon in 1968:

> In response to shouts of protest from anguished parents, whose children have discovered the effects of marijuana and LSD, the straight society pursues its course of persecuting hallucinogenic drug users … Yet at the same time pscyhedelia pushes every product from cars to clothes at the ever-

avid consumer. Beardsley posters proclaim not only love-ins but "Dodge fever." We watch TV via our "turned-on" channel. Radios broadcast hit parade songs which describe the "highs" that various drugs give. The straight society gladly accepts the trappings of the drug culture. Perhaps it doesn't realize that the brightly-colored swirls and paisleys of psychedelia represent, although palely, the hallucinations seen under acid.[135]

Psychedelic artwork and graphic design were ubiquitous in the 1960s, influencing, for a time, the look of the *Carillon* masthead.[136] The paper also published advertisements that played on and manipulated countercultural themes. Mining company Rio Algom/Rio Tinto tried to recruit employ-

9 November 1962

3 February 1967

1 March 1968

The *Carillon* masthead had various designs during the sixties. It went psychedelic (above, centre) for ten issues in 1967, beginning with 3 February 1967 and ending with 10 April 1967.

Carillon, 16 October 1970

ees with the pitch: "join our young Rock Group."[137] Coca-Cola advertised "what the world needs today are containers that re-cycle." It promoted its returnable bottle as "the answer to an ecologist's prayer."[138] Player's cigarettes exploited the sixties penchant for individual self-expression: "In your own way. In your own time. On your own terms. You'll take to the taste of Player's Filter."[139] Contac-C promised relief "for those 12-hour sit-ins,"[140] and coyly intimated that "most co-eds take the capsule."[141] Even local businesses got into the act. A Regina stereo outlet ad showed a nude couple, with the caption, "The world's second best reproduction system."[142]

The ads represented the commercialization of the counterculture, but they also probed its complexity. There was something in the counterculture that the "system" could work with. Rock music was both a vehicle for protest and a multi-million dollar industry. Woodstock was both a be-in and a blockbuster movie. As Arthur Marwick observes, the sixties were associated with an "outburst of entrepreneurialism, individualism, doing your own thing."

Carillon, 9 October 1970   Carillon, 9 March 1973

Facing page, this page and following page: Big business used the counterculture to appeal to the youth market.

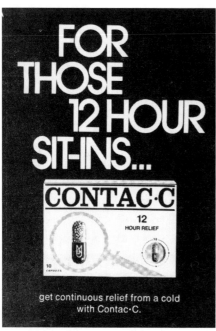

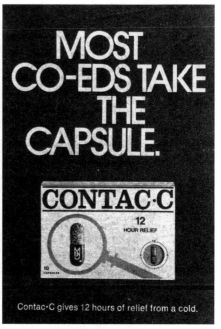

Carillon, 26 February 1971   *Carillon*, 4 December 1970

Carillon, 19 October 1973

He refers to "the founding of theatres, clubs, boutiques, modeling and pho-tographic agencies, book shops, cafes, restaurants, art galleries, 'arts labs,' pornographic and listings magazines, and design studios."[143] Roger Lewis adds that the head shops selling funky clothes, hand-made leather goods, pots, posters, books, pipes, and other counterculture paraphernalia were all part of the web of entrepreneurial capitalism.[144] It's not just that commerce corrupted the counterculture; there was an element of commerce already built into it. For all the rhetoric about altered consciousness, self-actualiza-tion and building a new society, the counterculture of sex, drugs and rock and roll contained a hedonistic element. While the counterculture opposed major tenets of mainstream culture, it also had a potential point of contact with liberal individualism and capitalism. Capitalism is highly adaptable and dynamic. It found a way to transform the celebration of human freedom and individual self-expression into a lifestyle based on hip consumerism.

The *Carillon* intuited the ambiguity. While praising and endorsing the counterculture, it was aware of the political and economic implications. It interpreted rock music as the product of a highly profitable industry, reduced Woodstock to a commercial proposition, analyzed the debate about drug le-galization in terms of the interests of the beer and liquor industry, and called attention to the impact of psychedelic culture on Madison Avenue. The *Caril-lon* supported the counterculture, but kept the focus on politics. Regina Cam-pus students were true to their Saskatchewan roots. They lived in a political city in a political province, and that was a heritage they could not easily escape.

CHAPTER 8

1968: The Year the Sixties Changed

Historian Mark Lytle summarizes what he calls the conventional narrative of the sixties:

Once upon a time, Americans lived in a world of social conservatism and political consensus. Preoccupied with the Communist menace, the nation's leaders refused to acknowledge fundamental domestic problems, including the second-class status of African Americans, Latinos, homosexuals, and women. Along came a generation of grassroots social, political, and cultural movements. Inspired by John Kennedy and their own youthful idealism, they insisted that the nation live up to its democratic, egalitarian ideals. While the power elite tried to accommodate and channel these movements, it got the country bogged down in a morally ambiguous Southeast Asian war. Everything came to a head in 1968. Protest brought down some of the war makers and made the war increasingly unpopular. After that, the extreme behaviors of political and social protest groups provoked widespread resentment and government repression. Unable to achieve their idealistic goals, movements became increasingly frustrated, fragmented, and polarized. Richard Nixon, the enigmatic man who ruled by dividing the nation, saw his presidency collapse from its abuse of power. After that everyone was so tired, they had to take a break.[1]

The narrative identifies 1968 as the pivot, the year the sixties changed. It has a common-sense appeal that is well supported by the evidence. In early April 1968, Martin Luther King, Jr., went to Memphis, Tennessee, to lend his support to a garbage collectors' strike. Most were black and underpaid. They marched with placards that read, "I am a Man." On the evening of April 3, King delivered his "I Have Been to the Mountaintop" speech. He said that he had never expected to live a long life (he often remarked that he did not think he would live to see his 40th birthday—he died at age 39), but that this was not a matter of great concern to him. The important thing was *how* you lived, not *how long*. As for him, he said he had been to the mountaintop and had seen the Promised Land. The next night, April 4, 1968, stepping out onto his motel balcony, he was gunned down. As news of the assassination spread across America, riots broke out in more than one hundred cities. Forty-six people were killed, 3,000 injured, and 21,000 arrested. Black power advocate Stokely Carmichael commented ominously: "When white America killed Dr. King, she declared war on us."[2]

Meanwhile, at Columbia University in New York, that same month, students occupied the classroom and administration building and the library. The SDS (Students for a Democratic Society), who led the action, ended their letter to university president Grayson Kirk with the sentence: "Up against the wall, motherfucker, this is a stick up."[3] The students were opposed to the university's plans to build a gymnasium in Morningside Park, which would deprive poor children in the neighbourhood of playground space. They also objected to the weapons development being carried on at Columbia's Institute for Defense Research. The students occupied President Kirk's office, rummaging through his files, drinking his sherry, and smoking his cigars. They also burned the research notes and book manuscript of a history professor, whose work they did not approve of. After a week, Kirk called in the police. They dragged the students out, banging their heads on the stairs and beating them severely. The university was in chaos, and shortly afterwards, Kirk resigned.

In Paris, students demanded reforms to the rigid and elitist education system. They occupied the Sorbonne and settled down to a "festival of talk," with slogans such as: "It is prohibited to prohibit. Liberty begins with one prohibition: that against harming the liberty of others," "The dream is reality," "Be realistic, demand the impossible," and "I am a Marxist, Groucho tendency."[4] For a time it appeared that Communist trade unions, pursuing their own agenda of better pay and a shorter workweek, would join forces with students to bring down the government. In the end, however, the unions thought better of it. They feared the anarchist element in the New Left that seemed to want to destroy everything, including the machinery in factories that workers depended on for their livelihood. By the end of May 1968, it was all over, but for a while it looked as though France would suffer a complete breakdown.

The American political system also experienced a crisis, largely the result of the continuing casualties from the Vietnam War. On March 31, 1968, President Lyndon Johnson announced that he would not stand for re-election. His failure to find a solution to the war had doomed his candidacy. Senator Eugene McCarthy, the peace candidate who wanted to pull out of Vietnam, did surprisingly well in the New Hampshire primary (42% of the vote),[5] prompting Bobby Kennedy to make a run for the Democratic party nomination. On June 5, 1968, while celebrating his victory in the California primary at the Ambassador Hotel in Los Angeles, Kennedy was shot and killed. The assassination, coming so soon after that of Martin Luther King, sent waves of grief and despair through America and beyond. Kennedy had been the one person who seemed capable of bridging the differences in a deeply divided country. His appeal extended to students, blue-collar workers, women, blacks, the middle class and the poor. Now the hope of peaceful reconciliation was gone. America entered a dark period of its history.

As the August 1968 Democratic party national convention approached, Chicago prepared for the worst. Radical groups planned massive demonstrations, while Mayor Richard Daley vowed to prevent long-haired freaks from disrupting the city. The yippies (Youth International Party) threatened to put LSD into the water system and predicted that thousands of young people would float nude in Lake Michigan and make love in the parks and on the beaches. They also nominated a pig as their candidate for the presidency. Daley put in place some 12,000 police, 6,000 Illinois National Guardsmen, and 7,500 army personnel, some of whom had just returned from Vietnam.[6] On August 28, 1968, police charged and indiscriminately clubbed protesters, bystanders and reporters. The student demonstrators chanted, "The whole world is watching."[7] The majority of Americans (those Richard Nixon called the "silent majority") had growing doubts about the Vietnam War, but they were even more appalled at the unruly, disrespectful conduct of the yippies. Nixon ran on a law-and-order platform and was elected president in November.

Trajectory of the Student Movement

For the student movement, too, the year 1968 was a turning point. Its trajectory mirrored that of the sixties as a whole. The SDS began hopefully in the early 1960s as the signature New Left organization. As we have seen, the Port Huron statement in 1962 offered an idealistic vision for the renewal of democracy in America. At Berkeley in October 1964, the Free Speech Movement was triggered by the university's decision to ban political activity on campus. Traditionally, students had a space where they could set up tables, solicit funds and distribute literature. Many of them had been in Mississippi during the summer of 1964, working to register African American voters. When they returned to school in the fall, they wanted to continue their involvement in the civil rights movement. They saw the ban on politics as an indirect attack on these activities.

On October 1, 1964, the police arrested Jack Weinberg, a former Berkeley student and civil rights activist, who had set up a table in the prohibited area. Several hundred students surrounded the police car, preventing it from

Free Speech Movement Café, today a hub of the Berkeley campus, University of California.
AUTHOR PHOTO

Plaque at the Free Speech Café, memorializing Berkeley student leader Mario Savio. AUTHOR
PHOTO

leaving the campus. The protest demonstration continued for thirty-two hours, as students (having first taken off their shoes), one after the other, climbed to the top of the car to give speeches. They quoted Greek philosophers and spoke of the struggle for liberty at the time of the French Revolution. All they had been learning in their philosophy and political science classes suddenly had a practical and direct application. The university administration finally agreed to negotiate, and the demonstration was suspended.

By November, university president Clark Kerr had reneged on his commitment. Student leader Mario Savio delivered what became one of the most frequently quoted speeches of the student power movement (it was reprinted in the *Carillon*): "There is a time when the operation of the machine becomes so odious, makes you so sick at heart that you can't take part; you can't even tacitly take part, and you've got to put your bodies upon the levers, upon all the apparatus, and you've got to make it stop. And you've got to indicate to the people who run it, to the people who own it, that unless you're free, the machine will be prevented from working at all."[8] One thousand students moved into Sproul Hall for a sit-in. At four o'clock in the morning, 600 police entered the building and made arrests. Almost 800 students were taken into custody, the largest mass arrest in California history.[9] The protests continued through the fall of 1964 until finally, in January 1965, the university conceded the students' right to set up tables and carry on political activities on university property.[10]

The Berkeley protests had massive media coverage and resonated with students across North America. The *Carillon* acclaimed the victory of the Free Speech Movement: "Berkeley demonstrated that legitimate grievances would receive attention from administrators only if the students showed that they would not be ignored. They could only show their concern by taking mass action, by striking. They could only take action after organizing themselves into a flexible, viable body of people who drew strength from their convictions and acted upon them with vigour."[11] The paper then drew a direct lesson for Regina. "This university is run by the same kind of men who ran Berkeley. They have the same notions about university; what a university should be. They have similar ideas as to what a student is and should learn, how and what he should think." Students at Regina Campus were advised to respond as the students at Berkeley had done—to think seriously about what they wanted from a university education and make sure they made their views known to the faculty and the administration.

The student movement in North America made steady gains through the mid-1960s, fuelled in part by opposition to the Vietnam War. This was especially true in the United States where students were subject to the draft. The SDS protests grew increasingly militant, as it became evident that peaceful marches and singing "We Shall Overcome" were not going to stop the war. The strategy shifted from protest to resistance; from "Hell no, we won't go" to "Hell no, nobody goes." Students in 1967 tried to shut down the Oakland Induction Center. They sat down in the middle of the street, expecting the police to drag them away. Instead, the clubs came out and the protesters were badly injured.[12] The FBI mounted a counter-intelligence program (known as Cointelpro) against the SDS and other allegedly subversive organizations. This went beyond the mere collection of information to the spread of misinformation and the infiltration of organizations by agents-provocateurs. It became a moot point as to who was more responsible for the escalating violence—the protesters or the FBI seeking to discredit them.

The mood in the student movement changed in 1968. The assassinations of King and Kennedy had a devastating effect. It seemed that the regular, lawful channels to bring about change did not work. As soon as a leader emerged who promised to take the country out of the morass into which it had sunk, he was murdered. Meanwhile, the war continued, and the casualties mounted. Radical students began to ask themselves: If I had been a German in World War II what would I have done—obey the government or try to stop the war and the holocaust by any means possible?[13]

This was the backdrop to the disastrous SDS national convention in Chicago in June 1969..Frustrated at the continuation of the war and infiltrated by Marxist-Leninist sects and Cointelpro agents, the organization split apart in an atmosphere that combined ideological warfare with psychodrama. Out of the chaos emerged the Weatherman (later renamed the Weather Underground), the faction that managed to wrest control of the SDS. They decided that there were no non-violent options. To do nothing was to consent to the violence being visited upon the Vietnamese and the other oppressed peoples of the Third World. Their solution was to meet violence with violence.

At this point, the sixties were transmuted, in the words of historian and former SDS leader Todd Gitlin, from "years of hope" to "days of rage."[14] The Weather Underground staged a riot in Chicago, October 8, 1969, involving 200 to 300 people. They trashed cars, broke storefront windows, and fought the police. Extremists then embarked on a bombing campaign, targeting such

institutions as the Harvard Center for International Affairs. To ste
selves for the bombings and to rid themselves of lingering "bourgeois inhi-
bitions," they performed such exercises as smashing tombstones in a cem-
etery and killing and eating a cat. In accordance with the principle "people
who live together and fight together fuck together," couples were separated
and everybody was ordered to sleep with everyone else—women with men,
women with women, and men with men.[15] In March 1970 in a New York
townhouse, three members of the Underground blew themselves up while
trying to build a bomb. The bombings continued, but as time passed and the
Vietnam War came to a close, most of the Weathermen turned themselves in,
served jail terms and eventually re-entered society. The SDS later claimed:
"We were the conscience of America; we saved the soul of America."[16] While
there is some truth to this, since the organization was in the forefront of the
anti-war movement, civil rights, and women's liberation, it is also true that
the SDS produced the Weather Underground, the dark, pathological under-
side of the sixties.

Tragedy struck Kent State University in Ohio in May 1970. President
Nixon's decision to send troops into Cambodia ignited demonstrations at
hundreds of campuses. At Kent, a small city not far from Cleveland, students
lit a bonfire in the downtown business district, smashed windows and threw
beer bottles at police cruisers. The next day, May 2, 1970, they set fire to the
ROTC (Reserve Officer Training Corps) building. When the fire trucks arrived, the protesters cut the hoses to prevent the firemen from putting out the
blaze. The governor of Ohio called in the National Guard, who occupied the
campus, setting up tents on the football field and patrolling the grounds with
jeeps and other military vehicles. On Monday, May 4, students assembled on
the commons shouting anti-war slogans and "Pigs Off Campus." What happened next remains unclear, but at the end of a series of confrontations the
National Guard opened fire for thirteen seconds, killing four students and
wounding nine. Some of the students were shot in the back. They were on
their way to class and had no involvement in the demonstration.[17] A photo
taken that day showed a student lying dead on the ground, another student
kneeling in grief over her body. The *Carillon* reproduced the picture, super-
imposing a memo from the associate registrar of Kent University: "This is to
inform you information has been received that Allison Beth Krause, Student
Number 220 58 6598 9, died May 4, 1970. She was admitted to the College of
Education the Fall Quarter 1969 and transferred to the College of Fine and

INTER-DEPARTMENTAL CORRESPONDENCE

KENT STATE UNIVERSITY.
KENT, OHIO

TO   Distribution List

FROM   John K. Garrett   DATE. May 13, 1970

SUBJECT Allison B. Krause
         220 58 6598 9

This is to inform you information has been received that Allison Beth Krause, Student Number 220 58 6598 9, died May 4, 1970.

She was admitted to the College of Education the Fall Quarter 1969 and transferred to the College of Fine and Professional Arts January 1970.

It is recommended that this student's name be deleted from routine mailing lists.

John K. Garrett
John K. Garrett
Associate Registrar

JKG:ves
Distribution:

    Data Processing
    College of Education
    College of Fine and Professional Arts
    Bursar
    Art Department—Mr. Lapola
    English Department—Barbara Agte
    Sociology & Anthropology Department—
      Dr. Dennis G. Cooke
    Political Science—Dr. Peter N. Crossland
    On Campus Housing

The *Carillon*, 14 May 1971, mourning four students shot and killed by the National Guard at Kent State.

Professional Arts January 1970. It is recommended that this student's name be deleted from routine mailing lists." [18]

Nothing like the Kent State massacre happened in Canada. There was unrest and disruption, but no loss of life. At Simon Fraser University, the Political Science, Sociology and Anthropology Department (PSA) was in turmoil.[19] When five graduate students were dismissed in March 1967 for participating in a demonstration, the student body rallied to support them. The board of governors backed down and the five students were reinstated. Student president Martin Loney advocated a policy of confrontation with the university authorities ("out of confrontation comes consciousness"). Crisis followed crisis, and the radicals in 1968 called for the abolition of the existing board of governors and its replacement by a body controlled by the students and the public at large. The police had to be summoned to evict students from the university president's office, and the PSA department was placed under trusteeship. Several faculty members and teaching assistants went on strike, offering free courses with titles like "Studies in Guerrilla Warfare" and "How Does Our Culture Fuck Us."[20] Another occupation ended with a massive police intervention in September 1969 and the arrest of 114 students.

At Sir George Williams University in Montreal, a committee met on January 29, 1969, to investigate allegations of racism that had been levelled against a professor in the biology department. Racial problems, brewing for some time, had been inflamed by the visit to the campus of black power activists Bobby Seale and Stokely Carmichael. Students disrupted the meeting of the committee and charged that the proceedings were rigged. They occupied the faculty club, ransacked the cafeteria, and on February 11, 1969, set fire to the computer centre.[21]

The Regina Campus did not experience violence and destruction of property, but the underlying dynamic of its student movement resembled that of other universities in Canada and the United States. There was a slow buildup to 1968-1969, followed by a splintering of the movement into ideological factions, a disengagement of the radical element from the mass of the student body, and a gradual fading out of protest and a return to, if not normalcy, at least equilibrium. In this way, the pattern of the Regina student movement was congruent with that of the sixties era as a whole: years of hope leading to a crisis in 1968, after which came a gradual subsidence. The difference was that at Regina Campus the 1968-1969 crisis took a milder form. The dynamic was the same, but in a lower register.[22] Regina, of course, was not unique in this respect. Even in the United States, campus violence was the exception, not the rule. At Wellesley College, student president Hillary Rodham made the transition from Goldwater Republican to anti-war Democrat. The supercharged year of 1968, she said, brought "a sense of tremendous change, internationally and here at home, which impacted greatly how I thought about things."[23] For some, the change led to violent action; for others, a new way of seeing the world.

Critique of Mass Education

At the root of the 1960s student movement was a critique of university education and the role of the university in society. Student activists contended that the university had tied itself too closely to government and big business, thereby compromising its mission as the independent upholder of human values. During the Vietnam War, for example, it was alleged that universities were engaged in scientific research of direct benefit to the American war machine. More subtly, it was alleged that the university had turned itself into an apologist for the status quo. The so-called "value-free" social sciences were not, in fact, neutral. They trained students to take their place in the technocratic/bureaucratic order as human relations managers, consultants, clinicians, pollsters, advertisers, and other behavioral experts, whose real job was to manipulate people into doing things that they otherwise would not have done. The university was failing to ask the basic questions: What is justice? What is truth? What is the good society?

Instead, it carved up knowledge into small, departmental units, failing to bring the pieces together to form a meaningful whole. Students took courses in individual disciplines—political science, anthropology, biology, etc.—each of which was a specialized world unto itself. The undergraduate curriculum failed to impart a coherent body of knowledge or an integrated worldview. As a result, technical and professional training in specific, job-oriented fields had replaced broadly-based liberal arts education. Student activists also bemoaned the lack of "relevance" in the curriculum. It failed to address the pressing problems that students would have to deal with as citizens: nuclear arms, environmental pollution, racism and poverty.

This led student activists into a contradiction. On one hand, they wanted the university to disengage from what, for lack of a better term, might be called the military-industrial complex, but, on the other, they saw the university as an agent for social change. In either case, the university was denied its traditional function as a place where truth is pursued for its own sake. Radicals wanted to substitute one form of politics for another. They were the mirror image of the enemies they attacked. Neither group was a friend of the university as the home of free, scholarly inquiry. Thus, the student movement harboured a latent authoritarianism based on the belief that it alone had a privileged pathway to the truth. This resulted in attacks on research that students did not approve of. It even led, at Cornell, to a situation where students, armed with rifles and shotguns, with bandoliers of shells draped around their necks, patrolled the hallways.[24]

Such issues were fodder for the *Carillon*. An article titled "The Student, His Power and Potential," September 24, 1965, asked whether the university was a hospitable place for the student "who wants to question, evaluate and challenge the status quo, to shape a satisfying and useful place for himself in society." The article criticized the compartmentalization of knowledge in "the hierarchical arrangements of the departments—the specialized, somewhat exclusive empires that the divisions seem to have become. Is this the best fashion in which to organize and handle the transferral of the great body of knowledge which man has accumulated throughout the centuries? Is the university, as is, able to develop and free the creative potential of the student to understand the forces which have shaped our world and each of us within it?"[25]

Student Ruth Warick confessed to feeling somewhat disillusioned with the university experience. While still in high school, she dreamed of what it would be like: "On one hand I pictured it as an Oxford idyll. There you have distinguished, elderly gentlemen who dress conservatively, and think and talk brilliantly … A totally different perspective lies in the Harvard-McGill-Berkeley combination. Here the professors are 'one of the boys,' several looking the part, all having striking personalities." Instead, she found something more like a factory: "Like cans of soup, students go through the stages of development, then go out into the world—a product,

Student Ruth Warick, author of insightful *Carillon* articles critiquing technocratic, job-oriented university education.

labelized, etc." The crux of the problem, she said, "is that the university is not just a place to learn, but a means to an end. The end is tied up in a good job and a good social position." Her solution was to find a real education outside the classroom in what she called the "unofficial university"—"things like working on the school newspaper, a non-credit theology class with supper included, listening to guest speakers ... going to the Ecumenical Conference for a week-end, developing your own film and pictures for the first time ... reading the odd book at the odd time, meeting new people and listening to people who have something to say."[26]

In a second article, Warick took a more pro-active stance. Rather than merely accepting the status quo and trying to work around it, she welcomed the signs of a rising student movement. "A nation of students have grown up," she declared, "a nation of students have decided, have been deciding all along that it wants something it is not getting, something which by rights it should be getting and this is precisely a university education." The existence of widespread discontent was proof "that everywhere thousands of students are trying to build a university. The cry of the university is not the cry of a few radicals searching for a kind of lost dream they had once—while they slept. It is the cry of students, like you and I, who came here to learn, to live and who want so desperately to learn and live." She thought that Regina Campus, being so new, had a unique opportunity. The students, she felt, had "a great amount of power to build the kind of university we want, that is, if we care enough ... We are the ones for whom the university exists. Surely an administration and a government must realize that they have to respect our wishes because what is a university without students?"[27]

The disaffection that Warick articulated inspired two striking front pages. The cover of the September 26, 1969, issue of the *Carillon*, "The University as Factory," displayed an anguished, alien-looking figure with a quote from T.S. Elliot's "The Hollow Men":

> This is the dead land
> This is the cactus land
> Here the stone images
> Are raised, here they receive
> The supplication of a dead man's hand
> Under the twinkle of a fading star.[28]

Carillon front page, 26 September 1969, protesting the impersonality and soulless-ness of mass education.

The March 10, 1972, edition featured a doctored image of a Nazi-era Nuremberg rally, a biting commentary on allegedly authoritarian teacher-training methods practised in the Faculty of Education.[29]

Jerry Farber, an English teacher at a Los Angeles college, wrote "The Student as Nigger," a diatribe that compared students to African American slaves:

> What school amounts to then, for white and black alike, is a 12-year course in how to be slave. What else could explain what I see in a freshman class? They've got the slave mentality: obliging and ingratiating on the surface but hostile and resistant underneath. As do black slaves, students vary in their awareness of what's going on. Some recognize their own put-on for what it is and even let their rebellion break through the surface now and then. Others—including most of the "good students"—have been more deeply brain washed. They swallow the bullshit with greedy mouths. They honest-to-God believe in grades, in busy work, in General Education requirements. They're like those grey-headed house niggers you can still find in the South who don't see what all the fuss is about because Mr. Charlie "treats us real good."[30]

The piece was reprinted in the *Carillon*, and thereafter student writers made frequent reference to it. University president John Spinks was referred to as "Mr. Charlie," the plantation boss, and the campus itself as the "watermelon patch."

Cyril Levitt in *Children of Privilege: Student Revolt in the Sixties* attributes much of student discontent to the bureaucratic, impersonal nature of universities, which were struggling to keep pace with rapidly growing baby-boom enrolments. As Levitt says, "Students who had been expecting a first-class passage on a luxury-liner soon discovered that they were second-class passengers on a tramp steamer."[31] At Regina Campus, student registrations outstripped the projected figures. In 1961, when full-time enrolment was 653, Principal William Riddell predicted that by 1967 it would climb to between 1,200 and 1,500 students.[32] The actual number was 3,400.[33] Students stood

Carillon, 10 March 1972, satirizing teaching methods in the Faculty of Education.

in interminable lines waiting to register for classes or to rent a locker. John Conway wrote in 1966:

> Registration (and examinations) communicate clearly just exactly what the members of the academic community are, what they are doing and for whom they are doing it. The shuffling lines of subdued, flat-eyed students made the metaphor of "knowledge factory" crudely expressive. They are the raw materials which, through various processes (including the initial selections made during registration), are transformed into commodities. The academic staff, seated at various tables along the line, are the workers whose skills are necessary for the transformation. The Administration are the foremen, agents of the entrepreneur. The technologi-

"— — degrading, but unavoidable, or so the folk wisdom goes."

Long lines for class registration, *Carillon*, 23 September 1966.

cal society, with its insatiable need for well-trained, perhaps a little skilled, obedient functionaries, is the entrepreneur. Such are perhaps the origins of the cynical, "make-out" mentality characterizing most students and staff in the university.[34]

Students enrolled in Logic 100 in the fall of 1968 found a tape recorder at the front of the classroom instead of a professor. The head of the department explained that the professor had to give the same lecture three times a day to three sections of the same class. To save the trouble of repeating himself, he recorded the lecture and then showed up in class once a week to answer questions. Midway through the class, Don Kossick, a CUS (Canadian Union of Students) fieldworker, walked in and wrote on the blackboard, "Is this Education?" About a third of the class walked out, and made an appointment to see the professor.[35] As a result, the students were allowed to vote on the question: "Is a tape recorder a satisfactory substitute for a teacher?"[36]

"Liberal Arts Dead at Regina" called for "a hard look at the examination and grading systems": "Socrates did not give examinations or grades. So our professors think they are better than the greatest teachers of history?" The article argued that "testing should be done only as an aid to teaching, not as a final evaluation, not as punishment for an academic weakness." The grading system only served to "produce people who are constantly producing A's or B's for some overlord." It did not "produce educated people, capable of independent work." If examinations were abolished, "we might find the universities turning out mature, emotionally balanced men and women instead of the hypertense, nerve-wracked organization man which is the typical product of the modern university."[37] Some experimentation did occur. For example, Dr. Arthur Gladstone allowed students to decide for themselves what grade they thought they deserved for one-third of their mark in introductory psychology.[38]

The physical environment of Regina Campus did nothing to allay discontent. It was a jolt for both faculty and students to move from the old brick buildings and park-like surroundings of the downtown campus to the new site at the periphery of the city. There was not a tree in sight. The new buildings had a stark, modernistic appearance. The *Carillon* panned the architecture and décor ("off-white ceilings, off-white walls, off-white floors, and colorfully interspersed black furniture"). It quoted an instructor in the

The park-like ambience of the old Regina Campus (above) and the contrasting stark, "space-age" modernity of the new campus (below). PHOTOGRAPHY DEPARTMENT, UNIVERSITY OF REGINA

Above: Library at the old campus, 29 January 1954. SASKATCHEWAN ARCHIVES BOARD R-B6680

Below: Library at the new campus. PHOTOGRAPHY DEPARTMENT, UNIVERSITY OF REGINA

psychology department, who said: "I'm not sure if I'm a monk in a monastery or a madman in a padded cell. But I guess in some ways I'm lucky—if I had working-class background I'd also have to worry about whether or not I'm in jail."[39] A student poet contributed the lines:

> Walking through hallways of
> solid glass
> One wonders what totalitarian
> impulses
> Created this landscape of void
> This vacuum of invention.[40]

Social and recreational facilities were in short supply, and the cafeteria was overcrowded.[41] The SRC took matters into their own hands and fitted up a room in the Classroom building as an improvised lounge and lunchroom. They put out an appeal for second-hand couches and chairs to furnish it.[42] The university did not provide a student services building until 1969, and, even then, it was a temporary, sub-standard structure.[43] The *Carillon* derided it as a "Quonset hut" and a "parody" of a Students' Union Building.[44]

Physical surroundings, especially social space, have a direct bearing on the formation of community. Regina Campus students tried to create for themselves a sense of belonging.[45] For them, this issue was tied up with the relationship of Regina Campus to the university in Saskatoon. As early as 1963, the *Carillon* campaigned for the creation of separate university in Regina. It maintained that Regina's growth would be stunted "as long as the funds and the policy making body is in Saskatoon." Regina had "to sever its parental connection with Saskatoon and thereby be allowed to develop along its own lines."[46] Students facetiously proposed the name, "University of Southern Saskatchewan, Regina," (USSR for short) for the new university.[47] When the first buildings were officially opened in October 1965, a group of protesters stood silently with placards that said, "Regina Campus Needs Autonomy":

> The sun was shining, the birds were singing, and the bu-
> reaucrats were haranguing us. T'was the official opening
> of the new Regina Campus. Ten (TEN?) stood, clear-of-eye
> and stern-of-jaw, mutely protesting the crushing of Regina

Above: Overcrowded cafeteria at the new campus. UNIVERSITY OF REGINA ARCHIVES AND SPECIAL
COLLECTIONS

Below: The "temporary" student services building under construction, *Carillon*, 29 November 1968.

Campus beneath the rifle butts of Saskatoon. The entire student body stood forth as one man and said nothing ... Make your wishes known ye masses and you shall be heard. IT CANNOT FAIL.[48]

1968: Turning-Point Year at Regina Campus

The student movement heated up across Canada in 1968. Students at Waterloo boycotted classes when two professors were fired, a thousand Quebec students took to the streets to protest delays in processing student loan applications, anti–Dow Chemical demonstrators caused disturbances at the University of Toronto, and University of Windsor students rallied in support of a free student press.[49] At a meeting of the Association of Universities and Colleges of Canada in July 1968, university presidents discussed pending upheavals. According to a briefing note that had been prepared for them, "world wide disturbances" had been planned for the coming fall: "... those for Canada will take several forms—student power demands in B.C., Toronto and McMaster, refusal to pay fees elsewhere, repetition of McGill sit-ins, but on a Montreal-wide scale so as to saturate police effort, destruction of one or more administrative offices (à la Stanford), multiple upsets in classrooms."[50] The report stated that the strategy of the radicals was to pick some local dispute as a pretext to foment unrest. The specific issue was immaterial, because the whole point of the exercise was not to solve a problem, but rather to provoke a confrontation. If the university granted concessions, the radicals would simply escalate their demands. The ultimate goal was to destabilize the university and bring about a revolution.

Principal Riddell in June 1968 prepared contingency plans for a student uprising at Regina Campus. He thought that the administration had to strike a balance between not doing enough and over-reacting: "Any delay in the face of revolt or any lack of decision or even firmness seems to have led to a loss of control. On the other hand the resort to force through police action may bring forth the cry of police brutality and cause the conservative students to make common cause with the activists." If students occupied university buildings, the plan was to have staff members withdraw and set up headquarters off campus. The university resolved to suspend the leaders of the revolt, along with faculty members who assisted them, but the police were not to be called in except as a last resort.[51] Riddell and Regina police chief Arthur Cookson agreed on a secret code word to be used if the university wanted to call in reinforcements. This was to guard against the possibility of students summoning the police in order to provoke an incident.[52]

Regina Campus officials in August 1968 invited representatives of the media for a briefing. Vice-Principal Thomas McLeod asked the reporters not to give the radicals undue attention. They represented but a fraction of the student population, and the press had a tendency to exaggerate their importance by giving them excessive coverage. However, the media were less than receptive to McLeod's advice. One journalist commented that "[student] unrest was a relief from the apathy and materialistic approach of the former generation," while another observed that, "dissent was healthy, but we must do everything possible to avoid a violent expression of it."[53]

Just before the start of the 1968 fall semester, Regina Campus students, including *Carillon* editor Norm Bolen, attended the annual Congress of the Canadian Union of Students in Guelph, Ontario. The delegates "worked out an anti-capitalist and anti-imperialist critique of society—although they balked at a four-square stand for socialism—labelled corporate capitalism as the cause of repressive instincts in Canadian universities, and demanded that student unions have control over 'the learning process and university

Annual congress of the Canadian Union of Students in Guelph, Ontario, *Carillon*, 13 September 1968, editor Norm Bolen at far right.

Left: Canadian Union of Students presi- dent-elect Martin Loney at Regina Campus, *Carillon*, 20 September 1968.

Facing page: Students gathered to hear Martin Loney, *Caril- lon*, 20 September 1968.

CUS President-Elect Martin Loney and SRC President Dave Sheard. Campus P.R.O. Lyn Goldman looks on.

decision-making.'" Another resolution "condemned the imperialistic and genocidal war currently being waged against Vietnam by the United States of America and its allies" and endorsed the Vietnamese National Liberal Front in its "struggle for national liberation."[54] Shortly after the congress, CUS president-elect Martin Loney addressed a crowd of 500 students at Regina Campus. He said that unless students were prepared to back up their talk with militant action, their activities were meaningless. Heckled by a group of engineering students, he retorted that "students aren't going to change things by shouting at one another. They're going to change things by talking to each other intelligently."[55] That same month the *Carillon* published a dia- gram with instructions on how to make a Molotov cocktail.[56]

Also in September 1968, Dean of Arts and Science Alwyn Berland an- nounced his resignation. An expatriate American who had come to Canada partly because of his opposition to the Vietnam War, Berland generally sup- ported the objectives of the student movement. He attributed his decision to resign partly to the lack of autonomy of the Regina Campus and partly to the "shocking inadequacy" of the physical plant and facilities at the campus relative to its enrolment. He also felt that the administration had failed to defend the academic freedom of the university with sufficient vigor when, in October 1967, Premier Thatcher had tried to assert direct control over the

ɔome of the 500 students who heard Martin Loney
Wednesday.

budget.[57] The students seized on his resignation as an opportunity for a confrontation with the president and board of governors. The annual meeting of the Student's Union, attended by over 850 students, voted overwhelmingly in favor of a resolution demanding a say in the selection of the new dean.

According to existing procedures, appointments fell within the purview of a committee consisting of the Regina Campus principal, a member of the board of governors, two deans, and the president of the university, who served as chair. The committee gave a recommendation to the board of governors, who had the final authority to make the appointment. The students proposed an alternative process involving a committee comprising three students and three professors, whose nomination would have to be ratified by both the Students' Union and the Faculty Association. The goal was to shift power from the board of governors to the students and faculty. This was known, in the parlance of the day, as the "democratization" of the university. The students issued an ultimatum to the administration demanding a response to their proposal no later than 12:30 p.m., October 3, 1968.

Principal Riddell made it clear that, while open to dialogue with students who had constructive ideas, he had no use for the opinions of those who were interested only in "confrontation, incidents and even violence." He said that "those willing to stay and work for a better University, one that is well prepared for the education of students of the twenty-first century are welcomed; the others should go elsewhere or set up their own institution that they can run as they wish or can."[58] With equal bluntness, President John Spinks informed an assembly of 500 students that he placed no confidence in their recommendation of a candidate for dean. He warned that "students and staff had better get wise to the 'train-wreckers' who wished to destroy our universities as part of their aim to destroy our western society."[59] Student Ron Thompson wrote a column satirizing the meeting as a theatrical performance: "The play was set in modern-day Saskatchewan. Rather than stage sets of cotton-fields and slave hovels, the players used available materials—desks, concrete and some managed to turn rakes and hoes into pencils"; "noted perennial outside pacifier, J.W.T. Spinks shone in his role as Uncle Charlie. There were no whips, no storming, no fuming. Just a quiet day on the plantation."[60] The *Carillon* portrayed Spinks as a latter-day Louis XIV, proclaiming, "The University? I Am The University."[61]

Rising tuition costs and concerns about the administration of the student loan program sparked the largest student demonstration of the decade. It took place at the grounds of the provincial legislature on October 2, 1968. Over 1,200 students, including two busloads of students from Saskatoon, shouted slogans and waved signs at Prime Minister Pierre Trudeau, who was in Regina to unveil a statue of Louis Riel.[62] Trudeau told the students they were being selfish for asking that student loans be made available to all academically qualified students. The protesters were polite until the last ten minutes or so, when they started to heckle and impede Trudeau from reaching his waiting limousine. The RCMP suggested he leave by the back door of the Legislative Building, but Trudeau refused, preferring to make his way through the hostile crowd with the assistance of a police escort. He was then spirited off to the airport.[63]

Students had mixed opinions about the demonstration. Rick Hesch confessed to some disillusionment with the student loan campaign because the loans largely benefited the middle class and were of very little use to the working class. "If we are only fighting because we are somewhat poorer than we were last year," he wrote, "then we're being selfish and Prime Minister Trudeau is correct in his accusation. But if we are fighting for the issue that education is a right, not a privilege, and if we are truly fighting for those

Facing page: *Carillon*, 13 September 1968, denounces university president J.W.T. Spinks' top-down administrative style.

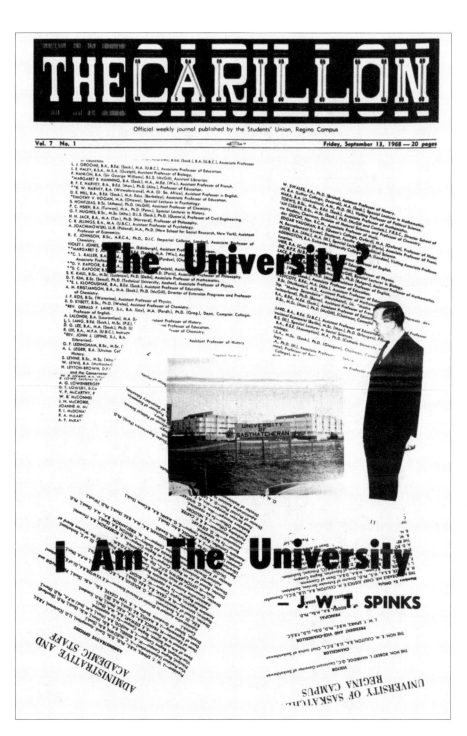

Peace my son. It's for your own good.

Left: Cartoonist's protest against an $80 tuition hike and inadequate student loans, *Carillon*, 2 February 1968.

Below: Annual meeting of Students' Union, more than 850 students in attendance, *Carillon*, 27 September 1968.

Facing page: The largest Regina student demonstration of the 1960s, *Carillon*, 4 October 1968.

1200 STUDENTS MARCH FOR LOANS

—By BOLEN, CAMERON AND GRAHAM

Over twelve hundred Saskatchewan university students went to get answers from Premier Ross Thatcher and Prime Minister Trudeau Wednesday, but all they got was vague political platitudes.

The students, comprising the largest y o u t h demonstration ever held in Saskatchewan, were mainly from Regina Campus, although two busloads of Saskatoon students joined in.

During his unveiling speech in honor of a statue of Louis Riel, Trudeau said, "In the end, democracy is judged by how the majority treats the minority." Following the unveiling of the statue of Louis Riel, Ross Thatcher told the student protestors that the Prime Minister would speak to them from the steps of the Legislature.

Trudeau spoke, but the students wanted answers and were not swayed by the impish smile and the vague generalities that seemed to be all that the Prime Minister had to offer.

Mr. Trudeau was met by a mass of chanting, placard carrying students. He told them that the students were selfish for asking that student loans be made available to all academically qualified students.

Then Mr. Trudeau informed the mass of students that all of the funds allocated by the Federal government to the student loan plan were not being used. This, he explained, meant

that all those students who met the established criteria received their loans. This explanation was met by loud shouts of 'change the criteria'.

Sensing a malaise in his audience, Mr. Trudeau threw out a political smokescreen by stating that education is a Provincial rather than a Federal matter and then stating that he was sure that he got the student's message.

Mr. Trudeau and Ross Thatcher were presented a brief by Mr. Dave Sheard, the president of the Regina Campus students Union. This brief outlined the concern of the students with the inadequacies of the Student Loan Program.

After the Prime Minister returned to the inside of the building the students began a chant of 'we want Ross', hoping that the Premier would also speak. However, it was announced by one of the Premier's aides that Mr. Thatcher wished to send off the Prime Minister at the airport, and that he would speak to the students at 'some later date'.

Don Mitchell, an SRC councillor relayed this information to the students on the Legislature steps, and the chant was immediately changed to 'we want Ross now'.

After a delay of about five minutes, the dignitaries were escorted through the dissatisfied crowd by a massive police cordon. The police met with

considerable resistance from the crowd, but were eventually able to reach the limousines safely. Mr. Thatcher was the safest of all, crouching low on his way out of the building. The students parted peaceably and let the official party depart. The police behaved well throughout the entire demonstration.

Dave Sheard, SRC president, issued a statement to THE CARILLON after the demonstration.

In the statement Mr. Sheard said, "I think that the turnout and the actual march were both excellent except for the last ten minutes. The students handled themselves very well." Mr. Sheard also said that he was

very disappointed with Mr. Trudeau's statements. At the same time Mr. Sheard expressed approval of the manner in which the police acted. He also thanked all those students who turned out. "The demonstration, he said, showed that those who turned out were aware of the problems and were willing to do something about them."

"There is a time when the operation of the machine becomes so odious, makes you so sick at heart that you can't take part; you can't even tacitly take part, and you've got to put your bodies upon the levers, upon all the apparatus, and you got to make it stop. And you've got to indicate to the people who run it, to the people who own it, that unless you're free, the machine will be prevented from running at all. . . ."

—MARIO SAVIO

who cannot be here with us, then our cause is good and just."[64] W.D. Harvey was more forthright in his criticism. He attacked the "power-hungry" New Left, who labored under the delusion that they had been "called by John Q. Taxpayer to take over the present Campus administration if they can only find an excuse … They couldn't care less what a degree is practically worth upon graduation. They won't be looking for a job in present society's mainstream."[65] A group of 75 "moderate students," most of them in the faculties of administration and engineering, formed an association to express their concern about the direction in which the campus was heading. They felt that the SRC had been "captured by a group of radicals."[66]

However, the moderates had limited impact, and the momentum continued to be with the more radical element. At the fall convocation, October 26, 1968, graduating student Ron Thompson asked permission to speak to the assembly. He wanted to correct some of the insinuations that had been made by the honorary degree recipient, Graham Spry, about the alleged fascist tendencies of the student movement. When he was denied the microphone, Thompson refused to accept his degree and walked out of the ceremonies. The reception buzzed with comment about the incident: "That filthy hippy.

If they would have let him speak, I would have gotten up and left … three thousand nice kids at the campus, and some like that … And that's the type of thing they're going to play up on television and the paper."[67] The *Carillon* produced a dramatic front page showing a clenched fist and the slogan in bold letters: "THIS UNIVERSITY BELONGS TO THE STUDENT! DIG IT."[68]

Student activist Ron Thompson (right) at Regina Campus convocation, 26 October 1968.

Thompson looks askance as SRC President Sheard tries to tell him he should have accepted the degree at the Fall Convocation. "But then I guess I really am closer to the Moderates," said Sheard (wearing tie, not beads) as the two chatted at the convocants' tea.

The clenched fist of student power, *Carillon*, 25 October 1968.

The crisis came to a climax when the *Carillon* published an anatomically explicit drawing of a woman giving birth, causing the board of governors to suspend the collection of student activity fees.[69] Student activists attempted to broaden the conflict from freedom of the press to a debate about the structure of the university. They argued that the board of governors was answerable ultimately "to a small but powerful minority—the business interests," who were closely connected to the governing Liberal party. The paper said the time had come to transform the university so that it served the needs of the people as a whole, not just the elite:

> There was a time when students looked upon the university as a training school for the privileged. After graduating from university, students went on to fill high-income slots in the elite of society. Most students no longer accept this role. They want to see the university changed so that it serves all the people, not just the wealthy. They don't want to go out into society and become part of a privileged elite. They want to join with farmers, workers, teachers, and housewives to build a society of equals, and to make sure the university plays its proper role in that society.[70]

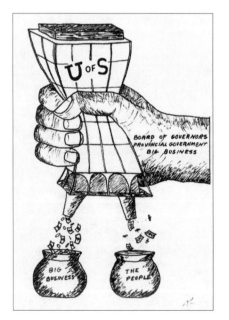

To reinforce the point, the *Carillon* produced a table indicating the occupation and political affiliation of the members of the board of governors. Most of them were businessmen or professionals who supported either the Liberal or Conservative party.[71] Another article cited the statistic that in Canada only 25 per cent of university students came from families earning $7,000 or less, but 53 per

Student radicals claimed that big business controlled the university for their own purposes, not those of ordinary citizens, *Carillon*, special edition, February 1969.

cent of all tax revenues came from families in that group.[72] Len Wallace of the Retail, Wholesale Department Store Union received a "thundering ovation" at a student teach-in when he said, "If you win the fees fight you've just got back what you had. Changing the whole method of running this place, and changing the kind of people it turns out, is a long-term battle and one that labor unions will help you with."[73]

The board of governors, after lengthy negotiations, signed an agreement to collect the fees. The *Carillon* celebrated the victory with a satirical advertisement for a two-act farce titled "Regina Campus," based on the cartoon character Mickey Mouse. Produced by Ross Thatcher and directed by J.W.T. Spinks, it featured Bill Riddell as Uncle Tom plus a cast of four thousand (students). The price of admission was a semester's tuition fee.[74] The students' victory masked a defeat. They won their battle to control the newspaper and the Students' Union, but they failed in their attempt to radically restructure and "democratize" the university. There was little support for this project. The *Carillon* crisis, in retrospect, represented the high point of the student power movement. At that moment, there was solidarity between radical activists and the mass of students. Thereafter, the two groups fell apart. In this sense, the year 1968-69 was a turning point for Regina Campus, as it was for the sixties era as a whole.

Carillon, 1 April 1969, satirizes the "Mickey Mouse" tactics of the university administration.

Decline of the Student Movement

The SRC in September 1969 urged students not to pay their fees until a strategy could be developed to protest the tuition increases. The emergency meeting called to discuss the matter was not well attended, and the activists resorted to calling the apathetic students "card players" and "coffee drinkers." Don Mitchell, student president 1966-67 and "grandfather" of the student movement, said he missed the wars of the old days.[75] The *Carillon* lapsed into a hectoring tone: "Students on this campus really don't want radical change in this society, a fact which should have been obvious to us. They want to simply vegetate here for three years, picking up their meal ticket (degree) in the process. They are not interested in political or social analysis, but rather how to fit into a profit-orientated system that denies many of its citizens—the poor, the Indians and Métis—a fair shake. It is only a small minority (a phrase the news media uses quite often) that is interested in reforming this institution to make it more humanely serve the people in it."[76]

The fire had left the student assemblies; they became tired and ritualistic. *Carillon* columnist "Tamerlane" in September 1969 identified three "teams" on campus:

> … the right-wing fascist imperialistic racist pigs (the straight clean-shaven ones, or, anyone in an Administration or Engineer's jacket); the wishy-washy Charlie Brown moderates (anyone who half agrees with anyone else); and, the anarchist left-wing radical pie-in-the-sky Marxist revolutionary (the crooked ones, or, anyone who hates Admin. and Engineering students). Added together, these groups constitute a minority. The majority of students form a neutral, or non-playing, block generally known as the apathetic card-playing mass. This group is used to determine, through their votes at General Meetings (playoffs), the winners of the game.[77]

The typical campus crisis followed a predictable cycle. First, the administration committed some kind of faux pas, which led to a banner headline in the *Carillon*, followed by an emergency SRC meeting. "The debate rages. It seems like forever, and it just might be. Then … the big vote … will they or won't they… tension mounts … it's passed!!! THERE WILL BE A GENERAL

MEETING AT 2:00 WED. TO DISCUSS THE ... CRISIS." Everyone storms into the cafeteria for a "litany of revolution and reaction." "Now begin the interminable speeches, the countless amendments; the mind wanders. The card games to your right and left continue undisturbed, except for the bodies packed in around them." Three hours pass. "The only cool thing is watching the girls, or maybe that card game. God, what a drag." It's time for a vote; the quorum is rapidly disappearing. "The winners cheer loudly and head for the pub. But it's not over yet; 3 or 4 meetings, with a steadily dwindling attendance, will be necessary before the issue is finally beaten to death. A rest comes to pass; orgasm is complete. The hunt begins for another inane action by someone. The cycle is complete; the ritual begins again."[78]

Student politics became increasingly dogmatic and ideological; sloganeering replaced real debate. The author of an article titled "Caged Conformity" asked, "What does the concerned student do under such coercive types of programmed conformity? ... If among the radicals, he must compete ... by shouting his protests at the correct number of decibels; include the prescribed number of four-letter words; invent new slogans for posters that will be adequately provocative; and memorize the right quotations from the right authors." If he chose to align himself with the conservatives, he faced similar pressures. "Here the style trends must be adhered to, the right places visited with the right company and nothing said to cause ripples in the placidity

of the group. In both cases, to some extent he surrenders his right to retain his critical faculties. He literally enters a cage—perhaps by imperceptible stages, but before he knows it he is caged and getting out of either one means putting up with garbage-cans of abuse."[79] Ideological rigidity and factionalism were typical of this period, not just at Regina Campus, but across the board. This helps explain

Regina Campus student Lorne Nystrom, 22 years old, in 1968 the youngest Member of Parliament in the history of Canada.

What's That You Said?

—PHOTOS AND INTERVIEWS BY ZENON AND ENA

Do you think that the Student Union should take a stand on political issues and questions?

Jim Hadfield, Admin. 2

I don't think the SRC should take a stand supporting a particular political party. However, they should take a stand on issues if they go to a meeting and get support from the students. An example of doing this was the way the SRC brought the question of the FLQ and Quebec to meetings recently.

Ron Blackburn, A&S 5

I have no objection if they do, but find it difficult to see how since their "representation" of me is rather limited. Frankly, I don't give a damn because I feel it is irrelevant. I am here to get out as fast as I can.

Above and facing page: Clashing views on Students' Union involvement in politics, *Carillon*, 30 October 1970.

Alice Flach, Ed. 4

Yes, they should. People in the university should get involved in political matters. They are the intellectual element and are thinking about these questions and problems. If they don't take a part through the Students' Union much of what they could do as far as legislation, etc., is concerned would just get lost. It's well known that one can't do anything alone, that we have to do things together. If we don't speak through the Students' Union then those who have opinions but aren't vocal would just never be heard, and this would be a loss for everybody. Through the union taking stands a few people can bring forward what many people think and feel, thus giving it effect.

Rick Pearce, Eng. 1

No, I don't think so unless they have 75 to 80 per cent support. To get this, those asking support should submit a proposal which could be voted on in referendum. Why 75 per cent? Because anything less, say 52 to 48 per cent, is too close and means there is too much opposition.

Randy Nimetz, Campion 1

They should take stands on those issues and questions that affect students and are matters over which students, here, in university in Canada, are concerned. On anything else they should not take a stand. If some people want to use the union to further their own ends, that's their problem and the union should have nothing to do with it. It's difficult to give a general rule that would classify, but it should be easy to see on specific questions. For example, the union should take a stand on the War Measures Act because students were being arrested in Montreal.

Kathy Stokes, A&S 3

Well, that's a hard question to answer. . . . Generally, no. Because it's easier for the union to get those things students need—when they have to deal with political figures—if it doesn't take stands. I approve of backing the Sheldon-Williams 12, not that I agree with them, but because they are students the union should support them. I wouldn't want to see the union sponsor a demonstration against the War Measures Act, but if it did and people were arrested I think then the union should support them.

Friday, October 30, 1970

CAFETERIA

DUH...
VIETNAM?
POLLUTION?
QUEBEC?
WAR?

Carillon, 14 February 1972, lamenting student apathy.

the 1969 break-up of the SDS, the dissolution of the Student Union for Peace Action in 1967, and the collapse of the Canadian Union of Students in 1969.[80]

The student movement at Regina had one last bravura moment. The 1972 fall semester began quietly enough, with only 200 students showing up for the annual Students' Union general meeting, a far cry from the 600 to 800 who could be counted upon to attend in the mid to late 1960s. The *Carillon* sourly pronounced, "Student Apathy Alive and Well."[81] An issue began to generate controversy in the social sciences division of the Faculty of Arts. The division council passed a motion, October 27, 1972, requiring all departments in the division to implement the "parity" principle, which meant equal representation of faculty members and students at department meetings. Dean of Arts and Science G. Edgar Vaughan ruled the motion out of order on the grounds that it was the prerogative of each department to determine how many student representatives it wanted to have. He said the division did not have the authority to force parity upon unwilling departments.[82]

On the afternoon of November 16, 1972, about one hundred students occupied the office of Dean Vaughan and demanded that he retract his ruling. When he refused, the students escalated their protest on November 20 by occupying the office of A. B. Van Cleave, dean of graduate studies.[83] He informed the students that if they used force to eject him, he would lay assault charges. One of the students slipped by, jumped over a desk, and removed the screens from the windows, enabling the others to get inside. Van Cleave then surrendered: "We left the office about 4:30 p.m. for the curling rink, where I regret to say, I was no more successful than I had previously been in defending my office."[84] The next day he realized that he had left in his office papers that were needed for a student's Ph.D. examination:

THE VOTE FOR VAN CLEAVE'S OFFICE

Above: Students vote to occupy the office of A.B. Van Cleave, dean of graduate studies, *Carillon*, 24 November 1972.

Below: Regina Campus student elections 1973, *Carillon*, 16 February 1973.

Last friday's S.R.C. Executive elections. The winners from left Bill Wells, Pam Wallin, Ted Leaker, Larry Kowalchuk

Some of the required documentation for his defence was in my inner office, which had not, as far as I knew, been occupied. I proposed to get these documents without admitting the so called "Liberators" to my inner office, as I saw no reason why one student should be denied his right to defend his thesis at the appointed time. I am happy to report that I entered my inner office alone, secured the necessary documents and left it again while the "brave" army of occupation were asleep in the outer office. Mr. Louman successfully defended his thesis on Wednesday morning.[85]

The campus was tense for a couple of days as the occupiers continued their siege. The *Carillon* published a "special occupation edition" including a clenched-fist poster urging students to "FIGHT FOR A DEMOCRATIC UNIVERSITY."[86] In the end, the crisis was defused without untoward incidents or destruction of property. Principal John Archer on November 22, 1972, offered to appoint a committee to review the nature and level of student participation in university decision making. The committee was to be composed of equal numbers of students, faculty and members of the general public.[87] The students held a general meeting the same day and voted to accept Archer's proposals and end the occupation. The Tri-Partite Committee

Just some of the students attending the Occupation Steering Committee.

Student strategy session during the failed bid to win "parity" in university decision making, *Carillon*, 24 November 1972.

delivered a majority report in May 1973, which stated that the number of student representatives in a department "may be equal" to the number of faculty members.[88] The "may" told the story. Departments did not have to implement parity if they did not wish to. A minority report from three faculty members on the committee opposed parity for three reasons: students often lacked the knowledge and experience required for making sound judgments with respect to university policy; they could not be held accountable for decisions in the same manner as faculty; and they did not have the time to engage in effective committee work.[89]

Although the students had failed to attain their goal, they raised only a token protest. There was no depth or breadth of student support for the parity demand. The great crusade ended with a whimper, not a bang. Although the issue was briefly resurrected in February 1974 in campus council, the motion to recognize the right of students to "equal participation in decision making at all department levels" was defeated.[90] A *Carillon* editorial and cartoon lamented the outcome, but there was no follow-up action or continuation of student demands.[91]

This was partly because the university had made strategic concessions. It allowed extensive student participation, though not universal parity, on departmental committees, and the University Act was amended to allow two Regina student representatives on the senate and one on the board of governors.[92] Moderate students were satisfied, even if the radicals were not. The student movement reached its zenith in 1968-1969, when the university moved aggressively against the autonomy of the Students' Union and the student newspaper by suspending the collection of student activity fees. The action mobilised the students in a way that no other issue or action was able to do. When the radicals attempted more ambitious projects, such as overhauling the board of governors and giving "power to the people," the majority of the students were not interested. It wasn't that the mass of students did not want reform—their actions proved that they did—it was just that they did not want revolution. To the extent that they desired change, namely a voice in running the university and respect for the rights of the Students' Union, they were successful in achieving their goals.

There were two other compelling reasons for the decline of the student movement, both of which help explain why the highs and lows of protest at the Regina Campus copied the rhythms of the sixties era. One was the fading impact of the baby-boom demographic on the university system. By 1970, the

The lasting legacy of the student movement was reform, not revolution. PHOTOGRAPHY DEPART-
MENT, UNIVERSITY OF REGINA

cutting edge of the boomers were 25 years of age or older. The enrolment at
the Regina Campus peaked at 4,345 full-time students in 1969-70[93] and declined or remained about the same until the early 1980s. The power of youth
in the sixties had always been a function of the heft of their numbers. When
the numbers faltered, so, too, did their influence. Also, the economy began
to slow down in the early 1970s. Articles in the *Carillon* deplored the difficulty students were having finding summer jobs and full-time positions after
graduation. The account of spring convocation in 1971 bemoaned the dim
prospects: "a cloud hung over the proceedings … the gloom associated with
a rather lean future. No longer do graduates go from Convocation to corporate boardrooms and the suburbs. No more steak barbecues on the patio with
the boss—only dreary trips to the unemployment office."[94] Unemployment
or the prospect of unemployment took the wind out of the sails of the sixties
generation. 1968 had been the peak year. Although it was not the end of the
sixties, it was the beginning of the end.

CHAPTER 9

Homeland of Today:
The Legacy of the Sixties

T he sixties has always been contested terrain. Some see it as a golden age, a brief shining moment when humanity glimpsed a better way to live; others regard it as a blighted time, the source of our present troubles. The negative interpretation is based on the belief that the sixties brought about a cultural revolution that eroded traditional morals and values. Margaret Thatcher declared in 1982, "We are reaping what was sown in the sixties … fashionable theories and permissive claptrap set the scene for a society in which old values of discipline and restraint were denigrated."[1] Newt Gingrich, celebrating the election of a Republican majority to the United States Congress in 1994, proclaimed, "There are profound things that went wrong starting with the Great Society and the counterculture and until we address them head-on we're going to have problems."[2] George W. Bush, too, has attacked the "if it feels good, do it" culture of the sixties. He sees the cultural revolution of the era as a "national calamity," the source of widespread family breakdown and all the social problems that attend it.[3]

The Sixties Condemned

Scholars and social commentators have had plenty to say on the subject. Roger Kimball sums up the sixties as "Dionysus with a credit card and a college education."[4] He says that we live in a world shaped by its "hedonistic imperatives and radical ideals … a trash world: addicted to sensation, besieged everywhere by the cacophonous, mind-numbing din of rock music, saturated with pornography, in thrall to the lowest common denominator wherever questions of taste, manners or intellectual delicacy are concerned."[5] Allan Bloom also sees the sixties as a descent into barbarism. He is particularly devastating in his criticism of rock music, which he dismisses as "junk food for the soul." Its triumph was "not only an aesthetic disaster of gigantic proportions: it was also a moral disaster whose effects are nearly impossible to calculate precisely because they are so pervasive."[6]

Bloom perceives a totalitarian impulse in the New Left. As so often in revolutionary movements, the call to liberation leads in practice to tyranny. The behavior of student radicals in America reminds him of what happened in Germany in the 1930s: "Whether it be Nuremberg or Woodstock, the principle is the same. As Hegel was said to have died in Germany in 1933, Enlightenment in America came close to breathing its last during the sixties."[7] Canadian author George Woodcock makes a similar observation. He cites a student leader of the sixties who quoted, to rapturous applause, an Italian leader of the 1920s saying: "… the status quo was intolerable, an Establishment was stifling all progress, the Spontaneous Anger of all the Young Forces of the Nation had to rise up and smash the Old System and release all the pent-up forces of Renewal and Revolution." The Italian leader was Mussolini. The radical, anti-bourgeois rhetoric of the New Left echoed the radical, anti-bourgeois speech of the fascists. Woodcock noted other similarities: allegiance to charismatic leaders, the cult of violence, vague utopianism, and blind faith in the efficacy of revolution. Both movements appealed to the same constituency—disaffected, half-educated, middle-class youth—and both tended towards tribalism and irrationalism.[8] The soft legacy of the totalitarian strain in the sixties New Left is "political correctness," defined as the suppression of views that do not conform to left-liberal orthodoxy.[9]

Harvey Mansfield delivers an equally sweeping indictment. While avoiding comparisons to Nazism, he condemns the sixties as a "comprehensive disaster." The sex revolution was folly ("sex without inhibition is loveless as well as shameless"); feminism has failed ("less happiness comes from being liberated into a *job*. Congratulations, women, on getting what you asked for!"); drugs are a plague ("they claimed that drugs were 'mind-expanding,' a delusion so pathetic that one can hardly credit that it was once held"); rock music is vulgar ("[it] glorifies sex to adolescent children who are not ready for it in any way except physically"); education has been corrupted ("the grade inflation that dates from the sixties is the clearest sign that teachers do not take their jobs seriously"); and affirmative action is a joke ("the college football team is the most honest part of the university.")[10]

Rounding out the jeremiad, Mansfield laments the impact of the sixties on the American family. The percentage of illegitimate births rose from 5.3 in 1960 to 28 in 1990, single-parent families increased from 9.1 per cent of all families in 1960 to 28.6 in 1991, the divorce rate increased from 9.2 per thousand married women in 1960 to 20.9 in 1991, and abortions went from an unknown figure prior to legalization in 1973 to 24.6 in 1991 as a percentage of the total number of pregnancies.[11] It amounts, he says, to the collapse of the traditional American family, which, "left-wing claptrap" to the contrary notwithstanding, "*is* the family, undermined and diminished by being called traditional. The hippie communes of the radical era were a complete flop and are no longer heard of."[12]

Myron Magnet argues that the real victims of the sixties cultural revolution were the poor, particularly urban, minority poor. The middle class has been able to withstand the assault on the traditional virtues of personal responsibility, self-control, and deferral of gratification. For those with less margin of error, such as those living in poverty or on the brink of poverty, the valorization of self-indulgence has often proved disastrous. Those trapped in self-destructive behavior need more than housing and handouts. They need "a strong message of work, sobriety, and personal responsibility from the surrounding culture."[13] This explains the mystery of the "panhandler begging outside McDonald's, right under the *Help Wanted* sign."[14] A culture that systematically devalues "the disciplines of work and family and citizenship" and elevates "rights and entitlements" above responsibilities will reap what it sows. As Irving Kristol puts it, "It's hard to rise above poverty if society keeps deriding the human qualities that allow you to escape from it." Instead of telling the poor "to take wholehearted advantage of opportunities that were rapidly opening, the new culture told the Have-Nots that they were victims of an unjust society and, if they were black, that they were entitled to restitution, including advancement on the basis of racial preference rather than personal striving and merit."[15]

Historian Gertrude Himmelfarb agrees that the sixties was a mistake, and, in retrospect, the fifties look much better. The counterculture was supposed to liberate everyone from "sexual repression and patriarchal oppression, bleak conformism and quiet desperation."[16] Instead, it had a destabilizing and demoralizing effect. It is no accident, Himmelfarb claims, "that the rapid acceleration of crime, out-of-wedlock births, and welfare dependency started at just the time that the counterculture got underway."[17] The "very idea of morality—even the word itself—has become suspect, redolent of puritanism, conformism, repression, small-mindedness and narrow-mindedness."[18] As Himmelfarb points out, the sixties was an international phenomenon, and, accordingly, its effects are not confined to the United States. "Out-of-wedlock births ratios, for example, between 1960 and 1990 rose from 5 per cent to 28 per cent in the United States and the United Kingdom; from 4 per cent to 24 per cent in Canada; from 6 per cent to 30 per cent in France; from 8 per cent to 46 per cent in Denmark; and from 11 per cent to 47 per cent in Sweden."[19]

Canadian critics of the sixties have taken up the cudgels, though, it must be said, not with the subtlety and panache of their American counterparts. William Gairdner levels his guns on the decade when "hordes of leftists and credit-card hippies, one-worlders, draft-dodgers, feminazis, homosexual activists, and liberal dreamlanders of all stripes from all parties commandeer[ed] the instruments of power."[20] Link Byfield deplores the decline in moral standards. He regrets that in a fit of misguided "moral tolerance" parliament in 1969 amended the Divorce Act, unleashing a "tidal wave of divorce," and then "declared open season on the unborn." The sixties, he continues, introduced a vocabulary of "rights," in which everyone is equal, but some ("historically disadvantaged groups") are more equal than others. Canada took a wrong turn, betraying the core values that had enabled it to "win two world wars and build the most prosperous nation in human history."[21]

Rex Murphy is sour on the sixties, an era he dismisses as "a dreadful stew." He describes the milestone of Bob Dylan's 60th birthday as a "kind of boomers' Rapture—the undiscriminating in full pursuit of the unintelligible."[22] Margaret Wente explores the cultural background of Canada's low fertility rate, which is holding steady at 1.5 children per woman (the replacement rate is 2.1). "It's fashionable," she says, "to blame the birth dearth on the loss of values in our secular, postmodern culture. Why have kids if people live only for themselves, nobody believes in sacrifice, and life is meaningless? The West has lost its way and we're committing cultural suicide." Wente goes on to say that fertility rates are plunging all over the world, even in poor countries. Children are no longer seen as an asset, but an expense. According to demographic estimates, more than half the world's population may now live in countries with "sub-replacement" fertility rates.[23]

The Sixties Celebrated

Not everyone is down on the sixties. The era also has its unabashed apologists. Paul Berman waxes eloquent on the "utopian exhilaration" of 1968: "The exhilaration was partly a fury against some well-known social injustices, and against some injustices that had always remained hidden. Partly it was a belief, hard to remember today (except in a cartoon version), that a superior new society was already coming into existence."[24] He admits that the euphoria of 1968 was ephemeral. In the aftermath "was an undertow of analysis and self-criticism among the rebels themselves. The undertow pulled steadily at the old left-wing political ideas, and one by one drew them out to sea, where they quietly drowned. And where the old ideas had been, newer thoughts silently bobbed to the surface … In place of the old aspirations for direct democracy and revolutionary socialism you could begin to see a much livelier appreciation of liberal democracy, social-democratic style (for some of us) or free-market style (for some lamentable others), but committed to Western-style political institutions in either case."[25]

Berman acknowledges that post-1968 developments have disconcerted recalcitrant leftists: "… to everyone who still adhered to the leftist funda-mentals, the fading away of the old revolutionary aspiration was a dismal thing to behold, and the entire trajectory from leftist to liberal was pathetic, and events have gone steadily downhill since 1968."[26] Disillusioned radicals regret the betrayal of the sixties. George W. Bush was elected president twice, and a war is being fought in Iraq that resembles all too closely what hap-pened in Vietnam. The Berlin Wall came down, and communism fell into decline, except for a few holdouts, like Cuba and North Korea. In the guise of globalization, capitalism extends its influence throughout the world. Protest demonstrations are so institutionalized and predictable that they have lost their meaning. Even the icons of the sixties are de-sanctified. The image of Che Guevara is plastered on everything from CDs, coffee, berets, downhill skis, and cigars to T-shirts and Taco Bell burritos.[27]

Between the two extremes—the "sixties-betrayed" and the "sixties-as-blight-on-our-times" camps—are those who see the sixties as partly good and partly bad. Arthur Marwick belongs to this school. He says that, as a result of the sixties, "Life became more varied and enjoyable. With less rigid conceptions of marriage and new opportunities for divorce, with changing attitudes to fashion and to education, with the abandonment of comfortable fictions about the nature of beauty and the arrival of informal, body-hugging clothing, there was a healthier openness to ordinary living, less need for lies, fewer cover-ups … The testimony that the new universal language of rock was genuinely liberating, and not just for the young, is overwhelming."[28] At the same time, he dismisses what he calls the "Great Marxisant Fallacy: the belief that the society we inhabit is the bad bourgeois society, but that, fortunately, this society is in a state of crisis, so that the good society which lies just around the corner can be easily attained if only we work systematically to destroy the language, the values, the culture, the ideology of bourgeois society."[29] Overall, Marwick is pleased that the sixties happened and he could not be persuaded, on any account, to return to the fifties.

A classic articulation of the pro-sixties viewpoint is the frequently cited *New York Times* editorial "In Praise of the Counterculture." Written in December 1994 in response to Newt Gingrich's denunciation of the sixties as a moral wasteland, the article celebrates the era's "morality-based politics that emphasized the individual's responsibility to speak out against injustice and corruption … It was a repudiation of the blind obedience and reflexive cynicism of politics as usual. It was about exposing hypocrisy, whether personal or political, and standing up to irrational authority."[30] The accomplishments were many: opposition to the Vietnam War, the civil rights crusade, the environmental, women's and gay rights movements. Did anyone seriously want "to go back to the days of blatant, sanctioned discrimination against African Americans and women, to a world deprived of all the 60s ingredients that still simmer in the cultural stew"? The message of the *New York Times* editorial was that we live in the world the sixties created and are much the better for it.

This theme is presented allegorically in the film *Pleasantville* (1998). Two teenagers (played by Toby Maguire and Reese Witherspoon) are suddenly transported from the 1990s into a 1950s television sitcom. It is a black-and-white world, both literally (the movie is filmed in black and white) and metaphorically (everything is cut and dried, all moral questions have simple solutions, and everybody fits into a prescribed role). Nobody harbors a subversive thought or says anything unexpected. The geography teacher puts on the blackboard a map showing the streets of the town. When Reese Witherspoon asks where Main Street leads to, if you leave the town, there are audible gasps and excited murmurings. The students can't imagine that anything exists outside their comfortable world. All the books in the library are blank, until the two visitors from the 1990s start explaining what they are about. In one key scene, Toby Maguire relates the plot of *Huckleberry Finn*. He says that it's about Huck and the slave Jim going on a journey to find freedom. In doing so, they realize they already are free. Some roads don't go in a circle. They just go on and on (more gasps). The allusion is to Kerouac's *On the Road*, the Beat literary classic that launched the counterculture.[31]

As the film continues, the characters begin to have epiphanies, that is, they begin to live in the sixties. As they do so, they are transformed on screen from black-and-white to color. The model housewife awakens to her sexuality and leaves her husband. The waiter at the soda fountain discovers a talent for art. Reese Witherspoon, the boy-crazy glamor girl, begins reading books and seriously engages the world of ideas. Toby Maguire, who had previously yearned for the certainty and conformity of the fifties, finds the courage to stand up to redneck bullies and defends equal rights for blacks. The film does not pretend that the world of the sixties is perfect or even always pleasant. On the contrary, the apple of discord has entered the Garden of Eden. But at least life in the sixties is real. People suffer and struggle; they are not automatons following somebody else's script. Living in color is always better than living in black and white.

The Sixties as Homeland of Today

Despite the wide diversity of opinion about the sixties, there is one point that almost everybody agrees on. The sixties are the homeland of today. Arthur Marwick puts it this way: "… the various counter-cultural movements and subcultures, being ineluctably implicated in and interrelated with mainstream society while all the time expanding and interacting with each other, did not *confront* that society but *permeated* and *transformed* it."[32] The sixties did not defeat the fifties or vice-versa; rather, the sixties blended in or melted into the fifties, creating something new.[33] Thomas Frank calls it the "conquest of cool" or the "rise of hip consumerism." He writes: "Our televisual marketplace is a 24-hour carnival, a showplace of transgression and inversion of values, of humiliated patriarchs and shocked puritans, of screaming guitars and concupiscent youth, of fashions that are uniformly defiant, of cars that violate convention and shoes that let us be us."[34] Burger King advises, "Sometimes You Gotta Break the Rules"; Apple Computer exalts "The Crazy Ones. The Misfits. The Rebels. The Troublemakers"; Lucent Technologies boasts that it is "Born to be Wild"; Nike borrows the cachet of Beat writer William S.

Burroughs and the Beatles song "Revolution"; *Wired* magazine adopts Jefferson Airplane color schemes; Coca-Cola incorporates Ken Kesey's Merry Prankster multi-coloured bus in its "Fruitopia" ad campaign; and R.J. Reynolds puts the peace symbol on a brand of cigarettes.[35]

This might be dismissed as mere co-optation of the sixties, a sell-out of the inner essence. However, the case can be made that consumerism, in its latest iteration, is a logical outcome of the sixties. The sixties were partly about freedom, the quest for the new, rejection of the old, hunger for experience, and desire for self-expression. Capitalism responds to these needs through niche marketing and an endless stream of innovative products tailored to individual preferences. People don't consume to keep up with the Joneses, but rather to prove that they are different from the Joneses. The capitalist system finds no particular advantage in consumers who are conservative, hidebound, and conformist. It thrives when they are addicted to change and continually rediscovering themselves, in other words, immersed in the ethos of the sixties. Sixties-oriented advertising is not necessarily fake or phony, a devious attempt to degrade the counterculture by pretending to agree with it. On one level, it *does* agree with it. Rebel youth culture is the "cultural mode of the corporate moment."[36]

Daniel Bell argues that the decline in the Protestant ethic, which emphasizes work, sobriety, and frugality—attributes conducive to high levels of economic productivity—spells trouble for capitalism. The counterculture's "preachments of personal freedom, extreme experience ('kicks' and 'highs') and sexual experimentation,"[37] are not likely to keep the worker's nose to the grindstone. According to Bell, "the characteristic style of industrialism is based on the principles of economics and economizing: on efficiency, least cost, maximization, optimization, and functional rationality. Yet it is this very style that is in conflict with the advanced cultural trends of the Western world, for modernist culture emphasizes anti-cognitive and anti-intellectual modes which look longingly towards a return to instinctual sources of expression."[38] However, as Thomas Frank makes clear, the "preachments of personal freedom" and the yearning for "instinctual sources of expression," while dysfunctional from the point of view of production, are highly functional in their impact on consumption. Capitalism needs consumers, and it has been remarkably successful in harnessing the search for authenticity and the desire for self-expression to the purchase of consumer goods and services. Hip consumerism means the willingness to try something new, the quest for the product or experience perfectly in synch with one's authentic self: the "double espresso, half decaf-half caffeinated, with mocha and room for milk," "the right organic fibre shirt in the perfect tone of earth brown (the production of which involved no animal testing),"[39] the "serious" hiking boot, and the ecologically enlightened vacation. Shopping has become a vehicle for self-exploration and means of self-expression.[40] Viewed from this perspective, the counterculture was but a stage in the evolution of consumer capitalism.

As Frank explains, when the counterculture was in its prime in the sixties, business culture underwent a transformation. Douglas McGregor's *The Human Side of Enterprise* (1960) signaled a shift from management theory predicated on tactics of control ("procedures and techniques for telling people what to do, for determining whether they are doing it, and for administering rewards and punishments") to theory based on teamwork and relationships ("the creation of an environment that will encourage commitment to organizational objectives and which will provide opportunities for the maximum exercise of initiative, ingenuity, and self-direction in achieving them").[41] Individualism and creativity were seen as the keys to productivity, displacing the previously revered values of hierarchy and efficiency.[42] Frank, in his analysis of advertising and the men's clothing business in the late 1950s and early 1960s, shows how American business saw the counterculture, not as "an enemy to be undermined or as a threat to consumer culture, but as a hopeful sign, a symbolic ally in their own struggles against the mountains of deadweight procedure and hierarchy that had accumulated over the years."[43] The leaders in these industries critiqued their over-organization, conformity, and routines of established power, in much the same way that countercultural radicals criticized the institutions of society as a whole.

The new management culture of the sixties flows into the present, especially in information-age sectors such as high technology, the media, advertising and design. Companies have upended William Whyte's "Organization Man," whose virtue was efficient compliance with the workings of the corporate machine. The machine metaphor has been replaced with that of the organic network, which is fluid and ever changing. Companies boast of abolishing job titles because they imply stuffy hierarchy, cutting layers of management, putting together small, flexible teams assigned to complete a task in the way they see fit. CEOs speak of leading by example, working collaboratively, and encouraging creativity in others, rather than wielding authority and laying down the law.[44]

Then, too, the digital revolution has a distinctly sixties flavour. It was no accident that the Bank of Montreal chose "The Times They Are A' Changin'" as the theme for its promotion of on-line banking. The Internet empowers individuals by giving them direct access to information, entertainment and products; it is a leaderless free-for-all with no centralized authority.[45] Gatekeepers are circumvented, and hierarchical structures crumble. Dell markets its computers with the slogan, "Power to the People."[46] Nortel features Carlos Santana, strumming a guitar and sounding like John Lennon: "A road to a world with no borders, no boundaries, no flags, no countries. Where the heart is the only passport you carry."[47] *New York Times* columnist and author Thomas Friedman declares that the world is flat. "Everywhere you turn," he writes, "hierarchies are being challenged from below or are transforming themselves from top-down structures into more horizontal and collaborative ones."[48] The merging of the sixties *Zeitgeist* with the Internet revolution descends to parody when William Shatner hymns the glories of e-commerce in adapted versions of "The Age of Aquarius" and "I Want You to Want Me."[49] Sixties media philosopher Marshall McLuhan coined the term "global village" and predicted a wired world. Fittingly, his name appears in the masthead of *Wired* as "Patron Saint: Marshall McLuhan."[50]

The Internet is a radically youth-centred culture. Children teach their parents the mysteries of the computer, and young millionaires recruit middle-aged executives to work for them.[51] Youth is where the action is, just as it was in the sixties. Change is constant, relentless, almost overbearing. The sixties taught us to embrace change, and that is what we have done. Appropriately, Bill Clinton, the first American baby-boomer president, chose for his campaign song, "Don't Stop Thinking about Tomorrow."

Leftists dismiss the argument that the counterculture has, to some extent, penetrated mainstream culture, on the grounds that vague talk about the *Zeitgeist*, new management theories, and hip consumerism are mere fluff, irrelevant to the basic structure of capitalism, which remains intact. Capitalists still own the means of production, maximize profits, and, in the Marxist analysis, exploit workers. At one level, the leftists are right. The sixties did not bring about revolution in the basic structure of capitalism, but it did bring about far-reaching social and cultural changes to the society in which we live. The sixties are the "source of the styles and tastes and values that define our world."[52] It is said that the past is a foreign country, but the fifties are more foreign to us than the sixties. The world of *Father Knows Best* and *Leave it to Beaver* is not our world.

Rereading the *Carillon* of the sixties, we find more that is recognizable than is strange, and as we move forward from the late 1950s to the early 1970s, the more familiar the terrain becomes. The paper both mirrored the general trends of the period—student power, liberation movements, opposition to the Vietnam War and American imperialism, the counterculture—and gave them distinctive expression. Just as the legacy of the sixties is best understood at the macro-level as a merging of the dominant culture and the counterculture, so, too, the University of Regina today represents a fusion of traditional and sixties values. The role of student government, student participation in university decision making, the place of women and minority groups, the existence of the First Nations University on campus, the range of non-traditional content in the curriculum, the opportunities for individual self-expression and non-conformity—all these are outcomes of the sixties. At the same time, the radical vision of a fully "democratized" university acting as a revolutionary agent to overthrow the capitalist order did not materialize. The university remains essentially a liberal institution serving the liberal, democratic society of which it is a part. As with society at large, the sixties transformed the university, but did not overturn it.

The sixties begin and end with the baby boomers in the prime of their youth. The boomers knew that their numbers commanded attention and gave them power. This was evident in the *Carillon* headline, November 9, 1962, "THE GIANT AWAKENS!" The students sensed their potential, as yet untapped and without clear definition. The headline in the next issue read, "WAR IS DECLARED!" Although the matter in dispute—student rates on city buses and at movie theatres—hardly justified the inflated rhetoric, it portended things to come. The students wanted to be noticed, and they wanted to do something worthy of notice.

It did not take them long to find causes to fight for. First, they refashioned student government. The SRC in the 1950s had been a modest, unassuming operation, concerned for the most part with the coordination of social and athletic events, the supervision of campus clubs, and the production of a newspaper and yearbook. According to the constitution, the SRC president was accountable to the dean of the college for the conduct of student government. The student body voted in 1965 to approve a new constitution, one that created a Students' Union, independent of the university administration, whose mandate extended beyond the management of extra-curricular activities. It addressed a wide range of student needs and interests—lower tuition rates, a better student loan program, construction of a Students' Union building, curriculum reform, improved teaching methods, and a voice in university governance. Students no longer arrived at the university with the idea of accepting passively whatever the institution had to offer. They acquired a sense of ownership, a consciousness that the university belonged to them, as much as it did to the faculty, the administrators or the taxpayers who footed most of the bill.

Radicals wanted a more drastic and thoroughgoing overhaul of the university structure. They claimed that the Board of Governors, appointed in the majority by the provincial government, represented the business elite, not the "ordinary" people of the province. The majority of students had no interest in this project. At the height of the *Carillon* crisis in 1969, when students mobilized to defend their right to control the Students' Union and the newspaper, the radical element made an attempt to broaden the struggle to demand a revolutionary restructuring of the university. The effort failed, and, thereafter, the radicals found it difficult to establish meaningful solidarity with the mass of the student body, despite a brief outburst in 1972 when administrative offices were occupied. Student activists demanded parity, that is, equality of representation with faculty, on university committees, but when the university administration rejected the demand, the radical minority was not able to rally support to continue the fight.

It is too simple, however, to say that in the big picture the university authorities "won" and the students "lost." Instead, the two sides compromised on middle ground. The students did not achieve parity, but they were given the right to participate in university decision making at every level. Student government in the 1950s had been under the supervision of the senior administration. Now, students not only controlled their own government, but also had a voice in the running of the entire institution. They sat on departmental committees, participated in faculty councils, and elected representatives to the Senate and Board of Governors. It was now considered normal for students to express their opinions about tuition fees, post-secondary funding, programs of study, and higher education policy in general. The policy of *in loco parentis*, the notion that universities exercised quasi-parental control over students, was abandoned.

The sixties concept of the citizen-student also applied to the world beyond the university. The main purpose of the student newspaper prior to the 1960s was to report on campus activities. Students were regarded as adults-in-training, participating in extra-curricular clubs and organizations, honing their leadership and social skills, preparing for the day when they would enter the real world and begin making a contribution to society. Regina Campus students annually elected a mock parliament, where they play-acted the roles of real politicians and engaged in simulated debates. Students in the sixties consciously enlarged the concept of citizenship. They did not think it was necessary to wait until they graduated before they took political action, whether this meant an editorial supporting Aboriginal rights, a protest march against the Vietnam War or the establishment of a women's centre on campus. As Regina Campus SRC President Ralph Smith stated in October 1967, "We have to assume responsibility for the society in which we live. It is in our interest to assume that responsibility now—for if we don't do it now while we are in the university, we probably will never do it."[53] That we no longer find such a statement remarkable or controversial is a measure of how the sixties changed student expectations and the university environment.

Civil rights was one of the first issues to grip the sixties imagination. The 1962 *Carillon* discussed the desegregation of the University of Mississippi, and a 1967 report covered the race riots in Detroit. Black Panther Fred Hampton spoke to students at the campus in 1969, just two weeks before Chicago police killed him. The *Carillon* drew the connection between African-American rights in the United States and Aboriginal rights in Canada, and the paper's emphasis on First Nations and Métis issues was a distinctive feature of how it presented the sixties. Less attention was given to the geographically more distant Quiet Revolution in Quebec, with the notable exception of the October Crisis in 1970. The *Carillon* denounced the imposition of the War Measures Act and expressed support for the goals, if not the tactics, of the FLQ. In the late 1960s, the women's liberation movement came to the fore. Despite the fact that all the editors of the paper in this period were men, women's liberation received prominent and sympathetic treatment. In short order from about 1966 to 1971, campus discourse on women's issues changed completely.

The effects of the liberation movements of the sixties continue to the present day. Québécois are no longer second-class citizens in their own province; they do not have to give up their language to get a good job. Women have more opportunities in education and the workplace, and they continue to strive for full equality. Aboriginal rights are near the top of the national agenda. "We have a dream, too," Matthew Coon-Come, National Chief of the Assembly of First Nations, declared in 2001, echoing Martin Luther King's 1963 speech.[54] The gay rights movement, an after-echo of the sixties, has made substantial gains. The liberation movements of the sixties have not reached their end point; they are works in progress.

The Quiet Revolution, women's liberation, and Aboriginal rights have all been the subject of landmark royal commissions—the Royal Commission on Bilingualism and Biculturalism (1968), the Royal Commission on the Status of Women (1970), and the Royal Commission on Aboriginal Peoples (1996). Even more significant, the Charter of Rights and Freedoms (1982) codified the social movements of the sixties. It enshrined official bilingualism, recognized equal rights for women, and entrenched existing treaty and Aboriginal rights. Appropriately, it was primarily the handiwork of Pierre Trudeau, who, with his phrase, "we must build a just society," embodied the sixties spirit in Canada.

The legacy of the peace movement is more difficult to interpret. The *Carillon,* as we have seen, agonized in the early 1960s over the possibility of a nuclear war. Regina Campus students protested the Cuban missile crisis in October 1962 and the testing of nuclear bombs in the Aleutian Islands in 1969 and at Amchitka in 1971. Although Canada did not send troops to Vietnam, we assisted the United States through the sale of military goods. The issue preoccupied *Carillon* writers, who did not let go of the subject until the war finally came to an end in 1975. At a deeper level, the Vietnam War was not just about Vietnam, but also about the role of the United States in the world. The issue has reappeared in Iraq and, more generally, in the debate about globalization. Anti-globalization protesters are the spiritual heirs of the anti-Vietnam War marchers, and, sometimes, they are the same people, now in advanced middle age. However, the crusade against globalization has not captured the imagination of the post–baby boomer generation. Unlike the protesters of the sixties, they are not gripped by the belief that the winds of change are with them.[55] Who is the Bob Dylan of today?

The counterculture, too, has left a mixed legacy. The sexual revolution

was real enough. Today's standards of speech and conduct are vastly different from what they were in the 1950s. At the same time, the bolder promises
of the sexual revolution (liberation equals no more hang-ups) have not been
fulfilled, and the impact on family life has been negative, if not disastrous.[56]
Sex was a weapon in the battle between the generations, a means for rebellious youth to taunt the establishment, and an excuse for the establishment
to crack down on youth. The *Carillon* used obscenity (though it was mild in
comparison to what was being published elsewhere) to provoke the Board of
Governors, who, in turn, used obscenity as the pretext for shutting down the
newspaper. The students fought back and won a victory for freedom of the
press and control over their own newspaper.

If the fallout from the sexual revolution is problematic, the legacy of the
drug culture is even more so. Saskatchewan was a leader in LSD research; indeed, the very word "psychedelic" was coined in the province. This helps explain why the *Carillon* had so much to say about drugs, most of it favorable.
LSD proved not to be the shortcut to nirvana its advocates hoped for, while
marijuana use continues to roil public opinion.[57] Rock and roll, by contrast, is
not contentious any more. It has penetrated popular culture so successfully
that it is robbed of rebel significance. The rock music industry today is "a
global colossus, a commercial juggernaut whose cash flow rivals the arms industry."[58] Music in the sixties was a "declaration of difference,"[59] the cultural
idiom of youth. It was experienced as "a spontaneous epic poem produced
miraculously by [their] peers for immediate use, something that could help
you make sense of the senselessness of it all by helping you come to your
senses, heightening them."[60] As rock entered the mainstream, it ceased to
be a "declaration of difference." The mainstream cannot rebel against itself.
Though young people today are umbilically connected to their CD players
and Ipods, their music is not a vehicle for revolt. The fate of rock epitomizes
the synthesis of mainstream and countercultural influences in the formation of contemporary society. The *Carillon* anticipated this development to
a degree by placing the counterculture in its political and economic context.
When others hailed Woodstock as the apotheosis of peace, love and the-uni-
verse-unfolding-as-it-should, the paper coolly pointed out that Woodstock
was also a mass-market movie raking in millions of dollars. The *Carillon* sixties were generally more political than they were countercultural. In this respect, the paper reflected the milieu of the city and province of which it was
a part.

Today, it does not matter how long your hair is, what clothes you wear or what music you listen to. This was not true of the 1950s, when it was assumed that those who were different—married women who did not want to be housewives, racial minorities, cultural rebels—were misfits and pariahs. They were expected to conform and fit in as best they could. The shoe is now on the other foot. Society bends over backward to make sure that everyone feels included and nobody is subject to harassment.[61] When we read the *Carillon* of the sixties era, we are not so much studying a bygone era as glimpsing the beginnings of the present. The sixties did not overwhelm the status quo, but neither did the status quo reject the sixties. Each absorbed elements of the other, and they melted into one another. Liberation movements have transformed society, and the cultural norms of personal authenticity and expressive individualism—the right to be who you are and "do your own thing"—are solidly established. On the other hand, the sixties made no dent in the basic structure of capitalism. The dreams of hippie communes, sharing of property, "power to the people," socialist revolution, and overthrow of the American Empire have come to nothing. The aspects of the counterculture that enhanced individualism were widely embraced, but collectivist ideals were largely spurned. The free market economic system remains intact; indeed, on a global scale, it has made major gains. The cultural transformations of the sixties enhanced the existing liberal order, rather than overturning it. People who had been on the outside were brought inside the circle, and individual freedom acquired a new psychological and cultural dimension.

The core principle of liberalism is freedom, and the main shortcoming of the sixties was the failure to explore adequately the question: "What is freedom for? What are human beings meant to do with their freedom?" The sixties too often forgot that freedom is not the answer; it is the beginning of the question. Richard Fairfield writes, "Freedom is a difficult thing to handle. Give people freedom and they'll do all the things they thought they never had a chance to do. But that won't take very long. And after that? After that, my friend, it'll be time to make a meaningful life."[62] The sixties were too quick to dismiss the possibility that there is a right life for human beings, "a life in accord with nature, a life that most fully realizes our potential for freedom, dignity, happiness" and that "we have three or four millennia of philosophers and poets trying to tell us what the right life is, three or four millennia of history to see how our predecessors tried to accomplish it."[63]

The students of the sixties and the writers of the *Carillon* had their faults. At times, they were self-righteous and self-indulgent. Yet, when we see them trudging through the snow to the Saskatchewan Legislative Building in March 1964 to demand lower tuition fees and an independent university, or waving peace placards during the Cuban missile crisis in October 1962, or marching through the streets of Regina to oppose a war being fought five thousand miles away, we cannot help but feel a twinge of admiration. At least they were *doing* something, standing up for their opinions, asking to be heard. They did not, as George Grant wrote, "crawl through university simply as a guarantee of the slow road to death in the suburbs."[64] The students of the sixties made history, and they shaped the world we live in today.

Photo Credits

page 47 • College Avenue campus, August 1961 • Photographer: Gibson • University of Regina Archives and Special Collections 84-11-96

page 51 • Minoru Yamasaki, Conferring of Honourary Degree at Fall Convocation, Darke Hall, October 14, 1967 • Photographer: Brigdens Photo/Graphics Ltd • University of Regina Archives and Special Collections 75-18-7

page 52 • Site of the future campus, August 4, 1961 • Photographer: unknown • University of Regina Archives and Special Collections 84-11-67

page 53 • Cornerstone-laying ceremony, September 26, 1963 • Photographer: unknown, photograph courtesy of the Saskatchewan Archives Board • University of Regina Archives and Special Collections 86-42-3

page 54 • First buildings constructed on new campus: classroom, laboratory, and library • Photography Department, University of Regina, 70-037-1

page 54 • Aerial view of the campus, after 1973 • Photographer: Photography Department, University of Regina • University of Regina Archives and Special Collections 91-31-2

page 74 • Saskatchewan Archives Board R-B8403

page 219 • Saskatchewan Archives Board R-B6489

page 251 • Ruth Warick • Photographer: Dave Furman • University of Regina Archives and Special Collections 84-11-1004

page 258 • College Avenue campus • Photography Department, University of Regina, 71-084-4

page 258 • New campus • Photography Department , University of Regina, 69-007-1

page 259 • College Avenue campus library • Saskatchewan Archives Board R-B6680

page 259 • Library at the new campus • Photography Department, University of Regina, 73-017-7

page 261 • Students in Lab Building cafeteria, July 1966 • Photographer: Neil J. Baisi • University of Regina Archives and Special Collections 84-11-933

page 282 • Grafitti on Physical Education Building • Photography Department, University of Regina, 72-043-2

REPRODUCTION OF UNIVERSITY OF REGINA YEARBOOK AND CAMPUS NEWSPAPER PAGES:

Pages or portions of pages from the *Sheet*, the *Tower*, and the *Carillon* were either directly scanned or photographed by the Photography Department, University of Regina.

Endnotes

INTRODUCTION

1   Bob Dylan, "Chimes of Freedom," first release, *Another Side of Bob Dylan*, 1964.

2   Arthur Marwick, *The Sixties: Cultural Revolution in Britain, France, Italy, and the United States, c.1958-c.1974* (New York: Oxford University Press, 1998), 7.

3   Terry Anderson, *The Movement and the Sixties: Protest in America From Greensboro to Wounded Knee* (New York: Oxford University Press, 1995), preface, not paginated.

4   Joyce Johnson, review of *A Strong West Wind: A Memoir*, *The New York Times Book Review*, 2 April 2006.

5   Robert J. Glessing, *The Underground Press in America* (Bloomington: Indiana University Press, 1970), 3.

6   Julius Duscha and Thomas Fischer, *The Campus Press: Freedom and Responsibility* (Washington, D.C.: American Association of State Colleges and Universities, 1973), 1.

7   *The Student Newspaper*, Report of the Special Commission on the Student Press to the President of the University of California (Washington, D.C.: American Council on Education, 1970), 47-55.

8   Duscha and Fischer, 6, 19, 20, 23.

9   Doug Owram, *Born at the Right Time: A History of the Baby Boom in Canada* (Toronto: University of Toronto Press, 1996), 241.

10 David Adams, "Are You A Radical?" *Carillon*, 16 October 1964.

11 "Carillon One of CUP's Best Papers," *Carillon*, 26 January 1968.

12 *Carillon*, 1 March 1968.

13 "Story Creates Nation-Wide Interest," *Carillon*, 15 March 1968.

14 Nick Bromell, *Tomorrow Never Knows: Rock and Psychedelics in the 1960s* (Chicago: University of Chicago Press, 2000), 5.

CHAPTER 1

1   Doug Owram, *Born at the Right Time: A History of the Baby Boom in Canada* (Toronto: University of Toronto Press, 1996), 306.

2   "Annual Inflation Rate—Canada, 1971-2004," http://www.oia.ucalgary.ca/cpi/tables/Canada.pdf.

3   Terry Anderson, *The Movement and the Sixties: Protest in America From Greensboro to Wounded Knee* (New York: Oxford University Press, 1995), preface, not paginated.

4   Owram, 217.

5   James Laxer, "The Americanization of the Canadian Student Movement," in Ian Lumsden, ed., *Close the 49th Parallel Etc: The Americanization of Canada* (Toronto: University of Toronto Press, 1970), 276-286.

6   Owram, 4-5; Canada, *Statistics Canada*, CANSIM, matrices 0001 and 0004 (10 August 2000); F.H. Leacy, ed., *Historical Statistics of Canada*, 2nd ed., (Ottawa: Statistics Canada, 1983), series B1-14).

7   Mary Louise Adams, *The Trouble with Normal: Postwar Youth and the Making of Heterosexuality* (Toronto: University of Toronto Press, 1997), 29.

8   Owram, 17.

9   Ibid., 17-18.

10 Adams, 26.

11 Owram, 159.

12 Ibid., 33.

13 Ibid.

14 Ibid., 124-128.

15 Ibid., 88.

16 Ibid., 96-99.

17 Veronica Strong-Boag, "Home Dreams: Women and the Suburban Experiment in Canada, 1945-60," *Canadian Historical Review*, 72, 4, December 1991, 487.

18 Ibid., 504.

19 Malvina Reynolds, "Little Boxes," Schroder Music Company, 1963.

20 Owram, 140.

21 Todd Gitlin, *The Sixties: Years of Hope, Days of Rage* (New York: Bantam, 1993), 37.

22 David P. Szatmary, *Rockin' In Time: A Social History of Rock-and-Roll*, 4th edition (Upper Saddle River, New Jersey: Prentice Hall, 2000), 6.

23 Ibid., 16.

24 Ibid.

25 Ibid., 21.

26 Ibid.

27 Ibid., 32.

28 Ibid., 33.

29 Ibid., 45.

30 *The History of Rock 'n' Roll*, produced and directed by Susan Steinberg, Time-Life and Warner Brothers, 1995.

31 James Gilbert, *A Cycle of Outrage: America's Reaction to the Juvenile Delinquent in the 1950s* (New York: Oxford University Press, 1986), 183-185.

32 Adams, 56; Gilbert, 66.

33 Gilbert, 65.

34 Ibid., 185-189.

35 *The Source*, a film by Chuck Workman, Beat Productions, 1996, explores the links between the Beats and the sixties counterculture.

36 *The Fog of War*, DVD, a Radical Media & Senart Films production, Sony Pictures Classics, 2003.

37 Norman Mailer, "The White Negro: Superficial Reflections on the Hipster," in Norman Mailer, *Advertisements for Myself* (New York: G.P. Putnam's Sons, 1959), 339.

38 John Leland, *Hip: The History* (New York: HarperCollins, 2004), 147.

39 Steven Watson, *The Birth of the Beat Generation: Visionaries, Rebels, and Hipsters, 1944-1960* (New York: Pantheon, 1995), 3.

40 Leland, 143.

41 Ibid., 144.

42 Watson, 136-137.

43 Ibid., 253.

44 Jack Kerouac, *On the Road* (New York: Penguin, 1976), 195.

45 Ibid., 209-210.

46 Ibid., 179-180.

47 Matt Weiland, "You Don't Know Jack," review of *Why Kerouac Matters: The Lessons of 'On the Road' (They're Not What You Think)* by John Leland, *The New York Times Book Review*, 19 August 2007.

48 Richard Kindleberger, "Poems and Bottles at Kerouac's Grave," *The Boston Globe*, 23 October 1999.

49 "Kerouac on the Block," *The New York Times*, 24 May 2001.

50 Kathryn Shattuck, "Kerouac's 'Road' Scroll is Going to Auction," *The New York Times*, 22 March 2001.

51 Kerouac, *On the Road*, 117.

52 Allen Ginsberg in *The Source*, a film by Chuck Workman, Beat Productions, 1996.

53 Allen Ginsberg, *Howl and Other Poems* (San Francisco: City Lights Books, 1959).

54 Michael McClure in *The Source*, a film by Chuck Workman, Beat Productions, 1996.

55 Bill Morgan, *The Beat Generation in San Francisco: A Literary Tour* (San Francisco: City Lights Books, 2003), 9.

56 Normal Mailer in *The Source*, a film by Chuck Workman, Beat Productions, 1996.

57 The phrase is from Jason Shinder, ed., *The Poem That Changed America: "Howl" Fifty Years Later* (New York: Farrar, Straus & Giroux, 2006).

58 F.H. Leacy, ed., *Historical Statistics of Canada*, 2nd ed. (Ottawa: Statistics Canada, 1983), series W340-438.

59 Owram, 179-181.

60 Paul Axelrod, *Scholars and Dollars: Politics, Economics, and the Universities of Ontario, 1945-1980* (Toronto: University of Toronto Press, 1982), 102.

61 David Bercuson, Robert Bothwell, and J.L. Granatstein, *Petrified Campus: The Crisis in Canada's Universities* (Toronto: Random House, 1997), 16-17.

62 Owram, 309.

63 Ibid., 171.

64 George Parkin Grant, *Technology and Empire: Perspectives on North America* (Toronto: House of Anansi, 1969), 65.

65   Port Huron Statement in James Miller, *Democracy is in the Streets: From Port Huron to the Siege of Chicago* (New York: Simon and Schuster, 1987).

66   Sociologist C. Wright Mills published *The Power Elite* in 1956, which argued that a small group of men who held senior positions in government, the military and business corporations "made the decisions that reverberated into each and every cranny of American life." Mills was a strong intellectual influence on the New Left. See John H. Summers, "The Deciders," *New York Times Book Review*, 14 May 2006.

67   Dominick Cavallo, *A Fiction of the Past: The Sixties in American History* (New York: St. Martin's Press, 1999), 204.

68   Ibid., 199.

69   Ibid., 198.

70   James Harding, "SUPA: An Ethical Movement in Search of An Analysis," in *Our Generation Against Nuclear War*, edited by Dimitrios Roussopoulos, (Montreal: Black Rose, 1983), 343.

71   Owram, 231-232.

72   Michael Valpy, "RCMP Infiltrated Agency that Spawned Future Star Politicians," *Globe and Mail*, 18 March 2002.

73   Ibid.

74   "The Waffle Manifesto" in H.D. Forbes, ed. *Canadian Political Thought* (Toronto: Oxford University Press, 1985), 402-405.

75   Robert A. Hackett, "The Waffle Conflict in the NDP," in Hugh G. Thorburn, ed., *Party Politics in Canada* (Scarborough: Prentice-Hall, 1979), 4th edition, 196.

76   Ibid., 193.

77   Peter Borch, "The Rise and Decline of the Saskatchewan Waffle, 1966-1973," MA thesis, University of Regina, 2005, 116.

78   Hackett, 198.

79   Arthur Marwick, *The Sixties: Cultural Revolution in Britain, France, Italy, and the United States, c.1958-c.1974* (New York: Oxford University Press, 1998), 12.

80   Theodore Roszak, "Youth and the Great Refusal," *The Nation*, 25 March 1968.

81   Theodore Roszak, *The Making of a Counter Culture: Reflections on the Technocratic Society and Its Youthful Opposition* (New York: Doubleday, 1969), 48-49.

82   Rebecca E. Klatch, *A Generation Divided: The New Left, the New Right, and the 1960s* (Berkeley: University of California Press, 1999), 134-135.

83   Bradford James Rennie, *The Rise of Agrarian Democracy: The United Farmers and Farm Women of Alberta, 1909-1921* (Toronto: University of Toronto Press, 2000), 5-11.

84   Raymond Mungo, *Famous Long Ago: My Life and Hard Times with Liberation News Service* (Boston: Beacon Press, 1970), 24.

85   Marwick, 480.

86   Owram, 210.

87   Martin A. Lee and Bruce Shlain, *Acid Dreams: The Complete Social History of LSD: The CIA, The Sixties, and Beyond* (New York: Grove Press, 1992), 180.

88   Gitlin, 209-210.

89 Klatch, 135-136; James Pitsula, "Bolen Still Channeling Change," *The Third Degree*, Spring 2000, vol. 12, no. 1, 13.

90 Klatch, 141.

CHAPTER 2

1 Pamela Wallin, *Since You Asked* (Toronto: Random House, 1998), 47.

2 Michael Hayden, *Seeking a Balance: The University of Saskatchewan 1907-1982* (Vancouver: University of British Columbia Press, 1983), 250.

3 Kenneth Heineman in his book on the peace movement on American campuses found that liberal arts and social science majors predominated in the ranks of the protesters. He attributed this to the fact that "these studies encourage critical approaches towards analyzing authority (and attract critical students), offer no specific avenues to jobs, and require sensitivity to, and reflection on, social problems." Kenneth J. Heineman, *Campus Wars: The Peace Movement at American State Universities in the Vietnam Era* (New York: New York University Press, 1993), 78.

4 University of Regina Archives (URA), Office of the University Secretary Files, 78.5, 307.0, "Analysis of Faculty by Nationality," 15 March 1971.

5 Saskatchewan Archives Board (SAB), Oral History Project, no. 87, "Student Unrest at the University of Saskatchewan, Regina Campus in the 1960s and 1970s," tape R-10, 321, interview with Joe Roberts, 7 April 1987.

6 J.L. Granatstein, *Canada 1957-1967: The Years of Uncertainty and Innovation* (Toronto: Mc-Clelland and Stewart, 1986), 186.

7 Newspaper clippings in *A World Away: Stories From the Regina Five*, produced and directed by Mark Wihak (Chat Perdue!, MGR: 2001).

8 Clement Greenberg, "Painting and Sculpture in Prairie Canada Today," *Canadian Art*, March/April 1963.

9 URA, Ken Lochhead Papers, 86-29, Correspondence, Ted Godwin, Art McKay, 1974-1985, Ted Godwin, "Ancient Days of Yore."

10 *Leader* (Regina), 26 October 1911.

11 James M. Pitsula, *An Act of Faith: The Early Years of Regina College* (Regina: Canadian Plains Research Center, 1988), 135.

12 SAB, T.C. Douglas Papers, R-33.1 V224 (5-3) 7/11, J.F. Leddy to J. Foster, 24 May 1955; J. Foster to "Sir or Madam," 11 May 1955.

13 Dianne Lloyd, *Woodrow: A Biography of W.S. Lloyd* (The Woodrow Lloyd Memorial Fund, 1979), 164-170.

14 SAB, W.S. Lloyd Papers, R-61.3, E-25, 36/37, minutes of a meeting of the university senate, 8 July 1959.

15 URA, Publications Section, University of Saskatchewan Senate minutes, 8 July 1959.

16 URA, Publications Section, University of Saskatchewan: Organization and Structure: Report of a Committee on the Organization and Structure of the University, as Amended and Adopted by the Senate of the University of Saskatchewan, 4 November 1966, 9.

17 URA, Principal's/President's Papers, 80-38, 100-5.4, convocation, spring 1972, address by President J.W.T. Spinks.

18   URA, Dean's/Principal's Office Files, 75-7, 102.1-4, "Wascana Center: A Center for Gov-
     ernment, Education, Arts and Recreation in Regina, Saskatchewan."

19   "Famous Architect Likely Wascana Centre Planner," *Leader-Post* (Regina), 18 July 1961.

20   URA, Dean's/Principal's Office Files, 75-7, 103.2, Minoru Yamasaki and Thomas Church,
     "Report on Wascana Centre."

21   Ibid.

22   "Regina Campus Master Plan Passed," *Leader-Post* (Regina), 4 January 1962.

23   URA, Publications Section, University of Saskatchewan, Board of Governors minutes, 4
     January 1962.

24   "Realization of Visions of Many for 60 Years," *Leader-Post* (Regina), 9 October 1965.

25   URA, John Archer Speeches and Reports, 80-35, FP 80-004, v. 1, John H. Archer, "Address
     Delivered at the Opening of the Library Building," 14 October 1967.

26   URA, Principal's/Dean's Office Files, 78-3, 200.2, statement concerning the Students'
     Union Building, 6 August 1968.

27   URA, Principal's/Dean's Office Files, 78-3, 101.10-2, J.W.T. Spinks to W.A. Riddell, 8 Octo-
     ber 1968.

28   URA, Publications Section, University of Saskatchewan, Board of Governors minutes, 2
     May 1968.

29   Mary Ann Dzuback, *Robert M. Hutchins: Portrait of an Educator* (Chicago: University of
     Chicago Press, 1991), 110-134.

30   Ibid., 240, 260.

31   URA, Principal's/Dean's Office Files, 78-3, 102.7, W.H. Ferry, "Why the College is Failing"
     (paper presented to the Association for Higher Education, NEA, Detroit, 1 July 1963).

32   URA, Dean's/Principal's Office Files, 75-7, 102.1-12, Dallas Smythe, "A Few Comments on
     the Liberal Arts Situation at Regina."

33   URA, Principal's/Dean's Office Files, 78-3, 102.6-1, A.B. Van Cleave, "Some Thoughts,
     Problems, and Suggestions Regarding the Development of Regina Campus," November
     1963.

34   Jack Mitchell, guest editorial, *The Carillon*, 13 March 1964.

35   "The Role of the University," "The New Student," *Carillon*, 20 September 1960.

36   David Orr, "The Student as Instrument," *Carillon*, 12 September 1966.

37   URA, Principal's/President's Papers, 80-38, 302.11-1, "Address by Premier W.S. Lloyd,
     Laying of Cornerstone," 26 September 1963.

38   URA, College/Faculty of Arts and Science, University of Saskatchewan, Regina Campus
     Files, 85-54, 102.1, J.L. Wolfson, "Concerning the Proposal to form a Faculty of Natural
     Sciences and Mathematics: A Minority Report."

39   URA, Principal's/Dean's Office Files, 78-3, 600.1, "Summary of New Curriculum as Ap-
     proved by Arts and Science Faculty," September 1965.

40   Paul Axelrod, *Scholars and Dollars: Politics, Economics, and the Universities of Ontario, 1945-
     1980* (Toronto: University of Toronto Press, 1982), 103-105.

41   Patricia Jasen, "'In Pursuit of Human Values (or Laugh When You Say That)': The Student
     Critique of the Arts Curriculum in the 1960s," *Youth, University and Canadian Society: Essays*

in the Social History of Higher Education, edited by Paul Axelrod and John G. Reid (Kingston/Montreal: McGill-Queen's University Press, 1989), 254-262.

42   URA, Principal's/Dean's Office Files, 78-3, 400.18, "Analysis of the Briefs Received by the Task Force Enquiring into the Desirability of Establishing a Faculty of Science and Mathematics"; A.B. Van Cleave, "Re: Proposed Faculty of Science and Mathematics," 30 January 1968.

43   URA, Principal's/Dean's Office Files, 78-3, 400.18, "Analysis of the Briefs Received by the Task Force Enquiring into the Desirability of Establishing a Faculty of Science and Mathematics"; Dallas Smythe to Faculty of the Division of Social Sciences, draft brief to Senior Academic Committee, 26 January 1968.

44   URA, Publications Section, University of Saskatchewan, Regina Campus, Faculty of Arts and Science minutes, 9 July 1968.

45   URA, College/Faculty of Arts and Science, University of Saskatchewan, Regina Campus Files, 85-54, 104-18, F.H.A. Rummens to the Faculty of Arts and Science, notice of motion, 8 September 1970.

46   URA, College/Faculty of Arts and Science, University of Saskatchewan, Regina Campus Files, 85-54, 104-18, F.H.A. Rummens, Report on the "Liberal Arts Education Policy," 15 January 1971.

47   URA, College/Faculty of Arts and Science, University of Saskatchewan, Regina Campus Files, 85-54, 104-18, J. Pachner to Michael Scholar, 29 September 1971.

48   URA, College/Faculty of Arts and Science, University of Saskatchewan, Regina Campus Files, 85-54, 104-18, Dallas Smythe to Michael Scholar, 5 February 1971.

49   URA, College/Faculty of Arts and Science, University of Saskatchewan, Regina Campus Files, 85-54, 104-18, G. Edgar Vaughan to D. Pogany, 4 January 1972.

50   URA, Publications Section, University of Saskatchewan, Regina Campus, "Summary Expenditure Establishment and Student Class Registration, November 1973."

51   URA, Publications Section, Regina Campus Council minutes, 20 and 21 October 1965.

52   URA, Publications Section, University of Saskatchewan: Organization and Structure: Report of a Committee on the Organization and Structure of the University, as Amended and Adopted by the Senate of the University of Saskatchewan, 4 November 1966, 14.

53   University of Saskatchewan, Annual Report of the President, 1968, 1.

54   University of Saskatchewan, Annual Report of the President, 1968, 10.

55   University of Saskatchewan, Annual Report of the President, 1969-70 to 1973-74.

56   Hayden, 250.

57   Archives of the University of Saskatchewan (AUS), President's Office Records, series 4, C4, Archer, J.H., J.W.T. Spinks to J.H. Archer, 27 January 1971.

58   AUS, President's Office Records, series 4, C4, Archer, J.H., J.H. Archer to J.W.T. Spinks, 12 May 1972, attached resolution.

59   "Spinks Says Gov't Aim to Control University," *Leader-Post* (Regina), 11 April 1973.

60   Report of the Royal Commission on Organization and Structure, 22 December 1973.

61   SAB, A.E. Blakeney Papers, R-565, III 137b, J.W.T. Spinks to G. MacMurchy, 16 January 1974, comments on Hall Commission Report.

CHAPTER 3

1   Don Mitchell, "Cafeteria Comments," *Carillon*, 15 October 1966.

2   "Carillon One of C.U.P.'s Best Papers," *Carillon*, 26 January 1968.

3   University of Regina Archives (URA), Dean's/Principal's Office Files, 75-7, 400.4, Student Elections; 75-7, 300.1-7, nominees proposed by the nominating committee for standing committees for the year 1958-59, 9 September 1958.

4   URA, Publications Section, Students' Union Ephemerae, "The Constitution of the Students' Representative Council of Regina College of the University of Saskatchewan."

5   "Editorial," *The Sheet*, 16 February 1962.

6   URA, Dean's/Principal's Office Files, 75-7, 400.1-1, "Re: *The College Record*, March/51 from Kinsman."

7   Ibid.

8   Ibid.

9   G.K. Piller, "Food for Thought," *College Record*, 29 January 1948.

10   I. Kreel, "A Real Education," *College Record*, 19 March 1948.

11   "Men's Residence," *Sheet*, 1958.

12   College Record, February 1955; *Sheet*, first edition, 1956.

13   "Censored," *College Record*, December 1955.

14   URA, Dean's/Principal's Office Files, 75-7, 400.1-1, S.R.C. financial statement.

15   "S.R.C. Budget," *Sheet*, December 1957.

16   "S.R.C. Budget, 1962-63," *Carillon*, 9 November 1962.

17   "Students' Union Financial Statement," *Carillon*, 24 September 1971.

18   *Carillon*, 9 February 1973.

19   "Editorial Policy, 1961-62," *Sheet*, 30 March 1962.

20   *Sheet*, 2 February 1962.

21   Don Barker, "Editorial," *Sheet*, September 1962.

22   "Why the Carillon?" *Carillon*, 26 October 1962.

23   *Carillon*, 17 January 1964. The masthead in the late sixties and early seventies shows that the *Carillon* also subscribed to the Liberation News Service, Underground Press Syndicate, and Last Post News Service.

24   Ken Mitchell, "Student Journalism: Policies of University Papers Change," *Leader-Post* (Regina), 22 January 1965.

25   "S.R.C. Report," *Carillon*, 12 October 1962.

26   "Constitution Changes," *Carillon*, 13 February 1964.

27   *Carillon*, 6 March 1970.

28   "The By-Laws of the Students' Union of the University of Saskatchewan, Regina Campus," *Carillon*, 20 September 1968.

29   Ron Verzuh, *Underground Times: Canada's Flower-Child Revolutionaries* (Toronto: Deneau, 1989), 20.

30 "Editorial Policy," *Carillon*, 20 September 1965.

31 Ibid.

32 "An Open Letter to Advertisers," *Carillon*, 1965.

33 *Carillon*, 15 October 1965.

34 "Conway," *Carillon*, 22 October 1965.

35 "Answer to Carillon Critics," *Carillon*, 15 October 1965.

36 "Kelly," *Carillon*, 22 October 1965.

37 National Archives of Canada (NAC), Records of the Canadian Security Intelligence Service, Record Group 146, vol. 2774, part 2, 8 December 1965, file number removed pursuant to the *Access to Information Act*.

38 Saskatchewan Archives Board (SAB), Oral History Project, no. 87, "Student Unrest at the University of Saskatchewan, Regina Campus in the 1960s and 1970s," tape R-10, 319, Don Mitchell interview, 8 April 1987.

39 Clint Bomphray, "Good-bye to All That," *Carillon*, 27 February 1967.

40 "Follow the Leader," *Carillon*, 9 February 1968.

41 "Follow the Leader," *Carillon*, 16 February 1968.

42 "Follow the Leader," *Carillon*, 21 May 1970.

43 Ibid.

44 "Follow the Leader," *Carillon*, 18 September 1970

45 For an account of this incident, see Roberta Lexier, "Economic Control Versus Academic Freedom: Ross Thatcher and the University of Saskatchewan, Regina Campus," *Saskatchewan History*, 54, 2, Fall 2002, 18-30.

46 URA, Principal's/Dean's Office Files, 78-3, 302.7, Potashville Educational Association, annual convention, Regina, 18 October 1967, speech by Premier Ross Thatcher.

47 "Is the University a Scapegoat?" *Carillon*, 3 November 1967.

48 *Carillon*, 17 November 1967.

49 URA, Principal's/Dean's Office Files, 78-3, 2000.3, J.W.T. Spinks to W.A. Riddell, 16 November 1967.

50 Archives of the University of Saskatchewan (AUS), President's Office Records, Series 4, C38, Regina Campus, Riddell, W.A., 1964-69, W.A. Riddell to J.W.T. Spinks, 28 November 1967.

51 AUS, President's Office Records, Series 4, C38, Regina Campus, Riddell, W.A., 1964-69, J.W.T. Spinks to W.A. Riddell, 3 January 1968.

52 URA, Principal's/Dean's Office Files, 78-3, 302.7, Allan Guy to W.A. Riddell, 4 January 1968.

53 URA, Dr. W.A. Riddell Papers, 84-31, 40, W.A. Riddell, diary, 1 February 1968.

54 URA, Principal's/Dean's Office Files, 78-3, 2000.3, note to file, W.A. Riddell, 15 February 1968.

55 "Guy Claims NDP Tool of Campus Protesters," *Leader-Post* (Regina), 6 February 1969.

56 "Principal Concerned About Guy Story," *Carillon*, 1 March 1968.

57   "Copy of Letter Sent from Principal Riddell to Ralph Smith, S.R.C. President," *Carillon*, 8
      March 1968.

58   "Students' Union Threatened," *Carillon*, 8 March 1968.

59   URA, Dr. W.A. Riddell Papers, 84-31, 40, W.A. Riddell, notes on council meeting, 29 Febru-
      ary 1968.

60   URA, Principal's/Dean's Office Files, 78-3, 2000.3, W.A. Riddell, "Statement to Council,"
      18 October 1968.

61   "Censor the Carillon?… Scold the Faculty?… Develop a 'Good Public Image?…'" *Carillon*,
      15 November 1968.

62   Liz Sorsdahl, "Carillon Distributed in Downtown Regina," *Carillon*, 18 October 1968.

63   URA, Principal's/Dean's Office Files 78-3, 302.1-4, statement re: Students' Representative
      Council, W.A. Riddell, 13 November 1968.

64   Ibid.

65   The Toronto underground newspaper, *Harbinger*, also came under attack for a cover illus-
      tration of a woman giving birth. The ensuing obscenity trial bankrupted the newspaper.
      See Ron Verzuh, *Underground Times: Canada's Flower-Child Revolutionaries* (Toronto: De-
      neau, 1989), 112.

66   URA, Principal's/Dean's Office Files, 78-3, 2000.3, note to file, 10 December 1968.

67   AUS, J.W.T. Fonds, unprocessed accession, Student Unrest, W.A. Riddell to J.W.T. Spinks,
      16 December 1968.

68   URA, Principal's/Dean's Office Files, 78-3, 302.1-4, Allan Tubby statement.

69   "The Strange Story of Political Obscenities in the *Carillon* or How to Suppress a Paper
      Without Appearing to Try…" *Carillon*, 24 January 1969.

70   URA, Principal's/Dean's Office Files, 78-3, 2000.1-3, Students' Representative Council to
      fellow students, 2 January 1969.

71   "Labor, SFU Rap Governors," *Leader-Post* (Regina), 6 January 1969.

72   URA, Principal's/Dean's Office Files, 78-3, 2000.1-3, *Leader-Post* (Regina), 3 January 1969.

73   "Union Supporters," *Carillon*, 8 January 1969.

74   URA, Principal's/Dean's Office Files, 78-3, 2000.1-3, *Leader-Post* (Regina), 4 January 1969.

75   URA, Principal's/Dean's Office Files, 78-3, 2000.1-2, G.E. Ross Sneath to Allan Tubby, 31
      December 1968; 78-3, 2000.3, letter signed by 25 clergymen.

76   "Editorial," *Carillon*, 8 January 1969.

77   "Referendum Supports Union," *Carillon*, 13 January 1969.

78   Ibid.

79   NAC, Canadian Security Intelligence Service, Record Group 146, Vol. 2774, part 4, 16 Janu-
      ary 1969, file number removed pursuant to Access to Information Act.

80   "Referendum Supports Union," *Carillon*, 13 January 1969.

81   URA, Principal's/Dean's Office Files, 78-3, 2000.1-3, notes on negotiations between the
      Board of Governors Committee and the S.R.C. Committee, 3 February 1969; "Students
      Take Story to Public," *Carillon*, 14 February 1969.

82   "Public Won't Stand for Outrageous Acts," *Leader-Post* (Regina), 6 February 1969.

83   "Guy Claims NDP Tool of Campus Protesters," *Leader-Post* (Regina), 6 February 1969.

84   "Thatcher Attacks Students," *Carillon*, 7 February 1969.

85   URA, Principal's/Dean's Office Files, 78-3, 2000.1-4, S.C. Atkinson to Board of Governors, 6 December 1968.

86   URA, Principal's/Dean's Office Files, 78-3, 2000.1-3, S.C. Atkinson to J.W.T Spinks, 6 January 1969.

87   URA, Principal's/Dean's Office Files, 78-3, 2000.1-4, S.C. Atkinson to Members of the Board of Governors, 7 January 1969.

88   URA, Principal's/Dean's Office Files, 78-3, 400.20, S.C. Atkinson to J.W.T. Spinks, 17 January 1969.

89   *Carillon*, 9 February 1973.

90   SAB, Oral History Project, no. 87, "Student Unrest at the University of Saskatchewan, Regina Campus in the 1960s and 1970s," tape R-10, 319, Don Mitchell interview, 8 April 1987

91   URA, Principal's/Dean's Office Files, 78-3, 302.1-3, "Basis of Agreement between the Students' Union and the University; Union Agreement Expected Wednesday," *Carillon*, 3 March 1969.

92   URA, Principal's/Dean's Office Files, 78-3, 2000.3, John E. Chappell, Jr. to W.A. Riddell, 14 March 1969.

93   URA, Publications Section, University of Saskatchewan, Board of Governors minutes, 8 July 1971.

94   "Students Defeat Occupation Motion," *Carillon*, 26 September 1969.

95   "Can Participatory Democracy Work Without Participation?" *Carillon*, 24 October 1969.

96   Barry Lipton, "Prairie Fire History Illustrates Struggles of the Alternate Press," *Briarpatch*, May 1980, 35.

97   *Carillon*, 25 June 1971.

98   "Students' Union to Support Saskatchewan Workers," *Carillon*, 13 March 1970; "Another T. Eaton Branch in Regina," *Carillon*, 3 October 1970; "A Worker-Student Alliance," *Carillon*, 20 March 1970; "Government Moves to Place Construction Workers Under Bill 2," *Carillon*, 2 July 1970; "Colonel Thatcher Attacks Labour," *Carillon*, 4 December 1970; "Strike at Parkside Nursing Homes Goes into Third Week," *Carillon*, 30 July 1970.

99   "Farmers' Bust," *Carillon*, 21 November, 2 December 1969; "Farmers' Union—Opposition to Thatcher," *Carillon*, 14 May 1971; "NFU Informs Consumers About Kraft Boycott," *Carillon*, 26 November 1971.

100 "Aftermath: Regina Court Fire," *Carillon*, 29 October 1971; "Groups Organizing to Protect Tenants," *Carillon*, 23 March 1973.

101 "Suggests Referendum Be Held on Carillon," *Carillon*, 5 March 1971.

102 Gerard Matte, letter to the editor, *Carillon*, 25 June 1971.

103 "More on Administration Backlash," *Carillon*, 29 October 1971.

104 Heintz, "Graffiti," *Carillon*, 15 October 1971.

105 "Larry Schultz: An Interview with the SRC President," *Carillon*, 8 September 1971.

106 "Editor's Note," *Carillon*, 19 October 1973.

CHAPTER 4

1   Helen Lefkowitz Horowitz, *Campus Life: Undergraduate Cultures from the End of the Eighteenth Century to the Present* (Chicago: University of Chicago Press), 11-20. I have modified Horowitz's nomenclature somewhat, but the essential concepts are the same.

2   Ibid., 118.

3   Victor Hugo, *Les Miserables* (Harmondsworth: Penguin, 1982)

4   Sara Z. Burke, *Seeking the Highest Good: Social Service and Gender at the University of Toronto, 1888-1937* (Toronto: University of Toronto Press, 1996), 31-32.

5   Ibid., 46-47.

6   Ibid., 57-59.

7   Ibid., 33-34.

8   R. MacGregor Dawson, *William Lyon Mackenzie King: A Political Biography* (Toronto: University of Toronto Press, 1958), 34-35.

9   A.B. McKillop, *Matters of Mind: The University in Ontario, 1791-1951* (Toronto: University of Toronto Press, 1994), 242.

10 Paul Axelrod, *Making a Middle Class: Student Life in English Canada during the Thirties* (Montreal & Kingston: McGill-Queen's University Press, 1990), 135.

11 Ibid., 146.

12 Paul Axelrod, *Scholars and Dollars: Politics, Economics, and the Universities of Ontario, 1945-1980* (Toronto: University of Toronto Press, 1982), 16, 18.

13 J.D. Herbert, "What Price Education?" *College Record*, 1 May 1945.

14 Peter Neary, "Canadian Universities and Canadian Veterans of World War II," in Peter Neary and J.L. Granatstein, eds., *The Veterans Charter and Post-World War II Canada* (Montreal & Kingston: McGill-Queen's University Press, 1998), 133-134.

15 This was true at McMaster University. See Charles M. Johnston and John C. Weaver, *Student Days: Student Life at McMaster University from the 1890s to the 1980s* (Hamilton: McMaster University Alumni Association, 1986), 81-91.

16 More recently, the sixties abandonment of the university's *in loco parentis* role has been challenged. In 2002, the parents of Elizabeth Shin, a student at M.I.T. who took her own life, filed a $27 million wrongful death suit against the university. The parents claimed that M.I.T., overly concerned with protecting Elizabeth's right to privacy, failed to act "*in loco parentis* to the diseased." Deborah Sontag, "Who Was Responsible For Elizabeth Shin?" *New York Times*, 28 April 2002.

17 Dean W.A. Riddell, "To All Students," *College Record*, March 1955.

18 "A Letter to the Editor," by "A Student," *College Record*, February 1955.

19 Bert Promislow, "Presenting True Democracy," *College Record*, 18 November 1947.

20 "Tories Win Campus Vote with Stand on Weapons," *Leader-Post* (Regina), 24 November 1962.

21 "Blow Out," *Carillon*, 5 November 1963.

22 Linda Sponsler, "Mud, Splinters & Feathers," *Carillon*, 23 September 1966.

23 "Frosh Week…," *Carillon*, 6 October 1967.

24   *Carillon*, 3 October 1969.

25   "Bacchus Festival," *Carillon*, 1 March 1968.

26   "Our Cup Runneth Over," *Carillon*, 17 March 1967.

27   "Official Rules For The Carillon Hotel Inspection Tour (CHIT—'72), *Carillon*, 3 March 1972. Drinking games continue to be popular among college students. According to four recent academic studies that surveyed more than 6,000 students in the United States, 50 to 80 per cents said they have played them. A favourite is beer pong. In this game, "each team stands at the end of a table in front of a triangle of cups partially filled with beer. Players pitch the ball into the other team's cups. When a player sinks the ball, the other team must chug the beer and remove the cup from the table. When one side runs out of cups, they lose." Beer companies promote the game, as do companies that sell beer pong tables. Jeffrey Gettleman, "As Young Adults Drink to Win, Businesses Get In on the Game," *New York Times*, 16 October 2005.

28   "Mitchell and the Mountain," *Carillon*, 9 November 1962.

29   "Holiday Thoughts," *Carillon*, 18 December 1963.

30   "Editorial," *Sheet*, January 1959.

31   "Anybody else disagree?" *Sheet*, April 1959.

32   "Few Decent Citizens at Regina Campus," *Sheet*, 3 November 1961.

33   "WAR IS DECLARED!" *Carillon*, 16 October 1962.

34   University of Regina Archives (URA), Dean's/Principal's Office Files, 75-7, 400.1-2, A.G. Cookson to W.A. Riddell, 5 November 1962.

35   "THE GIANT AWAKENS," *Carillon*, 9 November 1962.

36   "Snake Dance Leads to Police Warning," *Leader-Post* (Regina), 1 November 1962.

37   Keith Walden, "Respectable Hooligans: Male Toronto College Students Celebrate Hallowe'en, 1884-1910," *Canadian Historical Review*, 68, 1, 1987, 10-16.

38   *Leader* (Regina), 4 February 1915.

39   URA, Publications Section, Regina College Register, December 1923.

40   "Hijinx," *College Record*, first issue, fall 1951.

41   *College Record*, 8 December 1962.

42   Elaine Hamilton, "Arts and Science," *Sheet*, November 1959.

43   Doug Owram, *Born at the Right Time: A History of the Baby Boom in Canada* (Toronto: University of Toronto Press, 1996), 159-161.

44   "Editorial," *Carillon*, 23 November 1962.

45   B. Wigmore, "Letter to the Editor," *Carillon*, 15 March 1963.

46   URA, Dean's/Principal's Office Files, 75-7, 400.1-2, S.R.C. Social Directorate, 22 February 1955.

47   URA, Dean's/Principal's Office Files, 75-7, 400.1-2, Report of the Student Activities Committee, no date.

48   URA, Dean's/Principal's Office Files, 75-7, 400.1-2, W.A. Riddell to Mike Badham, 18 December 1962.

49   URA, Principal's/Dean's Office Files, 78-3, 400.2-1, Ken Mitchell to Mr. Bain, 7 April 1965.

50   "Editor of 'Sheet' Charges Riddell with Interfering," *Leader-Post* (Regina), 28 February 1962.

51   "Welcoming Message," *Carillon*, 17 September 1964.

52   "Students Adopt New Constitution," *Leader-Post* (Regina), 23 February 1965.

53   "The Proposed Constitution and Bylaws," *Carillon*, 22 January 1965.

54   Under the new constitution, the Students' Union was the official name for the students' organization. The S.R.C. was the board of directors of the Union consisting of the president, first vice-president, and second vice-president, who were elected by the students at large, and a general council of no less than ten and no more than twenty members elected by students of the various colleges.

55   Ron Thompson, "The Waiting Game—Its Facts and Failure," *Carillon*, 2 March 1965.

56   URA, Principal's/Dean's Office Files, 78-3, 302.1-2, Frederick Alexander to Stuart Mann, 27 February 1967.

57   Ron Thompson, "Student Boycott," *Carillon*, 16 September 1964.

58   "Regina Campus Students Want Royal Commission on Autonomy," *Leader-Post* (Regina), 20 March 1964.

59   *Carillon*, 15 October 1965.

60   "Time for an End to $ Waste on Yearbook," *Carillon*, 21 October 1966.

61   "Student Unionism Boosted; Becomes Campus Priority," *Carillon*, 30 September 1966.

62   "Demonstration Airs Student Grievances," *Carillon*, 20 January 1967.

63   URA, Principal's/Dean's Office Files, 78-3, 2000.1-2, Don Mitchell to J.W.T. Spinks, no date.

64   URA, Principal's/Dean's Office Files, 78-3, 2000.1-2, J.W.T. Spinks to Don Mitchell, 24 February 1967.

65   "Senate Representation Possible," *Carillon*, 17 February 1967.

66   Student Power cartoon, *Carillon*, 13 October 1967.

67   "Past…" *Carillon*, 6 March 1967.

CHAPTER 5

1   Pierre Vallieres, *White Niggers of America*, translated by Joan Pinkham (Toronto: McClelland and Stewart, 1971).

2   Peter Gzowski, "This is Our Alabama," *Maclean's*, 6 July 1963.

3   Maurice Isserman and Michael Kazin, *America Divided: The Civil War of the 1960s* (New York: Oxford University Press, 2000), 32.

4   Hans Kieferle, "The 'Know Nothings,'" *Carillon*, 12 October 1962.

5   *Carillon*, 4 December 1964.

6   Isserman and Kazin, 29-31.

7   Mark Hamilton Lytle, *America's Uncivil Wars: The Sixties Era from Elvis to the Fall of Richard Nixon* (New York: Oxford University Press, 2006), 74-76.

8   Isserman and Kazin, 34; Lytle, 121-126.

9   Lytle, 134-137.

10   Martin Luther King, Jr., "I Have A Dream," 28 August 1963, www.stanford.edu/group/ King/publications/speeches/address_at_march_on_washington.pdf

11   Lytle, 152-160.

12   Saskatchewan Archives Board (SAB), W.S. Lloyd Papers, R-61.8 XXI 125b ½, J.H. Brockel-bank to Mrs. James J. Reeb, 17 March 1965.

13   Lytle, 160

14   Isserman and Kazin, 133-139.

15   Malcolm X, "The Ballot or the Bullet," in Alexander Bloom and Wini Breines, *"Takin' it to the Streets": A Sixties Reader*, second edition (New York: Oxford University Press, 2003), 108.

16   Lytle, 187.

17   Ibid., 235.

18   Ibid., 189.

19   Ibid., 234.

20   De Jong, "Dateline Detroit," *Carillon*, 22 September 1967.

21   "The Black Panther Platform," in Alexander Bloom and Wini Breines, *"Takin' it to the Streets": A Sixties Reader*, second edition (New York: Oxford University Press, 2003), 125-128.

22   Lytle, 237.

23   Keith Reynolds, "Black Panthers," *Carillon*, 21 November 1969.

24   *Carillon*, 7 November 1969.

25   Carl Singleton, ed. *The Sixties in America*, vol. 2 (Pasadena: Salem Press, 1999), 338-339.

26   Monica Davey, "Chicago Divided Over Proposal to Honor a Slain Black Panther," *New York Times*, 5 March 2006.

27   James M. Pitsula, "The Saskatchewan CCF Government and Treaty Indians, 1944-64," *Canadian Historical Review*, vol. 75, no. 1, March 1994, 36.

28   Sally M. Weaver, *Making Canadian Indian Policy: The Hidden Agenda, 1968-1970* (Toronto: University of Toronto Press, 1981), 26.

29   Ibid., 187.

30   James M. Pitsula, "The Thatcher Government in Saskatchewan and Treaty Indians, 1964-1971: The Quiet Revolution," *Saskatchewan History*, vol. 48, no. 1, Spring 1996, 14.

31   Ibid., 12.

32   Howard Adams, *Prison of Grass: Canada From the Native Point of View* (Toronto: New Press, 1975), 176.

33   Ibid., 214.

34   *Leader-Post* (Regina), 2 April 1969.

35   *Globe and Mail* (Toronto), 26 July 1967. The sentence does not appear in the final, published version of the report. See *Indians and the Law*, a survey prepared for the Honorable Arthur Laing, Department of Indian Affairs and Northern Development, by the Canadian Corrections Association, August 1967.

36 *Leader-Post* (Regina), 26 July; 5 August 1967.

37 In April 1969 Adams had been elected president of the Metis Society, the organization that supplanted the Saskatchewan Native Action Committee. See James M. Pitsula, "The Thatcher Government in Saskatchewan and the Revival of Metis Nationalism, 1964-1971," *Great Plains Quarterly*, vol. 17, no. 3 and 4, Summer/Fall 1997, 227.

38 *Leader-Post* (Regina), 4 May 1970.

39 *Prairie Fire*, 25 November-2 December 1969.

40 SAB, Allan Guy Papers, R-47 I 3, "Métis Society of Saskatchewan," presented to the Liberal Party of Saskatchewan annual convention, 30 November 1970.

41 "Racial Prejudice and the Regina Indian," *Carillon*, 15 March 1963.

42 "Civil Rights Tested in Montmartre," *Carillon*, 29 September 1967.

43 Barbara Cameron, "A Study in Frustration," *Carillon*, 13 September 1968.

44 Harvey Linnen, "Winter of Our Discontent," *Carillon*, 29 September 1967.

45 "Neestow Appeal for Funds," *Carillon*, 21 January 1966.

46 Ibid.

47 N. Bolen and K. Healy, "Read or Riot," *Carillon*, 26 January 1968.

48 *Carillon*, 15 November 1968.

49 Rene Levesque, Interviewed by Richard M. Alway, *Canadian Public Figures on Tape*, The Ontario Institute for Studies in Education, n.d.

50 Robert Bothwell, Ian Drummond, and John English, *Canada Since 1945: Power, Politics and Provincialism* (Toronto, University of Toronto Press, 1989), 265-273.

51 David Charters, "The Amateur Revolutionaries: A Reassessment of the FLQ," *Terrorism and Political Violence*, 9, 1, Spring 1997, 141.

52 FLQ Manifesto, reprinted in John Saywell, *Quebec 70: A Documentary Narrative* (Toronto: University of Toronto Press, 1971), 46-51.

53 Charters, 155.

54 Ibid., 156.

55 Ibid., 159.

56 Robert Bothwell, Ian Drummond, and John English, 372.

57 Ibid.

58 "Trudeau's Our P.E.T.," *Carillon*, 20 June 1968.

59 John Gallagher, "Sympathy For FLQ," *Carillon*, 16 October 1970.

60 "Declaration of Editorial Intent," *Carillon*, 23 October 1970.

61 "Part of the crowd…," *Carillon*, 23 October 1970.

62 John Gallagher, "The Story is Wearing Thin," *Carillon*, 30 October 1970.

63 Doug Owram, *Born at the Right Time: A History of the Baby Boom in Canada* (Toronto: University of Toronto Press, 1996), 253.

64 Canada, Department of Labor, *Women at Work in Canada* (Ottawa, 1964); Canada, Labor Canada, *Participation*, part 1 of *Women in the Labor Force* (Ottawa, 1983).

65 Ibid.

66 Mongi Mouelhi, "University Enrolment Trends," *Education Quarterly Review*, vol. 2, no. 1, 1995, 37.

67 "Queen is Best," *Carillon*, 17 January 1964.

68 Miss Saskatchewan Roughrider photo, *Carillon*, 2 October 1964.

69 "Tap-Way," *Carillon*, 2 October 1964.

70 "Bondage A-Go-Go," Carillon, 29 October 1965.

71 Linda Sponsler, "Do I Hear a Bid?" *Carillon*, 10 November 1966.

72 Valerie J. Korinek, *Roughing It in the Suburbs: Reading Chatelaine Magazine in the Fifties and Sixties* (Toronto: University of Toronto Press, 2000), 326-330.

73 Ibid., 312.

74 Nancy Adamson, Linda Briskin, and Margaret McPhail, *Feminist Organizing for Change: The Contemporary Women's Movement in Canada* (Toronto: Oxford University Press, 1988), 39.

75 Elaine Tyler May, *Homeward Bound: American Families in the Cold War Era* (New York: Basic Books, 1999).

76 John English, *The Worldly Years: The Life of Lester Pearson*, vol 2: 1949-1972 (Toronto: Alfred A. Knopf, 1992), 245.

77 Monique Begin, "The Royal Commission on the Status of Women in Canada: Twenty Years Later," in Constance Backhouse and David H. Flaherty, eds., *Challenging Times: The Women's Movement in Canada and the United States* (Montreal & Kingston: McGill-Queen's University Press, 1992), 23.

78 Ibid., 22.

79 Kimberly Speers, "The Royal Commission on the Status of Women in Canada, 1967-1970: Liberal Feminism and its Radical Implications, in Sharon Anne Cook, Lorna R. McLean, and Kate O'Rourke, eds., *Framing Our Past: Canadian Women's History in the Twentieth Century* (Montreal & Kingston: McGill-Queen's University Press, 2001), 256.

80 Janine Brodie, Shelley A.M. Gavigan, and Jane Jenson, *The Politics of Abortion* (Toronto: Oxford University Press, 1992), 21.

81 Myrna Kostash, *Long Way From Home: The Story of the Sixties Generation in Canada* (Toronto: James Lorimer & Company, 1980), 176.

82 Ibid., 178.

83 Alison Prentice et al., *Canadian Women: A History* (Toronto: Harcourt Brace Jovanovich, 1988), 365.

84 Adamson, Briskin, and McPhail, 44.

85 Ibid., 55.

86 Ibid., 56.

87 "Fratenitas: The Role of Women in Canadian Society," *Carillon*, 15 March 1963.

88 Letter to the editor from May Archer, *Carillon*, 8 October 1965.

89 May Archer, "Mothers Arise!" *Carillon*, 29 October 1965.

90 University of Regina Archives (URA), Principal's/Dean's Office Files, 78-3, 2001.11, Barb Cameron and Maija Crane, "University of Saskatchewan, Regina Campus, Day Care

Centre," September 1969; URA, 78-3, 2001.11, Roy Borrowman, report of the daycare centre, 1 May 1970.

91   Wilma Brown, "Status of Women," *Carillon*, 13 September 1968.

92   "Facts on Working Mothers Released by Department of Labor," *Carillon*, 30 July 1970; Wilma Brown, "Status of Women," *Carillon*, 4 October 1968; Pat Hall, "What's The Ugliest Part of Your Body?" *Carillon*, 25 October 1968; Maija L. Crane, "Social Implications of Birth Control and Abortion," *Carillon*, 31 October 1969.

93   "Women's Caucus and the Birth Control Pamphlet," *Carillon*, 19 September 1969.

94   Ibid.

95   "Women's Liberation and the Frosh Queen Contest," *Carillon*, 10 October 1969.

96   "Violence flared...," *Carillon*, 19 November 1971.

97   "Women's Centre on Campus," *Carillon*, 14 May 1971.

98   Ibid.

99   Colleen Slater, "Women's Liberation: Hog Wash and Lye Soap," *Carillon*, 21 November 1969.

100   Ibid.

101   Regina Women's Liberation, "Hogwash and Lye Soap Revisited," *Carillon*, 2 December 1969.

102   "Motion Aborted," *Carillon*, 15 September 1972.

103   "Aquarius... Club With a Future," *Carillon*, 24 October 1969.

104   "What's That You Said?" *Carillon*, 16 October 1970.

105   Owram, 121.

106   Barry Lipton, "View From the Bottom," *Carillon*, 29 March 1974.

CHAPTER 6

1   Reg Whitaker and Gary Marcuse, *Cold War Canada: The Making of A National Insecurity State, 1945-1957* (Toronto: University of Toronto Press, 1994), 161-187.

2   Rex Weyler, *Greenpeace: How A Group of Ecologists, Journalists and Visionaries Changed the World* (Vancouver: Raincoast Books, 2004), 35-36.

3   "It's a Fact," *Sheet*, 5 January 1962.

4   "Announces November 11 March," *Sheet*, 3 November 1961.

5   Peter McCallum, "Canada—A Theoretical State," *Sheet*, April 1961.

6   Ibid.

7   "Varsity Students March 'Protesting Everything,'" *Leader-Post* (Regina), 25 October 1962.

8   Sylvia Meier, Letter to the editor, *Carillon*, 9 November 1962.

9   "Not from Cuba," *Leader-Post* (Regina), 20 November 1962.

10   Garth Hibbert, "Nuclear Disarmament," *Carillon*, 7 December 1962.

11   *Leader-Post* (Regina), 4 December 1964.

12   "More is Enough!" *Carillon*, 2 October 1964.

13   Stanley Karnow, *Vietnam: A History* (New York: Penguin, 1997), 185.

14   Robert Bothwell, "Canada and the Vietnam War," in Bob Hesketh and Chris Hackett, eds., *Canada: Confederation to Present* (Edmonton: Chinook Multimedia Inc., 2001).

15   Ibid.

16   Karnow, 295.

17   Ibid., 36.

18   Bothwell, "Canada and the Vietnam War," 7.

19   John Gallagher, "SRC Supports U.S.," *Carillon*, 12 February 1965.

20   "CUCND Changes Name, States Purpose," *Carillon*, 15 January 1965.

21   "SUPA Hits Americans," *Carillon*, 12 February 1965.

22   "SUPA Marches on Gov't," *Carillon*, 19 February 1965.

23   Robert S. McNamara, *In Retrospect: The Tragedy and Lessons of Vietnam* (New York: Vintage Books, 1996), 174; Karnow, 468.

24   Charles DeBenedetti and Charles Chatfield, *An American Ordeal: The Antiwar Movement of the Vietnam Era* (Syracuse: Syracuse University Press, 1990), 4.

25   Ibid., 389.

26   "Manifestation Deserves Support," *Carillon*, 25 October 1968.

27   Letter from Ray Freed, *Carillon*, 8 November 1968.

28   Keith Reynolds, "The Moratorium," *Carillon*, 21 November 1969.

29   Warren Carragata, "Dr. Benjamin Spock Says People Must Resist Government Injustice," *Carillon*, 30 October 1970.

30   "Students Demonstrate Against U.S. Army Band," *Carillon*, 21 May 1970.

31   "Torontonians Telegram Baker Asking that Charges Be Dropped," *Carillon*, 25 September 1970.

32   "Political Charges by the Political Police," *Carillon*, 18 June 1970.

33   "Final Defendant in 'Riot' Case Found Not Guilty," *Carillon*, 2 October 1970.

34   Victor Levant, *Quiet Complicity: Canadian Involvement in the Vietnam War* (Toronto: Between the Lines, 1986), 51-62; Douglas A. Ross, *In the Interests of Peace: Canada and Vietnam, 1954-1973* (Toronto: University of Toronto Press, 1984), 299-303.

35   Levant, 55

36   *The Helpful Fixer: Canada and the Vietnam War*, a special series on *As It Happens*. CBC Radio, Part III, "Partners in Conflict," 26 April 2000.

37   Letter from H. Schlotter, *Carillon*, 21 November 1969.

38   J.L. Granatstein, *Yankee Go Home? Canadians and Anti-Americanism* (Toronto: HarperCollins, 1996), 176.

39   Denis Smith, *Gentle Patriot: A Political Biography of Walter Gordon* (Edmonton: Hurtig, 1973), 323.

40   Granatstein, 181.

41   Ibid., 174.

42   McNamara, 253-254.

43   John Hagan, *Northern Passage: American Vietnam War Resisters in Canada* (Cambridge: Harvard University Press, 2001), 25.

44   Ibid., 38.

45   Ibid., 39.

46   Ibid., 41.

47   Ibid., 45.

48   Ibid., 34.

49   Ibid., 139.

50   "Regina Committee to Aid Deserters," *Carillon*, 13 November 1969.

51   Saskatchewan Archives Board (SAB), Oral History Project, no. 87, "Student Unrest at the University of Saskatchewan, Regina Campus in the 1960s and 1970s," tape R-10, 323, Terry Zimmer interview, 30 March 1987.

52   Karnow, 683.

53   Ibid., 11; Robert Mann, "Despite All, Vietnam Still Likes Americans," *New York Times*, 29 May 2002.

54   Bothwell, "Canada and the Vietnam War, 12; Karnow, 36.

55   Gabriel Kolko, *Anatomy of a War: Vietnam, the United States and the Modern Historical Experience* (New York: Pantheon Books, 1985), 76.

56   Norman Podhoretz, *Why We Were In Vietnam* (New York: Simon and Schuster, 1983), 198.

57   Stephen J. Morris, "The War We Could Have Won," *New York Times*, 1 May 2005.

58   Karnow, 34.

59   Podhoretz, 14.

60   Kolko, 72.

61   Bothwell, "Canada and the Vietnam War," 7-8.

62   "Graduating from University this Spring?" *Carillon*, 23 January 1970.

63   "American Empire: The Company With the Human Faces," *Carillon*, 8 September 1971.

64   "Petition," *Carillon*, 22 January 1971.

65   "Continentalism is Treason!" *Carillon*, 9 July 1971.

66   "Students Protest Aleutian Blast," *Carillon*, 3 October 1969.

67   University of Regina Archives (URA), Principal's/President's Papers, 80-38, 4000.1-1, J.H. Archer, memo to file, 29 October 1971.

68   "American Empire Will Eat You Up," *Carillon*, 5 November 1971.

69   "Environmental Teach-in," *Carillon*, 16 October 1970.

70   *Carillon*, 16 January 1970.

71   "Pollution Group Formed," *Carillon*, 30 January 1970.

72   "Corporate Obscenity—The Rape of the Environment," *Carillon*, 7 March 1969.

73   Keith Reynolds, "Pollution Probe Urges University to Reconsider use of Styrofoam Cups," *Carillon*, 18 September 1970; "There's No Pollution Problem in Saskatchewan," *Carillon*, 16 July 1970; Don Humphries, "Pollution Talk," *Carillon*, 23 January 1970; "Green Peace Too Mission," *Carillon*, 5 November 1971.

74   Jon Lee Anderson, *Che Guevara: A Revolutionary Life* (New York: Grove Press, 1997), 129.

75   Ibid., 545.

76   Jorge G. Castaneda, *Companero: The Life and Death of Che Guevara* (New York: Vintage, 1998), 100.

77   Anderson, 753.

78   P. Uhl and R. Howard, "Che... 'A New Form of Man?'" *Carillon*, 3 November 1967.

CHAPTER 7

1   Arthur Marwick, *The Sixties: Cultural Revolution in Britain, France, Italy, and the United States, c.1958-c.1974* (New York: Oxford University Press), 11.

2   John Tomlinson, *Globalization and Culture* (Chicago: University of Chicago Press, 1999), 18.

3   Ibid., 20.

4   Marwick, 12.

5   Letter to the editor, *Leader-Post* (Regina), 28 May 1968.

6   Letter to the editor, *Leader-Post* (Regina), 3 June 1968.

7   David Brooks, *Bobos in Paradise: The New Upper Class and How They Got There* (New York: Simon and Schuster, 2000), 69, 78.

8   Allan Bloom, *The Closing of the American Mind: How Higher Education Has Failed Democracy and Impoverished the Souls of Today's Students* (New York: Simon and Schuster, 1987), 78.

9   Roger Kimball, *The Long March: How the Cultural Revolution of the 1960s Changed America* (San Francisco: Encounter Books, 2000), 147.

10   Marwick, 18.

11   Ibid., 8

12   Beth L. Bailey, *From Front Porch to Back Seat: Courtship in Twentieth-Century America* (Baltimore: The Johns Hopkins University Press, 1989), 80.

13   Ibid., 111.

14   Veronica Strong-Boag, "Home Dreams: Women and the Suburban Experiment in Canada, 1945-1960" *Canadian Historical Review*, 72, 4, December 1991, 475.

15   University of Regina Archives (URA), Dean's/Principal's Office Files, 75-7, 401.4, Regulations, Women's Residence, Regina Campus, University of Saskatchewan, 1962.

16   URA, Public Relations Office Files, 84-11, 181, academic faculty minutes, 27 February 1953.

17   Beth Bailey, *Sex in the Heartland* (Cambridge, Mass.; Harvard University Press, 1999), 200-215.

18   Bailey, *From Front Porch to Back Seat*, 2.

19   Bailey, *Sex in the Heartland*, 202-205.

20   "Statement of Purpose," *Sheet*, 1 December 1961.

21   "Sex Education," *Sheet*, 1 December 1961.

22   "Sex Attitudes," *Sheet*, 1 December 1961.

23   "Some Protest Sheet Policy," *Sheet*, 5 January 1962.

24   Ron Chapdelaine, "Newman Club Speaks," *Sheet*, 5 January 1962.

25   "More Thoughts on Sex," *Sheet*, 19 January 1962.

26   Hal Lieren, "That 'Obscene' Book May Be Back for University Students to See," *Leader-Post* (Regina), 9 December 1961.

27   "Carillon Counsellor," *Carillon*, 2 December 1963.

28   "Carillon Counsellor," *Carillon*, 15 February 1963.

29   "Sex—The Great Escape Act," *Carillon*, 19 November 1963.

30   "Think For Yourself," *Carillon*, 31 January 1964.

31   Doug Owram, *Born at the Right Time: A History of the Baby Boom in Canada* (Toronto: University of Toronto Press, 1996), 267.

32   "The Carillon Birth Control Survey," *Carillon*, 17 March 1967.

33   "'I Don't Want To Talk About It,'" *Carillon*, 9 November 1973.

34   Bailey, *Sex in the Heartland*, 157.

35   David Allyn, *Make Love Not War: The Sexual Revolution, An Unfettered History* (Boston: Little, Brown, and Company, 2000), 220.

36   Ibid., 119, 125-126, 128.

37   Stefan Braun, "Freedom of Expression v. Obscenity Censorship: The Development of Canadian Jurisprudence," *Saskatchewan Law Review*, 50, 1, 1985-1986, 50.

38   Robert Bothwell, Ian Drummond, and John English, *Canada Since 1945: Power, Politics, and Provincialism* (Toronto: University of Toronto Press, 1989), revised edition, 160.

39   Braun, 52.

40   In the mid-1980s the Mulroney government tried to revise the Criminal Code to include a more precise definition of pornography, but the effort floundered and the bill died on the order paper. Reg Whitaker, "Chameleon on a Changing Background: The Politics of Censorship in Canada," in Klaus Peterson and Allan C. Hutchinson, eds., *Interpreting Censorship in Canada* (Toronto: University of Toronto Press, 1999), 34-35.

41   "I haven't got time to vote…," *Carillon*, 22 February 1967.

42   "Share…," *Carillon*, 6 March 1967.

43   Front page, *Carillon*, 22 March 1968.

44   "Happy New Year From The Carillon," *Carillon*, 6 December 1968.

45   Gary Kinsman, *The Regulation of Desire: Homo and Hetero Sexualities* (Montreal: Black Rose Books, 1996), 2nd edition, revised, 263-264.

46   Ibid., 276.

47   "Gay Liberation Center," *Carillon*, 29 October 1971.

48   "Gay Group Organizes On Campus," *Carillon*, 2 February 1973.

49   David Farber, *Chicago '68* (Chicago: University of Chicago Press, 1988), 221-222.

50   Owram, 197-198.

51   Ibid., 203.

52   Martin A. Lee and Bruce Shlain, *Acid Dreams: The Complete Social History of LSD: The CIA, The Sixties, and Beyond* (New York: Grove Press, 1992), xviii-xix.

53   Humphry Osmond in *Hofmann's Potion*, Connie Littlefield, director, National Film Board of Canada, 2002.

54   Lee and Shlain, 49-50.

55   Humphry Osmond in *Hofmann's Potion*.

56   Lee and Shlain, 48.

57   Ibid., 54-55.

58   Roy F. Baumeister and Kathleen S. Placidi, "A Social History and Analysis of the LSD Controversy," *Journal of Humanistic Psychology*, 23, 1983, 29.

59   For an account of the work of Osmond, Hoffer and Blewett, see Patrick Barber, "Chemical Revolutionaries: Saskatchewan's Psychedelic-Related Experiments and the Work of Abram Hoffer, Humphry Osmond and Duncan Blewett," MA thesis, University of Regina, 2006.

60   Dianne Leibel, "My Experience Under LSD," *Carillon*, 1 March 1963.

61   "Letter of Do-o-o-o-m…," *Carillon*, 17 January 1964.

62   "Psychedelic Research Smothered By Fear," *Carillon*, 18 November 1966.

63   Lee and Shlain, 77.

64   Ibid., 161.

65   Ibid., 177-178

66   URA, Principal's Papers, 75-2, 1500-14, "City's Flower Children Bloom at Campus Courtyard Love-In," *Leader-Post* (Regina), September 1967.

67   Lee and Shlain, 176.

68   Ibid., 194.

69   Baumeister and Placidi, 37.

70   Jay Stevens, *Storming Heaven: LSD and the American Dream* (New York: Grove Press, 1987), 274.

71   Baumeister and Placidi, 41.

72   Duncan Blewett in *Hofmann's Potion*.

73   "Drug Symposium," *Carillon*, 21 November 1969.

74   Ibid.

75   Stevens, 280.

76   "Timothy Leary's Dead. No He's Outside Looking In," *Carillon*, 9 February 1973.

77   John Gallagher, "Pot—and the Law," *Carillon*, 22 March 1968.

78   "Results on the Referendum," *Carillon*, 2 December 1969.

79   James Miller, *Flowers in the Dustbin: The Rise of Rock and Roll, 1947-1977*, (New York: Simon and Schuster), 1.

80   Myrna Kostash, *Long Way From Home: The Story of the Sixties Generation in Canada* (Toronto: James Lorimer & Company, 1980), 111.

81   Owram, 282.

82   *The Travellers: This Land is Your Land*, video, National Film Board of Canada, 2001.

83   Gary Robertson, "Folk-Singing," *Sheet*, 17 November 1961.

84   Ad for the Travellers, *Carillon*, 25 September 1963.

85   "Lightfoot—Folksinger and Patriot 'Maybe,'" *Carillon*, 17 March 1967.

86   Greil Marcus, *Like a Rolling Stone: Bob Dylan at the Crossroads* (New York: Public Affairs, a member of the Perseus Books Group, 2005), 157.

87   Bob Dylan, *Chronicles: Volume One* (New York: Simon & Schuster, 2004), 103.

88   Bob Spitz, *The Beatles: The Biography* (New York: Little, Brown and Company, 2005), 533.

89   David P. Szatmary, *Rockin' in Time: A Social History of Rock-and-Roll* (Upper Saddle River: Prentice Hall, 2000), 4th ed., 89.

90   Ibid., 93.

91   *No Direction Home: Bob Dylan*, DVD, a Martin Scorsese picture, Spitfire Holdings, Inc. Educational Broadcasting Corporation, Grey Water Park Productions, Inc., 2005.

92   Marcus, 33.

93   Bob Dylan, "Like a Rolling Stone," *Highway 61 Revisited*, 1965.

94   Dylan, *Chronicles: Volume One*, 117.

95   Ibid., 120.

96   Spitz, 534.

97   Blewett, "Records," *Carillon*, 27 September 1968.

98   Blewett, "Records," *Carillon*, 25 October 1968.

99   John C. McWilliams, *The 1960s Cultural Revolution* (Westport, Connecticut: Greenwood, 2000), 74-75.

100   James J. Farrell, *The Spirit of the Sixties: The Making of Postwar Radicalism* (New York: Routledge, 1997), 214.

101   J.G., "Capitalism on Wheels Gone Hip," *Carillon*, 30 July 1970.

102   "A Pink Think With the Floyd," *Carillon*, 16 October 1970.

103   Larry Day, "A Cold Prairie Blizzard For a Warm Joni Mitchell," *Carillon*, 22 March 1974.

104   Quine, "The Wax Factory Rides Again," *Carillon*, 6 March 1970.

105   Glenn Garry Darling, "Hendrix: A Eulogy," *Carillon*, 9 October 1970.

106   Quine, "Joplin: Dead But Not Forgotten," *Carillon*, 9 October 1970.

107   Farrell, 204.

108   John Leland, *Hip: The History* (New York: HarperCollins, 2004), 5.

109   Ibid., 20.

110   Ibid., 152.

111   *Sheet*, November-December 1960.

112   "Noon Hour Concerts," *Sheet*, 3 November 1961.

113   Farrell, 203; Lee and Shlain say that Caen coined the word in 1967 after the Golden Gate Park be-in, Lee and Shlain, 163.

114   Mitchell, "New Coffee House Compatible," *Carillon*, 29 January 1965.

115   Yehudi, "On Chianti," *Sheet*, 1 December 1961.

116   "Ever since I can remember, I have been running...," *Carillon*, 7 November 1969.

117   Howard Halpern, "Some People Talk About the Weather," *Carillon*, 3 March 1972.

118   Thomas J. Burns, "Pedestrian Kills Car!" *Carillon*, 26 November 1971.

119   James Henshaw, "Movie Reviews: Easy Rider," *Carillon*, 31 October 1969.

120   Peter Larson, "Movie Reviews: Easy Rider," *Carillon*, 31 October 1969.

121   "Horace Greeley," "Half Truths in Brief," *Carillon*, 20 March 1970.

122   "Archer's Defence of Students Hit By Judge Brownridge," *Carillon*, 18 June 1970.

123   "Principal Archer Did Well," *Carillon*, 18 June 1970.

124   Steve Hewitt, "'Information Believed True,': RCMP Security Intelligence Activities on Canadian University Campuses and the Controversy Surrounding Them, 1961-1971," *Canadian Historical Review*, 81 (2000): 195.

125   National Archives of Canada (NAC), Records of the Canadian Security Intelligence Service, Record Group 146, vol. 2774, part 2, 18 October 1966, file number removed pursuant to the *Access to Information Act*.

126   NAC, Records of the Canadian Security Intelligence Service, Record Group 146, vol. 2775, part 10, Re: Education—Canada, University of Saskatchewan (Regina Campus), Appendix "B," file number removed pursuant to the *Access to Information Act*.

127   "Investigations Must Stop," *Carillon*, 18 December 1963.

128   RCMP poster, *Carillon*, 6 April 1973.

129   "Cookie on Commies," *Carillon*, 18 June 1970.

130   "Freaks and Shorthairs Unite," *Carillon*, 28 May 1971.

131   "Mace—the Anti-People Gas," *Carillon*, 13 September 1968.

132   Heintz, "Graffiti," *Carillon*, 22 October 1971.

133   Thomas Frank, *The Conquest of Cool: Business Culture, Counterculture, and the Rise of Hip Consumerism* (Chicago: University of Chicago Press, 1997), 16.

134   Michiko Kakutani, "The Conquest of Cool: When Madison Avenue Donned Its Love Beads," *New York Times*, 5 December 1997.

135   Interested student, "Straight Society Persecutes," *Carillon*, 22 March 1968.

136   Masthead, *Carillon*, 17 February 1967.

137   "A Great Young Rock Group," *Carillon*, 16 October 1970.

138   "This is the Bottle for the Age of Ecology," *Carillon*, 9 October 1970.

139   "In Your Own Way...," *Carillon*, 9 March 1973.

140   "For Those 12 Hour Sit-Ins," *Carillon*, 26 February 1971.

141   "Most Co-eds Take the Capsule," *Carillon*, 4 December 1970.

142   "The World's Second Best Reproduction System," *Carillon*, 19 October 1973.

143   Marwick, 17.

144   Roger Lewis, *Outlaws of America: The Underground Press and its Context: Notes on a Cultural Revolution* (Harmondsworth: Penguin, 1972), 110.

CHAPTER 8

1   Mark Hamilton Lytle, *America's Uncivil Wars: The Sixties Era From Elvis to the Fall of Richard Nixon* (New York: Oxford University Press, 2006), 2.

2   Ibid., 251.

3   Ibid., 253.

4   Arthur Marwick, *The Sixties: Cultural Revolution in Britain, France, Italy, and the United States, c.1958-c.1974* (New York: Oxford University Press, 1998), 610-611.

5   Lytle, 249.

6   Maurice Isserman and Michael Kazin, *America Divided: The Civil War of the 1960s* (New York: Oxford University Press, 2000), 241.

7   Lytle, 262.

8   Cited in James J. Farrell, *The Spirit of the Sixties: The Making of Postwar Radicalism* (New York: Routledge, 1997), 161.

9   Lytle, 172.

10 Carl Singleton, ed., *The Sixties in America* (Pasadena: Salem Press, 1999), 294-295.

11 "Berkeley Approach Seems Answer to Student Problems," *Carillon*, 4 October 1966.

12 Lytle, 242-243.

13 *The Weather Underground*, DVD, a documentary film by Sam Green and Bill Siegel, The Free History Project, New Video Group Inc., 2004.

14 Todd Gitlin, *The Sixties: Years of Hope, Days of Rage* (New York: Bantam, 1993)

15 Ibid., 393-395.

16 SDS member quoted in *Rebels With a Cause*, DVD, a film by Helen Garvy, Zeitgeist Video, 2003.

17 *13 Seconds: The Kent State Shootings*, video, Partners in Motion, Regina, Saskatchewan, distributed by Single Spark Pictures, Santa Monica, California, no date.

18 Kent State photo, *Carillon*, 14 May 1971.

19 An account of the PSA affair may be found in Hugh Johnston, *Radical Campus: Making Simon Fraser University* (Vancouver: Douglas & McIntyre, 2005), 293-329.

20 Doug Owram, *Born at the Right Time: A History of the Baby Boom in Canada* (Toronto: University of Toronto Press, 1996), 247.

21 Ibid., 287.

22 For an account of the student movement at Regina campus, see Roberta Lexier, "Student Activism at the University of Saskatchewan, Regina Campus, 1961-1974," MA thesis, University of Regina, 2003.

23 Mark Leibovich, "In Turmoil of '68, Clinton Found a New Voice," *New York Times*, 5 September 2007.

24 Lytle, 344

25 Michelle Pohatyn, "The Student His Power and Potential," *Carillon*, 24 September 1965.

26 Ruth Warick, "Illusions of University," *Carillon*, 28 October 1966.

27 Ruth Warick, "Illusion? Myth? Or Reality?" *Carillon*, 10 February 1967.

28 "The University as Factory," *Carillon*, 26 September 1969.

29 "As Dean of the Faculty of Education…," *Carillon*, 10 March 1972.

30 Jerry Farber, *The Student as Nigger: Essays and Stories* (New York: Pocket Books, 1970).

31 Cyril Levitt, *Children of Privilege: Student Revolt in the Sixties* (Toronto: University of Toronto Press, 1984), 34.

32 "Regina Campus Takes Big Jump," *Leader-Post* (Regina), 7 September 1961.

33 Michael Hayden, *Seeking a Balance: The University of Saskatchewan 1907-1982* (Vancouver: University of British Columbia Press, 1983), 250.

34 John Conway, "University of the Absurd," *Carillon*, 23 September 1966.

35 "James Restun," "Tapes Substituted for Teachers," *Carillon*, 15 November 1968.

36 "Students to Vote on Tape Recorder Teaching," *Carillon*, 22 November 1968.

37 "Liberal Arts Dead at Regina—Killed by Semester System," *Carillon*, 2 December 1966.

38 "Experimental Teaching—Psychology 100," *Carillon*, 9 February 1968.

39 "Grow Vines!" *Carillon*, 20 September 1965.

40 "Letter to the editor," *Carillon*, 13 September 1968.

41 University of Regina Archives (URA), Principal's/Dean's Office Files, 78-3, 2000.2, statement re: Student Services Building, 6 August 1968.

42 "Lounge for Students," *Carillon*, 15 September 1967.

43 The "temporary" Students' Union Building opened in 1969 and lasted until 1997 when a new building was finally constructed.

44 "Quonset Hut," *Carillon*, 29 November 1968.

45 "All Work and No Play Makes Jack Adjust," *Carillon*, 16 September 1966; "The Place," *Carillon*, 27 January 1967.

46 "Editorial," *Carillon*, 29 March 1963.

47 "Why Not?" *Carillon*, 25 September 1963.

48 *Carillon*, 15 October 1965.

49 John Kelsey, "January: How Went the War?" *Carillon*, 9 February 1968.

50 URA, Principal's/Dean's Office Files, 78.3, 400.20, board of directors, AUCC, report, 10 July 1968.

51 URA, Principal's/Dean's Office Files, 78-3, 2001.9, W.A. Riddell memo, 17 June 1968.

52 URA, Principal's/Dean's Office Files, 78-3, 400.20, meeting with City officials to discuss University unrest, 26 August 1968; Saskatchewan Archives Board (SAB), Oral History Project, no. 87, "Student Unrest at the University of Saskatchewan, Regina Campus in the 1960s and 1970s," tape R-10, 320, W.A. Riddell interview, 4 April 1987,

53 URA, Principal's/Dean's Office Files, 78-3, 400.20, press conference, 7 August 1968.

54 "CUS Congress Mounts Attack on Society," *Carillon*, 13 September 1968.

55 "Loney Outlines Student Power Philosophy," *Carillon*, 20 September 1968.

56 "Molotov Cocktail Recipe," *Carillon*, 13 September 1968.

57 Archives of the University of Saskatchewan (AUS), Series 4, C5, Arts and Science, 1963-69, statement by Alwyn Berland, 18 September 1968.

58   URA, Principal's/Dean's Office Files, 2000.1-2, W.A. Riddell statement, 3 October 1968.

59   URA, Publications Section, University of Saskatchewan, Board of Governors minutes, 14 November 1968, Exhibit D, J.W.T. Spinks speech to students, 3 October 1968.

60   Ron Thompson, "Foot and a Half," *Carillon*, 11 October 1968.

61   "The University? I Am the University," *Carillon*, 13 September 1968.

62   The statue was later removed at the insistence of the Métis Society. James M. Pitsula, "The Thatcher Government in Saskatchewan and the Revival of Metis Nationalism, 1964-1971," *Great Plains Quarterly*, Summer/Fall 1997, vol. 17, no. 3 and 4, 227.

63   Bolen, Cameron and Graham, "1200 Students March For Loans," *Carillon*, 4 October 1968; National Archives of Canada (NAC), Canadian Security Intelligence Service, Record Group 146, vol. 2774, part 4, W.L. Higgett to D.B. Beavis, 19 November 1968.

64   Rick Hesch, "Disillusioned," *Carillon*, 11 October 1968.

65   W.D. Harvey, "Demonstrators Attacked," *Carillon*, 11 October 1968.

66   "Moderates Organize," *Carillon*, 11 October 1968.

67   "Thompson Challenges Convocation," *Carillon*, 8 November 1968.

68   "This University Belongs to the Student! Dig It," *Carillon*, 25 October 1968.

69   "This is Your Union," *Carillon*, 8 January 1969.

70   "Editorial," *Carillon*, February 1969.

71   "Who Runs the University of Saskatchewan?" *Carillon*, February 1969.

72   "You Foot the Bill for the University But Do You Really Benefit?" *Carillon*, February 1969.

73   "Union Leader Urges Publicity," *The Carillon*, 7 February 1969.

74   "Regina Campus," *Carillon*, 1 April 1969.

75   "Students Defeat Occupation Motion," *Carillon*, 26 September 1969.

76   "Can Participatory Democracy Work Without Participation?" *Carillon*, 24 October 1969.

77   Tamerlane, "Machiavelli's Manor," *Carillon*, 8 September 1969.

78   Ibid.

79   "Caged Conformity," *Carillon*, 2 December 1969.

80   Doug Owram, *Born at the Right Time: A History of the Baby Boom in Canada* (Toronto; University of Toronto Press, 1996), 234, 293-294.

81   "Student Apathy Alive and Well," *Carillon*, 27 October 1972.

82   URA, College/Faculty of Arts and Science, University of Saskatchewan, Regina Campus Files, 85-54, 303, G. Edgar Vaughan to F.W. Anderson, 9 November 1972.

83   "Democratic University," *Carillon*, 21 November 1972.

84   URA, Principal's/President's Papers, 80-38, 4000.6, personal statement by A.B. Van Cleave to members of the Regina Campus Council, 24 November 1972.

85   Ibid.

86   "Fight for a Democratic University," *Carillon*, 21 November 1972.

87   URA, Principal's/President's Papers, 80-38, 4000.6, John Archer statement, 22 November 1972.

88   URA, College/Faculty of Arts and Science, University of Saskatchewan, Regina Campus Files, 85-54, 103-5-1, J.H. Archer to Council, 18 May 1973, Report of the Tri-Partite Committee.

89   URA, College/Faculty of Arts and Science, University of Saskatchewan, Regina Campus Files, 85-54, 103-5-1, J.H. Archer to Council, 18 May 1973, Report of a Minority of the Tri-Partite Committee.

90   "Students Shafted Again," *Carillon*, 1 February 1974.

91   "Soft Chairs, Soft Heads," *Carillon*, 1 February 1974.

92   *Carillon*, 6 March 1970, 2 April 1971.

93   University of Saskatchewan, *Annual Report of the President*, 1969-1970.

94   "That's Not Performance," *Carillon*, 28 May 1971.

CHAPTER 9

1   Arthur Marwick, *The Sixties: Cultural Revolution in Britain, France, Italy, and the United States, c.1958-c.1974* (Oxford: Oxford University Press, 1998), 4.

2   Nick Bromell, *Tomorrow Never Knows: Rock and Psychedelics in the 1960s* (Chicago: University of Chicago Press, 2000), 7.

3   Myron Magnet, *The Dream and the Nightmare: The Sixties' Legacy to the Underclass* (San Francisco: Encounter Books, 1993), 8-9.

4   Roger Kimball, *The Long March: How the Cultural Revolution of the 1960s Changed America* (San Francisco: Encounter Books, 2001), 248.

5   Ibid., 261.

6   Ibid., 33.

7   Allan Bloom, *The Closing of the American Mind* (New York: Simon & Schuster, 1987), 314.

8   George Woodcock, "Fascism or Freedom? A Radical Dilemma," in Tim and Julyan Reid, eds., *Student Power and the Canadian Campus* (Toronto: Peter Martin Associates, 1969), 59.

9   Kimball, 23.

10   Harvey C. Mansfield, "The Legacy of the Late Sixties," in Stephen Macedo, ed., *Reassessing the Sixties: Debating the Political and Cultural Legacy* (New York: W.W. Norton, 1997), 21-45.

11   Ibid., 30.

12   Ibid., 31.

13   Magnet, 2.

14   Ibid., 13.

15   Ibid., 17-18.

16   Gertrude Himmelfarb, *One Nation, Two Cultures: A Searching Examination of American Society in the Aftermath of Our Cultural Revolution* (New York: Alfred A. Knopf, 1999), 13.

17   Ibid., 18.

18   Ibid., 28-29.

19   Ibid., 19.

20   William D. Gairdner, *On Higher Ground: Reclaiming a Civil Society* (Toronto: Stoddart, 1996), 28.

21   Link Byfield, " 'Narrow-Mindedness Goes National," *Globe and Mail* (Toronto), 25 October 1999.

22   Rex Murphy, "If I Had a Hammer, I'd Swat the Sixties," *Globe and Mail* (Toronto), 26 May 2001.

23   Margaret Wente, "Mommies on Strike," *Globe and Mail* (Toronto), 13 May 2006.

24   Paul Berman, *A Tale of Two Utopias: The Political Journey of the Generation of 1968* (New York: W.W. Norton & Company, 1996), 7.

25   Ibid., 13-14.

26   Ibid., 15.

27   Gordon H. McCormick, "The Revolutionary Odyssey of Che Guevara," *Queen's Quarterly*, vol. 105, no. 2, Summer 1998, 170.

28   Marwick, 803.

29   Ibid., 10.

30   "In Praise of the Counterculture," *New York Times*, 11 December 1994.

31   *Pleasantville*, video, New Line Productions, 1999.

32   Marwick, 13.

33   David Brooks, *Bobos in Paradise: The New Upper Class and How They Got There* (New York: Simon and Schuster, 2000), 43.

34   Thomas Frank, *The Conquest of Cool: Business Culture, Counterculture, and the Rise of Hip Consumerism* (Chicago: University of Chicago Press, 1997), 4-5.

35   Ibid., 110-111.

36   Ibid., 4.

37   Daniel Bell, *The Cultural Contradictions of Capitalism* (New York: Basic Books, 1976), 79.

38   Ibid., 84.

39   Brooks, 98, 101.

40   Ibid., 101.

41   Douglas McGregor, *The Human Side of Enterprise* (Toronto: McGraw-Hill, 1960), 132.

42   Frank, 20.

43   Ibid., 9.

44   Brooks, 112, 128, 132.

45   Stewart Brand, "We Owe It All to the Hippies," *Time*, Special Issue, Spring 1995, vol. 145, no. 12.

46   *Globe and Mail* (Toronto), 15 January 2000.

47   *Globe and Mail* (Toronto), 24 February 2000.

48   Thomas L. Friedman, *The World is Flat: A Brief History of the Twenty-First Century* (New York: Picador/Farrar, Straus and Giroux, 2007), 48.

49   Chris Reidy, "Beam U.S. Up, Scotty, Kirk's Singing Again…" *National Post* (Toronto), 21 January 2000.

50 Robert Fulford, "Spirit of McLuhan Looks Over TED City," *National Post* (Toronto), 8 June 2000.

51 Dawn Walton, "Dot-Com Teens Recruit Big Hitters," *Globe and Mail* (Toronto), 18 May 2000.

52 Frank, ix.

53 University of Regina Archives (URA), Principal's/Dean's Office Files, 78-3, 2000.1-2, Ralph Smith report, October 1967.

54 Matthew Coon Come, "We Have a Dream, Too," *Globe and Mail* (Toronto), 31 January 2001.

55 The phrase is borrowed from Michael Burleigh, *Earthly Powers: The Clash of Religion and Politics in Europe from the French Revolution to the Great War* (New York: HarperCollins, 2005), 39.

56 Magnet, 7; James J. Farrell, *The Spirit of the Sixties: The Making of Postwar Radicalism* (New York: Routledge, 1997), 230-231.

57 Allison Dunfield, "Marijuana Activists Incensed," *Globe and Mail* (Toronto), 22 April 2002; According to the Monitoring the Future Study conducted by the University of Michigan Institute for Social Research, 13.6 per cent of all high school seniors graduating in 1997 had tried LSD and 49.6 per cent had tried marijuana. Bromell, 9.

58 John MacLachlan Gray, "Rock 'n' Roll: We Thought It Was the End of History," *Globe and Mail* (Toronto), 20 September 2000.

59 Alice Echols, *Scars of Sweet Paradise: The Life and Times of Janis Joplin* (New York: Henry Holt, 2000), 14.

60 Bromell, 5.

61 Doug Owram, *Born at the Right Time: A History of the Baby Boom in Canada* (Toronto: University of Toronto Press, 1996), 314-315.

62 Cited in Terry Anderson, *The Movement and the Sixties: Protest in America from Greensboro to Wounded Knee* (New York: Oxford University Press, 1995), 286.

63 Magnet, 5.

64 George Grant, "A Critique of the New Left," in *Canada and Radical Change*, edited by Dimitrios I. Roussopoulos (Montreal: Black Rose Books, 1973), 59.

Index

Wallin, Pamela, 44

War Measures Act (1970), 10, 151–153, 181, 295

war resisters, 183–185

Warick, Ruth, 251–252

Wascana Centre Authority, 50

Wascana Hotel, 117

Wascana Lake, 47, 50

Wascana Park, 51, 233

Water, Roger, 224

Waterloo, University of, 8, 263

Waters, Muddy, 23

Watkins, Melville, 38, 181

Watts riots, 140

Wayne State University, 51

Weather Underground, 206, 246–247

Weathermen, 246–247

Weinberg, Jack, 243

welfare state, 35, 39

Wellesley College, 250

Wente, Margaret, 286

Westell, Anthony, 157

Western Ontario, University of, 64

Westinghouse, 152

White Panther Party, 206

Who, the, 214

Whyte, William, 291

Wiffen, Dave, 131

Wigmore, Barry, 124

Wild One, The, 25

Wilson, Sloan, 21

Windsor, University of, 64, 263

Winters, Margaret, 159

Wired magazine, 290, 292

Wisconsin, University of, 139

Witherspoon, Reese, 288–289

Wolfe, James, 150

Wolfson, Joseph, 62

Wolof (African language), 226

women

discrimination against, 158, 288

as oppressed in capitalist system, 12, 34, 135, 162, 296

status of, 19, 157

violence against, 158

in workforce, 154

women's liberation movement

conflicting views on, 86, 164

as event of sixties, 2, 16, 71, 153, 247, 288, 295

as societal problem, 56, 135, 247

legacy of, 296

see also Carillon, on women's liberation

Wood, Natalie, 25

Wood, Robertson, 147

Woodcock, George, 284

Woodstock, 2, 15, 43, 218, 237, 297

commercialization of, 239, 223–224

Woolworth's (Greensboro), 137

World Trade Center, 51

World University Service SHARE campaign, 208

Wretched of the Earth, The, 145

Wright, Rick, 224

Yale University, 139

Yamasaki, Minoru, 50–53

York University, 64, 184

Youth International Party (yippies), 242

YWCA, 157

Zwerg, Jim, 138